CONTINGENT MA

Contingent Maps

Rethinking Western Women's History and the North American West

Edited by

SUSAN E. GRAY and GAYLE GULLETT

THE UNIVERSITY OF ARIZONA PRESS
TUCSON

The University of Arizona Press
www.uapress.arizona.edu

Printed in the United States of America
19 18 17 16 15 14 6 5 4 3 2 1

Cover designed by Nicole Hayward

Chapters 1 through 10 originally appeared in *Frontiers: A Journal of Women Studies* and are reprinted with permission from the University of Nebraska Press.

Library of Congress Cataloging-in-Publication Data
Contingent maps : rethinking Western women's history and the North American West / edited by Susan E. Gray, Gayle Gullett.
pages cm. — (Women's Western voices)
Summary: "*Contingent Maps* is an appeal to all who care about the history of women in the North American West. Susan E. Gray and Gayle Gullett, former co-editors of *Frontiers: A Journal of Women Studies*, offer in this collection a new approach to women's history that is firmly rooted in a fresh understanding of place"—Provided by publisher.
Includes bibliographical references and index.
ISBN 978-0-8165-2889-9 (paperback)
1. Women—West (U.S.)—History. 2. West (U.S.)—History. I. Gray, Susan E., 1952– II. Gullett, Gayle Ann.
HQ1438.W45C66 2014
305.40978—dc23

2014007747

∞ This paper meets the requirements of ANSI/NISO Z39.48–1992 (Permanence of Paper).

To the writers, reviewers, and readers who
have supported *Frontiers* since 1975.
The journal owes its life to you.
Thank you.

CONTENTS

Acknowledgments ... ix

Introduction ... 3

Part I. Identities and Place ... 23

Chapter 1 The Woman's Lodge: Constructing Gender on the Nineteenth-Century Pacific Northwest Plateau ... 28
MARY C. WRIGHT

Chapter 2 Mindful Masquerades: Que(e)rying Japanese Immigrant Dress in Turn-of-the-Century San Francisco ... 46
AMY SUEYOSHI

Chapter 3 Latitude in Mass-Produced Culture's Capital: New Women and Other Players in Hollywood, 1920–1941 ... 80
BRETT L. ABRAMS

Chapter 4 Saying "Nothin'": Pachucas and the Languages of Resistance ... 110
CATHERINE S. RAMÍREZ

Part II. Colonized Places ... 143

Chapter 5 The Erotics of Racialization: Gender and Sexuality in the Making of California ... 147
YOLANDA VENEGAS

Chapter 6 Elle Meets the President: Weaving Navajo Culture and Commerce in the Southwestern Tourist Industry ... 171
LAURA JANE MOORE

Chapter 7 Working on the Domestic Frontier: American Indian Domestic Servants in White Women's Households in the San Francisco Bay Area, 1920–1940 ... 194
MARGARET D. JACOBS

Part III. Networks and Place 229

Chapter 8 Docile Children and Dangerous Revolutionaries: The Racial Hierarchy of Manliness and the Bisbee Deportation of 1917 232
KATHERINE BENTON-COHEN

Chapter 9 ILGWU Labor Organizers: Chicana and Latina Leadership in the Los Angeles Garment Industry 254
MARÍA A. GUTIERREZ DE SOLDATENKO

Chapter 10 *Esperanza v. City of San Antonio*: Politics, Power, and Culture 276
AMY KASTELY

Editors and Contributors 293

Index 297

ACKNOWLEDGMENTS

Contingent Maps was Laura Woodworth-Ney's idea, and we thank her for it. As consulting editor for the Women's Western Voices series at the University of Arizona Press, she suggested that we, co-editors of *Frontiers: A Journal of Women Studies* from 2003 to 2012, prepare a reader of essays recently published in the journal that explored the intersectionality of place, race, and gender in the history of the North American West. Kristen Buckles, acquiring editor at the University of Arizona Press, subsequently guided us through the review process. We thank her, as well as the anonymous reviewers, who embraced the concept of the volume and provided such thoughtful suggestions for strengthening the manuscript.

We especially thank the authors who submitted their articles in Western women's history to *Frontiers*. We were the editors when most of these pieces came to the journal, but some were published when Susan Armitage, our immediate editorial predecessor, managed *Frontiers*. We thank Sue for choosing and supporting such excellent work. No doubt these scholars thought of *Frontiers* as the place to publish their work because of the long, close, and highly fruitful relationship between the journal and Western women's history.

The founding of *Frontiers* in 1975 was virtually coeval with the creation of Western women's history, and it was the work of many of the same actors. Susan Armitage gave the keynote address at the 1983 Women's West conference that launched the field.[1] She and Elizabeth Jameson produced its first anthology, *The Women's West*, largely a collection of papers from the conference, almost half of which were originally published in *Frontiers*. Armitage and Jameson both served on the original editorial collective of *Frontiers*. Susan Armitage, the journal's editor from 1996 to 2003, made a particularly important contribution to the field by developing special issues of *Frontiers* featuring racial ethnic women of the regional West. Several of the special issues also became anthologies.[2] Looking back from 2014, we are deeply mindful of the many hands, heads, and hearts that contributed to the making of *Frontiers* and the development of Western women's history as a field. But we must express particular gratitude to Sue and Betsy, whose creativity, vision, inclusive politics, and feminist commitment so profoundly shaped both journal and field. We are pleased and humbled that our anthology will take its place next to theirs on a shelf reserved for Western women's history.

Notes

1. Susan Armitage, "Through Women's Eyes: A New View of the West," in *The Women's West*, eds. Susan Armitage and Elizabeth Jameson (Norman: University of Oklahoma Press, 1987), 9–18.

2. Following Elizabeth Jameson, we use the term "racial ethnic" to emphasize that the concepts of race and ethnicity are both constructed and overlapping. See Elizabeth Jameson, "Looking Back at the Road Ahead," *Pacific Historical Review* 79, no. 4 (November 2010): 575, n. 4. For special issues concerned with racial ethnic relations in the West, see *Frontiers* 5, no. 2, "Chicanas en el Ambiente Nacional/Chicanas in the National Landscape" (1980); *Frontiers* 6, no. 3, "Native American Women" (1981); *Frontiers* 11, no. 1, "Las Chicanas" (1990); *Frontiers* 14, no. 2, "Chicana Identity" (1994); *Frontiers* 17, no. 3, "Rethinking Frontiers" (1996); *Frontiers* 20, no. 1, "Latina/Chicana Leadership" (1999); *Frontiers* 21, nos. 1–2, "Asian American Women" (2000); *Frontiers* 22, no. 2, "Indigenous Women" (2002); *Frontiers* 24, nos. 2–3, "Gender on the Borderlands" (2003). For readers, see Yolanada Flores Niemann, ed., *Chicana Leadership: The Frontiers Reader* (Lincoln: University of Nebraska Press, 2002); Linda Trinh Võ and Marian Sciachitano, et al., eds., *Asian American Women: The Frontiers Reader* (Lincoln: University of Nebraska Press, 2004); Antonia Castañeda et al., eds., *Gender on the Borderlands: The Frontiers Reader* (Lincoln: University of Nebraska Press, 2007).

CONTINGENT MAPS

Introduction

Western women's history emerged as a field about thirty-five years ago. Despite its brief life, the field has produced an outpouring of important work, illuminating pivotal questions regarding the West and transforming the way historians think about issues fundamental to us as a nation.[1] Yet those who write Western women's history do not praise its progress, or even register pride in its achievements. Quite the opposite. In articles, published conference roundtables, and anthologies, they regularly engage in often harsh criticism of the field, calling, sometimes despairingly, for new, indeed transformed, scholarship.[2] Part of the reason for this lack of confidence in the field is its awkward status as the stepsister to both U.S. women's history and the New Western history, an intellectually fraught position directly related, in our view, to how Western women's historians, and Western historians generally, understand place. This understanding, in turn, helps to explain why Western women's history remains unhappily chained to Frederick Jackson Turner's identification of the frontier—for him, the meeting ground of savagery and civilization—as the master narrative of both the West and the nation.

From the beginning, Western women's historians have denounced the Turner thesis, and they continue to do so today.[3] But they have not been able to replace it with a better story, either as national and regional mythology or as scholarly narrative. We make no pretenses in this volume to offering a new imaginary for the next hundred years of Western history, but we do have a potentially liberatory story, or rather stories, to tell about Western women's history.[4] These stories revolve around what it has meant for Western women to live in place as well as time. We take our cues from the work of feminist geographers, who have taught us to consider the spatiality of all social relations and how the stories they tell can be simultaneously national and regional, global and local. The unboundedness of this thinking, we believe, can help free Western women's historians from the shackles of Turner's frontier. For from its beginning, Western women's history has literally been a problem of place.

We offer our stories about Western women's history because of our experiences as co-editors of *Frontiers: A Journal of Women Studies*, a journal linked to Western women's history since its first issue in 1975. In 2003, we came to *Frontiers* with our own research interests in the field and the determination to make place one of its categories of analysis.[5] Over our nine years as editors, we published a number of excellent articles in Western women's history, prompting an ongoing conversation between us about what we saw as an unwarranted state of despair among practitioners about the field, the usefulness of place as an analytical category, and the potential of place to revitalize Western women's history. In this anthology we share with you the fruits of our thoughts and editorial decisions.

A brief guide to this book: in the introduction we first survey Western women's history as a field, focusing on its problematic relationship with Turner's frontier and one particular consequence of that relationship—the absence of place as an analytical category. We next explore the insights of feminist geographers that we believe most useful for developing new understandings of the histories of women in the West. Ten recent *Frontiers* articles that examine the intertwined histories of the region, women, and gender follow the introduction, grouped into three thematic sections—"Identities and Place," "Colonized Places," and "Networks and Place." These themes enable us to see how considerations of place can transform our understanding of the history of women in the North American West. In all of the essays in this volume, place serves as both a subject and, in varying ways and degrees, an analytical category. We therefore begin each section with a brief discussion of the relationship between the place-based theme as informed by feminist geography and Western women's history. We welcome you to our conversation.

Western Women's History, Turner's Frontier, and Place

Western women's historians have remained unhappily chained to Frederick Jackson Turner's frontier for several complicated reasons. The Turner thesis gave Americans a national-origins myth that reinforced and reified American exceptionalism, the notion that the founding of the United States represented a break with a feudal past and the forging of a democratic future. In Turner's telling, America emerged not from Europe but from the American frontier. As white frontiersmen subdued Indigenous societies and turned forests into farms, they transformed themselves into distinctive American men, individualists who created a new kind of democracy. Developed on the frontier with the blessing of God, American national identity rested on the supremacy of the white race and the courage of white manhood.

At the turn of the twentieth century, Americans widely accepted Turner's frontier as the place that had created America and white American manhood. The meeting ground between savagery and civilization, the frontier was both place and process, at once a locus of and a mechanism for making a nation and its men. The persuasiveness of Turner's argument owed much to the fact that in 1893, when he delivered his seminal paper, "The Significance of the Frontier in American History," Americans already believed in the ability of the frontier to remake effete males into the vigorous men who had made, and were making, America.[6] Exhibit A in this thinking was Theodore Roosevelt. In the early 1880s, some ten years before Turner presented his paper, Roosevelt left New York City for the Dakotas to remake himself into an authentic American man. He then published books attesting to his transformation: memoirs of his rugged ranch life and a multivolume popular history of the West. In these works, Roosevelt declared that a new white race had developed on the American frontier; men of European descent became American men as they battled Indigenous savages. In his frontier thesis, Turner affirmed this popular racialized and gendered view of American history. The American public and professional historians alike embraced his argument in large part because it conferred scholarly authority on what they already believed about America, the West, and American manhood.[7]

Why were Turner and so many other Americans so taken with the frontier in the late nineteenth century? And why were their frontier stories narratives of masculine rebirth? The United States in this period was undergoing a dramatic transformation; industrialization, urbanization, and immigration were turning the nation into a modern world power, and the West was being incorporated into the modern nation. Railroads, barbed wire, and telegraph lines extended across the western plains, taut lines that increasingly pulled the West into national and international markets. Some men, particularly white middle-class men of the urban East, experienced these changes as threats to their manhood. They saw themselves as reduced from independent producers, the backbone of the republic, to middle managers, intimidated by organized labor and frightened by rising numbers of immigrants who seemed as dangerous as they were foreign. They also worried about their wives, daughters, and sisters who, individually and in organized movements, were leaving their homes and pushing their way into public arenas. Such worries prompted many white middle-class males to reassess their notions of manhood, to shift from an older standard of moral manliness, which prized self-control and piety, to a new, more physical, aggressive, and sexual manhood, which they labeled masculinity.[8]

Many men also took up reading western dime novels. Transported to the West in stories where, in struggle with the elements and Indians, white men became fully masculine—real men; they escaped temporarily the fearful, emasculating world in which they lived. Deeply entangled in these popular narratives, Turner's frontier has remained ever green. His imagined frontier West has lived on in pulp fiction and serious novels alike, and in films, radio shows, and television dramas from the late nineteenth century to the present.

Born after World War II, the baby boom generation grew up watching Westerns. They had little choice. Westerns dominated movies and television from the late 1940s through the early 1960s. Films such as *High Noon* (1952) and *Shane* (1953) gained critical applause, won Oscars, and sparked the production of more Westerns, as films and television series. In 1959, eight of the top ten television shows were Westerns. Observing that Westerns gained their largest audiences during the Cold War, commentators at the time and since have debated the links between the glorification of American conquest in Westerns and American acceptance of Cold War ideology. Perhaps, as scholars Lee Clark Mitchell and Stephen Tatum suggest, Westerns were popular because they could serve as parables for so many political positions. *High Noon*, for example, could be interpreted as both a pro- and an anti-McCarthy film. Baby boomers grew up listening to people argue about the lessons that Westerns offered for the present day. "Would a Wyatt Earp," wrote one man in *The American Mercury* in 1958, "stop at the 38th Parallel, Korea when the rustlers were escaping with the herd? Ridiculous!"[9]

Asked by reporters soon after 9/11 about the goals of the federal government regarding Osama bin Laden, President George W. Bush responded that the United States wanted the al-Qaeda leader "dead or alive." Bush anchored this national objective in his baby boomer's memory of the West: "I just remember, all I'm doing is remembering when I was a kid, I remember that they used to put out there in the old West, a wanted poster. It said: 'Wanted, Dead or Alive.'"[10] Since most Americans in the early twenty-first century had only seen these posters in movies or on television, Bush was utilizing ideas from an imaginary place to explain and legitimate national foreign policy. "The Western," observes American Studies scholar Stephen McVeigh regarding this 9/11 incident, "took on a relevance that it had not known since the era of the Cold War."[11]

Thus, for more than a century, the zeitgeist that Turner's thesis refracts has proved bigger than the man or his ideas about the origins of American democracy. So big, indeed, that Western women's historians have remained chained to the thesis even as they have denounced its racism and its reduction of women's experience to a handful of sexual stereotypes. Indeed, from the outset, Western women's historians have relied on the frontier to establish the significance of their field. Susan Armitage and Elizabeth Jameson began their "Editors' Introduction" to the first anthology of Western women's history,

The Women's West (1987), by declaring that the frontier West is central to the national narrative. It was the exceptional importance of the frontier that allowed them to argue strenuously that Western women must be included in histories of the West and in histories of U.S. women. This claim, however, better describes the western imaginary than Western history.[12]

Despite Western women's historians' insistence that the history of women in the West was of foundational importance for American history, U.S. women's historians in the 1980s generally neglected women in the West as subjects of scholarly inquiry. They did so partly because they believed that the key events for U.S. women occurred in the Northeast and the South. This belief, which was linked to their understanding of American racial history as a black-white binary, further reduced their interest in the histories of women in the West, including the narratives of Indigenous, Mexican American, and Asian American women. To the extent that U.S. women's historians thought about the American West, moreover, they, like the Western women's historians, were appalled by Turner's thesis, which further diminished their interest in Western women's history.[13]

Not coincidently, as Western women's historians struggled in the 1980s for ways to link their histories to some consistent, nationally significant notion of the West, the "New Western history" challenged the older field of coonskin caps, wagon wheels, and six-shooters.[14] New Western historians, whose professional influence reached its apogee in the late 1980s and early 1990s, contended that the West that historians should study was not the frontier but the regional West, meaning the United States west of a line running from the Canadian border through the Dakotas and on south through eastern Texas. Exactly where the West began depended on who was drawing the line. New Western historians argued that their focus on region, on the West as a place, cleansed Western history of Turner's celebration of the "frontier" as a triumphal process of white conquest and settlement.[15] Patricia Limerick, one of the founders of the field, famously dubbed the frontier the "new F word."[16]

New Western historians made region, which they understood as a particular kind of place, the cornerstone of their field. Distinctive factors, they declared, created the West, and the study of such factors would illuminate the region's great significance to the nation's history. New Western historians generally agreed that these factors included racial diversity, the conquest of Indigenous peoples, the formative role of the federal government, the boom and bust economy, and the degradation of the environment.[17] But as many scholars have pointed out, this definition of a region according to a laundry list of supposedly unique traits meant that, when they studied the West, Western historians could only reaffirm what they already knew to be characteristic of the place.[18] When the New Western historians considered the West as a region, they evoked an intellectual container already full of predetermined traits. Their place-making actually limited the analytical possibilities for exploring Western history. Another blow to the field came as scholars demonstrated that the allegedly distinctive western characteristics were not unique to the West. The West is racially diverse, for example, but not more so than other American regions. For all these reasons, the attractions of the New Western history, as a field for established scholars and new graduate students alike, began to fade in the late 1990s.[19]

Western women's historians responded to the decline of the New Western history with mixed feelings.[20] Devotees of the New Western history had proved remarkably uninterested in women or gender. Yet their claim that the West was an exceptional region and therefore an, if not the, essential part of an exceptional national history, bolstered the significance of the West for all who studied it, including Western women's historians. Indeed, from the beginning, Western women's historians linked their field to one of the supposedly distinctive factors of the region, racial diversity.

In their 1980 article, "The Gentle Tamers Revisited," which did so much to legitimatize and energize the new field of Western women's history, Joan Jensen and Darlis Miller asserted unequivocally that the field must be multicultural. Otherwise, Western women's historians would be confined to Turner's frontier and thus limited to the study of white women as appendages of white men, whether as wives or prostitutes.[21] Eight years later, Elizabeth Jameson, in another key article, concurred with Jensen and Miller's assessment of the significance of multiculturalism for the field.[22] This was the first—and one of the only—contributions to Western women's history to be published in *Signs: Journal of Women in Culture and Society*, a leading interdisciplinary feminist journal.

In her article, tellingly entitled "Toward a Multicultural History of Women in the Western United States," Jameson pointed out additional reasons for historians to adopt multiculturalism as feminist politics and scholarly praxis. Dedication to multiculturalism, she argued, would encourage historians to develop new conceptual frameworks for the field, frameworks that would enable them to link analytically gender, race, and ethnicity in the West in fruitful ways. Jameson thought, for example, that although Western women's historians' longstanding strategy of comparing Eastern and Western women's experiences remained useful, they should also compare women of different ethnicities and racial backgrounds in a single place, including a place then largely ignored by U.S. historians of the West, the U.S.-Mexico border. She also contended that multiculturalism would encourage historians to break away from the Turnerian periodization in which Western history ended with the "closing" of the frontier in 1890. How else, she reasonably asked, could historians examine the full history of American Indian women?[23] This new emphasis on the history of the twentieth-century West has been widely shared by Western women's historians and New Western historians alike. But Western women's historians have held particularly high hopes for multiculturalism as an instrument that would conceptually develop and strengthen their field.

Jameson and Armitage's second anthology, *Writing the Range: Race, Class, and Culture in the Women's West* (1997), stands as the ultimate statement of the commitment of Western women's history to multiculturalism. This massive volume of 656 pages catalogs the racial and ethnic diversity of Western women's history over twenty-nine essays and six extensive bibliographies. Despite their significant and obvious achievement, however, Jameson and Armitage puzzled in their editors' introduction over how best to shape a new narrative for Western history that would bring the "countless combinations of race, ethnicity, class, gender, age, religion, and many other factors" into a "common focus."[24]

Their concern about finding a unifying narrative for Western women's history reflects the fact that multiculturalism has not served the field as well as its practitioners had hoped. As Antonia Castañeda and Margaret Jacobs have observed, while multiculturalism celebrates diversity, as an analytical approach it does not lead scholars to investigate how and why inequalities of power are created and sustained. Commitment to multiculturalism, for example, did not prompt historians to examine the power that accrued with whiteness.[25] Historians of Western women's history correctly saw multiculturalism as foundational for their field. But they did not see how to develop the field to include all racial and ethnic histories and to synthesize these histories into a unified narrative that explained power inequities.

Multiculturalism proved disappointing to Western women's historians for another reason. They had hoped that historians of race and ethnicity in the West would acknowledge the shared goals and scholarly significance of their field and that of Western women's history. But what occurred was something quite different, almost the opposite. Beginning in the 1990s, and especially since the turn of the century, scholars who write racial ethnic histories located in the U.S. West have taken up the study of gender, women, and sexuality. As historian Karen Leong has recently argued, however, scholars identified with Western women's history do not necessarily see racial ethnic histories set in the West as part of their field, while practitioners of racial ethnic history do not regard their work as part of "Western history." Leong attributes both perceptions to the strength of the "western imaginary," which is to say, to the lingering strength of Turner's conception of the West.[26] In other words, although their work literally shares the same ground, Western women's and racial ethnic historians do not see their fields as connected because they do not share the same understanding of the West as a place.

Historians who study race and ethnicity in the West and who use gender and sexuality as categories of analysis generally identify themselves as historians of the United States. Their histories of racial ethnic women have become, and rightly so, part of American women's history. As a result, U.S. women's history has become more racially and ethnically diverse, moving beyond its earlier, limited focus on black-white racial dynamics. In contrast, U.S. women's historians' interest in the history of women in the West as *Western* women remains slight, and Western women's history as a field remains underdeveloped.

Searching for a tool that allows historians of the American West to study race, gender, and power, historians Antonia Castañeda, Patricia Limerick, and Margaret Jacobs have argued that the best way to study the West is as part of the history of global colonialism.[27] All three historians see colonialism as a valuable framework because it demands that historians pay attention to the unequal power dynamics of empire building, dynamics that are fundamentally intertwined with gender, class, and race. Moreover, by encouraging comparative global perspectives, the study of colonialism curbs our reflexive faith in American exceptionalism and enhances our ability to locate the common factors that have shaped our many histories.[28] Compared to scholars of European empires, however, American historians have been slow to consider U.S. nation-building as an intrinsically colonial project. The American colonial past has traditionally been relegated to the "colonial period" before 1776 and to a series of overseas engagements beginning in 1896. But there is increasing recognition that American history is a history of internal colonialism and domestic empire to which the experience of Indigenous people is central.[29]

This position we embrace wholeheartedly in this volume. But while we believe that colonialism is an important theme in the history of the American West, we do not think that it is the only possible analytical framework. Colonialism can be closely intertwined with migration and global capitalism, for example, but it does not necessarily tell us all we need to know about either topic. If a generation of Western women's history has taught us anything, it is to be wary of the ability of any single analytical category to define the field.

The West, Western Women, and Place

We propose, instead, that the field of Western women's history add the analytical category of place to the toolbox of other vital categories for studying the North American West, such as gender, sexuality, class, colonialism, and race. Our particular hope is that this reader will encourage many conversations about how the study of place can transform the field of Western women's history. Rooted in places ranging from the Pacific Northwest Plateau to

Hollywood and from the Navajo homeland to San Antonio, the articles in this volume certainly consider place as a factor in the construction of gender and race, but they do not do so in a way that encourages readers to think systematically about Western women's history. Reading the essays while foregrounding concepts of place enhances their already considerable analytical reach by suggesting the possibilities of synthesizing history and geography. We therefore now turn to explicating our understanding of place in relation to the histories of women in the regional West. Our ideas owe a great debt to the work of feminist geographers, particularly Doreen Massey, from whom we have borrowed several concepts.

We begin with a definition of place. In everyday life, we define the West and places within the region as physical locations, but that is not our concern here. Instead, to paraphrase geographer Tim Cresswell, we define place as a way of understanding, as an epistemology.[30] We see place, and thus the West, as created by an infinite variety of social relations. Critic Stephen Tatum gives us some examples of social relationships that have been important for the West (and many other places), contending that we should think of Western places "as *sites* produced by the circulation of peoples, of technologies and commodities, and of cultural artifacts, including of course images, stories, and myths" (italics in the original).[31] Place is socially constructed, and social construction is also our means of understanding place.

Places are always under construction. The social networks of which they are composed are intertwined with cultural, economic, and political power relations, and power, by nature, is fluid. Because people are always contesting each other, ideas, and institutions, their notions of place are also always contested and contingent. As geographer Linda McDowell observes, the power relations that produce places draw boundaries, and boundaries often lead to contests over who belongs and who does not.[32] In other words, places are generally constructed in ways that give more power to one group and less to others. Colonialism provides us with an easy-to-visualize example of this concept at work. As historians Tony Ballantyne and Antoinette Burton postulate, "Empire was a *self-consciously* spatializing project, with colonizers attempting both to impose their own topographies on conquered space and . . . to unmake preexisting maps of native communities or refashion them to suit their own political, economic, and military ends" (italics in the original).[33] Those who would wield power over others must seize and hold their physical and mental territories. All of which is to say that we should think of place as a verb, as something that is performed, something that actively creates and maintains power relations. Place does not simply mirror society; place and society are mutually constituted.[34]

Social networks, constantly dividing and connecting, growing and declining, create different kinds of places at particular points in time. Neither are places in time themselves fixed; what seems to be one place can be many places because people understand their locations in time and space differently. Standing at different intersections of gender, class, sexuality, and race, they will have unequal access to power. They will therefore contest the meaning of places. Some places will be ephemeral and others long-lasting, but all places are contingent. Literary critic Blake Allmendinger captures this contingent sense of the West when he writes, "All of us recognize a West whose history is represented by certain dates and hard facts; whose literary heritage is embodied by a canon of literature; whose images are communally recognized, shared, and experienced; whose geographic identity is sketched as a series of immobile boundary lines. But at the same time, each of us makes up the West for ourselves."[35] We see the West as something that can never be contained by lines on a map, but that will always be in flux.

The social networks or power relations that shape a particular place are not contained by that place, or bounded. The local is also global. Social networks facilitate movements of people, ideas, and things—from local to global and back again—that shape places. Mining towns in the American West, for example, were and are shaped both by international commodity markets—the price of copper, silver, and gold—and local factors, such as physiography and the availability of labor. The interaction of local and global forces creates places where notions of race and gender take shape.[36] Feminist geographers use the concept of "scale" to explain how every place is simultaneously local and global and many places in between. Scale is not an exogamous variable, an analytical construct imposed upon a place. Living in social networks, people themselves create and experience scale, whether they are fully aware of its effects or not. People create scale by drawing boundaries as self-conscious members of households, neighborhoods, communities, regions, and nations. The spatial reach of the power relations in which their lives are enmeshed varies from place to place and changes over time.

How do such concepts change how we think about the West and western identity? When people speak or write about the West, they commonly refer to it as a region. In our view, region should be seen as a special kind of place, socially constructed as are all places, yet in some ways transcending location in time and space. We follow historian Katherine Morrissey in understanding regions as "mental territories" in which the "boundaries that govern the residents are those they draw themselves." In this context, "region" "connotes something that is largely cognitive and emotional," as Andrew Cayton and Susan Gray have concluded about the Midwest.[37] To refer to the "West" and "Western history," in other words, is to evoke a place-based political identity midway between locality and nation.

As we have seen, in the 1890s, Frederick Jackson Turner developed the idea of a pre-modern West, a place where white frontiersmen lived as authentic men, as a counter to the industrialized, urbanized East, a modern place that many affluent white men perceived as threatening to their manhood. To this day we often think of the East and West as binary terms that construct each other and thus our understandings of America. Literary critic Krista Comer, for example, points to the debate that raged in 1962 between East and West over whether the Nobel Prize for literature that year should have gone to a westerner, John Steinbeck.[38] Regional identities matter emotionally and intellectually. They are, as Cayton and Gray contend, stories that we tell about ourselves in order to understand where we are and who we are.[39] To understand the West as region is to understand how Americans construct personal identities in relation to American nationalism.

To this day, practitioners of Western women's history lament that no matter how much they denounce Turner, they have not yet cleansed their field of his influence. Such laments are acknowledgements of an intellectual impasse from which there seems to be no escape. But Western women's history, and Western history in general, can be something more than a tenacious—some would say pernicious—narrative of regional identity. If we use the tools of feminist geographers, the narratives of the West can become a multitude of stories about unbounded social networks that continually shape and re-shape human experience in the "West" and the rest of the world. Thus contextualized, there is no need to replace the western narratives with the container-model of the New Western history. Masculinity in twenty-first-century Los Angeles is as much a part of the realm of Western women's history as white women trudging across the plains in the 1840s. What matters is the place in time. All maps are contingent.

Mapping Western Women and Modernity

To see these concepts in action and to gauge their ramifications for Western women's history, let us now turn to the articles themselves. Many were published during our co-editorship of *Frontiers: A Journal of Women Studies*; all are relatively recent. We chose these ten essays more for their quality than because they address a particular theme related to gender, place, and the American West, yet, considered as a group, they cohere topically, spatially, and temporally. Five longstanding themes of Western women's history—racial ethnic diversity, colonization, global capitalism, immigration, and modernity—dominate the collection as a whole. Nearly all of the essays are set in the period from the late nineteenth century to the post–World War II era, during which the United States first emerged and then triumphed as a modern world power. The essays can be read as gendered narratives of the modern West. Metaphorically and literally, their stories of the West begin in the late nineteenth century, when Frederick Jackson Turner and many others declared the frontier closed. The twentieth century, the era of American history given short shrift in traditional histories of the West, is the focus of this anthology. The articles open the doors to the modern Wests, invite us in, and provide us with maps (all contingent, of course) to guide our explorations.

Situated in the American West during the long turn of the last century, the essays can also be read as meditations on the nature of modernity. As feminist scholar Rita Felski observes, modernity can refer to a time period, but it can also signal the changes wrought by capitalism and the experiences of those changes. Collectively, the articles depict the emergence of the modern West through such modernizing processes as industrialization, urbanization, the development of mass transportation, and the growth and centralization of the state. Several articles focus directly on these processes, but others explore the human experience of modernity, a world of continual, confusing, heart-stopping change, a world where you may feel free today but trapped tomorrow. Modernity is a place where "all that is solid melts into air," as Marshall Berman writes, quoting Karl Marx on the collapse of the old order.[40] An ambiguous yet invaluable concept, modernity thus signals the modernizing forces that characterize the period and people's experience with those forces, such as the economic booms and busts that made and re-made the West.[41]

Using modernity as a conceptual rubric helps us to identify the linkages among economic, political, and cultural networks created by modernizing forces in particular times and places.[42] As modernity shaped the West, as transcontinental railroads were built, as ranching, mining, and logging industries developed and for the first time sent significant amounts of their products to national and international markets, the region was incorporated into the national economy, which in turn helped to make the United States a world power. At the same time, modernity meant the growth of western cities. By 1880, the West was the most urban region in the country, a place where great cities dominated vast open spaces.[43] San Francisco then reigned as the largest city in the West and the ninth-largest city in the United States. It was overtaken in the 1920s when Los Angeles became the region's largest, and the nation's tenth-largest, city.[44] Western cities, like all cities, were the most intense sites of modernity, the places where many of the modernizing processes intersected. Five of the essays in this volume consider experiences of modern urban life in San Francisco or Los Angeles. A common theme is how growing numbers of urban women chose to challenge traditional sexual norms, their decisions provoking reactions ranging from dread to delight on the part of the women and others. Thanks to the feminist geographers' tool of scale, we can understand modernity in the West as the integration of the region into the nation and as women's transformative sexual experiences in urban settings.

Besides modernity, the articles are concerned with three other themes related to gender and place—identities and place, colonized places, and networks and place—and we have grouped the essays accordingly. These topics highlight significant themes of Western women's history as illuminated by attention to place. Within each section, we have arranged the articles in roughly chronological order, the better to allow readers to evaluate the impact of time as well as place. Read through the lenses of place in time, each group of essays directs us toward new ways of thinking about Western women's history.

Many historians, including Frederick Jackson Turner, have associated the West as a region with personal identities. The four articles in "Identities and Place," however, seek to explain the role of place in the construction of gendered Western identities. All of the essays demonstrate the foundational concept of feminist geographers that gender and place are mutually constituted and illuminate their mutual transformation under the impact of such forces of modernization as immigration and urbanization. Modernization created upheavals; modernity entailed people attempting to bring order to their disrupted places. The articles scrutinize the many ways that people in the West—women and men, citizens and immigrants—scrambled for a social equilibrium favorable to their interests. They drew and contested boundaries that created multiple kinds of identities, equal and unequal. As narratives of western modernity, the essays depict the contentious creations of western places and identities.

The articles in "Colonized Places" examine how colonization shaped the West after military conquest. Colonization was inextricably linked to the emergence of modernity in the region. Control of land and people was the first step in the creation of the modern West. To mask the violence of their appropriation of Indigenous labor and resources, colonizers evoked an imaginary West, where the cost of conquest in blood and treasure was slight and where the conquered, as "primitives," were already doomed by the forces of modernity. As the essays in this section show, versions of this imaginary appeared in many places, including works of literature, restored "historic" sites, railroad trackside displays of Indigenous handicrafts promoted by railroad companies, and federal Indian assimilation policies. As the articles also demonstrate, however, the imaginary was not simply imposed upon and accepted by Indigenous people. The essays depict the struggle of Indigenous women to create and defend autonomous lives and identities within the confines of colonial power relations.

Spanning the twentieth century and reaching into the new millennium, the three articles organized under the rubric of "Networks and Place" trace the multidimensional connections among global capitalism, immigration, and social movements. These essays use the by now well-established notions of power operating in place and of scale to examine how modernity forged transnational networks. Each article focuses on a city and the many networks moving capital, labor, goods, and information between there and other cities and nations.

Notes

1. For an excellent bibliography of the field, see the notes in Susan Lee Johnson, "Nail This to Your Door: A Disputation on the Power, Efficacy, and Indulgent Delusion of Western Scholarship that Neglects the Challenge of Gender and Women's History," *Pacific Historical Review* 79, no. 4 (November 2010): 605–17. For a succinct historiography of the field, see Elizabeth Jameson, "Looking Back to the Road Ahead," *Pacific Historical Review* 79, no. 4 (November 2010): 574–84. Also useful is Vicki Ruiz, "Shaping Public Space/Enunciating Gender: A Multiracial Historiography of the Women's West, 1995–2000," *Frontiers: A Journal of Women Studies* 22, no. 3 (November 2001): 22–25.

2. For some examples of critical assessment, see "The Contributions and Challenges of Western Women's History: Four Essays by Sarah Deutsch, Virginia Scharff, Glenda Riley, and John Mack Faragher," *Montana: The Magazine of Western History* 41 (Spring 1991): 58–73; Karen Anderson, "Work, Gender, and Power in the American West," *Pacific Historical Review* 61, no. 4 (1992): 481–500; Antonia I. Castañeda, "Women of Color and the Rewriting of Western History: The Discourse, Politics, and Decolonization of History," *Pacific Historical Review* 61, no. 4 (1992): 501–34; Virginia Scharff, "'Else Surely We Shall All Hang Separately': The Politics of Western Women's History," *Pacific Historical Review* 61, no. 4 (1992): 535–56; Susan Lee Johnson, "'A Memory Sweet to Soldiers': The Significance of Gender in the History of the 'American West,'" *Western Historical Quarterly* 24, no. 4 (November 1993): 495–517; Elizabeth Jameson and Susan Armitage, eds., *Writing the Range: Race, Class, and Culture in the Women's West* (Norman: University of Oklahoma Press, 1997); Valerie J. Matsumoto and Blake Allmendinger, eds., *Over the Edge: Remapping the American West* (Berkeley: University of California Press, 1999); Susan Armitage, "Turner's Ghost: A Personal Retrospective on Western Women's History," in *The Practice of U.S. Women's History: Narratives, Intersections, and Dialogues,* eds. S. Jay Kleinberg, Eileen Boris, and Vicki L. Ruiz (New Brunswick: Rutgers University Press, 2007), 126–45; Elizabeth Jameson and Sheila McManus, eds., *One Step over the Line: Toward a History of Women in the North American Wests* (Alberta: University of Alberta Press, 2008); Elizabeth Jameson, Margaret D. Jacobs, Susan Lee Johnson, and Karen J. Leong, "If Not Now, When?: Gender, Power, and the Decolonization of Western History," *Pacific Historical Review* 79, no. 4 (November 2010): 573–628.

3. Joan M. Jensen and Darlis A. Miller, "The Gentle Tamers Revisited: New Approaches to the History of Women in the American West," *Pacific Historical*

Review 49 (1980): 173–213; Castañeda, "Women of Color," 501–34; Jameson, "Looking Back to the Road Ahead," 575.

4. Thanks to Karen Leong for the term "Western imaginary." See Karen J. Leong, "Still Walking, Still Brave: Mapping Gender, Race, and Power in U.S. Western History," *Pacific Historical Review* 79, no. 4 (November 2010): 618–28.

5. Susan Gray is interested in settler colonialism and the intersections of race and gender. Her work is focused on the U.S.-Canadian borderlands. Gayle Gullett studies the relationships of urban modernity, gender, and race; her focus is early twentieth-century Los Angeles.

6. Frederick Jackson Turner, "The Significance of the Frontier in American History," in *History, Frontier, and Section: Three Essays* (Albuquerque: University of New Mexico Press, 1993), 59–92.

7. Alan Trachtenberg, *The Incorporation of America: Culture and Society in the Gilded Age* (New York: Hill and Wang, 1982), 11–37; Gail Bederman, "Theodore Roosevelt: Manhood, Nation, and 'Civilization,'" in *Manliness and Civilization: A Cultural History of Gender and Race in the United States, 1880–1917* (Chicago: University of Chicago Press, 1995), 170–215. See also Michael Lansing, "Different Methods, Different Places: Feminist Geography and New Directions in US Western History," *Journal of Historical Geography* 29, no. 2 (April 2003): 239–43.

8. Bederman, "Theodore Roosevelt"; Johnson, "'A Memory Sweet to Soldiers.'"

9. For the information regarding television Westerns in 1959, see Jane Tompkins, *West of Everything: The Inner Life of Westerns* (Oxford: Oxford University Press, 1992), 5. As quoted in Gary A. Yoggy, "When Television Wore Six-Guns: Cowboy Heroes on TV," in *Shooting Stars: Heroes and Heroines of Western Film,* ed. Archie P. McDonald (Bloomington: Indiana University Press, 1987), 230. Lee Clark Mitchell, *Westerns: Making the Man in Fiction and Film* (Chicago: University of Chicago Press, 1996), 2–13; Stephen Tatum, "The Classic Westerner: Gary Cooper," in *Shooting Stars: Heroes and Heroines of Western Film,* ed. Archie P. McDonald (Bloomington: Indiana University Press, 1987), 78–79; John G. Cawelti, *The Six-Gun Mystique Sequel* (Bowling Green, OH: Bowling Green State University Popular Press, 1999), 92–98; Stanley Corkin, "Cowboys and Free Markets: Post-World II and U.S. Hegemony," *Cinema Journal* 39, no. 3 (Spring 2000): 66–91; Richard Slotkin, *Gunfighter Nation: The Myth of the Frontier in Twentieth-Century America* (New York: Atheneum, 1992).

10. As quoted in Stephen McVeigh, *The American Western* (Edinburgh: Edinburgh University Press, 2007), vii.

11. McVeigh, *The American Western*, viii. For further discussion regarding Bush, 9/11, and the American West, see Susan Kollin, ed., *Postwestern Cultures: Literature, Theory, Space* (Lincoln: University of Nebraska Press, 2007), ix–x.

12. Susan Armitage and Elizabeth Jameson, "Editors' Introduction," in *The Women's West*, eds. Susan Armitage and Elizabeth Jameson (Norman: University of Oklahoma Press, 1987), 3–6.

13. For a critique of the neglect of Western women's history by American women's historians, see Ellen Carol DuBois and Vicki L. Ruiz, "Introduction," in *Unequal Sisters: A Multicultural Reader in U.S. Women's History,* eds . Ellen Carol DuBois and Vicki L. Ruiz (New York: Routledge, 1990), xi–xii. For a similar discussion regarding race, region, and American literature, see Krista Comer, *Landscapes of the New West: Gender and Geography in Contemporary Women's Writing* (Chapel Hill: University of North Carolina Press, 1999).

14. The founding texts of the New Western history were Patricia Nelson Limerick, *The Legacy of Conquest: The Unbroken Past of the American West* (New York: W. W. Norton & Co., 1987); Donald Worster, *Rivers of Empire: Water, Aridity, and the Growth of the American West* (New York: Pantheon, 1986); William Cronon, *Nature's Metropolis: Chicago and the Great West* (Chicago: W. W. Norton & Co., 1991); and Richard White, *"It's Your Misfortune and None of My Own": A New History of the American West* (Norman: University of Oklahoma Press, 1991).

15. For an excellent review of the foundational works of New Western history, see Robert D. Johnson, "Beyond 'The West': Regionalism, Liberalism, and the Evasion of Politics in the New Western History," *Rethinking History* 2, no. 2 (June 1998): 239–42.

16. For Limerick's inaugural indictment of the "F" word, see her essay, "The Adventures of the Frontier in the Twentieth Century," in Richard White and Patricia Nelson Limerick, *The Frontier in American Culture,* ed. James R. Grossman (Berkeley: University of California Press, 1995), 72–80. For further discussion, see Kerwin Lee Klein, "Reclaiming the 'F' Word, or Being and Becoming Postwestern," *Pacific Historical Review* 65, no. 2 (May 1996): 179–215.

17. For a classic formulation of the factors that supposedly constitute the West as a distinctive region, see Limerick, *The Legacy of Conquest.*

18. See Lansing, "Different Methods"; Johnson, "Beyond 'The West.'"

19. The sharp rise and decline in the production of dissertations in Western history between 1988 and 2006 is quite striking. Between 1988 and 1994, the *Western Historical Quarterly* reported, on the basis of annual searches in *Dissertation Abstracts International,* an average of 115 dissertations completed per year in Western history. Then, abruptly, the number shot up to 167 dissertations (an increase of 74 over the previous year) in 1995, peaked at 288 in 1996, with an average annual production of 187 dissertations in Western history between 1995 and 2001. Then, again abruptly, the number of dissertations plummeted from 191 in 2001 to a mere 82 the following year, with an annual average of 102 dissertations between 2002 and 2006. Numbers of dissertations in Western women's history (coded as gender and sexuality beginning in 2007) mirrored the trajectory of the field as a whole, annually averaging nearly 6 between 1998 and 1994, nearly 11 between 1995 and 2001, and 6 again between 2002 and 2006. These last numbers are not a true count of dissertations in Western women's history, however, because dissertations featuring women as subjects have frequently been coded in racial/ethnic categories. These figures have been tabulated from the following: Kim M. Gruenwald and Christiane

A. Mitchell, "A List of Dissertations," *Western Historical Quarterly* 19, no. 3 (August 1998): 313–20; Christiane A. Mitchell and Kathryn Morse, "A List of Dissertations," *Western Historical Quarterly* 20, no. 3 (August 1989): 323–30; Kathryn Morse and Renée M. Sentilles, "A List of Dissertations," *Western Historical Quarterly* 21, no. 3 (August 1990): 341–49; Renée M. Sentilles et al., "A List of Dissertations," *Western Historical Quarterly* 22, no. 3 (August 1991): 335–42; Dan Moos and John A. Hardcastle, "A List of Dissertations," *Western Historical Quarterly* 23, no. 3 (August 1992): 355–61; Andrew M. Honker and Kevin D. Hatfield, "A List of Dissertations," *Western Historical Quarterly* 24, no. 3 (August 1993): 383–91; Andrew M. Honker, "A List of Dissertations," *Western Historical Quarterly* 25, no. 3 (Autumn 1994): 377–82; Stephen Kent Amerman and James Wyatt Feldman, "A List of Dissertations," *Western Historical Quarterly* 26, no. 3 (Autumn 1995): 361–71; James T. Wyatt Feldman and Todd G. Anderson, "A List of Dissertations," *Western Historical Quarterly* 27, no. 3 (Autumn 1996): 359–72; Todd G. Anderson and Michael J. Lansing, "A List of Dissertations," *Western Historical Quarterly* 28, no. 3 (Autumn 1997): 389–99; Michael J. Lansing and Heather L. Block, "A List of Dissertations," *Western Historical Quarterly* 29, no. 3 (Autumn 1998): 371–81; Heather L. Block and Kyle T. Bulthuis, "A List of Dissertations," *Western Historical Quarterly* 30, no. 3 (Autumn 1999): 357–69; Kyle T. Bulthuis and Christian P. Peterson, "A List of Dissertations," *Western Historical Quarterly* 31, no. 3 (Autumn 2000): 347–57; Christian P. Peterson and Jesse T. Schreier, "A List of Dissertations," *Western Historical Quarterly* 32, no. 3 (Autumn 2001): 353–64; Jesse T. Schreier and Matthew Pehl, "A List of Dissertations," *Western Historical Quarterly* 33, no. 3 (Autumn 2002): 343–48; Matthew Pehl and John P. Barnes, "A List of Dissertations," *Western Historical Quarterly* 34, no. 3 (Autumn 2003): 355–61; John P. Barnes and Jennifer Holland, "A List of Dissertations," *Western Historical Quarterly* 35, no. 3 (Autumn 2004): 365–72; Jennifer Holland and Sarah A. Fox, "A List of Dissertations," *Western Historical Quarterly* 36, no. 3 (Autumn 2005): 359–66; Sarah A. Fox and Adam M. Luke, "A List of Dissertations," *Western Historical Quarterly* 37, no. 3 (Autumn 2006): 359–65.

20. Armitage, "Turner's Ghost."

21. Jensen and Miller, "Gentle Tamers." Susan Johnson repeated this same point in the early 1990s. See Johnson, "'A Memory Sweet to Soldiers.'"

22. Elizabeth Jameson, "Toward a Multicultural History of Women in the Western United States," *Signs: Journal of Women in Culture and Society* 13, no. 4 (Summer 1988): 761–91. Between 1988 and the present, *Signs* has published only one other essay that fits within Jameson's rubric of Western women's history. See Tanis Modleski, "A Woman's Gotta Do . . . What a Man's Gotta Do?: Cross Dressing in the Western," *Signs: Journal of Women in Culture and Society* 22, no. 3 (Spring 1997): 519–44. There are, to be sure, articles on Hispanic and Indigenous feminisms and on women and the U.S.-Mexico border, but they are not historical in nature. Finally, "Western" is simply not the point of Anita Clair Fellman's essay, "Laura Ingalls Wilder and Rose Wilder Lane: The Politics of a Mother-Daughter Relationship," *Signs: Journal of*

Women in Culture and Society 15, no. 3 (Spring 1990): 535–61, which appears in a special issue, "The Ideology of Mothering: Disruption and Reproduction of Patriarchy."

23. Jameson, "Toward a Multicultural History," 777, 788–91.

24. Jameson and Armitage, *Writing the Range*, 3–15.

25. Castañeda, "Women of Color"; Margaret D. Jacobs, "Getting Out of a Rut: Decolonizing Western Women's History," *Pacific Historical Review* 79, no. 4 (November 2010): 585–604.

26. Leong, "Still Walking." Following Elizabeth Jameson, we use the term "racial ethnic" to emphasize that the concepts of race and ethnicity are both constructed and overlapping. See Jameson, "Looking Back to the Road Ahead," 575, n. 4.

27. Jacobs, "Getting Out of a Rut"; Castañeda, "Women of Color"; Patricia Nelson Limerick, "Going West and Ending Up Global," *Western Historical Quarterly* 32, no. 1 (Spring 2001): 5–23.

28. Ann Laura Stoler, an anthropologist of Southeast Asia, has been particularly influential in encouraging American scholars to consider U.S. history in the context of global colonialism. See especially her "Tense and Tender Ties: The Politics of Comparison in North American History and (Post) Colonial Studies," *Journal of American History* 88, no. 3 (December 2001): 829–65; and her edited collection, *Haunted by Empire: Geographies of Intimacy in North American History* (Durham: Duke University Press, 2006). For further evidence of Stoler's influence, see "Domestic Frontiers: The Home and Colonization," a special issue of *Frontiers: A Journal of Women Studies*, guest edited by Victoria Haskins and Margaret D. Jacobs, 28, nos. 1–2 (2007).

29. See, for example, Linda Gordon, "Internal Colonialism and Gender," in Stoler, *Haunted by Empire*, 427–51. Two recent works of "Western" history that are also major contributions to the history of internal colonialism in the United States are Cathleen D. Cahill, *Federal Fathers and Mothers: A Social History of the United States Indian Service, 1869–1933* (Chapel Hill: University of North Carolina Press, 2011); and Margaret D. Jacobs, *White Mothers to a Dark Race: Settler Colonialism, Maternalism, and the Removal of Indigenous Children in the American West and Australia, 1880–1940* (Lincoln: University of Nebraska Press, 2009).

30. Tim Cresswell, *Place: A Short Introduction* (Malden, MA: Blackwell, 2004), 11–15.

31. Stephen Tatum, "Postfrontier Horizons," *Modern Fiction Studies* 50, no. 2 (Summer 2004): 460–61.

32. As quoted in Lansing, "Different Methods," 233.

33. Tony Ballantyne and Antoinette Burton, "Introduction: The Politics of Intimacy in an Age of Empire," in Tony Ballantyne and Antoinette Burton, eds., *Moving Subjects: Gender, Mobility, and Intimacy in an Age of Global Empire* (Urbana: University of Illinois Press, 2009), 2.

34. Comer, *Landscapes of the New West*, 26.

35. Matsumoto and Allmendinger, *Over the Edge*, 2.

36. See Antonia Castañeda, "'Que se puieran defender (So You Could Defend Yourselves)': Chicanas, Regional History, and National Discourses," *Frontiers: A Journal of Women Studies* 22, no. 3 (2001): 116–42.

37. Katherine G. Morrissey, *Mental Territories: Mapping the Inland Empire* (Ithaca: Cornell University Press, 1997), 8; Andrew R. L. Cayton and Susan E. Gray, "The Story of the Midwest: An Introduction," in *The American Midwest: Essays in Regional History*, eds. Andrew R. L. Cayton and Susan E. Gray (Bloomington: Indiana University Press, 2001), 4.

38. Comer, *Landscapes of the New West*, 20–25.

39. Cayton and Gray, "The Story of the Midwest," 4–17; for more on regional identity, or "regionality," see the essay by Kathleen N. Conzen, "Pi-ing the Type: Jane Grey Swisshelm and the Contest of Midwestern Regionality," in Cayton and Gray, *The American Midwest*, 91–111. David M. Wrobel and Michael C. Steiner make a compatible argument in their edited volume, *Many Wests: Place, Culture, and Regional Identity* (Lawrence: University Press of Kansas, 1997).

40. Marshall Berman, *All That Is Solid Melts into Air: The Experience of Modernity* (New York: Penguin Books, 1988).

41. We rely on Rita Felski for these definitions because of her clarity and because she understands that modernity is a deeply gendered concept. Prominent male geographers, such as David Harvey and Edward Soja, have contributed much to our understanding of modernity and place, yet, as Doreen Massey observes, because they do not include gender in their analysis, their work is incomplete. See Rita Felski, *The Gender of Modernity* (Cambridge: Harvard University Press, 1995), 9, 12–13; David Harvey, *The Condition of Postmodernity: An Enquiry into the Origins of Cultural Change* (Cambridge: Blackwell Publishers, 1990); Edward W. Soja, *Postmodern Geographies: The Reassertion of Space in Critical Social Theory* (New York: Verso, 1989); Doreen Massey, *Space, Place, and Gender* (Minneapolis: University of Minnesota Press, 1994), 212–48.

42. Felski, *The Gender of Modernity*, 9.

43. White, *"It's Your Misfortune and None of My Own,"* 391–93.

44. U.S. Census Bureau, "Population of the 100 Largest Cities and Other Urban Places in the United States: 1790 to 1990," Population Division Working Paper No. 27, 2013, http://www.census.gov/population/www/documentation/twps0027/twps0027.html.

PART I

Identities and Place

Places and identities are complexly and inextricably tied together. As feminist geographers Liz Bondi and Joyce Davidson write, "To *be* is to be some *where*" (italics in the original).[1] As humans we can only act in place. Constructing places is our intensely social way of experiencing the world.[2] Interacting with others, we create and re-create places and, in so doing, shape and reshape our identities. Place and identity are thus mutually constituted.

Mary C. Wright's essay, "The Woman's Lodge: Constructing Gender on the Nineteenth-Century Pacific Northwest Plateau," takes as its departure point the mutual constitution of place and gender, a concept she attributes to feminist geographers Gillian Rose and Linda McDowell. Wright's subject is the relationship between women's lodges and gender identity among nineteenth-century Indigenous peoples of the Pacific Northwest Plateau. As geographer Yi-Fu Tuan observes, buildings are cultural texts that depict beliefs about the social order and identities.[3] Native women assembled the materials to build the lodges and constructed and controlled them, all actions that attested to and reinforced women's power within the villages. The physical location of the lodges also communicated lessons: menstrual lodges, for example, were positioned away from the village to protect it from women's power. Inside the lodges, women conducted rituals for puberty, menstruation, and birth. There they also worked to make the trade goods, such as baskets, that connected one community with another. In this way, the women's lodges served as crucibles for the production and reproduction of gender, the foundation of a way of life.

Wright also draws on the geographers' insight that the women's construction of gender was deeply enmeshed in social networks experienced at different scales. For most of her essay, Wright examines power relations among Indigenous people within and between villages in the early nineteenth century when white settlers were relatively few. By the late nineteenth century, however, the impositions of the colonial state had destroyed the autonomy of Plateau Indians. Increasingly unable to pursue their traditional lifeways, women gradually gave up their lodges. Wright thus soberly concludes her article with the emergence of modernity and its effects on Indigenous identity.

The other three essays in "Identities and Place" focus on relationships between modernity and identity. In particular, they examine how gendered and racialized identities are constituted in modern cities. In her article, "Mindful Masquerades: Que(e)rying Japanese Immigrant Dress in Turn-of-the-Century San Francisco," Amy Sueyoshi analyzes relationships between the city and constructions of race and gender. She wants us to understand the power relations that underlaid San Francisco as the nation's ninth-largest city in 1900.[4] Sueyoshi depicts San Francisco as a place constituted by interlocking global and local networks, a city where one could experience what feminist geographer Doreen Massey calls a "global sense of place."[5] To illustrate what she means, Massey describes Kilburn High Road, a street in London where immigrants from places as different and far-flung as Ireland and India own shops. One cannot understand the street, she contends, "without bringing into play half the world and a considerable amount of British imperialist history."[6] Massey's contemporary London street is a place of "time-space compression," a place where rapid transportation and communication technologies have abridged physical distances, making possible a global sense of place experienced through such seemingly simple transactions as buying a newspaper from Ireland or a sari from India. How similar experiences shaped identities in San Francisco is the focus of Sueyoshi's essay.

Sueyoshi is especially interested in what she calls "mindful masquerades"—the performance of race and gender through dress. Time-space compression deeply influenced late nineteenth- and early twentieth-century San Francisco, a port city connected to the world by international shipping, transcontinental railroads, and the marvels of the telegraph and telephone. Immigrants from Japan, who read about the United States before they ever boarded ship, came to San Francisco believing they had a chance to become American Gilded Age financial success stories—Japanese American Andrew Carnegies—a possibility they linked to bolstering Japanese nationalism. Once they arrived in San Francisco, they quickly donned American clothing to advance their ambitions. They wanted to look American in the hopes of being accepted as Americans. Japanese brides in San Francisco wore white wedding gowns, not kimonos. In contrast, elite white women dressed themselves in kimonos to perform a Japanese femininity that they imagined as a temporary retreat from their identities as modern women; the white women believed that wearing kimonos would enable them to experience an identity that was pre-modern, exotic, and erotic. For Sueyoshi, then, the body is a place. She shows that both Japanese immigrants and affluent Euro-American women believed that by wearing new clothes they could embody new identities.

Just as geographers use place to mean not only physical location but also a way of knowing, so they use body or, more precisely, embodiment to refer not to physical bodies per se but to a way of thinking about them.[7] Embodiment is the process by which bodies are socially constructed and contested. Japanese immigrants in San Francisco failed in their attempt to claim citizenship by dressing like Americans. White Americans deemed Japanese bodies not only un-American but also unable to become American, to join the body politic.[8] But neither could Chinese immigrants, who, Sueyoshi makes clear, made little attempt to embody an American identity. At the same time, kimono-wearing affluent white women, as well as cross-dressing entertainers (another group examined by Sueyoshi) could perform different kinds of raced, gendered, and sexualized identities that were acceptable, precisely because they did not threaten the social order. Raced, gendered, and sexualized bodies in one city, San Francisco, thus created what historian Michael Lansing calls "places within places."[9]

Brett L. Abrams studies bodies and sexualities in another city, Hollywood, during the 1920s and 1930s. In his essay, "Latitude in Mass-Produced Culture's Capital: New Women and Other Players in Hollywood, 1920–1941," Abrams shows how a city dependent on one industry was shaped by that industry, from the built environment to the way the industry promoted itself and the city, both locally and across the nation. Abrams describes how a group he labels the "Hollywood players," women who cross-dressed, as well as lesbians and gay men, built a community in Hollywood. Frequenting the same nightclubs and parties, they "forged a concept of Hollywood as a place of latitude for unconventional figures." Prompted by the industry's publicity agents, the media during this era routinely covered the exploits of the "Hollywood players" to sell movies and newspapers. Together, the players and the media constructed Hollywood as a place where the culturally forbidden became permissible, where the unconventional sexuality of the players was neither censored nor condemned. Instead, publicity described the players as successful members of the industry who publicly enjoyed themselves, whether at work on the studio lot or in nightclubs. In either place they might be cross-dressed; wherever they were, they remade place and sexual identities.

Like Amy Sueyoshi, Catherine S. Ramírez is concerned with a city of intersecting global and local networks, immigration, and immigrants who embodied contested identities. In "Saying 'Nothin': Pachucas and the Languages of Resistance," Ramírez examines the zoot suit subculture of young, second-generation Mexican American men and women who wore zoot suits and spoke pachuco slang in 1940s Los Angeles. Hipsters who grew up in the barrios of Los Angeles, pachucos and pachucas sought modern urban pleasures. By embracing the city's nightlife, they sometimes flouted the strictures of their traditional Mexican parents and consistently confronted the racism of Anglo society. Their zoot suits were part of a youthful rebellion that signified, Ramírez declares, "difference and defiance." Ramírez's focus, however, is on another kind of rebellious embodiment: how the second generation spoke. Because they adopted a hybrid slang that was neither Spanish nor English, adults in both the Anglo and Mexican communities denigrated the pachucos and pachucas as neither fully Mexican nor American. The young Mexican Americans embodied highly contested identities that were linked to place and influenced place.

When male Chicano activists of the 1960s and 1970s looked at this earlier era of youthful rebellion, they romanticized the slang-speaking male—the pachuco in a zoot suit who performed a hip racialized masculinity. He was a "*vato de huevos*" (ballsy guy), experienced in the ways of (heterosexual) transgressive sexuality. Sexually active pachucas, on the other hand, were often labeled *putas* (whores). Despite their marginalization, pachucas resisted racism, second-class citizenship, and sexism. They also wore zoot suits, spoke pachuco slang, and hung out in the popular places where *pachuquismo* was performed. If called to testify in court against pachucos, the young women found ways to resist: refusing to answer questions or to cower. Pachucas refused to act as ladies. In contrast to late twentieth-century Chicano activists, for whom hip resistance was embodied as male, pachucas defied conventional notions of gender as well as race.

We began this section by commenting on the universality of the connection between place and identity: all humans create places to live that shape their identity. The articles in this section analyze a broad range of people who created places and thus identities, from Indian women on the Pacific Northwest Plateau in the nineteenth century to zoot-suiter women in Los Angeles during World War II. The experience of modernity—of immigration, urbanization, time-space compression, and transgressive sexuality—runs through the essays, tying them together. We hope that these pieces will help readers understand some of the ways modern identities were constructed and experienced in the West. The feminist geographers' tool of scale should also help readers to see how international and national factors shaped the West and vice versa. Modernity in the western United States is part of a global story.

Notes

1. Liz Bondi and Joyce Davidson, "Troubling the Place of Gender," in *Handbook of Cultural Geography,* eds. Kay Anderson, Mona Domosh, Steve Pile, and Nigel Thrift (London and Thousand Oaks: Sage Publications, 2003), 338.

2. Tim Cresswell, *Place: A Short Introduction* (Malden, MA: Blackwell, 2004), 18–24.

3. Yi-Fu Tuan, *Space and Place: The Perspective of Experience* (Minneapolis: University of Minnesota Press, 1977), 101–14.

4. U.S. Census Bureau, "Population of the 100 Largest Cities and Other Urban Places in the United States: 1790 to 1990," Population Division Working Paper No. 27, 2013, http://www.census.gov/population/www/documentation/twps0027/twps0027.html.

5. Doreen Massey, *Space, Place, and Gender* (Minneapolis: University of Minnesota Press, 1994), 146–56.

6. Massey, *Space, Place, and Gender*, 154.

7. Linda McDowell, *Gender, Identity and Place: Understanding Feminist Geographies* (Minneapolis: University of Minnesota Press, 1999), 34–70.

8. McDowell, *Gender, Identity, and Place.*

9. Michael Lansing, "Different Methods, Different Places: Feminist Geography and New Directions in US Western History," *Journal of Historical Geography* 29, no. 2 (April 2003): 236.

CHAPTER 1

The Woman's Lodge

Constructing Gender on the Nineteenth-Century Pacific Northwest Plateau

MARY C. WRIGHT

Gender and all manner of status and societal roles have come to be seen as constructed. People help define the categories of human groupings by their behavior, their expectations, their ideas, their resistance, and by the way they treat each other. The understanding of woman as a biologically determined being is challenged (some would say overturned) by cultural definitions resulting from human actions. And, of course, this defining of gender differs by group or culture and changes over time.

Female gender construction began at the woman's lodge among the Indigenous peoples inhabiting the Pacific Northwest Plateau at the beginning of the nineteenth century. A constellation of gender definitions, beliefs, and behaviors radiated from that place. In these woman-built structures all women passed their menstrual periods, girls' puberty rituals took place, children were birthed, baskets and other woman-produced articles were made, and teachings of what it meant to be a woman were passed from generation to generation.

The Plateau is an arid, often mountainous region drained by the Columbia, Fraser, and Snake rivers, or roughly occupying a region defined today by eastern British Columbia, Washington, and Oregon, all of Idaho, and parts of Alberta and Montana. A wide range of Indigenous peoples made their home in the region, such as the Nez Perce in Idaho state, the Yakama of Washington state, and the Thompson, Lillooet, and the Okanagan in Canada. All included a woman's lodge among their buildings and their cultural practices. In a 1930s project defining the Plateau as a distinct cultural area, anthropologist Verne F.

Ray found menstrual seclusion and girls' puberty rites, both sited in the woman's lodge, universal in the region. So much so, that he identified them as defining characteristics of Plateau culture.[1]

Investigating the women's lodge as a *place* and as *space* proves to be a productive approach to understanding how gender was constructed for Plateau women. Cultural geographers have long studied human spatial patterning. Feminist geographers, expanding cultural geography's study of human spatial patterning, find women's use of space different from men's and women's places endowed with special meanings, protections, and practices. Applying some of the same inquiries and considerations of gender and space for non-European peoples, in this case the Indigenous peoples of the Plateau, shows the profound impact of gender on human construction of place and, visa versa, of spatial implications for the construction of gender.[2]

Control of the woman's lodge indicates the overall importance of women in the society at large, even as it serves as a marker of that power. The societal and cultural importance of Indigenous Plateau women can be traced to their economic contributions and control of distribution, the strength of the bilateral kinship system (where heredity and identity are calculated along both male and female lines), equal spiritual opportunities, and other cultural markers such as mobility and access to divorce.[3] Underneath these outward manifestations of women's power in the community at large were those behaviors and beliefs constructed internally, among women themselves, in the woman's lodge.[4]

American Indian women of the Plateau region built and controlled significant space within Native culture.[5] Shelter took two forms among the Plateau people. The winter lodge, built in sheltered valleys, was a pit house entered by ladders in the center, with a dugout basement and overarching rafters covered with mats and earth. The summer or traveling lodge was smaller, more likely to be circular, without the deeply depressed flooring and with a different rafter structure. Women collected marshland tules and constructed mats needed for both structures. Buffalo robes later came to replace the mat covering for some groups. Women prepared the thirty to forty robes needed for the lodge and owned them.[6] The lodge's robes were valued at sixty to one hundred dollars total in mid-nineteenth-century currency.

Early-nineteenth-century fur traders and missionaries observed, often with surprise, the women's importance to the people's housing and the social practices that grew from that connection. Plateau women set up camp, including raising the mat lodges, then broke camp and dismantled the lodges when traveling and when returning to traditional villages. Their ownership of the lodge was recognized throughout the region. Upon divorce, a man's belongings were set outside the lodge door, while the woman retained the dwelling.[7]

A young woman built her own lodge for the puberty ritual. Later in her life, she would also build menstrual and birth lodges, as well as the dwellings needed for her family. These structures were built of materials the women gathered or produced, over the basement the women dug out themselves. The woman's lodges established the blueprint for the larger structures of the people, as well as providing the site for the important times and rituals of women's lives.

The Menstrual Lodge

The ritual practice of menstrual seclusion on the Plateau discloses the sited nature of girls' puberty rites. Passing on women's lore and wisdom occurred during puberty training. Women's training in the production of artifacts, such as basketry, leather goods, and quill (later beadwork) adornment was also spatially defined in the menstrual lodge. Delivery of the next generation took place in the woman's lodge, where births occurred. For many girls, the menstrual lodge was where they ensured a good future (that included health, prosperity, husband, and children) for themselves through ritual practices. The range of activities within the lodge and the weight of their importance for women mark the structure as culturally significant.

Given this cultural value, archaeologists have not assiduously searched for evidence of menstrual lodges within the Plateau or elsewhere. Remains of an excavated Yakima Valley village included small pits, eleven to thirteen feet in diameter, encircled with stones, located at the edge and downstream from the main housing site. These sites were not identified in the literature conclusively as menstrual lodges, yet they could be marks left by the women's lodges.[8]

These findings are substantiated by testimony gathered in the 1970s from Native women who tell about the lodges' former construction, physical structure, and setting, even though menstrual seclusion practices have declined. The nineteenth-century girl undergoing the puberty rite built the lodge herself, but women usually cooperated in the raising of other lodges. The lodge was usually a small circular pit house, with a dugout floor, pine poles, and mat covering. The menstrual lodge was secluded, or located downstream, at the edge of the winter village or summer encampment.

A Nez Perce elder reported in the 1990s, "They had a place to go when they were menstruating—menstrual lodge. . . . There is one in Kamiah. You can see [it] on the other side of the second church, that little creek over there. You can tell because it is indented. It's down deep." According to a Yakama woman interviewed in the 1970s, "Long time, the women put up a hut, keep her outside [camp] for five days. . . . She stays in that mat tipi."[9]

The terms of menstrual seclusion itself seem to have followed a geographic designation for some groups. "The first menstrual period is called *tlo'gamug* . . . [in] reference to the hole in the ground beneath the menstrual lodge . . . all after periods [were] *alitska* (going outside)," reported Charles Hill-Tout for the Lower Lillooet Indians. Other Plateau villages used *zo'met* (abstaining from fresh meat) as their term.[10]

Whatever the term for the seclusion, selecting the place to build the lodge was all-important. The away-from-camp location can be understood as ensuring the health of the community. There was concern about the power of menstruating women negatively influencing the health of the community and men's power, tools, and hunting abilities. Menstruating women did not go to fishing sites or ceremonies. There were ritual and herbal remedies if by chance a woman contacted a man, the lodge, or others during her menses. It was not an all-or-nothing matter, but grandmothers and other elder women trained the younger generation to be careful in this regard.[11]

Rather than see menstrual restrictions in a negative light, until recently the standard Euro-American interpretation, we might see seclusion both as an acknowledgment of women's power and a mechanism to contain its potentially negative forces. Among the Cherokee, argues historian Theda Perdue, blood was believed to contain a being's life or spirit and demanded to be treated with the ritual care, whether in menstruation, or a childbirth, or, for men, in hunting and warfare. That many of the same rules—seclusion, purification, prayer—were followed by men during their blood-related war or hunting activities as by women during menstruation underscores that the blood was at issue, not the sex of the human interacting with it.[12]

There were also male-female similarities in Plateau culture. In fact, men were believed to have formerly menstruated. Coyote's decision to change the matter was influenced by both gender and spatial considerations. In *Memoirs of the American Museum of Natural History*, James Teit recounts a Shuswap menstruation myth:

> Coyote Makes Women Menstruate: Formerly the men menstruated, and not the women. When Coyote was working in the world, putting things to right, he considered this matter, and said to himself. "It is not right that men should menstruate. It is very inconvenient, for they do all the hunting and most of the traveling. Women stay more at home, and therefore it will be better if they menstruate, and not the men." Whereupon he took some of the menstrual fluid from men, and threw it upon the women, saying, "Henceforth, women shall menstruate, and not men. They shall menstruate once a month or with every moon."

Perhaps it is not surprising then that in Plateau culture some practices transcended gender. Men also went into seclusion and purification before hunting or going to war. Both boys and girls underwent purification and were isolated when they sought a guardian spirit on the vision quest. Fathers followed restrictions, as did mothers, at birthing. Boys even let blood from cuts in their legs during a portion of their puberty training. It follows, then, as a wider cultural practice that women would go into isolation and undergo purification during this powerful time. Rather than see this as simply a pollution issue and a restriction of women, a broad societal pattern of spatial containment can be discerned.[13]

Just as shamans were honored and feared among the Plateau peoples, menstruating woman were revered and believed powerful. A modern contemporary Nez Perce woman reported in the 1980s:

> [A] Woman is strong when she is pregnant, [a] woman is strong on her moon [menstruating] . . . That's why she had to keep away from everybody. Women never went to medicine dances, war dances, stick games, or funerals. They were not supposed to be anywhere if they had their menstruation . . . that's how they were separated . . . Woman was very sacred when she had her menstruation or whenever she was pregnant.[14]

The lodge also may have been sited at a particular, secluded place due to its neutral or, alternately, supernatural qualities. A leading older woman who was respected in the community, one with appropriate powers and gifts, or the grandmother of the extended family chose the site and oversaw its construction. There might also have been spiritual reasons for building the menstrual lodge along a stream or by water. Two films give Native testimony on the spiritual power of Plateau water places. In *Place of Falling Waters*, the Salish people define a waterfall as a spiritual, powerful place. In *Everything Change, Everything Change*, a girl's guardian spirit power included using water to replicate the lake location where she acquired it. Menstrual seclusion and especially the girls' puberty rite carried significant metaphysical content. The by-the-water site of the menstrual lodge then might have been potentially powerful space.[15]

Girls' puberty rite activities radiated from the menstrual lodge base. One spiritually significant activity among the Thompson people of Canada was for a girl near the end of her menstrual training to peck pictographs into the surface of a spiritually important rock or to use red paint to mark the stone. The powerful pubescent girl linked the two places by traveling from the menstrual lodge to the place of a rock appropriate for spiritually significant markers. The designs she made on the rock included lodges, pines, trails, and basketry connected to her training ritual. Not only was the menstrual lodge geographically significant in itself, but many of the spiritually powerful symbols representing it were geographic icons, such as trails and lodges. These same trail, lodge, and tree designs appeared in the headbands, hats, and baskets women made throughout their lives, connecting them back to the puberty lodge.[16]

The spot to build the menstrual lodge changed, of course, as the people migrated from place to place on their seasonal food-procuring rounds. In May they may have been digging roots, but by late summer they would pick berries at another mountain location. In early spring and autumn they would congregate at the fishing sites, or alternately they hunted elk and deer. Some traveled to the Plains to hunt buffalo. In each of these seasons, there would undoubtedly be preferred camps with special places where the menstrual lodge or lodges would be built year to year, appropriately away from community activity. One wonders whether these spots elicited the kind of stories and teachings (and in this case, women's knowledge) that Keith Basso has noted in *Wisdom Sits in Places: Landscape and Language among the Western Apache*. The stories about menstruation, the puberty rite, and proper female behavior sited in these different locales throughout the region surely were part of the lore passed on by the elders or stories shared by women who occupied the lodges together.[17]

Women living in close proximity have been shown to develop similar menstrual cycles over time. In *Blood Magic: The Anthropology of Menstruation*, Thomas Buckley argues that this synchrony of women's menstrual seclusion among California's Yurok people may have served as the timing for community rituals and male training. Menstrual synchrony among Plateau women of the community or family may have been difficult to establish because of these same seasonal rounds and a fluctuation in attendance. If menstrual synchrony developed on the Plateau, it would seem logical that the winter village would be the time and place. The winter village was important in Plateau identity, and many of the tribal or band names by which the people are now known came from the rivers or valleys of their traditional winter village sites, or, alternately, the rivers were named for the people who resided nearby. If the women of the extended family who made up the winter village came, after several months, to menstruate at the same time, their joint seclusion would undoubtedly have been a powerful female ritual and community marker. Ethnographers have documented common menstrual lodges for the Tenino, Southern Okanagan, and the Nez Perce Plateau peoples.[18]

The girl or woman, then, built the menstrual lodge on an appropriate site using materials made by themselves or by other women of the community. It was a place of seclusion and ritual, a place of spiritual potential, and a space for passing on women's knowledge and rituals. This woman's lodge space was the center of Plateau women's gender identification.

Producing New Women

As a built environment on a selected site, the menstrual lodge was important woman's space where new women were also constructed. Girls were taught, guided, and imprinted by the puberty rite passed on to them by female ancestors and monitored by the families' or community's elder women.[19]

Christine Quintasket, a Colville woman from the late nineteenth century known by her pen name of Mourning Dove, defined from her own experiences the basic Plateau puberty rite. Traditional families of the Plateau, such as Quintasket's, still practiced the rite in the late nineteenth century. James Teit found its use had declined from earlier in the century, according to the elders whose testimony he collected for Franz Boas. Quintasket reported:

> A girl started her fast at the first sign of menstruation, usually at an age between twelve and fifteen. She was . . . not allowed to come in contact with her family for ten days. When she did return, she had to take several sweat baths and put on a complete change of clothes . . . A girl prayed about motherhood at this time.[20]

The puberty rite was the culmination of an extensive training regimen for Quintasket:

> When my mother and Teequalt [the elderly woman training her] began to anticipate my puberty, they became more serious in their instructions . . . I was told to bathe and take on more responsibilities around the house. I was also made to run uphill without stopping until I reached the top. . . . From then on, I had to carry all the water in the house . . . this was to give me energy for my lifework, my teacher explained. I carried all the firewood, worked beside my father in the fields, and went to round up the horses each day before my breakfast and daily cold water bath. While my sisters continued to play at will, I was obliged to do many duties about the tipi and cabin. It seemed I had to learn something new every day . . . My eating was carefully watched and I was never allowed to fill up at meals as I had previously.[21]

In contrast to Quintasket's extensive prepuberty instruction, the girls of the Thompson people (Canadian Plateau) usually trained one year and some longer after the first menstrual cycle. To support her during this arduous training period, a girl's family moved away from the main village and stayed closer to her secluded lodge to assist her. The first four days of the puberty rite were the most intense with fasting, physical exercise, ritual bathing, and instruction in women's traditional tasks. Imprinting or forecasting of health, ability, and good fortune of the girl's life seemed to be the goal of most of these practices. Intense physical activities such as running, digging trenches, going without sleep, washing with fir boughs, and continuous construction of basketry seem calculated to lure spiritual power, as well. Girls could attain such guardian spirits as basket, kettle, root digger, owl, porcupine, and huckleberry. With this training and the help of the spirits, a girl entered womanhood.[22]

Women from other Plateau groups also experienced intense training, according to recent informants. "At puberty time for a girl, the Nez Perce had those menstrual lodges where women would go . . . during her period . . . they go there, and they stay there, her grandmother or mother would take her there and help them, explaining about it. She would stay there during that time," recalled a Nez Perce woman in the 1980s.[23]

As appropriate to its important training function and spiritually powerful space, the puberty rite lodge contained implements designated solely for that place. Just as an altar, ciborium, and chalice help define the central ritual of the Christian church, so too do the drinking tube, the cup, and the scratching stick define the lodge rituals. Each had a defined purpose, as well as a supernatural and gendered meaning. Not only was the menstruating woman powerful to others, but also to the environment and to herself. "She couldn't touch her hair, and she had a certain cup to use, a special cup just for that," recalled one Yakama woman. "All the cups were made from cedar roots in those days."[24]

Water, a source or location of spiritual power, was mediated in the puberty rite lodge by utensils that separated the power of the menstruating girl from drinking water. When in seclusion, the woman never drank from a stream or touched the water directly, but used a straw to separate herself from the water. The straw, a hollowed out bone tube among the Thompson, "processed" the water for her use and helped circumvent negative impact from her to the water, or visa versa. Boys in puberty training among the Thompson also used a drinking tube. Shamans among some Plateau groups used straws in their healing ceremonies to "suck" the disease or evil intention from their patient.

Within the lodge, girls in training, and later menstruating women, used a special cup for drinking. It "contained" the water and its potential power that separated the woman's power from it. The cup was made of cedar root among some groups and birch bark painted red among others, both highly regarded materials used in fiber or basketry work by the women. While in menstrual seclusion within the woman's lodge, the care taken by the women for their own contact with water reinforced their caution necessary to protect men and community members from menstrual power.[25]

When using the lodge for puberty training, a girl was required to alter her diet. Among the Colville, "A woman could not eat any freshly killed game without impairing the hunter's luck." For the Yakama girl, "Her grandmother brings her food, just dry meat and fish and berries. She can't eat anything fresh . . . She can eat anything [afterward]. But they used to say it's an Indian rule: can't eat anything fresh during that time . . . that's to keep her stomach right." The Nez Perce girl "couldn't cook with or eat with anybody." The food allowed in the women's lodge, in other words, was "cooked" by only having a woman process it and was never in its raw or male-tainted state.[26]

Careful disposal of the menstrual refuse usually took place within the lodge. Normally, the refuse was buried within the hole dug inside the menstrual lodge itself. It was never burned. This practice corresponds to others in the culture, such as the careful collection of hairs shed throughout life and the burial of these with the person at death. Afterbirth was also carefully disposed of, either hidden up a tree or buried, to protect the health of a newborn. Medicine people with evil intentions could use parts from a person to cast curses or steal power, so in the powerful menstruation situation precautions were taken. Alternately, among the Thompson, in a ritual to increase a girl's power, a small amount of her first menses might be taken to a barren and rocky mountainside to be burned.[27]

Spiritual power or luck could be gained within the puberty lodge by the repetition of activities. For power the Thompson used the number four and the Yakama the number five. Some rituals were apparently performed in order to limit future menstrual flows to this prescribed number of days.

A scratching stick was another ritual tool used in the puberty rite. A girl was instructed never to touch herself, but instead to use the stick. Some of the same allusions listed above—mediating function, woman-made product—apply here as well. But in this case, the protection seems to be for a woman from her own power. How can that be?[28]

Other studies report that during the puberty rite the girls often collected wood or brought water for the entire camp. Obviously the supposed "contamination" from the girl could be stymied if she channeled it in appropriate ways through work and providing needed services to the wider community. In some groups, the girl ran the ridges near the village in the early dawn hours, apparently not only to build stamina but also to chart the village's space or claim the trails somehow. These and the productive work done in the puberty lodge may have "imprinted" the emerging woman with gender attributes and spatial command desirable to her life within the wider Plateau community.

Special attire and appearances within the women's lodge were also important, perhaps carrying spiritual but certainly gendered significance. Although the patterning might vary, girls from all groups painted their faces red. All wore knee and ankle fringes decorated with deer hoof rattles. Among the Thompson and some other groups, the girls wore their hair tied behind each ear and used a special headband or cap, had a special robe used for the first few days of the rite, and masked themselves when they emerged from their lodge at night.

These special implements, activities, rituals, and accomplishments helped transform the pubescent girl into a properly trained woman. She could now continue her training for matrimony. The Klamath of the Southern Plateau sponsored a community-wide dance to mark her new status, much as did the Luiseno of California and the Western Apache. Among the Yakama, she would now begin her string counting ball, marking important events by knotting the string and keeping it with her until death. For several Canadian Plateau groups, women's facial tattoos and ear or nose rings could now be worn. Her puberty training complete, the new woman would reenact elements of the rite whenever she was secluded.[29]

Perhaps most important as she progressed through her life cycle, the Plateau woman would carry forward the training and teachings of gender roles that she received from her own grandmother, other female family members, and community elders. Some of the values imparted in the puberty training were to "be pure, cleanly, honest, truthful, brave, friendly, hospitable, energetic . . . virtuous . . . kindhearted to friends, diligent . . . modest . . . charitable . . . faithful . . . industrious." Important lessons of female-male relationships were disclosed, childbirth discussed, and family advice shared.[30]

The puberty rite's menstrual lodge was a spiritually powerful place where womanhood was constructed. Emergent women were trained there in the use and containment of power, imprinting the future with benefits by appropriately using special ritual implements and enacting proper gendered activities. Beyond the creation of new women, the menstrual lodge was the place for other productive activities that tied the secluded woman to other women and their shared Plateau culture. It was in the woman's lodge that they first made baskets, containers, mats, skin clothing, and other women's products.

Powerful Products

The siting of the menstrual lodge at the edge of the village, downstream or near water, can be thought of as a pathway, gateway, or boundary marker on the way to somewhere else. This connective function can be viewed in two ways. First, the things produced within the menstrual lodge were often intended for others within the wider extended family, for use at giveaways, or in ritual exchanges. Secondly, the thriving trade network among women on the Plateau for these same woman-made goods connected the activities in one community to the larger region. The scarce and valuable time needed to produce these utilitarian works of art could be found, a few days at a time, in the menstrual lodge.[31]

"She could work on anything though. That was for all womens," reports a Yakama woman in the 1970s. "They were raised up and taken care of by grandmothers and aunts and taught to be good diggers, and how to make clothes, and do things like that," says a Nez Perce woman. "The only time [a married woman] received a vacation was during her menstrual period, when she retired to a hut built away from the encampment. While in the hut she might tan skins," explained Quintasket. The women's objects produced were traded by women and sought by other women. These goods, it was believed, showed a woman's talents and spiritual gifts.[32]

Because of their particular home territory and its varying resources, tribal women "specialized" in certain products. Klickitat baskets, Nez Perce sweet grass sally bags, Salish parfleches, or Canadian Plateau birch-bark baskets circulated in the region through the Indigenous trade fairs and at mutually used food resource sites. A talented tanner, quiller, or basket-maker became well known throughout the region and her work was sought after. She passed her knowledge and her skill to young women in her family or band.[33]

Each menstrual seclusion after the all-important puberty ritual reinforced the special manifestation of a woman's power in the production and decoration of these products. Women could use their "leisure" time in the menstrual lodge to make baskets, tanned-skin clothing, beaded objects, or the more mundane twine and tule mats. Perhaps the focus of much of the "work" done during the puberty rite was to train the hands—as the articulators of a woman's creative power made manifest in menarche—in proper duties or habits or relationships with the object they produced.[34]

A Birthing Place

The importance of the women's lodge in the construction of Plateau women's gender roles has been defined in three ways. First, the lodge was a woman-built structure using woman-made materials on a preferred site selected by women. Second, the lodge was the puberty ritual's site, where the elders trained up each generation in ways appropriate for women. Third, the lodge was a place of production, where skills were introduced to girls and where menstruating women made goods. Finally, the woman's lodge was also the site for another, equally significant, gender construction task. Birth is the fourth understanding of the lodge's importance.

It has been argued elsewhere that birthing and motherhood are powerful concepts for Indigenous women, central to the construction of their gender definition.[35] For women on the Plateau, the birthing experience replicated many practices of the puberty ritual itself. There was a very careful monitoring of foods consumed, behaviors were proscribed (no inappropriate looking, teasing the less fortunate, handling dead animals, or entering lodges backwards), and exercise and healthful living were required. In this case, however, the father as well as the mother followed strict rules. Among the Thompson, the birth mother did her hair up like a girl in puberty, was not to scratch herself, and for a first child both she and her husband "had to go through certain ceremonies similar to the puberty ceremonies." Among the Lillooet, after the birth, the entire family painted their faces red. The father and mother ritually bathed and sponsored a feast for family and friends.[36]

Perhaps most important, when a woman went into labor she used a woman's lodge for birthing. This lodge was constructed slightly larger than those used for menstrual seclusion. Otherwise, it followed the menstrual or puberty lodge schema. The woman might add a strap for gripping when contractions were intense. She might rely on an elder woman as a midwife. The afterbirth and any blood were handled in ways patterned by disposing of menstrual blood.[37]

Nez Perce testimony in the 1980s attests to enduring belief in the power of Plateau woman at the time of motherhood: "Woman is strong when she is pregnant, woman is strong on her moon [menstruating]. She is creator at time of pregnancy." Native women used the lodge in the nineteenth century not only to construct their definitions of gender and to produce new women, but also to bring forth new life and the people's future.[38]

Changes

It cannot be known precisely what challenged and changed the practices of nineteenth-century menstrual seclusion, Indigenous puberty rites, and the use of the birth lodge. Teit, whose ethnographic work has provided much of the detail for this analysis, noted the practices were already much reduced and some were lost by the end of the nineteenth century. He interviewed the Thompson people's eldest women for their memories and experiences, but was not as interested in outlining the then-current practices. He did not trace or consider how the new ways of the late nineteenth and early twentieth centuries might be old ideas or models wrapped in new ways. Instead, Teit writes, in 1906, "Customs in connection with puberty have fallen into disuse. A very few families still make the girls pass through a ceremonial purification, but in a much modified form."[39]

The forces of change can easily be conjectured, although to be certain a thorough investigation of these issues would be necessary. Apparently, contact with European and Euroamerican culture and peoples challenged Indigenous women's practices. Epidemics, market economy, Christian missionaries, settlers to the Oregon Country, and, after the 1846 boundary decision, the United States government all had an impact on Plateau cultural practices. In the later nineteenth century, the mining rushes and the building of the railroads both north and south of the boundary line brought increased Euroamerican populations and economic development to the interior. By taking girls away from their families and communities, boarding schools and Euroamerican education contributed greatly to the dissolution of traditional practices.

Taking a spatial perspective, however, is also instructive. The challenge to Indigenous control of territories, especially with Euroamerican population incursion, treaties with the United States that dissolved Indian title to the land, and the establishment of the reservations in the region, added to the pressure for change because some of the traditional places were no longer accessible, even with porous reservation boundaries and inventive Native circumvention of officialdom. The practice of seasonal food gathering rounds was challenged in the nineteenth century by settler takeover of fertile root grounds and fishing sites, for instance.[40] Perhaps the woman's lodge, as another index of the Plateau-built environment, foundered as the people's geography became circumscribed.

Contemporary Women

Despite these changes, the enduring power of Indian women today may be due, in part, to its grounding in the birthing and menstrual lodges of the past.[41] The construction of gender and the foundation of woman's power has shifted from the woman's lodge to new locations and situations. Awareness of the old ways and the woman's lodge tradition still circulates among the Plateau people, as much of the modern testimony cited in this study makes clear. Teaching young women the important values for women and appropriate gender roles continues despite the passing into disuse of the woman's lodge.

Today, young Indian women are singled out for important cultural roles. In first root ceremonies, they maintain traditional rapport with the land. As powwow and rodeo royalty, their beauty, traditional clothing, and honorable behavior represent the best of their culture to their tribe and to others. In shawl and jingle-dress dancing, women's innovations in powerful ritual practices are celebrated. New practices that challenge and train young Native women bestow honor on them in their people's eyes. These new roles seem to serve much the same function in constructing young women, as did the former puberty rites.[42]

Despite changes and modern challenges, Indigenous Plateau women continue in powerful gender roles. Their self-definitions, behavior, and contributions show what it means to be an Indian woman today. The birth lodge, the puberty rite lodge, the menstrual seclusion lodge, as well as the family dwelling built and owned by the woman, show that previously the Plateau-built environment was almost exclusively under women's purview.[43] Women's gender construction came from this space, but also from the life cycle connection established there between the newborn, the pubescent girl, the mature woman, and the elders. Their acquisition of spiritual power and their ritual practices were connected to their lodges' space and functions, as were societal honoring and male recognition of women's gender perogatives. Perhaps former female gender roles of responsibility for and honor from lodging has been transformed in today's world into responsibility for and honor from their work for the peoples' resistance, continuance, and power. As part of the larger Native American cultural renaissance, the woman's lodge might yet return as a place to bolster American Indian women's self-definition and construction of gender roles.[44]

Notes

A different version of this essay was presented in July 2000 at the Fifth Women's West Conference, Pullman, Washington. The author wishes to thank Sasha Harmon, Linda Heidenreich-Zuniga, Carol Williams, and Loraine Littlefield for their comments.

1. For an overview of the Northwest Plateau cultural area, see *Handbook of North American Indians*, vol. 12, *Plateau*, ed. Deward E. Walker Jr. (Washington, DC: Smithsonian Institution, 1998). For a shorter version see Alice Kehoe's textbook, *North American Indians: A Comprehensive Account* (Upper Saddle River, N.J.: Prentice Hall, 1992), 382–98; Verne F. Ray, *Cultural Relations in the Plateau of Northwestern America* (Los Angeles: Southwest Museum, 1939), 52–61; and "Cultural Element Distributions: XXII, Plateau," *Anthropological Records* 8:2 (1942): 202–6.

2. Good places to start in reviewing the literature of feminist geography are Gillian Rose, *Feminism and Geography: The Limits of Geographic Knowledge* (Minneapolis: University of Minnesota Press, 1993); and Linda McDowell, *Gender Identity and Place: Feminist Geographies* (Minneapolis: University of Minnesota Press, 1999).

3. Lillian Ackerman, "Kinship, Family, and Gender Roles," *Handbook of North American Indians*, vol. 12, 515–24.

4. Mary C. Wright, "Economic Development and American Indian Women in the Nineteenth-Century Pacific Northwest," *American Quarterly* 33:5 (1981): 525–35, and "The Circle, Broken: Gender, Family, and Difference in the Pacific Northwest, 1810–1850" (Ph.D. diss., Rutgers, New Jersey, 1996); Lillian Ackerman, "Complementary but Equal: Gender Status in the Plateau," *Women and Power in the Native North America*, ed. Laura A. Klein and Lillian A. Ackerman (Norman: University of Oklahoma Press, 1995), 75–100; and Lillian Ackerman, "Sexual Equality in the Plateau Cultural Area" (Ph.D. diss., Washington State University, 1982).

5. I will use Indian, American Indian, Indigenous, and Native American interchangeably in this essay, although some of the peoples discussed herein are Canadian, where First Nation is the appropriate term.

6. Mary C. Wright, "Places for the People: Indigenous Women as Builders in the Nineteenth-Century Pacific Northwest Plateau," paper presented at the Western Association of Women Historians meeting, May 2001, Portland, Oregon. For buffalo hide lodges, see Capt. E. F. Wilson, "Report on the Indian Tribes Inhabiting the Vicinity of the 49th Parallel of North Latitude," *Transactions, Ethnological Society of London* 4 (1866): 275–332; and Nicholas Point, *Wilderness Kingdom: Indian Life in the Rockies, 1840–1847*, trans. Joseph P. Donnelly, S. J. (New York: Holt, Reinhart & Winston, 1967), 145, 174. The Yakama Cultural Heritage Center in Toppenish, Washington, has an excellent exhibit of traditional Plateau housing, including nearly life-size models of a pit house and a tule mat lodge. Visit their Web site at http://www.ohwy.com/wa/y/ yakama.htm.

7. Peter Nabokov and Robert Eastman, *Native American Architecture* (New York: Oxford University Press, 1989), 174–87; Father Pierre de Smet, *Life, Letters, and Travels of Father Pierre Jean de Smet, S. J., 1801–1873*, ed. Hiram Martin Chittenden and Alfred Talbot Richardson (New York: Kraus Reprint, 1969), 1012; Point, *Wilderness Kingdom*, 145; and Father Gregory Mengarini, S. J., *Recollections of the Flathead Missions Containing Brief Observations both Ancient and Contemporary Concerning this Particular Nation*, trans. ed., Gloria Ricci Lothrop (Glendale, Calif.: Arthur H. Clark, 1977), 216–17 n. 19 and 20.

8. For a critique of archaeology's lack of interest in menstrual lodges, see Patricia Galloway, "Where Have All the Menstrual Huts Gone?" *Women in Prehistory: North and South America*, ed. Cheryl Claassen and Rosemary A. Joyce (Philadelphia: University of Pennsylvania Press, 1997), 47–62; and Kenneth M. Ames et al., "Prehistory of the Southern Plateau," in *Handbook of North American Indians*, vol. 12, 103–19; Dorothy Sammons-Lohse, "Features," in *Chief Joseph Dam Cultural Resources Project, Washington*, ed. Sarah K. Campbell (Seattle: University of Washington, 1985), 113; and Harlan I. Smith, "The Archaeology of the Yakima Valley," *Anthropological Papers of the American Museum of Natural History* 6:1 (1910): 51–57.

9. Caroline James, *Nez Perce Women in Transition, 1877–1990* (Moscow: University of Idaho Press, 1996), 80; and Helen Hersh Schuster, "Yakima Indian Traditionalism: A Study in Continuity and Change" (Ph.D. diss., University of Washington, 1975), 120.

10. Charles Hill-Tout as quoted in James Teit, "The Lillooet Indians," in *Memoirs of the American Museum of Natural History*, ed. Franz Boas, 4:5 (1906): 296, n. 8. In contrast, the euphemism for menstruation used among the Western Apache was "grandmother's visit." Keith H. Basso, "The Gift of Changing Women," *Bulletin 196* (Bureau of American Ethnology, Anthropological Papers) 76:113–73.

11. Issues of pollution and seclusion are addressed in Thomas Buckley and Alma Gottlieb, "A Critical Appraisal of Theories of Menstrual Symbolism," in *Blood Magic:*

The Anthropology of Menstruation, ed. Thomas Buckley and Alma Gottlieb (Berkeley: University of California Press, 1988), 3–50.

12. Theda Perdue, *Cherokee Women: Gender and Culture Change, 1700–1835* (Lincoln: University of Nebraska Press, 1998), 28–40.

13. James Teit, "The Thompson Indians of British Columbia," in *Memoirs of the Museum of Natural History*, ed. Franz Boas, 2:4 (1900): 305; James Teit, "The Shuswap," *Memoirs of the American Museum of Natural History*, ed. Franz Boas, 4:7 (1909): 589–90; and Teit, "Lillooet," 261.

14. James, *Nez Perce Women*, 80–81. For a full discussion of this interpretation of menstruation as power, see Buckley and Gottlieb, *Blood Magic*.

15. *Everything Change, Everything Change: Recollections of Ida Nason, An American Indian Elder*, prod. Patricia Branch Larson and Sandra Lewis Nisbet, dir. John Givens, 1986; Roy Bigcrane and Thompson Smith, *Places of the Falling Waters*, prod. Dan Hart, Native Voices Public Television Workshop and Salish Kootenai College, 1991.

16. Teit, "The Thompson Indians," 218, 228, 264, 314, plate 19. Teit was married to a Thompson woman, spoke the language, and lived among the people for many years before doing his ethnographic work for Franz Boas. For these reasons, and because he was a sensitive man, we have very complete information about women's customs in the Canadian Plateau. See also Wendy Wickwire, "Women in Ethnography: The Research of James A. Teit," *Ethnohistory* 40:4 (1993): 539–62.

17. Keith H. Basso, *Wisdom Sits in Places: Landscape and Language among the Western Apache* (Albuquerque: University of New Mexico Press, 1996). See also Steven Feld and Keith H. Basso, eds., *Senses of Place* (Santa Fe, N.Mex.: School of American Research Press, 1996).

18. Buckley, "Menstruation and the Power of Yurok Women," 187–209; and Ray, *Cultural Relations in the Plateau of Northwestern America*, 54.

19. For more about Plains women's puberty rites, see Marla Powers, "Menstruation and Reproduction: An Oglala Case," *Signs: Journal of Women in Culture and Society* 6:1 (1980): 54–65; Mark St. Pierre and Tilda Long Soldier, *Walking in the Sacred Manner: Healers, Dreamers, and Pipe Carriers—Medicine Women of the Plains Indians* (New York: Simon and Shuster, 1995), 67–76; and Marsha C. Bol and Nellie Z. Star Boy Menard, "'I Saw All That': A Lakota Girl's Puberty Ceremony," *American Indian Culture and Research Journal* 24:1 (2000): 25–42.

20. *Mourning Dove: A Salishan Autobiography*, ed. Jay Miller (Lincoln: University of Nebraska Press, 1990), 38–41, 67, 204, ns. 7, 8, 9.

21. Miller, *Mourning Dove*, 40–41.

22. Teit, "The Thompson Indians," 311–17.

23. James, *Nez Perce Women*, 80.

24. Schuster, "Yakima Indian Traditionalism," 120.

25. Teit, "Thompson Indians," 313, 317, "Shuswap," 587–88, 612, and "Lillooet," 264; and Schuster, "Yakima Traditionalism," 120.

26. Miller, *Mourning Dove*, 67; Schuster, "Yakima Traditionalism," 120; and James, *Nez Perce Women*, 80.

27. For refuse burial, see Miller, *Mourning Dove*, 204, n. 7; Schuster, "Yakima Traditionalism," 121, 165–79.

28. Teit, "Thompson Indians," 313, 314, 317; and Schuster, "Yakima Traditionalism," 120. For a picture of a scratching stick see Teit, "Thompson Indians," 312. The scratching stick was the only material aspect of the girls' puberty complex found universally throughout the American West. See Harold E. Driver, "Culture Element Distributions, XVII: Girls' Puberty Rites in Western North America," *Anthropological Records* 6:2 (1941): 51.

29. Verne F. Ray, "Cultural Elements Distribution, XXII: Plateau," *Anthropological Records* 8:2 (1942): 203; Teit, "Thompson Indians," 311–17; Ray, "Cultural Elements," 203–7; Joan Oxendine, "The Luiseno Girls' Ceremony," *Journal of California and Great Basin Anthropology* 2:1 (1980): 37–50; Basso, "The Gift of Changing Woman," 138–41; and Douglas Leechman, "String Records of the Northwest," *Indian Notes and Monographs* (New York: Museum of the American Indian, Heye Foundaton, 1921), 16: 5–47.

30. Teit, "Thompson Indians," 367; and Ackerman, *A Song to the Creator*, 22–23.

31. For examples of the creative work of Plateau women, as well as commentary on women's culture, see Ackerman, *A Song to the Creator*.

32. Schuster, "Yakima Indian Traditionalism," 120; James, *Nez Perce Women*, 80–81; and Miller, *Mourning Dove*, 67.

33. Ackerman, *Song to the Creator*, explains this phenomena well.

34. Ray, *Cultural Elements*, 203.

35. Susan L. Rockwell, "The Delivery of Power: Reading American Indian Childbirth Narratives," *American Indian Culture and Research Journal* 19:3 (1995): 71–85. Also see Margaret A. Kay, *Anthropology of Human Birth*, (Philadelphia: F. A. Davis, 1982) for essays by Veronica Evaneshko, "Tonawanda Seneca Childbearing Culture," 395–411; Beverly Horn, "Northwest Coast Indians: The Muckleshoot," 361–75; and Anne Wright, "Attitudes toward Childbirth and Menstruation," 377–94. For another perspective on First Nations' motherhood, see Jo-Anne Fiske, "Child of the State, Mother of the Nation: Aboriginal Women and the Ideology of Motherhood," *Culture* 13:1 (1993): 17–35.

36. Teit, "Lillooet," 260.

37. Teit, "Lillooet," 260–61, and "Shuswap," 584, and "Thompson Indians," 305–10.

38. James, *Nez Perce Women*, 80–81.

39. Teit, "Thompson Indians," 228, 294, 312, and "Shuswap," 267, 269.

40. Janet H. Gritzner, "Native American Camas Production and Trade in the Pacific Northwest and the Northern Rocky Mountains," *Journal of Cultural Geography* 14:2 (1994): 47.

41. Teit, "Thompson Indians," 228, 294, 312, and "Shuswap," 267, 269.

42. See Tina Billedeaux, "Young People Encouraged to Preserve Bitterroot Tradition," *Char-Koosta News: The Official News Publication of the Flathead Indian Nation*, June 12, 2000 (online at http://www.ronan.net /~ckn/fea.html).

43. Women also built the racks where salmon and meats were dried. The sweat lodge, elementary hunting lodges, and fishing weirs were built by men.

44. For an encouraging report from another Native community, see Shirley Williams, "Woman's Role in Ojibway Spirituality," *Journal of Canadian Studies* 27:3 (1992): 100.

CHAPTER 2

Mindful Masquerades

Que(e)rying Japanese Immigrant Dress in Turn-of-the-Century San Francisco

AMY SUEYOSHI

Introduction

In 1900 an actor sporting a hat and suit appeared on stage at the California Theater near San Francisco's Union Square. Singing "Rag Time Mixes My Brain," the performer, who might have appeared to be a man, actually was a woman named Mary Marble. While she sang about nonsensical American slang that fuddled the brain, her presence as a woman in man-drag likely signaled an additional "mix[ing] of the brain." Gender impersonators such as Marble particularly delighted theatergoers at the turn of the century.[1] Not far from the applause of the California Theater, recent immigrants from Japan gathered for a group photograph in Golden Gate Park. Nearly all of the thirty-six men wore Western-style outfits, three-piece ensembles of white collared shirts, buttoned vests, and matching blazers. Some had topped their outfits with ties or tailored hats. The event marked an important moment for these neatly dressed men.[2] Though separated by only a few miles, Mary Marble and the young immigrant men appeared worlds apart—one of performance and recreation and the other of community building in a harshly anti-Asian city. As much as the two realities appeared to exist on separate planes, they in fact shared one terrain, for they both enacted mindful masquerades. As performers beguiled audiences in their gender transformations, Japanese immigrants deliberately donned Western dress in hopes of transforming themselves into "Americans." Together, they revealed coexisting ideologies of passing and privilege that grew complicated along the axes of gender and race.

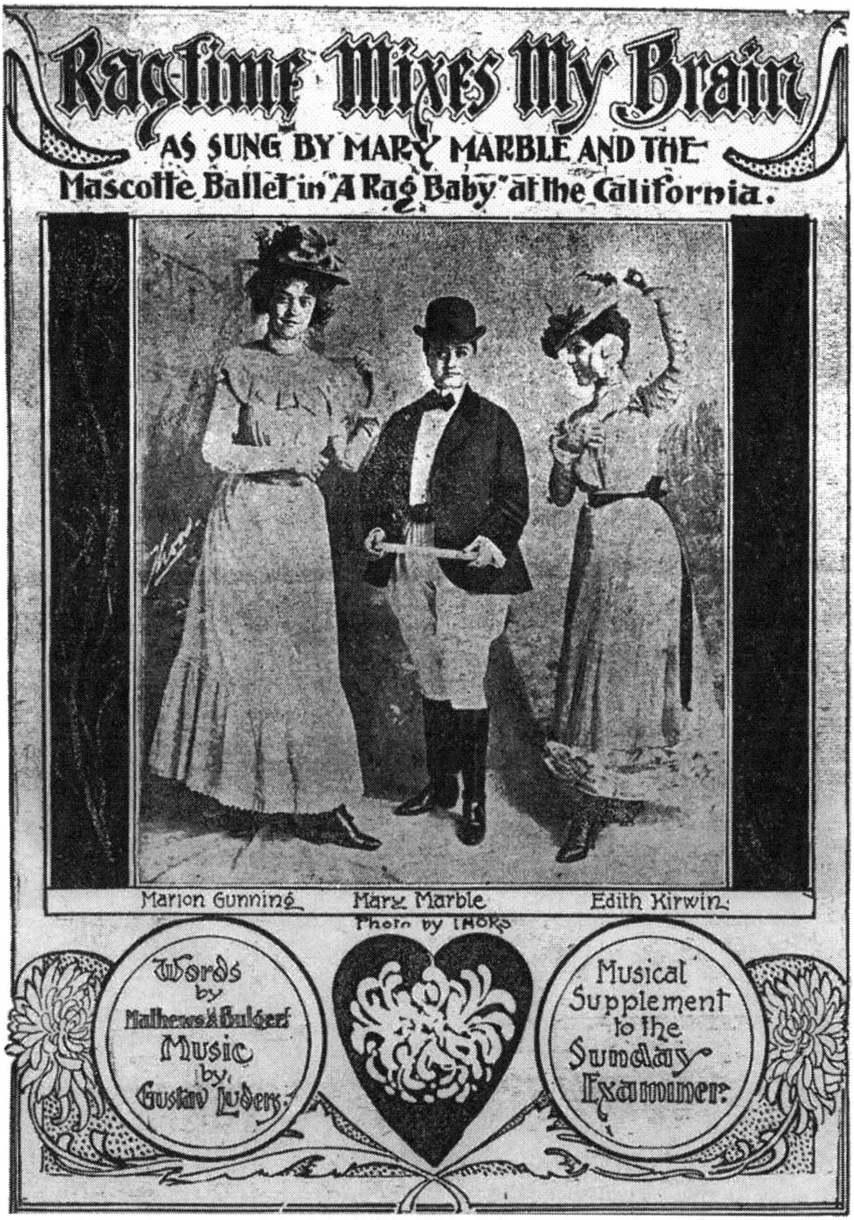

Figure 2.1. Mary Marble performing in man-drag at the California Theater. Gustav Luders, *Rag Time Mixes My Brain*, score, 1900, San Francisco History Center, San Francisco New Main Public Library, San Francisco.

By taking on deliberate presentations, both groups manipulated their identities visually to mask a perhaps physically unchangeable part of themselves. Gender illusionists who successfully passed as a different gender made gains at the box office. Japanese immigrants who wore Western dress less successfully transformed their race, despite their "American" appearance. Ironically, local whites who would not see Japanese immigrants as Americans celebrated the kimono and, specifically, the Japanese femininity it signified. Their embrace of Japanese dress as exotic amusement would only reinforce the "alien" status of Japanese San Franciscans. This essay suggests not only the historical normativity of a multiplicity of masquerades existing in turn-of-the-century San Francisco, but also calls into question the naturalness of American immigrants adopting Western dress. In the face of Chinese San Franciscans who less visually incorporated American items into their dress, Japanese abandonment of their ethnic dress might prove odd indeed.

Finally, juxtaposing theatrical gender impersonators with Japanese immigrants forges additional links between queer theory and ethnic studies scholarship. While queer theorists question the very foundational categories of power, gender, and sexuality in ethnic studies scholarship, they have conversely been criticized for their inability to address issues of race and apply their discursive theories on the material world.[3] Indeed, after the disassembling of categories, queer theory may appear to have little practical application. Scholarship on race, on the other hand, takes for granted fundamental categories of enfranchised and disenfranchised, men and women, white and nonwhite to address more pressing questions of social inequalities. Moreover, individuals at the turn of the century hardly questioned how their gender or race might be socially constructed. For many it might seem anachronistic to graft postmodern theories of sexuality and gender onto people of the past.

Yet que(e)rying Japanese immigrant dress, interrogating and questioning its normalcy in the face of accepted gender impersonators, illustrates not only the most obvious—how gender and racial categories operated differently in one moment of time—but also suggests the less decipherable intimate issue of how and why one method of accessing power and passing proved acceptable and others did not. Unquestionable categories of gender would allow for some degree of acceptance of male and female crossings, while embattled categories of race and its attending privileges foregrounded the confinement of Japanese in a nonwhite racial category. Ironically, daily realities demonstrated how crossing gender appeared much more possible than traversing the indelible marker of race. Gender impersonators for the most part passed and profited. Japanese immigrants, despite their Western dress, failed to convince the city or the nation of their "American" status and suffered from individualized assaults as well as larger discriminatory measures that restricted their

Figure 2.2. Immigrants posing in Golden Gate Park for a photograph. *Recent Arrivals*, 1900, Issei Project, National Japanese American Historical Society, San Francisco.

economic livelihood. While both groups used the potential power of masquerades to imagine themselves beyond the constraints of their physical bodies, only one convinced the American public to believe in its alternate identity. As a city openly discussing its varied gender expressions and diverse ethnicities for a brief window at the turn of the century, San Francisco proved to be a productive location to examine the concurrent development of gender and racial ideologies.

Gender Crossings

When Mary Marble crooned onstage in man-drag, she existed as one of many actors who acceptably crossed into different genders on stage. Gender impersonators were popular theatrical specialties across the country.[4] Particularly in San Francisco, gender impersonators took on aesthetic significance. More than just a prank, appearing on stage as a different sex signaled an impressive skill that drew praise from local reviewers. While the popularity of such performances appeared to signal an acceptance of fluidity in gender categories, additional representation of cross-dressing in the local press and in the courts revealed how rigid ideas of gender in fact undergirded San Francisco's delight in gender illusionists.

At first glance, the broad popularity and praise of gender impersonators in local publications seemed to signal gender fluidity, in the theatrical world at the very least. Reviews and representations of these performances frequently appeared in the city dailies such as the *San Francisco Chronicle*, the *San Francisco Call*, and the *San Francisco Examiner*. Widely circulated literary serials published outside the city, such as the *Overland Monthly*, elaborated not just on local performances but also on intriguing international events. The lesser-known *Wasp Magazine*, a local illustrated magazine of satire devoted to the local arts, regularly addressed several pages of its weekly to gender impersonations. Finally, theater records such as playbills, scripts, promotional material, and other items showed how gender impersonations on stage served as a serious aesthetic endeavor.

Local newspapers expressly commended crowd-drawing male and female impersonators as a popular form of entertainment. In 1897, a young man with very "shapely legs" skipped across stage at the Columbia Theater. *The Chronicle*'s theater critic described the play, *Devil's Auction*, as "capital entertainment," especially since the young man, in fact, was a woman.[5] At the Columbia Theater, "Stuart," the famous female impersonator, graced the stage in the production of *1492*.[6] In 1899, the *Wasp* praised Gladys Montague, the "champion cake walker and male impersonator of the Pacific Coast," who at seven years of age held a collection of medals.[7] Mary Marble herself reflected the popularity and utility of gender impersonation in performance. In a previous 1898 play, Marble, along with four other women actors, appeared in male attire at the Columbia Theater in *A Milk White Flag*.[8]

Moreover, critics praised gender impersonation as art, rather than regarding it as ridiculous comedy. In 1900, two curly-headed boys, Ellis and Edwin Smedley, enacted the tragic romance between Romeo and Juliet. The *Call* praised the "clever chaps" for their clarity and sincerity in acting. "Adult actors could take a lesson from them."[9] The *Chronicle* also commended Walter Leon, only eight years old, for his recitations, all given with the poses, mannerisms, and characteristic expressions of a little girl. "He is a strikingly handsome youngster [with] long golden curls. Gowned after the most approved feminine style, with his pretty ringlets fluffing about his delicate face, the clever little fellow will go through his really artistic work with perfect self-possession."[10] When the *Overland Monthly*'s Dora Amsden applauded men costumed as women in Japanese Noh Theater, she explicitly used the language of art as she described the Japanese male actors with "slender nut brown fingers" hypnotizing the audience as they balanced their personas between the masculine and feminine. She recounted how the spectators went "wild with excitement" and flung their personal accessories and clothes they wore at the feet of their favorite. She praised "Genoski, the great female personator, whose face has the delicate contour of the aristocratic Japanese woman." Though Amsden may have articulated Orientalist sentiments of Japan as a nation imbued with feminine gentility, she highlighted its refinement in its gender performance.[11] She privileged the theater by comparing it to the Delphic Oracles, Shakespeare, and theater of the Grecian days.[12] In these artistically acclaimed performances, successful passing into a different gender remained fundamental.

Sympathetic portrayals of women wearing male attire in local newspapers seemed to signal acceptability of gender fluidity further. Neither strongly sensational nor pejorative, both the *Call* and the *Chronicle* might have appeared sensitive even by twenty-first-century standards. Articles extolled these individuals and used pronouns that fit their immediate gender presentation.[13] The local dailies generally reported positively on women who wore male attire off the stage. In 1898, the *Chronicle* cited Mrs. William Kreiger, who attained local fame with her male attire. Despite initial notoriety, her community in Oakland quickly came to support her. The paper praised her as a "woman of great benevolence," "endear[ing]" to many.[14] In the previous year the *Call* praised twenty-two-year-old Clara Jensen's determination as a "full fledged knight of the road." Dressed in man's garb with a roll of blankets across her back, Jensen had footed it all the way from San Francisco to Fresno in April 1897. She was on her way to her parents' home in Fort Worth, Texas, after her husband of only one year had deserted her.[15]

For those who literally passed as men, reporters also wrote sympathetically. In 1897 the *Chronicle* put forth the idea that women should be allowed to ride racing horses, after a stable accident in England led doctors to discover an eighteen-year-old stable groom was a woman. The stable owner himself declared that it would be advantageous for women to race because of their light weight and devotion to the horses.[16] In the same year, Billy Johnson likewise received praise from both the *Call* and *Chronicle* for his "correct life," chopping and cording wood for money between jobs, despite his "tramping" lifestyle in a "dusty roads fraternity." Newspapers described Johnson as "good looking" and "affable." Johnson had been fired from a previous restaurant job when the owner's wife suspected something awry with his "smooth face" and "graceful movement." In their article, the *Chronicle* markedly referred to Johnson as "he" until "she" pleaded guilty to the charge of impersonation.[17]

While articles generally appeared receptive of real-life gender crossings in language, their very appearance in local publications may have signaled their primary worth as potent curiosities that would draw readers. The frequent portrayals in the local press then may have more accurately reflected publishers' capitalizing on gender fluidity's oddity rather than accepting it. In a favorable article on Babe Bean, a woman reporter who lived as a man, the *Chronicle* wrote, "The *Stockton Mall* has a special writer who is a curiosity in more respects than one."[18] Additionally, when three men and one woman robbed a bank, the *Chronicle* headline read "Woman Bandit in Male Attire." While the text of the article detailed only the robbery itself, the curiosity of a woman in male attire headlined the heist. The *Chronicle* likely hoped to profit from the titillation of a cross-dresser in a story about a perhaps otherwise usual bank robbery.[19]

The one derisive article depicting women passing as men revealed rigid boundaries of gender. In the retelling of Babe Bean's 1897 train accident in the *Chronicle*, the headline read "Miss Bean Not an Up to Date Young Man" and accused Bean of "trying to play the boy" by jumping off the train as it was moving. The article underlined Bean's feminine sex in light of her failed attempts at masculinity, which in turn highlighted the discrete categories of male and female in which Bean lived.[20] Additionally, even the clearly favorable reports subtly revealed how specific characteristics could be appropriate to only one sex. The *Call* praised male impersonator Alice Condon's performance on stage. For example, the fourteen-year-old's "strong," "true" voice and pleasing "carrying" quality made her "naturally adapted" for gender transformation. The "Native Daughter Should Have Been a Boy," the headline declared.[21]

Furthermore, illustrated representations of gender blurring or confusion more often became sites of comedy or ridicule rather than art. A 1900 full-page pictorial in the *Call*, entitled "How San Francisco Notables Look in Theatrical

Roles," assigned fourteen dignified urbanites to female bodies. Heads of San Francisco notables such as Judge W. W. Morrow, Mayor Phelan, David Starr Jordan, and Joaquin Miller perched atop bodies of famous female theatrical roles such as Cleopatra, Juliet, Cinderella, and Lady Macbeth.[22] As rugged bearded faces sat atop female gowned bodies, the jarring images more likely entertained readers by the misplaced juxtaposition rather than portraying a well-regarded aesthetic.

In an 1898 cartoon in the *Wasp*, Hannibal Flirtatious became the butt of a joke when he approached from behind an individual he believed to be a woman. As he stepped up to offer her an umbrella, he thought to himself, "Ah hah! I'll just ask that beauty to get in out of the wet." When she turned around, she revealed herself to be a male porter. The porter responded, "Naw, I don't want no umbrella, I'm waterin' dere plant see." Flirtatious jumped back in horror, dropping his umbrella and monocle. He was indeed "disillusioned," as the title of the cartoon read.[23] The humor that framed Hannibal Flirtatious's mistake defused the horror that gender fluidity might bring, the "wrong" gender in the pursuit of a romantic partner.

One illustrated frame in the *Wasp* on the newest fashion trends additionally demonstrated rigid categories of gender even in its most recent reconfiguration. "Where Shall the Line Be Drawn," read the title. Two women appeared, one in bloomers and a blazer and the other in a late Victorian dress. As they faced off, "Miss Primm" argued with "Miss Manly." While the labeling of the gowned woman as "Miss Primm" revealed disdain for lingering conservative dress, the articulation of "Miss Manly" equally revealed gender ideologies that had little tolerance for gender crossings.[24]

In a most telling cartoon in the *Chronicle*, individuals who did not necessarily fit discrete categories of male or female were derided. The strip titled "Personal Pronouns Up-to-Date" displayed three frames of images that defined gender. The first frame pictured a woman smoking a cigarette, dressed in a jacket, blazer, necktie, and bloomers. She wore short hair and a tailored hat. Under her image sat the caption "She." The second frame showed a man in a jacket, collared shirt, belted knickers, and a driving hat. He clutched a golf club and the caption underneath read "He." In the final image appeared an individual in an overcoat, an oversized bowtie, and a derby hat. Underneath this third image read the caption "It." Those who fell outside even the most up-to-date versions of gender became dehumanized.[25]

The city's commitment to distinct gender presentations becomes clearer with a San Francisco city ordinance adopted in 1903 that prohibited cross-dressing. Section one noted, "It shall be unlawful for any person to appear, upon any public highway in the dress, clothing or apparel not belonging to or usually worn by his or her sex." Courts convicted violators of a misdemeanor,

Figure 2.3. "Personal Pronouns Up-to-Date," *San Francisco Chronicle*, June 27, 1897.

with a maximum punishment of a $500 fine and six months in county jail.[26] Enactment of the code may have come as no surprise, because frequent articles on gender crossers and the rise of mannish attire in women's fashion likely aggravated anxieties. However, even before the law took effect, police had been arresting those who donned clothes of a different sex under laws that prohibited impersonation. When San Francisco detectives discovered Babe Bean was in fact a woman wearing male attire, Bean wound up at the police station explaining how traveling in trousers and a coat afforded "more protection than skirts."[27] Likewise, authorities arrested George Crowley when he wore his mother-in-law's dress and bonnet and accompanied his father-in-law to a nearby saloon.[28]

Thus San Franciscans to a large extent remained heavily invested in stable categories of male and female. Their beliefs perhaps coincided with a national consensus that supported discrete biological and moral definitions of male and female.[29] During this "golden age of impersonation," performers probably reinforced notions of polarized gender difference. Actors marketed themselves as magicians, performing the unimaginable feat of crossing into the role of the opposite sex. Gender cross-dressing sold as "magic" drew audiences who firmly believed in innate differences between the sexes. Social acceptance of performances such as that of the nationally acclaimed cross-dresser Julian Eltinge relied on this fundamental assumption that an impossible divide existed between men and women.[30] Though their physical performances seemed to muddy gender categories, men and women who impersonated the opposite sex in the early twentieth century did not profoundly challenge contemporary notions of gender among the middle-class audiences who enthusiastically and comfortably enjoyed their productions. Instead, these socially acceptable performances in

San Francisco likely mirrored and solidified existing gender norms as serious demonstrations of ideal femininity and masculinity.

Dressing "American"

As female and male impersonators profited by crossing apparently impermeable categories of gender, so Japanese immigrants donning Western dress or *youfuku* less successfully crossed into what they believed to be more permeable categories of "American."[31] Immigration records, newspaper images, family pictures, group photographs, and individual portraits trace Japanese adoption of *youfuku*, reflecting immigrants' hopes of gaining acceptance in the United States. Their dress diverged significantly from that of their Japanese contemporaries in Japan who customarily wore Japanese dress or *wafuku*. While upper-class men in Japan increasingly adopted Western style as a new trend signifying education and high culture, the vast majority in Japan remained in *wafuku*.[32] As Japanese San Franciscans recorded themselves on film, they participated in an American fascination with photography that had recently become accessible to the middle classes as well. Though the Western images did not depict the most up-to-date in American fashion or format, they nonetheless demonstrated their subjects' dedication to, if not success in, being perceived as "American."

Photographs of immigrants arriving at Angel Island Immigration Station before disembarking at San Francisco show that most individuals landed wearing Japanese rather than Western dress.[33] Without access to a clothier or beauty salon for a San Francisco coif, they remained in Japanese style or *wafuku* while being detained. In photographs documenting Angel Island, large numbers of Japanese women appeared in Japanese dress. In carefully crafted photographs, Japanese women posed in kimonos held together with neatly tied obi. In candid pictures, Japanese women in traditional hairstyles and *wafuku* stood overlooking the cove or on the roof of the administration building at Angel Island.[34] Interestingly, soon after authorities released women from the immigration detention center, Japanese women appeared in one- or two-piece skirt and dress ensembles. Several Issei, the first generation of Japanese to arrive in the United States, recalled a visit to the Western clothier shop as one of their first destinations after landing in San Francisco. In the group of recently arrived Japanese in Golden Gate Park, all posed in Western dress.[35]

In a thirty-eight-page spread congratulating Japan's military prowess in the annexation of Korea, the *Chronicle* included articles on the Japanese in the city as well as across the Pacific. A full-page pictorial displayed portraits of twenty-five "men of prominence" in the "local Japanese colony." All the men had their hair cropped short, appropriate to contemporary styles, and all wore Western suits. Nineteen of the twenty-five also dignified their visages by sporting the bushy mustache common among Americans in the early 1900s.[36] Brief captions accompanied the photographs detailing advanced degrees from prestigious universities.[37] Clearly all these men fit ideal American male aesthetics in their style if not in their skin color.

Family portraits consistently revealed wives and mothers wearing Western dress.[38] Parents also dressed children in Western clothes. Kay and Sawako Tsuchiya, two and five years old, wore dresses with trimmed collars and sleeves, holding delicately dressed dolls. A big white bow held Sawako's hair.[39] In a 1915 portrait, a cook and his wife who labored at the Leonard home on Fulton Street also posed in Western dress. While the man wore a suit, the woman wore a high-necked dress and puffed white hat that resembled a giant cotton ball.[40] Additionally, a 1922 photo of David Fukuda at one hundred days old pictured him in a white trimmed dress, an outfit reflecting lingering Victorian norms.[41]

Even in environments that specifically promoted Japanese culture, photographs revealed participants in Western clothes. In a 1909 photo of the Japanese language school on Sutter Street, adults and children wore appropriately gendered Western garb.[42] An illustration of a group of men at a kendo club showed Japanese men dressed in Western suits or protective kendo gear. Their collective identity based on ethnicity and culture proved important to the members, not only in their regular meetings for language or kendo training, but also in the taking of the group photograph.[43] Their cultural solidarity, however, did not motivate the men to wear Japanese garb. None wore *wafuku* in the group photograph.[44]

At wedding ceremonies as well, brides increasingly wore Western style wedding dresses, not flowing kimonos. In the Ichikawa wedding portrait, the groom wore a white bow tie and long tuxedo jacket, while the bride donned a frilly white dress with delicate trim. A veil, an elaborate hairpiece, and white gloves accessorized her outfit. Flowers bedecked her Mary-Jane shoes.[45] Some couples did exhibit more cultural fusion. In these cases, grooms typically wore tuxedos, but some women wore the more traditional black wedding kimonos. Even for these brides, though, a Western bridal hairpiece and a veil topped their ensembles. One bride wore white gloves with her wedding kimono. For many of the wedding portraits the only item "Japanese" besides the ethnicity of the individuals themselves may have been the decorative cherry blossoms that often accessorized the photo shoot.[46]

Japanese women also participated in the national trends of portraiture for young American society women. Beauty shots akin to debutante portfolios celebrated blossoming young womanhood. Photography studios such as Motoyoshi and Moriyama in Japantown developed headshots for young women to distribute among friends and family. Hana Ohama wore a lacy white dress, white gloves, and a hat with a big plume hanging over the side. As she sat upright, her positive posture pushed her breasts forward while her hands rested in her lap.[47] Kikuye Okuye's gloved fingers supported her slightly tilted head at the chin. Her dress fell across her shoulders to form a "V" down her front, where it was fastened with a brooch.[48] An additional photograph from the Uakahara family presented a profile of a woman peering out the window as she gently pulled back the curtain. Bedecked in a lacy beaded dress that flowed to the floor, she wore a white flower in her short wavy hair parted to the side. A large diamond ring conspicuously enveloped her left ring finger.[49]

For Japanese San Franciscans, their Western clothing probably reflected their efforts to gain American acceptance. Japanese Americanist Yuji Ichioka noted that Issei community leaders and Japanese government officials detailed a policy of fitting into its American population, which included dress.[50] Historian Eiichiro Azuma similarly noted that the Japanese community grew fearful of white American conflation of Chinese and Japanese into the same group. At the turn of the century, Chinese and Japanese who already shared a history of warfare hardly thought of themselves as allies, even in anti-Asian California, where both groups became targets of discrimination with little distinction between the two. Japanese government officials and other elites explicitly denounced "uncivilized" Japanese who lacked Western appearance and compared them unfavorably with the Chinese.[51] Migrating Japanese additionally left a home country where print media had already popularized narratives of "self-made men" such as Andrew Carnegie, Theodore Roosevelt, and Abraham Lincoln. Many young Japanese hoped to project these images of underprivileged, ambitious men who succeeded in rising from "empty pockets to millionaires" or "log cabin to the presidency." Part of achieving this goal meant adopting the very American dress that these self-made heroes wore.[52]

An 1899 Togasaki family portrait eloquently portrayed the aspirations of Japanese immigrants as they sought to enjoy a piece of the American pie. The young father wore a suit and tie, while the wife wore a dress with black plumed hat. The two children also wore Western clothes. Yet more telling than merely the Western-style clothes themselves were the detail and finishing touches of the children's presentations. The small boy donned an outfit reminiscent of a U.S. soldier's uniform. Both children clutched American flags. For Asian immigrants unable to naturalize, traditional symbols of American citizenship and nationalism, the U.S. flag and participation in the military, proved particularly ironic.[53]

Japanese immigrants who took great pride in their national origin less likely hoped to become actual white Americans and more likely hoped to take great advantage of American privileges. The Japanese in exodus at the turn of the century considered themselves to be both "emigrating" and "colonizing."

Figure 2.4. Photograph of Togasaki family, 1899, Issei Project, National Japanese American Historical Society, San Francisco.

Japanese immigrants who strove for acceptance and success on the West Coast remained invested in their Japanese identity, and their desire to assimilate then became a part of expressing Japanese nationalism.[54] In masquerade, they hoped for equal access to opportunities that racism would deny based on appearances that associated them as outsiders. For the Japanese, their masquerades became a more serious act of fitting into a city often fearful of the unfamiliar. They existed as mindful masquerades, constructed thoughtfully rather than arising "naturally" from living in San Francisco in hopes of acquiring their American dream.[55]

Notably, Japanese self-representations on film may have been not completely "American" in form. According to historian Alan Trachtenberg, American photographers had established a distinct sitting protocol for portraiture by the 1870s. Though the middle-class daguerreotype portraits from an earlier time hoped to capture bodies without regard to composure, by the late nineteenth century photographers moved to overcome the "intractable countenance," the face that would not "relax or mellow or glow with 'expression.'" In the late nineteenth century, photographer W. S. Haley explicitly instructed that "[the] posture of person sitting for the portrait should be easy and unconstrained; the feet and hands neither projecting too much, nor drawn too far back; the eyes should be directed a little sideways above the camera, and fixed upon some object there, but never upon the apparatus since this would tend to impart to the face a dolorous, dissatisfied look." Photographer Albert S. Southworth elaborated the chief goal of the portrait as a look of animation, intelligence, and inner character. The photographed should will themselves into a desired expression that matched their self-image and look anywhere but into the lens.[56]

However, few of Japanese San Franciscans' photographs from the early twentieth century displayed animation or mood-inspiring manipulation. Sitters sat stiffly, stared directly into the camera with an expressionless face, and presented what Haley undoubtedly would have criticized as an "intractable countenance." Though Japanese dressed in Western clothes, their poses for the most part remained frozen in a time that preceded 1900s San Francisco by at least two decades. Their poses may have replicated sitting styles of their picture-taking cohorts in Japan. In a photographic exposé by clothing scholars Etsuji Tanida and Mitsue Koike, images of Japanese in Japan from the 1890s and early 1900s all revealed expressionless faces staring directly into the camera.[57]

Japanese American portraiture appeared more conservative in content as well as form. Immigrant women did not appear in the most current styles during the earliest years of the twentieth century. Western dress for Japanese women meant enacting more traditional styles of American dress. While the city's trendiest female dressers donned fashionable bloomers, blazers, neckties, and vests that some commentators criticized as "mannish," Japanese women in San Francisco had themselves photographed in late Victorian gowns. More than just conservative, these outfits may have struck some San Franciscans as outdated in these more "modern" times of the "New Woman."[58] For the immigrant Japanese, dressing "American" more likely meant capturing an imagined, obviously occidental, aesthetic rather than keeping up with the most recent and sometimes hair-raising styles.

Dressing Japanese

As Japanese sought to abandon Japanese dress, San Francisco whites in fact embraced the kimono in literary and visual imagery as well as embodiment. While white writers eroticized Japanese women clothed in Japanese style, white women in particular clamored to dress Japanese. Articles on Japanese femininity appealed to white San Franciscans at a time when the meaning of womanhood was changing. Japanese womanhood symbolized a "lost" femininity in the shadow of the "New Woman." The ideal of Japanese femininity enhanced whites' personal lives on a very public level.[59] San Franciscans sympathetic to Japanese aesthetics would ask Japanese acquaintances to wear kimonos, as well. These demands ultimately imposed a second kind of cross-dressing on Japanese immigrants, reminding them of the alien status they sought to overcome.

Beginning in the mid-1890s, contributors to the *Overland Monthly* frequently set what they believed to be desirable Japanese traditional femininity in contrast to that of "American" women. In 1906 Charles Lorrimer described Japanese women as "rare exotics" with more patience than American girls.[60] Celebrations of Japanese women appeared in magazines, journals, and newspapers. In photographs, "pretty teahouse girls" dressed in kimonos gazed innocently into the camera. In poetry and short stories, "sweet" and "doll-like" Japanese women in "soft kimono" and "silken zori" arose from mystical settings such as a "tiny garden." Narratives wove tales of romantic love between Japanese women and white men that would nearly always end in the death of the Japanese women. Even in tragic endings, short stories would evoke the kimono, as the Japanese woman, for example, collapsed into a "bundle of silk."[61] Furthermore, in Olive Dilbert's 1907 short story of a Japanese woman's fall to doom, the protagonist Umeko-san wore Western dress as she deserted her more traditional husband for a more Western man. Wearing a big white plumed hat, Umeko sashayed out the door to run off with Satsumoto-san, a smooth talker who expounded on the virtues of divorce and women's independence.[62]

White women essayists also articulated Japanese women's sexual desirability while invoking Japanese feminine dress. While writers such as Hester A. Benedict spun smooth romances between a white male protagonist and a Japanese woman, others such as Grace Hibbard and Gertrude Holloway wrote of desiring Japanese women in the first person without the cover of a male pseudonym. Hibbard wrote a poem lamenting the affection of a Japanese woman, describing her as an exotic beauty. Holloway also wrote of carefully courting a Japanese woman, secretly desiring a kiss. Descriptions of flowing silk in these writings implicitly pointed to Japanese dress. Some included an even more explicit visual, including an illustration of a Japanese woman in a kimono, to accompany their writing.[63]

Despite the obvious homoeroticism of a white woman's longing for a Japanese woman, same-sex sexuality likely never entered the imagination for much of heteronormative San Francisco. No public cultural discourse on desire in terms of explicit heterosexual, homosexual, bisexual, or any sexual identity existed at the turn of the century. Underground literature on same-sex sexuality circulated in the United States with little notice from larger society.[64] Thus, the gender-impersonating Smedley twin boys could reenact a Shakespearean love story with little outrage over the sexual subtext of same-sex sexuality as well as incest.[65] Still, as innocent as performances of a woman declaring love for another woman may have appeared, they carried great potential for alternative readings during a time when "romantic friendships" between middle- and upper-class white women appeared relatively common.[66] These works reflected a web of romanticism about Japanese femininity that served not only the men who leafed through the *Wasp* but also the white women who may have desired to engage intimately in Japanese femininity.[67]

At afternoon teas, affluent San Franciscans threw parties dressed in kimonos. Japanese luncheons became intensely popular among society women weary of the monotony of English-style afternoon teas and matinée lunches. White women took great care in accessorizing their homes and bodies for these afternoon events. In full Japanese garb from the sandals to the haori, partygoers chatted and ate "suimono," "yakizakana," "sashimi," or a light snack with "kuchitorimono" and "chawan mori."[68] Items from the "Orient," including teacups from Turkey or China and even servants "only from Japan," added a distinct flavor to tea parties that left guests raving for days.[69] Department stores known for their "honest values," such as Marks Brothers on Market Street, kept their prices competitive for the popular trend by slashing their "lawn kimonas," normally fifty cents, to nineteen cents.[70]

Moreover, Japanese femininity enhanced American womanhood, even its most "classy" form. In 1907, Lady Teazle of the *San Francisco Chronicle* outlined the lives of rich and dignified women of the Bay Area on her "Society

Figure 2.5. San Francisco elites threw Japanese lunches to break up the monotony of English tea parties. "The Japanese Luncheon Fad," *San Francisco Call*, February 14, 1897.

Chat" page. In addition to her usual reports outlining the accomplishments of local society women, one day she featured large pictures of two women in her full-page column. One youthful brunette in her twenties, Mrs. B. O. Bruce, wore a tennis outfit and carried a racket while posing in front of the net. The other, Mrs. J. Parker Whitney, a heavier, silver-haired woman, posed stoically, clothed in more elegant attire. Sandwiched between these society women and serving as a backdrop to the two photographs, a drawing of a

Japanese woman in a kimono sprouted from an enlarged flower. She daintily held a rice paper umbrella over her shoulder as the rising sun of imperial Japan radiated behind her. Although Lady Teazle had not included even a sentence on an upper-class Japanese woman in San Francisco, she evoked the image of Japanese feminine gentility in the use of a Japanese woman in the backdrop. For Teazle and perhaps many of the well-to-do people of San Francisco, a Japanese woman's femininity represented an ideal that even white society women could not evoke.[71]

Japanese San Franciscans wearing kimonos proved to be a pleasing attraction for city elites enraptured with Japanese aesthetic. The San Francisco Women's Board of Foreign Missions sent Japanese American community leader Yonako Abiko a letter requesting that she wear her kimono when she volunteered for a weekend excursion in Bolinas. "I trust that you will find it convenient to take with you the Japanese costume. It will add so much to the joy of the girls."[72] In truth, wearing a kimono with its delicate fabric, many layers, and multiple ties around the waist would almost never be "convenient." Still, Abiko appeared familiar with this type of attention. When Abiko embarked on a cruise in 1907, the international passengers began applauding upon her entry into the grand ball. She had worn a kimono at the request of her fellow passengers.[73] European friends as well constantly raved about the beauty of the kimonos. Margherita Palmieri wrote:

> I scarcely need to tell you how pleased I should be to have [your photograph] in your pretty national costume if you have one to spare. In fact I am wearing one at this moment, and I think you would be rather amused if you could see it, as I was not able to get one thin enough for summer wear I have had one made of art muslin such as they use for curtains and I have made two paper chrysanthemums for my hair![74]

In perhaps a more unusual request among men, Western writer Charles Warren Stoddard expressed disappointment when Japanese immigrant poet Yone Noguchi appeared before him in a shirt and tie rather than a kimono.[75] For Japanese immigrants who purposely wore Western dress in their daily lives, fulfilling requests to wear kimonos became an obligatory second cross-dressing that underlined their visibly Japanese origin.

Probably few, if any, white women wanted to become ethnically Japanese. Even fewer would have believed that in wearing Japanese dress their race might be perceived as Japanese. Yet, many of the middle and upper classes embraced the signifiers of Japanese womanhood to enhance their own lives amid shifting gender trends. As the "New Woman" posed potential dangers of masculinizing women, white women enacted romantic femininity by incorporating gendered

Japanese bodies into their own lives, which remained securely white. Masquerades provided a way to express desire and fantasy, as San Franciscans hoped to enhance their most personal dimensions. For Japanese San Franciscans who hoped to be recognized as American with all of its attending privileges, Japanese dress imagined, enacted, and at times requested by whites no doubt reminded Japanese residents of their insurmountable alien status.

Dressing "Un-American"

While assimilationists might view adoption of Western clothes as the natural course of immigration, Japanese San Franciscans could also be construed as "queer," particularly in comparison to other immigrant groups who also had to undergo a distinct wardrobe change to accommodate American clothing mores. Chinese San Franciscans dressed less visually "American" than their Japanese counterparts by maintaining more of their Chinese clothing. Sinophobes focused on Chinese components of Chinese American dress to highlight their alien existence in America. Among the Chinese, community disdain for Western dress may have discouraged them from completely abandoning their ethnic dress, as did the Japanese. As Chinese in the city created clothing styles that reflected a fusion of both Western and Chinese influences, Japanese San Franciscans' wholesale absorption of Western dress might not appear so "natural" after all.

At Golden Gate Park and on the city sidewalks, Chinese men appeared with long queues, clothed in cotton tunics and Chinese shoes. On street corners and public benches, Chinese women wore matching pantsuit-like outfits and pulled their hair tightly back into neat buns.[76] In San Francisco, where men kept their hair cropped short and women wearing bloomers caused controversy, Chinese men wearing long braided queues and women wearing pants must have looked like a reversal of appropriate gender presentations.

While the wealthiest city inhabitants purchased exotic photographs of San Francisco Chinese from photographer Arnold Genthe, the less wealthy and the majority of the city participated in a more common discourse that poked fun at the odd Chinese.[77] In one 1901 illustrated satire in the *Wasp*, the Chinese queue became an "American plait" when a young white girl following a Chinese man eyed his queue, cut it off, and reattached it to her own head. In her appropriation of the Chinese queue, crossings became a mix of mockery, desire, and incorporation. In the image of a Chinese man wearing a gender marked braid, the cartoon likely underlined "odd" Chinese masculinity to white San Franciscans.[78] Through the last quarter of the twentieth century, short stories, newspaper accounts, and political propaganda in the San Francisco area evoked Chinese as a queer version of men.[79]

Many Chinese were aware of the negative impact of their obviously Chinese dress. One anonymous poet elaborated, "A loose gown with wide sleeves brings only scurrilous remarks. And it gets you nowhere, even if you are modern in education."[80] Attitudes toward Western dress held by the Chinese, who frequently associated it with sexual excess and immoral character, may have inhibited their adoption of such attire, despite the negative attention Chinese dress brought. In the Chinese newspaper *Chung Sai Yat Po*, Western dress often appeared in advertisements that offered remedies for sexually transmitted diseases. In December 1909, images of men wearing traditional Chinese clothing and advertisements sold goods and services in Chinese. On December 29, however, an ad appeared for "Scott's Santal Pepsin Capsules." In the top corner appeared a headshot of a very Western-looking man. Dignified in appearance, with cropped short hair and the requisite bushy mustache of the time, he wore a jacket with a collared shirt and tie. His race remained indiscernible. It was the only ad with the text appearing in both English and Chinese. "No cure, no pay," it read, "Curee quickly and permanently the worst cases of Gonorrhea and Gleet, no matter how long standing." For the Chinese, sexually transmitted diseases and their remedies held an American component articulated through the image of dress, style, and language.[81]

For writer Sui Sin Far, whom literary scholars have labeled the first Asian American writer, American dress signaled duplicitous character.[82] In her works from the turn of the century, only her Asian villains appeared often in Western dress. In "A Chinese Ishmael," Far depicts the villain as well-acculturated into white America. Lum Choy, a scarred man of little integrity who intends to pay a high bride price for Ku Yum, "curr[ied] the favor of white people," "w[ore] American clothes," and "when it suit[ed] his convenience passe[d] for a Japanese." Far's villain, Choy, notably in American dress, embodies a despicable man, adopting the image of Western masculinity through his attire. His duplicity is emphasized by his habit of passing as Japanese.[83]

Finally, poems in collected works published in San Francisco's Chinatown during the earliest years of the twentieth century reveal how American dress on Chinese women signified illicit sexual freedom. Western clothing incited ambivalent reactions among individuals who recognized both its sexually provocative qualities as well as its disregard for displaying "appropriate" Chinese femininity. "All dolled up. Strolling along the street. She's so elegant and sweet! She dresses half Chinese, half American, she ties her loose temple hair with a bright silk ribbon. She shows her fashion expertise, not her feminine disposition." The sex appeal of American gender presentation implicated prostitute-like qualities, as well. "We in the business of pleasing men must keep up with the trend. . . . Doll ourselves like beautiful American-borns; Surely the men will find us very pleasant."[84] For Chinese San Franciscans, cross-dressing into male or female American gender presentations held less than desirable connotations.

Still, as much as resident Chinese appeared alien to scrutinizing eyes, in fact their appearance embodied little of anything authentically or uniquely Chinese. Chinese San Franciscans' dress was not composed of wholly Chinese ensembles. Their outfits reflected a blend of the cultural influences that permeated San Francisco's Chinatown. In his detailed study of early San Francisco Chinatown photographs, historian John Kuo Wei Tchen observed that as alien as the Chinese seemed to white San Franciscans, the immigrants' physical appearance hardly reflected Chinese traditionalism. Photographs reveal the majority of the Chinese population in cotton tunic tops, cloth shoes, pants, and wide-brimmed hats. Though the tunics and cloth shoes came from China, the pants and Hamburg style felt hats did not. While Chinese immigrants did indeed adopt bits and pieces of American dress, such as wide-brimmed hats, they remained for the most part visibly Chinese to the San Francisco eye.[85] Sadly, anti-Chinese sentiment would not disappear with a mere wardrobe change. Western dress would have brought no substantive benefits from xenophobes who would have easily found another characteristic to condemn as Chinese intractability. For those Chinese who found comfort largely within San Francisco Chinatown, any shifts to more drastically abandon Chinese dress and risk alienation would have made less than perfect sense.

Interestingly, whereas scholars of Chinese America such as Judy Yung and John Kuo Wei Tchen never explain perhaps the more "natural" phenomena of retaining cultural markers in clothing, Japanese American historians such as Yuji Ichioka and Eiichiro Azuma take time to elucidate the adoption of Western dress among Japanese immigrants. If these scholars' decisions to dwell on certain transformations and not on others are any indication of which events are more worthy of explanation, then Japanese San Franciscans and their pervasive American masquerades might have been a unique immigrant phenomenon. Additional research by Barbara Kawakami, Daniel Masterson, and Sayako Funada-Classen also suggest that Japanese immigrants in Hawaii and Latin America during the same period largely chose to maintain Japanese dress when plantation work did not dictate what they could wear.[86] Though urban xenophobes declared the Chinese and their Chinese dress odd, Japanese San Franciscans may have in fact proved queer in their American masquerades. Moreover, que(e)rying Japanese immigrants' Western dress, questioning it and also highlighting its potentially odd nature in the face of other immigrants who did not shed their ethnic dress, draws attention to the assumptions and perhaps unfair expectations we continue to put on our newer Americans.

Still, even if San Francisco Japanese deliberately dressing Western proved odd, their masquerades became a very real and perhaps "natural" part of their identities—a mindful presentation of themselves that reflected the hardships they experienced in America. Their location in an urban setting, within a largely white American population, and their desire to gain equal access to privileges of American citizenship could logically add up to Western dress. *Youfuku* in San Francisco remained a clothing style borne out of the conflict inherent to Asian life in America and almost immediately became an ordinary part of Japanese immigrants' identity.

Conclusion

In the early twentieth century, gender and cultural impersonations existed in many forms and held various implications. Collectively, they illuminated the ways individuals used gender and sexual imagination to enhance their lives and create identities that physical bodies limited or to enact desires that social proscriptions prohibited.[87] Theatrical gender impersonators drew audiences by magically defying gender. Women who wore men's clothes in daily life accessed traditionally male spheres of public life. Urban whites sought to "color" themselves for entertainment, as they enacted Asian personae. For the Japanese who dressed Western, cross-dressing represented their hopes of accessing the "American dream" during xenophobic times. Masquerades appeared to have positive value as acts of self-determination.

Yet taken apart, gender impersonations carried implications distinct from those of race. While categories of gender appeared immutable, San Franciscans appeared less threatened at the theatrical gender crossings which appeared as magic. Both theatrical and daily gender masquerades enjoyed a degree of acceptability in which participants effectively passed. In theater, actors drew sold-out audiences and respectable fame. Individuals such as Mrs. William Krieger and Babe Bean enjoyed aspects of work and leisure that would have been unavailable to them in female dress.[88] While municipal laws prohibited wearing clothes of a different sex, those who dressed across gender profited to some degree.

Similarly, Japanese San Franciscans hoped to access privileges by passing as American through more conventional forms of cross-dressing. Their attire, though, held little novelty. Japanese immigrants' Western transformation on the streets of San Francisco hardly raised an eyebrow. Still, the social normalcy of a specific masquerade did not necessarily bring its due privileges, nor did it signal a successful crossing. While turn-of-the-century San Francisco remained largely mystified and complimentary about gender crossings, they perceived American masquerades by Asians as hardly impressive.[89] So banal would the course of assimilation appear that those who resisted it, such as the Chinese, would come under fire for their intractable alienness.

Notably, race-based impersonations in theater diverged significantly in their intent than did those of gender. While the success of gender crossing relied heavily on its authentic presentation, racial impersonation drew audiences precisely for its fictional mockery. In 1900 Little Blanche Trelease impressed audiences with her "laughable Chinese imitations" in *Brownies in Fairyland*.[90] In productions such as *The Geisha*, *The Mikado*, and *First Born*, all marked as "comedy," narratives mocked and infantilized Chinese as well as Japanese. Other cities, such as London, New York, and Chicago, criticized unfair depictions in theater, some going as far as to ban specific productions out of respect for the Japanese government. Japanese immigrant poet Yone Noguchi noted, "The vogue of the *Mikado* or the *Geisha*, a comic opera, made my true Japanese heart pained, as I thought it was a blasphemy against Japan; how often I wished to shout from the pit or gallery on its absurdity."[91] In their pejorative parody of Chinese and Japanese individuals, San Francisco whites seemed to care little about what Asians in America might think.

As different as gender and race impersonations appeared to be, they resemble each other in their relationship to power. As categories of gender and its access to power grew increasingly unstable through the 1920s, gender ambiguity appeared more threatening. Men obsessed with their masculinity more actively defended it against the rising tide of white-collar work, educated women, and female activists. Unconventional gender presentations grew more explicitly linked to "homosexuality" in popular thought.[92] Biographer Louis Sullivan noted that when Babe Bean found it increasingly unacceptable to be a "biological woman living as man," she changed her name to Jack Bee Garland to remake herself more deliberately as a man.[93] With the disintegration of "separate spheres," female impersonation no longer could appear as baffling and thrilling acts of pure magic. During the 1920s, impersonators increasingly became viewed as deviant performing homosexuals rather than as performance artists. By 1930 authorities banning theatrical cross-dressing forced most of America's thousands of female impersonators out of business.[94]

To xenophobic whites in 1900, however, unstable definitions of race may have proved more threatening than gender ambiguity. As more rigid categories of gender allowed gender impersonators to pass effectively and with approval, contestable legal categories of race appeared unstable, as evidenced by the constant reinforcement of nonwhiteness in the courts and in legislation.[95] As Japanese immigrants battled discriminatory naturalization laws, alien land laws, and antimiscegenation laws, white xenophobes likely sensed slippages in their hold on power and privilege. Ironically, visual categories of gender proved much more permeable than Japanese who remained marked "Mongoloid," even in Western dress.[96] As gender impersonators passed and profited, Japanese immigrants unable to pass successfully as "American" lost out. And though American xenophobes criticized the Chinese as unassimilable for their Chinese dress, they offered few favors to the Japanese for their Western dress.

As much as ethnic masquerades reinscribed relationships of racial power and gender and sexual normativity, they also unearthed the infinite contradictions embedded within the city's social hierarchies.[97] Though some local San Franciscans embraced the feminine kimono, Japanese in the city hardly felt welcomed by local residents. For Japanese San Franciscans, downplaying their ethnicity would prove to be one strategy of survival. For local whites, race would serve as a source of privilege to dabble in different cultures with few repercussions.[98] Fantasies of race and ethnicity may have additionally served as one vehicle for white men to express interracial romance and white women to express homoerotic as well as interracial desire.[99] Cultural critic Eric Lott thus noted how masquerades "became less of a repetition of power relations" and more of a "distorted mirror" that signified displacements and discontinuities and that illuminated a "peculiar American structure of racial feeling." Literary critic Laura Browder also highlighted the American tradition of "self-invention" and "testaments to the porousness of ethnic identity," particularly in California.[100]

Perhaps for some, identity proved porous. Yet for many more it did not. Precisely because limitations posed by biology and social proscriptions proved physically impermeable, San Franciscans resorted to their imaginations to escape or stretch social reality. Masquerades on many levels crossed various boundaries drawn by sociolegal prohibitions as well as physical bodies. As individuals committed these acts deliberately under the cover of social acceptability, masquerades revealed how imagination created viable virtual realities within constraining physical actualities. As much as racial categories and thus racial privileges appeared to constantly have potential for redefinition and redistribution, in fact its marker appeared more distinct and less permeable for the many San Franciscans who remained indelibly marked at the turn of the century. Scientists believed that innate characteristics distinguished not just men from women but also Chinese, Japanese, and African Americans from whites.[101] Though racial categories faced a legacy of public blurring through the contestations of language, biological reason, and mixed-race individuals, it would nonetheless be a racial fluidity more readily available for those who could pass as whites or even "dark white."[102]

For Japanese San Franciscans, their near future appeared more inflexible than for those who perceived California as a place of "porous ethnic identity."[103] After the enactment of the 1913 Alien Land Act, the first major anti-Japanese legislation in California banning Japanese land ownership and restricting their tenancy, the Japanese community began a new mission of assimilating Japanese immigrants. Titled *gaimenteki doka* or external assimilation, it required conforming physical appearance and environment to European American ways that paralleled what the "educated" Japanese had been advocating since the 1890s. By 1915 Japanese immigrant women passing through Angel Island most likely wore Western dress. When Michi Kawaii, an activist for the YWCA, visited California to educate herself on Japanese immigrants and their living conditions, she described picture brides as looking "queer," "for no one had told them their huge pompadours stuffed with 'rats' had long since gone out of style in America, and their efforts to beautify themselves with an excessive use of powders resulted only in giving an impression of uncleanness."[104] For Japanese who dressed in Western clothes, their masquerades signified only the beginning of a longer struggle between their optimism and the reality of overcoming a race-conscious society despite their visually marked bodies.

Notes

1. So popular did her musical number become that its song sheet appeared in the Musical Supplement Section of one *San Francisco Examiner* issue. Gustav Luders, "Rag Time Mixes My Brain," score, 1900, San Francisco History Center, San Francisco New Main Public Library, San Francisco.

2. Photograph of "recent arrivals" in Golden Gate Park, 1900, Issei Project, box 4, folder "Ogata, Shizuye," National Japanese American Historical Society, San Francisco. Hereafter, the project will be cited as the Issei Project.

3. For a brief overview of queer theory and critical race studies, see Annamarie Jagose, *Queer Theory: An Introduction* (New York: New York University Press, 1996); Kimberlé Crenshaw et al., ed., *Critical Race Theory: The Key Writings that Formed the Movement*, with a foreword by Cornel West (New York: The New Press, 1995); and Richard Delgado and Jean Stefancic, *Critical Race Theory: An Introduction* (New York: New York University Press, 2001). For criticism of queer theory, see E. Patrick Johnson, "'Quare' Studies, or (Almost) Everything I Know about Queer Studies I Learned from My Grandmother," *Text and Performance Quarterly* 21, no.1 (January 2001): 1–25.

4. Gender impersonations existed as a significant cultural phenomenon and had held a variety of social meanings since the Middle Ages if not earlier. In the United States specifically, racialized gender impersonations first took the nation by storm in the early nineteenth century through Vaudeville acts, including "blackface." For more on its history, see Valerie R. Hotchkiss, *Clothes That Make the Man: Female-Cross Dressing in Medieval Europe* (New York: Garland Publishing, 1996); Roger Baker, *Drag: A History of Female Impersonation in the Performing Arts* (New York: New York University Press, 1994); Eric Lott, *Love and Theft: Blackface Minstrelsy and the American Working Class* (New York: Oxford University Press, 1993); Robert Toll, *On with the Show* (New York: Oxford University Press, 1974).

5. "Entertainment in Play and Music," *San Francisco Chronicle*, January 19, 1897.

6. First Nighter, "The Theaters," *Wasp*, March 5, 1898, 19.

7. "Gladys Montague," *Wasp*, September 16, 1899, 6.

8. In *A Milk White Flag*, Ada Mansfield, Maud Harris, Eva Hill, and Ilma Pratt played the "messenger boys." "Mary Marble," *Wasp*, September 10, 1898, 13; Programme for *A Milk White Flag*, 1897, San Francisco Performing Arts Library and Museum, San Francisco.

9. "Two Clever Little Players," *San Francisco Call*, March 11, 1900.

10. While local publications similarly praised male and female impersonators with little distinction between the two, there appeared to be some anxiety regarding boys dressing up as girls on the New York stage. Though popular in San Francisco, New York authorities banned Leon's public performance. Boys impersonating girls appeared to be more of a novelty than the girls who dressed as boys. "The bright little girl in knickerbockers, impersonating the small boy, is familiar to the public, but the little boy arrayed in a frock and acting the part of a girl is something of a novelty." "A Boy Rival for Girl Actors," *San Francisco Chronicle*, February 14, 1897.

11. For more details on the definition and implication of Orientalism, see Edward Said, *Orientalism* (New York: Pantheon Books, 1978).

12. Amsden points to Noh with its gender impersonators as notable art, with an aesthetic value that could only have originated in the West. "Once more we find a parallel with the ancient Grecian methods which will ever remain the supreme standard of art, and which the aesthetic Orient unconsciously assimilated." Dora E. Amsden, "Dramatic Art in Japan," *Overland Monthly* 36, no. 212 (1900): 100–107.

13. The Gay and Lesbian Alliance against Defamation (GLAAD), founded in 1985, has been providing education to media on producing fair, accurate, and inclusive representation of individuals in the queer community. Two criteria among others include positive depictions and the appropriate use of pronouns that mark self-proclaimed gender identity rather than natal sex. GLAAD, "Media Resource Kit," http://www .glaad.org/media/resource_kit_detail.php?id=3163 (accessed July 7, 2005).

14. In a marital pact she had agreed to labor alongside her husband in the fields and other manual work. "Wore Male Attire for Years," *San Francisco Chronicle*, May 24, 1898.

15. Jensen had initially eloped with the man, who then took her to San Francisco before deserting her. "Goes as a Tramp in Man's Attire," *San Francisco Call*, April 5, 1897.

16. "Woman's New Occupation," *San Francisco Chronicle*, November 16, 1897.

17. "In Man's Attire This Girl Toiled," *San Francisco Call*, March 9, 1897; "Female Tramp in Male Attire—Peculiar Santa Rosa Case," *San Francisco Chronicle*, March 9, 1897.

18. "Babe Bean," *San Francisco Chronicle*, January 16, 1898.

19. "Woman Bandit in Men's Clothes," *San Francisco Chronicle*, August 22, 1897.

20. "Miss Bean Not an Up to Date Young Man," *San Francisco Chronicle*, August 31, 1897.

21. "Native Daughter Who Should Have Been a Boy," *San Francisco Call*, March 11, 1900.

22. "How San Francisco Notables Look in Theatrical Roles," *San Francisco Call*, February 1900.

23. "Disillusioned," *Wasp*, July 16, 1898, 20.

24. "Where Shall the Line Be Drawn," *Wasp*, August 12, 1897, cover.

25. "Personal Pronouns Up-To-Date," *San Francisco Chronicle*, June 27, 1897.

26. San Francisco General Ordinances (1915), ordinance no. 819.

27. "Wears Trousers But Her Tongue is Silent—A Mysterious Young Woman Who Lives in a River Ark at Stockton," *San Francisco Call*, August 24, 1897.

28. "Tried to Impersonate His Mother-In-Law," *San Francisco Chronicle*, November 15, 1897.

29. Peggy Pascoe described distinct gender roles based on innate differences between the sexes as facilitating missionary rescue homes. Peggy Pascoe, *Relations of Rescue: The Search for Female Moral Authority in the American West, 1874–1939* (New York: Oxford University Press, 1990).

30. For more on the social significance of cross-dressing, see Marjorie Garber, *Vested Interests: Cross-Dressing and Cultural Anxiety* (New York: Routledge, 1992); Lesley Ferris, ed., *Crossing the Stage: Controversies in Cross-Dressing*, (New York: Routledge, 1992). For more on Julian Eltinge, see Sharon R. Ullman, *Sex Seen: The Emergence of Modern Sexuality in America* (Berkeley: University of California Press, 1997), 45–71.

31. My use of Western versus Japanese dress might appear artificially imposed, since culture and therefore clothing is never constructed by an unchanging, essential set of values from a single source. Admittedly, cultures, clothing, and identities are constantly evolving and often have blurry origins in their "authentic" location. Yet I deliberately use perhaps theoretically contestable categories of Western versus Japanese dress by directly translating how the Japanese themselves described and continue to describe their clothes today. "Youfuku" means Western dress and "wafuku" signifies Japanese dress. What scholars might argue to be theoretically messy categories of labeling the culture by dress made perfect sense for the Japanese. Thus, I employ them here.

32. Etsuji Tanida and Mitsue Koike explained that the lack of women adopting Western dress could be attributable to their lesser involvement in public life. Etsuji Tanida and Mitsue Koike, *Nihon Fukushokushi*, (Tokyo: Koseikan, 1989). See also Mainichi Shimbunsha, *Sandai no Onnatachi* (Tokyo: Mainichi Shimbunsha, 1981). Feminist scholars might argue that women perceived as the bearers of culture and tradition have historically been socially pressured not to adopt newer, nontraditional cultural trends.

33. Angel Island, often referred to as the Ellis Island of the West Coast, served as the immigration processing station for immigrants arriving along the Pacific Coast.

Him Mark Lai, Genny Lim, and Judy Yung, *Island: Poetry and History of Chinese Immigrants on Angel Island, 1910–1940* (San Francisco: Hoc Doi, 1980).

34. Photograph of Angel Island Immigration Station, 1912, Issei Project, box 1, folder "Angel Island Immigration Station—S.F., Record Group 90 of National Archives."

35. Photograph of Japanese Women at Angel Island, 1916, and photograph of "recent arrivals" in Golden Gate Park, 1900, Issei Project, box 1, folder "Angel Island."

36. The six who did not have mustaches appeared to be in their twenties, perhaps signaling a new facial hair aesthetic as documented by historian John Kasson. John F. Kasson, *Rudeness and Civility: Manners in Nineteenth-Century Urban America* (New York: Hill and Wang, 1990).

37. "Men of Prominence: Local Japanese Colony," *San Francisco Chronicle*, October 22, 1911.

38. Photograph of Iwata family, December 6, 1920, Issei Project, box 2, folder "Iwata, Buddy"; Portrait of Father and Daughter, 1913 Issei Project, box "Strength and Diversity, JA Women, Prewar Years"; photographs of Abiko family, 1921, Abiko Family Papers, box 42, folder 4, Japanese American Research Project, Charles E. Young Research Library, University of California at Los Angeles, Los Angeles. The Abiko Family Papers are hereafter cited as AFP.

39. Photograph of Kay Okamoto, 1911, Issei Project, box 4, folder "Okamoto, Kay."

40. Photograph of cook and his wife, 1915, Issei Project, box 1, folder "California Historical Society."

41. Photograph of David Fukuda, March 28, 1922, AFP, box 42, folder 2.

42. Photograph of Japanese language school, 1909, Issei Project, box 1, folder "California Historical Society."

43. Philip Stokes notes that group photos demonstrated a greater need to mark solidarities, to take every possible step to map the forms of one's personal society. Philip Stokes, "The Family Photograph Album: So Great a Cloud of Witnesses," in *The Portrait in Photography*, ed. Graham Clarke (London: Reaktion Books, 1992), 193–205.

44. "How Japanese Warriors Are Made," *San Francisco Call*, January 17, 1897.

45. Photograph of Ichikawa wedding, February 28, 1915, AFP, box 43, folder 1.

46. Interestingly, even the blossoms could be arguably inauthentic, as they appeared to be artificial. Photographs of wedding, July 11, 1916? AFP, box 43, folder 1.

47. Photograph of Hana Ohama, February 12, 1912, Issei Project, box 4, folder "Ohama, Geo."

48. Photograph of Kikuye Okuye, October 4, 1915, AFP, box 43, folder 3.

49. Portrait from M. Uakahara, March 1921, AFP, box 44, folder 3.

50. Things Japanese had to be "eschewed" as much as possible. Outward appearances influencing how Americans perceived Japanese couples became important as officials advised wives to walk alongside their husbands rather than behind to avoid reinforcing the stereotype of the tyranny of Japanese husbands. Yuji Ichioka, *The Issei:*

The World of First Generation Japanese Immigrants: 1885–1924 (New York: The Free Press, A Division of Macmillan, 1988).

51. Eiichiro Azuma, "Interstitial Lives: Race, Community, and History among Japanese Immigrants Caught between Japan and the United States, 1885–1941" (PhD diss., University of California at Los Angeles, 2000), 87. See also Eiichiro Azuma, *Between Two Empires: Race, History, and Transnationalism in Japanese America* (New York: Oxford University Press, 2005).

52. Ibid., 48.

53. Photograph of Togasaki Family, 1899, Issei Project, box 4.1, folder "Togasaki, Family." The Nationality Act of 1790 limited the privilege of naturalization to "any alien, being a free white person." Asians, not being white, could become citizens only if they were born in the United States.

54. Azuma, "Interstitial Lives," 87.

55. Homi Bhabha described "mimicry" as being like a camouflage, not a harmonization of a repression of difference, but a form of resemblance that differs from or defends its presence through display. Homi K. Bhabha, *The Location of Culture* (New York: Routledge, 1994), 85.

56. Alan Trachtenberg, *Reading American Photographs: Images as History, Matthew Brady to Walker Evans* (New York: Hill and Wang, 1989), 26, 27.

57. Tanida and Koike, *Nihon Fukushokushi.*

58. For more on the "New Woman," see Jean V. Matthews, *The Rise of the New Woman: The Women's Movement in America, 1875–1930* (Chicago: Ivan R. Dee, 2003).

59. Though writers used Japanese femininity most frequently to discuss American womanhood, South Asians also appeared as models of ideal womanhood, particularly as relations with Japanese became more tense in the decades following the earliest years of the twentieth century. For example, see Jean Q. Watson and Frances L. Brown, "The Partheneia of University of California," *Overland Monthly* 67, no. 5 (May 1916): 359–364. When young San Francisco men of elegant leisure and abundant means hosted stag parties, they preferred provocative woman dancers in exotic garb from the "Orient." See also "A Favorite with Clubmen," *Wasp*, May 27, 1899, 9. "Orient" here refers to cultures from the Middle East.

60. Charles Lorrimer, "The Japanese Art of Flower Arrangement," *Overland Monthly* 47, no. 2 (February 1906): 116–123. Narratives of attractive Japanese geishas became particularly notable since previous depictions from the latter nineteenth century of women lacked similar tones of gender appeal. In 1897, a few anthropological narratives lingered amid a growing number of romantic geisha stories. See "Ancient Japanese Laws," *San Francisco Chronicle*, January 17, 1897. "Coaling Ships in Japan," *San Francisco Chronicle*, July 24, 1898.

61. "Our Oriental Neighbors," *Wasp*, February 25, 1899, 8; "The Tale of Fan," *San Francisco Chronicle*, February 21, 1897; Charles Brown, Jr., "The Geisha Girl's Tale," *Overland Monthly* 61, no. 3 (March 1913): 248; W. D. Tillotson, "The Houses Where Gods Do Dwell," *Overland Monthly* 46, no. 6 (December 1905): 562–573; Leonard

Franklin Sawvel, "Nita, Child of the Sun," *Overland Monthly* 52, no. 4 (October 1908): 378; Hester A. Benedict, "Kamako," *Overland Monthly* 37, no. 3 (March 1901): 779–785.

62. Olive Dilbert, "Umeko-san," *Overland Monthly* 50, no. 4 (October 1907): 343.

63. Hester A. Benedict, "Kamako," *Overland Monthly* 37, no. 3 (March 1901): 779–785; Grace Hibbard, "Japanese Love Song," *San Francisco Chronicle*, March 13, 1898; Gertrude Holloway, "A Coquette," *Wasp*, November 5, 1898, 8.

64. While legal and medical experts had explicitly addressed "sex inversion" and "homosexuality" within their professional fields, the larger public remained unengaged in discussions about diverse sexual desires until World War I. For more, see John D'Emilio and Estelle B. Freedman, *Intimate Matters: A History of Sexuality in America*, 2nd. ed. (Chicago: University of Chicago Press, 1997). Western writer Charles Warren Stoddard wrote of reading banned publications on erotic fraternal love from Europe. Roger Austen, *Genteel Pagan: The Double Life of Charles Warren Stoddard*, ed. John W. Crowley (Amherst: University of Amherst Press, 1991).

65. "Two Clever Little Players," *San Francisco Call*, March 11, 1900.

66. Caroll Smith-Rosenberg documented "romantic friendships" that formed among education- and reform-minded women. These socially acceptable relationships proliferated from the 1880s into the early 1900s, until critics grew increasingly concerned about the prevalence of homosexuality in America and discouraged female intimacy as "lesbianism." Caroll Smith-Rosenberg, "The Female World of Love and Ritual: Relations between Women in Nineteenth-Century Amerca," in *Disorderly Conduct: Visions of Gender in Victorian America* (New York: Oxford University Press, 1985), 53–73. For more on the homoerotic potential if not reality of stage performers, see Jennifer Costello Brezina, "Public Women, Private Acts: Gender and Theater in Turn-of-the-Century American Novels," in *Separate Spheres No More: Gender Convergence in American Literature, 1830–1930*, ed. Monika M. Elbert (Tuscaloosa: University of Alabama Press, 2000); Lott, *Love and Theft*.

67. Mari Yoshihara asserted that Massachusetts white women dressing Japanese and expressing desire for Japanese men enacted alternative sexual identities. For Yoshihara, these explorations of sexuality referred to white women, mimicking "Oriental" romance and desire. Her research pointed to an enacted "Japanese" sexuality as different from an "American" one, and thus it became alternative. In contrast, my examples of poetry by Hibbard and Holloway additionally suggest white women imagining same-sex sexuality through their romantic desire for white women. Mari Yoshihara, "Women's Asia: American Women and the Gendering of American Orientalism, 1870s to WWII" (PhD diss., Brown University, 1997). See also Mari Yoshihara, *Embracing the East: White Women and American Orientalism* (New York: Oxford University Press, 2003).

68. "The Japanese Luncheon Fad," *San Francisco Call*, February 14, 1897.

69. "Third Violet," *San Francisco Chronicle*, January 17, 1897.

70. "Sale of Lawn Kimonas," *San Francisco Call*, May 25, 1905.

71. Lady Teazle, "Society Chat," *San Francisco Chronicle*, October 13, 1907.

72. Woman's Board of Foreign Missions, San Francisco, to Abiko Yonako, October 14, 1922, AFP.

73. Diary of Yonako Abiko, 1906–1907, AFP.

74. Margherita Palmieri to Yonako Abiko, July 1908, AFP.

75. Yone Noguchi, "In the Bungalow with Charles Warren Stoddard: A Protest against Modernism," *National Magazine* (December 1904): 306.

76. Photographs of Chinese in San Francisco, 1905, Special Collections, Bancroft Library, University of California at Berkeley, Berkeley. Chinese SVP, Subject Viewing Prints, volumes 1–3. For three examples, see 1905.5278.77–PIC; 1905.7442–PIC; and 1905.17500.14:83–PIC.

77. Historian John Tchen documented how Genthe went as far as altering his photographs to project a more "Chinese" image. For more details, see Arnold Genthe and John Kuo Wei Tchen, *Genthe's Photographs of San Francisco's Old Chinatown* (New York: Dover Publications, 1984).

78. "How a Chinese Queue Became an American Plait," *Wasp*, December 21, 1901.

79. For more on depictions of Chinese men as odd, see Nayan Shah, *Contagious Divides: Epidemics and Race in San Francisco's Chinatown* (Berkeley: University of California Press, 2001); Robert Lee, *Orientals: Asian Americans in Popular Culture* (Philadelphia: Temple University Press, 1999).

80. Marlon K. Hom, *Songs of Gold Mountain: Cantonese Rhymes from San Francisco Chinatown* (Berkeley: University of California Press, 1987), 206.

81. *Chung Sai Yat Po*, December 29, 1909.

82. Sui Sin Far served as the pen name for writer Edith Maude Eaton. Eaton, whose father was white and mother was Chinese, was born in England and spent much of her childhood in Canada. While technically a mixed-race Chinese Canadian, Sui Sin Far came to define her Chinese identity through San Francisco Chinatown. For more details, see Xiao-huang Yin, *Chinese American Literature since the 1850s* (Chicago: University of Illinois Press, 2000); Dominika Ferens, "Edith and Winnifred Eaton: The Uses of Ethnography in Turn-of-the-Century Asian American Literature" (PhD diss., University of California, Los Angeles, 1999).

83. Sui Sin Far, "A Chinese Ishmael," *Overland Monthly* 34, no. 199 (1899): 43–49.

84. Hom, *Songs of Gold Mountain*, 229, 312.

85. Genthe and Tchen, *Genthe's Photographs*.

86. Barbara Kawakami, *Japanese Immigrant Clothing in Hawaii, 1885–1941* (Honolulu: University of Hawaii, 1993); Daniel M. Masterson with Sayaka Funada-Classen, *The Japanese in Latin America* (Urbana: University of Illinois Press, 2004).

87. Theorists noted ethnic and racial impersonations as reflecting "mixed and messy" cultural contradictions that reflect both racial "envy" and "insult." Lott, *Love and Theft*, 18; Jessica Munns and Penny Richards, "The Clothes That Wear Us," in *The Clothes That Wear Us: Essays on Dressing and Transgressing in Eighteenth-Century Culture*, ed. Jessica Munns and Penny Richards (Cranbury, NJ: Associated University Presses, 1999), 26.

88. The San Francisco Lesbian and Gay History Project argued that many women who passed as men obtained socioeconomic privileges that would not have been available to them as women. San Francisco Lesbian and Gay History Project, "She Even Chewed Tobacco," in *Hidden from History: Reclaiming the Gay and Lesbian Past*, ed. Martin Duberman, Martha Vicinus and George Chauncey, Jr. (New York: Meridian, 1989).

89. In the 1930s, city whites intrigued by Asians acting "American" flocked to nightclubs such as Forbidden City to see the novelty of Asian Americans performing Frank Sinatra, Sophie Tucker, and other "eye-popping, all-American extravaganzas." *Forbidden City, U.S.A.*, videocassette, directed, written, and produced by Arthur Dong (Los Angeles: Deep Focus Productions, 1989).

90. "Clever Child in Her Debut," *San Francisco Call*, March 14, 1900.

91. For the scripts of the three productions, see Owen Hall, *The Geisha* (London: Ascherberg, Hopwood & Crew, 1896); W. S. Gilbert, *The Mikado* (New York: Boni and Liveright, 1917); Francis Powers, *First Born: A Chinese Drama in One Act* (n.p., [1897?]). For the banning of certain productions and additional protest, see Hesketh Pearson, *Gilbert and Sullivan: A Biography* (New York: Harper and Brothers Publishers, 1935); "Casino," Theatre 12 (July–December 1910): 4; "'The Mikado' Barred," *Literary Digest* 34, no. 21 (May 27, 1907): 838; "Chinese Drama Controversy," *San Francisco Chronicle*, September 25, 1897; Yone Noguchi, *The Story of Yone Noguchi* (Philadelphia: George W. Jacobs, 1914).

92. For more on shifting gender ideologies and their social implications, see Gail Bederman, *Manliness and Civilization: A Cultural History of Gender and Race in the United States, 1880–1917* (Chicago: University of Chicago Press, 1995). For essays on the scientific correlation of gender ambiguity to homosexuality, see Vernon Rosario, ed., *Science and Homosexualities* (New York: Routledge, 1997).

93. Louis Sullivan's biography of Babe Bean suggested San Francisco may have exhibited some gender fluidity in the earliest years of the twentieth century. Louis Sullivan, *From Female to Male: The Life of Jack Bee Garland* (Boston: Alyson Publications, 1990).

94. Despite its censure in the 1920s, gender impersonators at the turn of the century appeared to have come a long way since its earliest days—from crass comedy embedded in misogyny to a reverent celebration of femininity in all of its gentility, modesty, and grace. Rising out of the shadows of vaudeville, drag enjoyed national acclaim as legitimate theater. Late Victorian vaudeville female impersonation affirmed and celebrated the most traditional middle-class norms. Baker, *Drag*, 161–162; Ferris, *Crossing the Stage*, 108–109.

95. For more on how Asians were excluded from naturalization, property rights, and interracial marriage, see Sucheng Chan, *Asian Americans: An Interpretive History* (Boston: Twayne, 1991).

96. Legal scholar Ian López noted how legal categories of race that could not be articulated with biological precision often defaulted to "common knowledge."

Thus, though Japanese might legally prove to be white or American according to its definition, the court used perceptions of the "common" individual to still mark them as nonwhite. Ian F. Haney López, *White By Law: The Legal Construction of Race* (New York: New York University Press, 1996).

97. The world of clothing and appearance well illustrates these cultural contradictions. England and France, at war for most of the century, admired, copied, and imported each other's fashions. Additionally, triumphant colonial expansion and control of trade markets brought new materials and styles to England and continental Europe. Though eagerly adopted, they also led to fears of cultural dilution and loss of national identity. Munns and Richards, "The Clothes That Wear Us," 26–27. Similar to its historical predecessors, turn-of-the-century San Francisco cross-dressing reflected existing social hierarchies and their internal contradictions, prevalent in communities grappling with social diversity.

98. For more on white privilege and cultural appropriation, see Mary C. Waters, *Ethnic Options: Choosing Identities in America* (Berkeley: University of California Press, 1990).

99. An additional story by Jean Armor Deamer suggested a white woman's attraction to a Chinese man who is in the end a white man in Chinese masquerade. Jean Armor Deamer, "The Lasting Escape," *Overland Monthly* 51, no. 4 (April 1908): 351. Covers of ethnicity enabling articulations of various desires certainly did not appear for the first time in turn-of-the-century San Francisco. Long before the Civil War white Americans enacted same-sex sexuality in blackface as they denigrated African Americans. Lott, *Love and Theft*, 162–164.

100. Laura Browder noted that during an age of theater of "blackface" and the "Wild West Show," identity had become something to be performed, rather than an essential quality. These productions permitted performers to slip between shades of brownness to find identities that were easier to live with than the ones they had been assigned at birth. She noted that from its beginnings, California had been a place where passage from one national and ethnic identity into another seemed possible. Laura Browder, *Slippery Characters: Ethnic Impersonators and American Literature* (Chapel Hill: University of North Carolina Press, 2000), 74, 76.

101. The notion that various ethnicities or races had biologically distinct origins dominated racial ideology throughout the nation. Scientists used this notion of innate differences to order various ethnicities into an evolutionary hierarchy, where whites not surprisingly occupied the upper tiers. E. Nathaniel Gates, ed., *Racial Classification and History* (New York: Garland Publishers, 1997); Matthew Frye Jacobson, *Whiteness of a Different Color: European Immigrants and the Alchemy of Race* (Cambridge, MA: Harvard University Press, 1997); Audrey Smedley, *Race in North America: Origin and Evolution of a World View*, 2nd ed. (Boulder, CO: Westview Press, 1999); Stephen Jay Gould, *The Mismeasure of Man*, rev. ed., (New York: Norton, 1996); Michael Adas, *Machines as the Mismeasure of Men: Science, Technology, and Ideologies of Western Dominance* (Ithaca: Cornell University Press,

1989); George W. Stocking, *Victorian Anthropology* (New York: Free Press, 1987); Matthew Frye Jacobson, *Barbarian Virtues: The United States Encounters Foreign People at Home and Abroad, 1876–1917* (New York: Hill and Wang, 2000).

102. I use the term "dark white" to point to literary critic Christina Mesa's use of the term when she referred to those individuals who accessed whiteness despite their dark pigmentation. Christina Mesa, "White Guise and Dark White Women: Purity and Miscegenation in Nineteenth Century American Culture" (PhD diss., Stanford University, 1999).

103. Brower, *Slippery Characters*, 74.

104. Azuma, "Interstitial Lives," 111–112, 120.

CHAPTER 3

Latitude in Mass-Produced Culture's Capital

New Women and Other Players in Hollywood, 1920–1941

BRETT L. ABRAMS

> *When Your Urge's Mauve, [go to] the Café International on Sunset Boulevard. The location offered supper, drinks, and the ability to watch boy-girls who necked and sulked and little girl customers who . . . look like boys.*

The 1940 guidebook *How to Sin in Hollywood* offered tourists this description of a commercial establishment that they could see when they visited the Hollywood area. On the opposite page, a cartoon featured two women in tuxedos above the caption "the little girl customers."[1] One smoked a cigar and both wore prominent lipstick. The description and cartoon presented images of women in the Los Angeles area who defied the culture's gender and sexual norms.

The description and cartoon of Café International suggested that the book's creators and readers accepted a link between the urban area of Hollywood, cross-dressing females, and homosexual women and men. Hollywood, the town, offered nightspots and other locations where Hollywood industry figures could act upon their non-normative gender and same-sex interests. Between the early 1920s and early 1940s, the Hollywood industry publicity departments and movie-making personnel, novelists of Hollywood, and the newspaper reporters and gossip columnists capturing Hollywood industry people's daily lives placed cross-dressing females and other people who defied the culture's prescriptions

Figure 3.1. Entering the Club International on Sunset Boulevard. Jack Lord and Lloyd Hoff, *How to Sin in Hollywood* ([Hollywood?], CA, 1940).

about proper gender and sexual behavior in their depictions of Hollywood people and places. These figures—in this article called Hollywood players—did not adhere to the automatic link between biological sex and gender behavior, such as females behaving in a conventionally feminine manner. They eschewed heteronormativity, or the cultural prescription that bound sexual activities to a man and a woman who were already married or intending to be wed soon. These female Hollywood players used nightspots, homes, parties, and studio lots in downtown Hollywood, along Sunset Strip, and in the exclusive areas of Hollywood Hills and Malibu Beach to pursue their interests, and they forged a concept of Hollywood as a place of latitude for unconventional figures. The representations of these female Hollywood players portrayed them as complex, successful figures, an unusual depiction for living persons and fictional characters who defied conventional sexual and gender norms.

These images flourished immediately after World War I because of changes in the culture and the industry. The United States witnessed the breakdown of genteel culture and its restrictions on topics of discussion in the aftermath of the war. The new "modern" culture invited greater presentation of sexual innuendo and sexuality in the mass media. Indeed, in the first era to revision sexuality around desire and fulfillment, the culture interpreted sex as central to personal identities. The entertainment for this culture would logically focus on presenting such an important topic to its audiences, and news media outlets attempting to describe celebrity personalities would focus on sexual identities, as well. By 1920, the movie studios changed their publicity approach. The divorces and other off-screen activities of several major stars forced the industry to shift from promoting stars as picture personalities, reflections off-screen of their on-screen characters. Instead, the studio publicity featured the star's supposed everyday life and personality, with the latter necessitating the discussion of the star's sexual behavior, which was considered central to personal identities.[2]

The number and variety of media that featured Hollywood movie people expanded significantly during the era. Newspaper coverage included regular articles about the industry's personalities, occupations, and products and daily gossip columns from the six major syndicated writers on the beat. General-interest magazines, such as *Time* and *Life*, and the fanzines, such as *Photoplay* and *Silver Screen*, reached millions of readers with their weekly photographs, features, and gossip items on Hollywood. During the late 1910s, the Hollywood novel changed its focus away from the technology of movie making to stories about characters within the industry. Hollywood movies about the industry increased as movie production solidified itself in the southern California climate.[3]

Recent scholarship has demonstrated the development of places in urban areas where people with same-sex sexual feelings could pursue their interests and even establish a degree of community. Some locations, including parks and bathhouses, offered only temporary and clandestine opportunities, predominately to males. Other locations, such as bars in vice or tourist areas, always faced the threat of official repression. A few spaces, including the social club Heterodoxy and basement apartments in areas like Greenwich Village, Harlem, and Chicago's South Side, offered regular meeting places for a subsection of the nonconformist population of these cities for a short time.[4] These places rarely appeared in the media, except during local authorities' efforts to drive the people who defied gender and sexual norms from local bars.[5]

Scholars have noted that the images of women in the media changed significantly during the 1920s and 1930s. The dominant image of the "New

Woman" during the 1920s was the flapper. While flappers enjoyed greater freedom in consumption and sexual awareness, much of their consumption and sexual gratification focused on pleasing males, not on engaging in same-sex sexuality. The flapper embraced a career for herself until she got married and rarely acted in other ways that defied the newly established gender norms of the era.[6] Images of women who defied the culture's dominant images, such as matrons, faced ridicule for representing Victorian rather than "modern" gender and sexual attitudes.[7] Figures who challenged sexual norms in literature of the era sparked censorship efforts, despite appearing as miserable characters who experienced emotional turmoil and became outcasts or suicide victims or who engaged in self-loathing and despair.[8] Despite the occasional movie that showed a successful independent woman, during the period before the establishment of the Production Code Administration in the mid-1930s, most of the adulterers, gold diggers, and other "fallen women" met unfortunate ends or were forced to redeem themselves at the end of the movie.[9]

Scholars writing in the 1980s and 1990s, including Vito Russo and Andrea Weiss, have observed that in most Hollywood productions from the early 1910s to the mid-1970s, homosexuals led lonely lives, experienced derision, and sometimes became victims of murder or suicide. Lesbians appeared as vampires who preyed upon innocent younger women.[10] Historians of the movie industry noted few instances of nonconformist imagery in news about the movie industry. Generally, they determined that the industry viewed these images as detrimental to the business and observed that the industry covered up gender and sexual nonconformity by mainstreaming the images.[11]

The depictions of Hollywood players created by the movie studio publicity departments, their movie-making personnel, newspaper and magazine reporters, and other observers of the movie industry belied the findings regarding the types of urban spaces available to nonconformists and their presentation within the media. The Hollywood players of the 1920s and 1930s illustrated that within the Los Angeles environs people engaged in alternative gender and sexual behaviors and used nightclubs, homes, parties, and studio lots as locations where they could act upon their interests. The media images depicted these figures throughout the period. The players appeared successful in their personal and professional careers, indicating that the capital of the world's mass-produced culture had a unique relationship to the "New Woman" and other gender and sexual nonconformists of the era.

Nightspots

The Café International nightclub appeared on one of Hollywood's most magical streets, Sunset Boulevard. During the 1920s Hollywood's population quadrupled as the area expanded west through Beverly Hills and north into the San Fernando Valley. Los Angeles developed a manufacturing base in automobiles and aircraft, expanded its oil refinery industry, and emerged as one of the top tourist locations in the country. Los Angeles also developed the Mediterranean and Spanish Revival architectural styles and Southland literature. Movie-making became the eleventh largest industry in the nation. The large studios transformed the "barn" structures of the early 1910s into the series of buildings and sets behind tall gates, giving the studios the look of fiefdoms. The production wings of the big eight studios functioned like factories. Each studio employed nearly three thousand people, and a single department, such as Metro-Goldwyn-Mayer's makeup department, could handle twelve hundred actors in an hour.

The growth of the movie industry brought more people and money to the Los Angeles area. As the movie industry grew, related industries, including costume and prop stores, expanded. Between 1917 and the early 1930s, the number of restaurants and lunchrooms quadrupled. They spread, as did nightclubs, from the Spring Street area in downtown Los Angeles to two major sections of Hollywood. The blocks around the intersection of Hollywood and Vine in downtown Hollywood contained luxurious hotels, elaborate beauty parlors, shops, and widely publicized restaurants such as the Brown Derby. The old town of Sherman, later to become West Hollywood, clustered its stores, nightclubs, and restaurants in groups along Santa Monica and Sunset Boulevards.[12]

Stars continued during the 1920s to go to towns like Vernon and Culver City to slum in the cabarets and speakeasies.[13] However, by 1930, Hollywood had "more Neon lights than Broadway. . . . It is gayer, newer, brighter, and younger than anything in the history of man."[14] The majority of the "in" places congregated along the Sunset Strip, a three-square-mile area that bordered Hollywood and Beverly Hills. The area remained outside the city of Los Angeles and was policed by the Los Angeles County sheriff. Many famous stars greeted the boys in the patrol cars by name in this unincorporated area of West Hollywood. Such familiar relationships reflected the power relationships of the city and the capacity of people from all walks of life to become star struck and led to a more relaxed attitude toward the enforcement of certain laws. The Sunset Strip gained notoriety as one of the most famous hot spots in the country. Of the nightclubs in the area, The Barn, La Bohème, the Club New Yorker, and the Back Yard Café all featured cross-dressing performers and clientele. Despite the protests of religious figures and other citizens that the bars and nightclubs, gambling houses, and houses of ill repute had invaded the best residential districts, the Strip drew the stars, the aristocracy, and the politicians. Hollywood, the industry, and the newspapers and magazines that covered it promoted these locations to maintain fan interest and boost the sales of its products.[15]

One of the most famous nightspots in Hollywood served its customers in a building shaped like a man's hat. The Brown Derby restaurant attracted actors, directors, producers, and screenwriters of the industry from noon until the early morning hours. The Vine Street location reserved its booths and the north wall front tables for stars and executives, while others sat in the center. All hoped to get noticed.[16] One of the earliest scenes in the movie *What Price Hollywood?* occurred inside this restaurant: Drunken motion picture director Max Carey walks in throwing gardenias he bought from an old woman outside. Smiling, he greets the people he knows. He briefly exits the screen. (The viewer sees a section of the restaurant as the shot switches from a medium to a long shot.) Carey continues walking around the restaurant and bumps into the mannishly attired woman as she rises from her table. His mouth drops as he steps back and says, "I beg your pardon, old man." As she straightens her suit jacket, Max slowly looks down then up her torso and rolls his eyes back in his head. Reaches out his hand and taps her elbow. "Pardon me, who's your tailor?" She turns her back and strides out as he smirks then carries on giving out the flowers.[17]

The creative team behind *What Price Hollywood?* (RKO, 1932) attempted to "tell the truth about Hollywood."[18] Producer David O. Selznick thought the "trouble with most films about Hollywood was that they gave a false picture, that they burlesqued it, or they oversentimentalized [*sic*] it. . . . And my notion . . . dialogue was actually straight out of life and was straight 'reportage.'" Evidently, Selznick and the movie-making personnel at RKO purposely included an image of a woman in men's attire in their movie because they thought it captured the essence of what occurred in Hollywood.

The movie places its audience inside the most famous Hollywood eatery in downtown Hollywood. The scene puts a variety of Hollywood types on display, including a lecherous agent, an egotistical actor, and a producer with his sycophant dining in a booth. The presence of the mannishly dressed woman indicates that these women are part of Hollywood nightlife. Her introduction differs from the presentation of other Hollywood types. Carey briefly exits before returning into view and immediately bumping into the woman in a man's suit. Of all the Hollywood types presented in this scene, the movie tries to surprise its viewers only when it introduces the Hollywood player.

The separation of this woman's image from the other industry types illustrates the significance of the role of Hollywood players in Hollywood nightlife. The image makes the restaurant seem like a wild and fantastic place. The woman's mannish dress hints that she had lesbian interests. The difference in her introduction indicates that the image represents a unique type of person and spurs the belief that Hollywood nightlife is wild because it contains special places where people who act on taboo interests dine. The player image provides audiences with the perception of Hollywood nightlife as fantastic by giving them the experience of seeing a person who pushes the culture's sexual boundaries beyond their everyday experience.

The scene at the Brown Derby and the image of the mannishly dressed, presumptively lesbian enhanced the picture's reputation for RKO. The scene corroborated the perception of Hollywood held by many people around the world. As critics for the trade magazine *Motion Picture Herald* informed theater owners, *What Price Hollywood?* was a serio-burlesque load of inside dope on what folks everywhere thought Hollywood was. The box office returns from most U.S. cities validated the trade reviewers' perceptions that the motion picture would fulfill audience expectations.[19]

The image sacrifices truth for entertainment value. The mannish female character's tailored suit is too large for her, prompting Carey's quip about wanting to know about her tailor. Among the Hollywood women wearing masculine tailored suits during the era, actress Marlene Dietrich, director Dorothy Arzner, and screenwriter Mercedes de Acosta wore suits with impeccably sharp lines and style. Certainly producer David Selznick, director George Cukor, and the four screenwriters knew about the sharp style affected by women in men's clothing. But the production team, wanting to add humor to the scene, chose to make her the object of the joke. Still, the mannish woman in the movie had more positive attributes than depictions of lesbians in the popular culture of the era: she had an attractive face and a torso that was neither overly boyish nor overweight; she treated herself well, dining at a hot spot; and she had a place within the motion picture industry community.

Hollywood women in masculine attire appeared occasionally in newspaper and magazine gossip columns. While validating the image from *What Price Hollywood?*, the gossip items exchanged information, fostered understandings of the conception of Hollywood, and created a community among its readers. With items such as "Director Dorothy Arzner, who favored 'man-tailored suits,' dined with actress friends at La Maze," "[Arzner] lunched with a variety of women friends, including actress Claudette Colbert, at the exclusive Vendomes," and "Director George Cukor and screenwriter Zoe Akins held a party for their friend actress Tallulah Bankhead [who frequently donned mannish attire] at a downtown French café"[20] they placed women in men's clothing at a variety of Hollywood's eateries and watering holes. Like the character in *What Price Hollywood?*, the gossip items associated Hollywood nightlife with the thrill of seeing women who defied the norm for women's attire. Frequently, adoption of such clothing signaled a same-sex sexual interest, so that readers also received the titillation of encountering females who pursued taboo sexual interests.

Items like the three above benefited the movie industry and the media organizations. The publicity focused readers' attention on movie industry figures. The items seemed to present specific knowledge about the women's activities, providing readers with what they wanted and presumably keeping them reading the news outlet for more information. As Richard Schickel argued in *Intimate Strangers*, readers wanted knowledge about celebrities in their daily lives. This desire defined Hollywood publicity departments and the media's presentation of celebrity pieces. The items could not be too sensational, or readers would disbelieve it and would not get the experience that they sought from reading. The disappointment would presumably motivate them to seek another source of information and thus stop reading the original media source.[21]

Figure 3.2. Marlene Dietrich, Paramount Pictures promotional shot, c. 1932. Mercedes de Acosta Collection, Rosenbach Museum and Library.

Publicity items about the mannishly attired women in Hollywood nightclubs and restaurants portrayed them as successful people, Hollywood players who enjoyed fine lives in Hollywood. Important industry figures, the women worked for the major movie studios on big-budget pictures, earning large salaries that enabled them to dine at exclusive nightspots. They forged friendships, attended and hosted parties, and built a community of like-minded women in Hollywood.

The image of the mannishly dressed woman in Hollywood nightlife reached its apex with the publicity featuring Marlene Dietrich. Certainly, people knew that Dietrich could cross-dress. In two other successful Hollywood movies, she wore tuxedos. As early as the fall of 1930, gossip columnist Louella Parsons noted Dietrich's preference for pants in her daily life. During those early years Paramount avoided discussing Dietrich's clothing preferences. However, in late 1932, Dietrich had a box office failure with her movie *Blonde Venus*. Paramount signed Dietrich to an expensive five-year contract and severed her relationship with the director, Josef von Sternberg. The studio sought an image with which to promote their star, and the studio's publicity department launched a huge publicity campaign for Dietrich's new movie, *Song of Songs* (1933). The publicists featured her clothing, knowing that most successful publicity campaigns revolved around an aspect of the star's personality, because, as noted earlier, that was the information that the public sought. As one industry columnist stated, "The truth about that masculine attire which Marlene Dietrich affects these days is this. She liked wearing that sort of clothes—trousers. Paramount objected. Marlene insisted on trotting about in pants. Finally they gave up. 'Oh well,' sighed Paramount, 'then we'll make a cult of it—exploit Marlene in men's clothes.'"[22]

Paramount's publicity department staged their events in the same places in downtown Hollywood and along the Strip where the earlier depictions of women in men's clothing occurred. In January 1933, a few articles and several industry columnists chronicled Dietrich's attire. A tabloid piece provided abundant detail about Dietrich's apparel. "Marlene Dietrich gave the photo snappers and autograph hounds a real thrill yesterday by appearing at the Brown Derby with long gray flannel trousers, blue sweater, cap to match, dark gray mannish coat and her attorney, Ralph Blum."[23] An item in the *Los Angeles Times* offered more context. "Lunching with Mamoulian [Dietrich was] still wearing trousers and coats and evidently having them made to order. It is said she has just ordered two or three Tuxedo suits to wear in the evening. It is also said that she ate considerable humble pie in coming back to Paramount."[24] Another tabloid item suggested a reaction to readers as it informed them that Dietrich's Hollywood nightlife style caused heads to turn. "Marlene Dietrich created a mild sensation when she arrived at the El Mirador hotel in Palm Springs. . . . She wore masculine attire for all occasions at the desert resort."[25] These items accomplished the studio's goal of having the star receive significant media coverage, and reporting the actress wearing men's clothing at Hollywood restaurants made Hollywood nightlife appear wild and decadent in a humorous manner.[26]

The studio offered readers an interpretation of these images that did not promote the connection between Hollywood nightlife and the star's romantic life. Paramount's publicity department framed this "new" Dietrich image as the start of a fashion trend. Despite clothing that stretched gender conventions for women, the publicity department still linked Dietrich's image with a cultural understanding of woman as display object of consumer culture products. Some contemporaries writing on Dietrich's masculine attire interpreted the image similarly. "'Will it be overalls next?' an industry columnist wondered. 'Depends probably on how much publicity Katharine Hepburn gets out of her favorite garb. Anyway, they seem to be organizing a publicity campaign on them. It's probably rivalry for Dietrich's trousers.'"[27]

Others perceived that the "new" Dietrich image offered hints about Dietrich's sexual activities. The images spurred readers to connect the star's romantic life with Hollywood nightlife, turning that nightlife into a site for fantasies.

Dietrich's occasional beau and confidant Maurice Chevalier expressed the star's interest in heterosexual males. "I told Marlene myself that if she would wear men's clothes and women's garments even to the extent of fifty-fifty, I would find it the most attractive and charming idea. . . . [S]he looks wonderful in men's attire."[28] Director Josef von Sternberg noted that Dietrich's adoption of masculine dress also appealed to another romantic interest. Von Sternberg described his motive for Dietrich in male tuxedos in two motion pictures. "The formal male finery fitted her with much charm, and I not only wished to touch lightly on a Lesbian accent, . . . but also to demonstrate that her sensual appeal was not entirely due to the classic formation of her legs."[29] The Dietrich image positioned the Hollywood player in Hollywood nightlife but also gave that nightlife an appeal to those readers with player interests of their own.

The Dietrich images revealed that Paramount's publicity department devised a campaign around presenting one of the industry's biggest stars as a Hollywood player. The decision to promote their star's habit of wearing tailored suits and slacks in restaurants and other locations illustrated both the studio's intentional use of Hollywood player imagery and the promotional value of the imagery. The Dietrich campaign worked. People remembered the images.

Other creators used the Dietrich Hollywood player image and connected it to Hollywood nightlife. In mid-1933, the great songwriting team of Richard Rogers and Lorenz Hart wrote "I'm One of the Boys" for the motion picture *Hollywood Party*. The song chronicled the activities of a woman "who was One of the Boys, girls. I go to the tailor that Marlene employs because no dresses from France are so modern as these. And under my pants are BVD's. . . . Now I take my brandy at the bar. Dice, cards, and tobacco are my favorite toys. . . ." The possibility that the song might appear in the movie caused the Studio Relations Committee's head to write to MGM executive Eddie Mannix. As the chief of the censorship organization for the industry, he advised Mannix not to play "I'm One of the Boys" in any way that might be suggestive of lesbianism.[30]

The Dietrich campaign proved successful because audience members remembered it. When readers visited Hollywood a few years later, they regularly asked whether Miss Dietrich really wore trousers. Guides told visitors that the Brown Derby would be a good place to see the star for themselves. The guides' advice confirmed the accuracy of the Dietrich publicity campaign. They also gave the visitors the chance to experience the Hollywood nightlife fantasy themselves.[31]

The city government tried to halt the cross-dressing of women and men in the nightclubs. The Los Angeles City Council passed a law that prohibited the appearance of people in drag within a café, unless employed by the café. Contemporary observers and current scholars observed the numerous raids on female and male cross-dressing nightclubs in late 1933 and thought the law would close these locations, but the existence of Club International in the late 1930s proved this incorrect. The fans' enjoyment of the Dietrich image and the chumminess of the Los Angeles Sheriff's Office offered key reasons as to why the policing effort failed.[32]

Women in men's clothing dined and drank in restaurants and nightclubs in downtown Hollywood and along the Sunset Strip. These female industry people influenced the perception of Hollywood, the town and the cultural symbol. Their appearance made Hollywood a place where women who did not abide by the culture's gender and sexual norms had a public presence on the town and in the media. They formed an unmistakable addition to the mystique of Hollywood nightlife. Their presence helped the restaurants and nightclubs appear wild and decadent, allowing Hollywood nightlife to stand apart from all other depictions of city nightlife in the media.

Houses

During the early 1920s, the growing movie industry and expanding city offered several women who worked in the other creative trades the opportunity to establish homes where they could be Hollywood players. Alla Nazimova, an accomplished violinist and Stanislavski-trained actress who became the leading interpreter of Ibsen on the Broadway stage before becoming known as a silent-film actress, ranked among the top stars in the annual *Photoplay* popularity poll in the late 1910s. The star moved west of downtown Hollywood, and her house at 8080 Sunset Boulevard made her a leader in the transformation of Sunset Boulevard into the Strip.[33] She formed a development company and turned her homestead into a complex of twenty-five bungalows that lined the largest swimming pool in Hollywood. She named the place the "Garden of Allah," adding the "h" to her given name to associate it with the garden hostelry of sacred and profane love in Robert Hichens's 1904 novel, *The Garden of Allah*.[34]

Nazimova's homestead influenced the development of Hollywood as a town and its conception as a place of latitude for women. A group of Nazimova's friends who met regularly at the star's home and enjoyed ribald activities became known as the "8080 Club." After Nazimova left Hollywood in the mid-1920s, her homestead became an apartment complex for many of the workers who came to Hollywood during the first years of the talkies.

Media descriptions of Nazimova's home revealed that her house offered the star the opportunity to display her cross-gender clothing and other aspects of her Hollywood player personality. As the head of her own production company, Nazimova decided that this type of publicity was beneficial to her image and would make her movies successful. An interviewer for *Photoplay* described her masculine attire in the living room of Nazimova's house:

> "She enters whistling," I observed aloud. Nazimova made a move and twirled into the corner of a divan, drawing her feet up after. The effect was boyish, shining black hair cropped very short and parted on one side, a white Eton collar over a dark blouse, a short plaid skirt and flat-heeled brogues, and an abnormally long cigarette holder properly functioning.[35]

Nazimova created a cross-gender look while she also appeared to be the "head of her castle." The interior décor of purple divans, crystal lights, and a mirror laced with gold reflected Nazimova's outsized personality. The reporter notes that within the house Nazimova revealed a dash of "diablerie" (wickedness) about her, so that one could not precisely say that heaven was her home.[36]

The star directed her publicity in a similar manner with newspapers. Newspaper coverage described Nazimova's home as a location where she could express another of her personality traits, a preference for the company of women. Nazimova brought a Hollywood player's defiance of gender norms to her friendships with young women, telling reporters that, "They call me Peter and sometimes Mimi." Nazimova's first nickname linked the actress to a male character, Peter Pan, while the latter nickname alluded to the tragic lover in La Bohème. One set of gossip items said that the star's swimming pool, crowded only with Hollywood ingénues, contained underwater lights that illuminated the water at night. The gossip united the physical display of female bodies around a swimming pool with a sensuous environment to suggest homosexuality at her Hollywood home.[37]

Nazimova used interviews at her home to publicly attack gender conventions. The movie star emphasized that a woman must live her own life: "A woman living a creative life is bound, necessarily, to do things sometimes defiant to convention. In order to fulfill herself, she should live freely." Nazimova's position regarding women's domestic role was unique even among women who identified themselves as feminists during the 1920s.[38] Scholars have observed that a few second-generation New Woman writers used their feminist language to attack conventions. However, their efforts sparked representations that depicted them as unnatural followed by criticism and the full brunt of social ostracism and legal censorship. Nazimova and other Hollywood players issued stinging attacks on gender and romantic conventions of the era and received little criticism from the media, politicians, or other industry people.[39]

Nazimova was not the only woman in Hollywood to use her house as a location for the expression of Hollywood player behaviors. Women dominated the industry's screenwriting departments throughout the 1920s. As career women who earned significant incomes, screenwriters faced questions about their attitudes toward their careers, motherhood, and family. Indeed, the sexual and gender behavior of these women was questionable enough that twenty years later F. Scott Fitzgerald noted in his last novel, *The Last Tycoon*, that successful screenwriter Jane Meloney received numerous labels, many focused on the private world of her sexuality. "The little blonde of fifty," he wrote, "could hear the fifty assorted opinions of Hollywood . . . a sentimental dope, the smartest woman on the lot, and of course, nymphomaniac, virgin, pushover, a Lesbian."[40] Most labels were generally not used by studio employees to attack but to understand the wealthy writer.

The extensive newspaper coverage of a bizarre love triangle in the late 1920s thrilled readers with revelations that some screenwriters pursued their Hollywood player interests in their homes. After the disclosure of her husband's death and his female biological sex, screenwriter Beth Rowland explained in the press that her marriage to Peter Stratford resulted from the love and respect that emerged during a two-year correspondence before Stratford declared "his" love for Rowland. The widow described her role as a platonic wife, nurse, and homemaker to a fastidious gentleman. However, the testimony of others, including Rowland's son, depicted Stratford as a healthy and active person, raising the suggestion that the pair shared a same-sex marriage. This appears more likely when one considers that Rowland used the term "infidelity" when she discovered Stratford wrote endearing letters to Rowland's screenwriter friend Alma Thompson.[41]

Alma Thompson appeared to live a player's existence in a ranch house in Hollywood. Thompson studied mysticism and claimed she wrote to Stratford out of sympathy for his affliction, but their letters contained appeals for a deeper love and carried the salutations "Dearest Lamb" and "Dear Pedar." Thompson sent Stratford secret rose petals and Stratford referred to Thompson as "my soul." The exchange of deeply emotional letters with a person she knew as the husband of her friend made Thompson the "other" woman. Whether Thompson knew herself to be part of a triangle of three females, the screenwriter actively engaged in an adulterous emotional affair with a person she believed to be a married man, or knew to be a woman living as a man. Fittingly, Alma Thompson's one screen credit came a few years later for the 1933 feature *I Loved A Woman*.[42]

Another screenwriter with few movie credits generated enough interest to appear in publicity pieces throughout the 1930s. The child of an aristocratic Spanish family from Cuba, Mercedes de Acosta's mother called her Rafael, dressed her in male clothes, and encouraged her to believe that she was a boy for several years. De Acosta married painter Abram Poole in 1921, but the pair led increasingly separate lives and were divorced in 1935. A novelist, playwright, poet, and Hollywood screenwriter, de Acosta achieved fame as a confidante and companion to several women in theatrical, artistic, and motion picture circles.[43] During de Acosta's first year as a screenwriter, Hollywood reporter Alma Whitaker visited de Acosta's home and offered a description of de Acosta in terms that revealed her Hollywood player nature. Whitaker noted that de Acosta was in her dangerously attractive late thirties and "affects the strictly tailored idea, even unto a genuine walking shoe."[44] The screenwriter crossed the culture's gender boundaries for clothing within her home.

After mentioning that de Acosta lived alone in Hollywood while her husband stayed in New York City, Whitaker noted, "Miss de Acosta has taken a delightful house at Brentwood Heights, where she is ensconced with her servants and her dogs and she says her stay is indefinite. She also owns a home in New York and an apartment in Paris."[45] The screenwriter expected a long, comfortable stay in her new, charming residence without her husband, whom she soon divorced. Afterward, she established a "family" in her Hollywood home over which she ruled. The image highlighted de Acosta as a Hollywood player. Unlike other images of screenwriters and their homes, the piece neither describes de Acosta's house in feminine terms, nor does it define the screenwriter's relationship to her home in a manner that the culture associated with females.[46] Readers discovered that the screenwriter created this life for herself in the hills of Los Angeles County, in an exclusive residential area north and east of Beverly Hills where stars like Gary Cooper and Shirley Temple lived.

De Acosta, like Nazimova, argued for the right to defy the culture's gender conventions. She told an interviewer, "Of course, I think matrimony is out of date. I don't approve of it at all. . . . Divorce . . . should be unnecessary. And if matrimony were abolished it would be." Then, de Acosta added that she had no children, noting that "she can imagine how some mothers will feel about me."[47] The Hollywood player challenged the prevailing family structure of the home during a time when the culture strongly encouraged women to limit their aspirations to husband, family, and domesticity. Still, de Acosta faced no repercussions within or outside the industry as the result of expressing her opinions.[48] She lived in Hollywood over the next decade, with Greta Garbo and Marlene Dietrich among her circle of friends.

For two decades Hollywood actresses and screenwriters used their homes to pursue their Hollywood player interests. They wore men's clothing as they relaxed in their private space, creating memorable images for reporters to share with the public. Nazimova held all-female pool parties in their expansive back yards, and Thompson engaged in sexual mysticism with her girlfriend's female husband in her small Hollywood bungalow, both notable examples of pervasive player activity. They used their porches to offer opinions to the press that challenged the culture's limits on the woman gender. Their presence made the Hollywood town a place where women owned and ruled large homes. Their appearance associated the Hollywood celebrity home with outsized personalities that carried overtones of the taboo, unique among the depictions of large homes in the media.

Parties

Private parties provided another Hollywood location where female Hollywood players acted upon their interests. A journalist of the era described these galas as "the last word in American social relaxation, rich with the super costly meats and drinks, alive with the unrestrained wit, whoopee and love-making of the Republic's most romantic characters."[49] During the 1920s, disclosures such as those from the trials of Fatty Arbuckle gave Hollywood parties a reputation as wild affairs.

A famous movie comedian, Fatty Arbuckle attended a large, exciting party in a San Francisco hotel during which former actress Virginia Rappe died under mysterious circumstances. Accused of causing her death, Arbuckle underwent three trials that received detailed coverage in metropolitan dailies from late 1921 through 1922. Despite an acquittal, the negative publicity ended Arbuckle's career. Scholars have used the Arbuckle affair to demonstrate that the industry strove to control scandal and the publicizing of unorthodox behavior.

The coverage of the Arbuckle incident illustrated the important difference between the Arbuckle image and the Hollywood player images. In the Arbuckle case, the industry struggled to control the dissemination of information and perspectives on the incident because the trial grabbed the nation's attention and granted opponents of the industry a weapon with which to advance their view that Hollywood was a pernicious influence upon American morals and values. Furthermore, Arbuckle's story did not allow for a humorous perspective that could put a spin on the matter that might benefit the industry. Other groups successfully argued that the Arbuckle affair was symptomatic of social problems that required collective legal action against the motion picture industry. Arbuckle might be a murderer, or at least, a menace to other people. This potential threat motivated the Hollywood industry to work to remove negative images from media and public attention as soon as possible and to placate opponents.[50] In contrast, the Hollywood player image represented Hollywood insider or semi-independent perspectives and did not create sparks that threatened the movie industry or the conception of Hollywood. The Hollywood players made Hollywood locations look fun and playfully decadent, but certainly not violent or harmful.

Two novels, one by Nina Putnam and another by Jim Tully, featured Hollywood private parties within five years of the Arbuckle affair. Each included depictions of Hollywood players that the editors and publishers deemed acceptable to present to readers. As observers of the Hollywood industry and its world, both authors sought to describe to the readers of their novels what each saw as the truth about Hollywood.

Author Nina Putnam included a Hollywood private party in *Laughter Limited*, her book about a young woman's attempt to become a movie star. Bonnie and her friend Anita meet a writer, who takes them to a famous director's house on Malibu Beach for a party. All kinds of pawing occurs after enormous amounts of great food and drink. "[When] Bonnie ran away as Tom Muro himself put a hand on her shoulder [publicity director Greg] Strickland tells Bonnie to come across and she'll get into pictures."[51]

The author depicts Hollywood private parties as a place of intense revelry. After sating their eating and drinking desires, all the partiers begin acting to satisfy their libidos. Hollywood private parties offered industry people and their guests locations where they could meet the upper echelon of the movie industry. They also served as places where the guests could engage in any sexual activity they desired. Many enjoyed these Hollywood player activities. Others, like the lead character in the novel, perceived the experience as a potential source of extortion. While this image suggested that some might see Hollywood player activities as coercive, it also suggested that other women enjoyed the revelry. In addition, none of the revelers at the party hurt their professional or social lives through participation in the party activities.

The novel received only a few reviews. Most respected Putnam's writing and thought the book entertaining. One reviewer concentrated on the experience of the main character and believed that the "age-old story" of the "job party" was beneath Putnam's capabilities. This reviewer likened the women at the party to the forty-niners going west to stake their claim to strike it rich and having as likely a chance at success. She saw no reason to doubt the party's realism but suggested that a focus upon the producers and directors who received the women's favors would prove as truthful and more interesting.[52]

In 1926, Jim Tully, one of the founders of the naturalist "proletarian" school of writers in the U.S. and former publicist for Charlie Chaplin, released his Hollywood novel, *Jarnegan*. The publisher promoted *Jarnegan* as the first honestly written novel about Hollywood. Tully's book sold well in its first printing but never went into a second printing. Over the remaining two decades of his life, Tully wrote novels and articles about Hollywood stars for magazines ranging from *Vanity Fair* to *The New Movie Magazine*.[53]

Near the end of the novel, the main characters set off to crash a large party. Jarnegan, his assistant director Jimmy, and two female friends drive into the

Hollywood Hills. Fueled by a strong anger over a fellow director's misbehavior with a female extra for whom he cared, Jarnegan goes to find the man. He walks into the petting party of a movie producer to see "women at the party were semi-nude, not in happy abandon, but in middle-class vulgarity."[54] The director's Hollywood private party offers guests splendid costly food, drinks, and the most beautiful people in the movie colony. Despite Jarnegan's jaundiced view of the affair, the private party provides the best of everything. Hollywood women can enjoy the lavish environment and also use the Hollywood party as a place to engage in a variety of sexual activities with other guests, regardless of marital status or sexual interests.[55]

Critics enjoyed the novel. They viewed the book as a vivid picture of life out of the commonplace and written directly from material observed at first hand. A story about a rough customer, the novel struck critics as part of the expansion of the scope and intensity that changed the formerly polite American novel. The reviewers saw the party as part of the depiction of a feverish populace's pursuit of wine, women, and song—and they cared little about missing the singing. While not addressing the truth of the presentation, reviewers noted that Tully's experience meant he should know of what he wrote.[56]

Both Putnam and Tully thought that describing Hollywood—the town and concept—required a scene featuring the lavish private parties thrown by the industry's creative people. The novels placed these private parties in the large homes along Malibu Beach and in the Hollywood Hills, exclusive residential areas in distinctive natural environments. Top movie people competed to own homes in these locations. Industry people who owned the limited number of places along Malibu Beach included a small percentage of the studio heads, directors, and top actors.[57] The homes were far away from everyday life and received little police surveillance, and an invitation to a private party there offered the guest the chance to escape. Both authors showed that in such an environment people established their own rules and provided male and female guests a place where they could engage in a variety of sexual activities with any other guest. According to both authors, the guests could partake in these activities without negative repercussions in their personal or professional lives. The party scenes mixed morality, titillation, and coercion. Some readers might have enjoyed the hint of sexual excitement and absorbed a moral lesson. Others could have felt titillation from the sexuality and a charge from the sense of coercive nature to the sexual exchanges. The party images offered the first set of readers a tonic to purify their excitement, while the latter set of readers received excitement and the fulfillment of potential fantasies.

When Clark Gable separated from his wife, Maria Langham, gossip columnists noted that he and actress Carole Lombard attended public affairs and places together. Knowing the media coverage and the stars' continued appearance together, MGM invited its star Gable to the movie premiere and party for the 1938 movie *Marie Antoinette* at a famous nightclub on the Sunset Strip. Lombard accompanied Gable, despite his status as a married man. A huge photograph in *Life* magazine showed the pair smiling as they sat at a table. The caption noted, "Carole Lombard and Clark Gable had the best time at the Trocadero. Always full of fun and careless of dignity, they are one of Hollywood's delightful couples. They can not marry because Gable's wife has refused to divorce him."[58] The style in which the information about the stars appeared and the positive presentation of Gable and Lombard's behavior encouraged readers to approve of the couple and their nonconformist sexual activity. The image also offered readers the opportunity to imagine themselves in this type of relationship.

A major media entity taking a photograph inside a studio party would most likely have occurred with studio cooperation. Usually, studios encouraged publicity when they believed that the image benefited the star and the industry. As noted earlier, the studios strove to link publicity images to either a real or imagined personality trait of the star. They also hoped to make the image something with which fans could identify so that they would feel closer to the star and continue coming to their movies.

MGM and *Life* proved to be correct, for both stars remained very popular. Gable went on to his biggest role in *Gone with the Wind*. Lombard made a few more successful movies with Paramount studios. Readers accepted Gable's image as a rogue, but what enabled them to accept Lombard's status as the other woman? Carole Lombard developed her popular screen persona based on several screwball comedies during the 1930s. After her short marriage to actor William Powell, Lombard forged an off-screen personality as a single woman—quirky, feminine, and independent. The actress was also well known for her big parties. Her party across the entire Venice Pier Amusement Park late in 1937 was a big hit with industry people. The party generated some racy publicity images, including photographs of Dietrich, Claudette Colbert, and Lombard showing their legs. After Lombard cut back on these affairs because of her relationship with Gable, many Hollywood insiders missed them. A fan magazine reporter summed up the attitude of some in Hollywood in an article entitled, "What ever happened to Carole Lombard?" Like Hollywood insiders who enjoyed her personality, many of her fans enjoyed Lombard's antics and lifestyle and presumably thought her an appropriate match for the rogue Gable.[59]

The image of the pair at the movie premiere party illustrated the degree of acceptance of Hollywood players. The studios invited Hollywood players to their premiere parties and did not force them to hide their nonconformist behaviors. In this instance, the studio featured the Hollywood players in their publicity about the studio party. The industry party offered Lombard a place to enjoy herself with her paramour and their friends. Lombard maintained her position as a movie star and as an admired person within and outside the movie community. Studios did not extend the same invitations to same-sex couples.

Studio Lots

Female Hollywood players did not have to confine their pursuit of their gender bending, adultery, or same-sex interests to their leisure time. The studio grounds also provided times and places where the women could behave as they wished. While the public could not often walk behind the studio gates, studio publicity departments, newspaper reporters and gossip columnists, and Hollywood novelists provided a public view of the lots and the women who defied gender and sexual norms.

Gossip columns about the movie industry devoted a significant amount of space to glimpses behind the scenes. Some of the earliest columns noted the presence of stars who crossed gender boundaries. Alla Nazimova, during the height of her popularity, appeared so comfortable around the studio that she wore her masculine attire. This prompted one columnist to report that "[There were] rumors around that Nazimova has adopted trousers while lounging at the studio." A decade later, another star with Metro studios made her private space on the lot reflect her defiance of gender norms: A magazine article characterized Greta Garbo's large dressing room, where the reclusive actress frequently rested between takes, as so lacking in decorations that the environment suffered from a masculine severity. The fan magazines ran a two-part piece a year earlier on Garbo's private life that included gender-bending decorations and actions. Indeed, MGM released a few publicity items regarding the star's cross-dressing, featuring a beret and tailored suits that she wore.[60]

MGM's *Bombshell*, a 1933 movie about the industry, argued that the producers went further than providing female Hollywood players space to be themselves on the lot; they helped to manufacture a player image for its female stars. The movie depicted the life of fictitious star Lola Burns, played by Jean Harlow. Burns, known to her fans as the "Blonde Bombshell," had an image as a wanton woman who loved and left all sorts of men. Jean Harlow was known for her platinum blonde hair and alluring figure, and the movie was based loosely on her real-life experiences.

In the movie, Burns dislikes her image and the daily demands she faces, and she wants to change everything. At work, the actress needs to shoot retakes of her last movie, because the Hays Office and the production codes deem some scenes too risqué. At home, she copes with a free-loading family and her two jealous suitors. In the media, she faces questions stemming from false stories about her liaisons. She seeks to change her public image, despite being told by the studio publicist, Space Hanlon (Lee Tracy) that romantic scandal is what her adoring public wants. Burns tries unsuccessfully over the course of the movie to replace the image of herself from that of a sexually aggressive woman to the picture of the girl next door. Hanlon does everything he can to undermine Burns's efforts and to continue promoting her image as a free-spirited woman.[61]

Bombshell offered a revelation about the activities within the studio and in the life of a movie star. The movie made fun of the creation of star images and the assumed link between a star's image in the movies and her or his off-screen life. Most strikingly, the movie depicted a female movie star whose studio wanted her to lead a Hollywood player existence. In its opening montage, the movie shows how a woman with this image can remain a popular star. Young and old commuters, housewives, and other people appear, eagerly reading a series of newspaper headlines that catalogue Burns's crossing the boundaries of sexual propriety. In the view of the director Victor Fleming and screenwriters John Lee Mahin and Jules Furthman, a spectrum of audience members enjoyed the Hollywood player antics and wanted to know the details about their favorite star's activities in Hollywood. The movie industry insiders behind *Bombshell* portrayed the studio publicity department actively promoting a star image of an actress as an unmarried woman having sex, sometimes with married men.

Critics generally praised the movie. Calling it adroit, markedly clever, and one of the best comedies of life in Hollywood, reviewers praised the cast's performances as well. The reviewers considered Burns a temperamental star who dabbled in everything, including relationships. They enjoyed the publicist character and relished the way he humorously used Burns's pseudorelationships and his imagination to grab any front-page headlines that he could. The public expressed mixed reactions. Although the movie did well in the big cities on the first week, it did not prove to have the box office power to last there for long. The movie grossed excellent box office receipts in midsized and smaller cities across the country.[62] It allowed audiences to view Lola Burns as a sexy, wild woman, yet having her attempt to change this image made it easier for audiences to like and accept her. Burns became the good bad woman, an obvious fantasy figure for many men but also one for those women who wanted to play this part.

By the early 1940s, the depiction of Hollywood players behind the scenes became much more infrequent. This change occurred because the industry as well as the U.S. government sought to diminish its focus upon Hollywood as a separate community during World War II. They established a branch of the Office of War Information to oversee the motion picture industry's output and located it in the center of Hollywood. The local government increased its policing activities. The Los Angeles Police Commission began reviewing nightclub performances before issuing the licenses that allowed the shows to appear. The first act they stopped was by Julian Eltinge, a popular female impersonator who had a great following among Hollywood movie stars. In addition, the understanding of the definition of homosexuals changed by the early 1940s, making this large group of Hollywood players less humorous and thus less useful to the entertainment industry.[63]

One of the last female Hollywood player images of the era appeared in Ann Bell's 1940 novel *Lady's Lady*. Lotus, a female star who finds the studio lot conducive to her sexual interests, falls deeply in love with Bunny, a woman she has picked from among the hundreds of extras while filming a scene in a movie. Bunny sleeps with Lotus but the extra's coolness causes the star to plead for renewed affection.

> My heart is aching. Whenever I close my eyes, I can see you in my imagination with other girls. I had planned and hoped never to have any more heartaches, but the way I feel about you is pitiable. I would give my life to be with you this very moment, just to feel you near me, to drift in the dreamland of heavenly bliss for only a few minutes. I would be happy if you would allow me to be with you once again . . . but regardless of anything and everything, I wish and am longing to hear your voice again. Darling, may I?[64]

This novel presented the sound stage as a place for performers to fulfill their romantic interests. Readers learned that a star could walk around the stage and exchange glances with hundreds of extra girls to decipher their level of interest to her and in her. The representation indicated that a star expressed little concern about engaging in this activity and exhibited little fear that one of these extra women or other studio workers might object to her Hollywood player activities. While Bunny might not have wanted to pursue the relationship beyond one night, her response to Lotus's letter makes it clear that Lotus could have chosen a different girl to fulfill her romantic desires. Lotus may fail to retain Bunny's love, but she maintains her position as a movie star and continues to receive the income and adulation associated with her status. Lotus has free reign of the studio to pursue her homosexual interests and faces no overt condemnation for this activity. The story also suggests that an unheralded extra could find romance with a wealthy, popular star, adding a Cinderella promise to romance behind the scenes in Hollywood.

Cross-dressing, free-spirited, and homosexual women appeared on the movie studio lots in downtown Hollywood, Culver City, and other neighboring areas. They lounged in their men's clothing, decorated their dressing rooms in masculine severity, and sought liaisons and potential relationships on studio stage sets. These women and their activities received a public presence through their appearance in the media. These depictions added to the mystique of Hollywood behind the scenes by bringing the taboo and forbidden pleasures to the mystery and glamour that dominated depictions of the studios as a workplace.

The Hollywood players had an extraordinary run of two decades. The depictions illustrated that the phenomenon's mass-produced cultural capital offered women who defied gender and sexual norms many places where they could act upon those interests. The Hollywood movie industry, its observers, and the organizations that reported on this world presented Hollywood players to the public, positioning media sources as places where the women also had a public presence. Media sources, as shapers of Hollywood's cultural image, used these images to add the taboo and forbidden pleasures to the mystique associated with these Hollywood locations.

The female Hollywood players appeared as successfully integrated into the Los Angeles-Hollywood world. They drank and dined in the restaurants and nightclubs in downtown Hollywood and along Sunset Boulevard. The women expressed their personalities in their homes in central Hollywood, along the Boulevard, and in the exclusive residential district of the Hollywood Hills. They partied with the upper echelon of the movie industry at private parties in the Hollywood Hills and in chic Malibu Beach. They pursued their personal interests in the dressing rooms and on the sets at the studio lots. The lifestyles they led raise issues about urban life for scholars of women, gender, and sexuality to consider.

The presentation of the Hollywood players offered them a public presence in the culture. As celebrity figures, many of the players likely attracted audience members' attention, and their words and deeds appeared more seductive to emulate. In the increasingly urbanized United States of the era, with its expanding mass-produced culture, the Hollywood players appeared as figures of a vibrant present and an exciting future. Unlike what scholars have previously found, that nonconformist figures who appeared in movies, literature, and newspapers led horrific lives, the media images of female Hollywood players leading successful lives offered audience members examples of alternative lifestyles that could be rich and rewarding. The players demonstrated that cultural gender and sexual norms did not represent the precipice beyond which lay an abyss of misery. This offered audience members, particularly those who crossed the boundaries themselves, great excitement and relief. This element in the representation of women in the media deserves further investigation.

The examples I have presented and others I have found indicate that the studios purposely created and presented Hollywood player images.

Newspapers, magazines, and the novels and movies about the motion picture industry in Hollywood presented them. As portrayed in *Bombshell*, young and old women and men bought the consumer products that the stars endorsed to identify with them, read the banner headlines of their activities to be in the know, pored over the feature articles and novels to acquire details about the players and their lives, and watched the movies that featured the player images to fantasize about them. The most striking images in the montage that opens *Bombshell* included one woman and one man, each lying down in their homes dreaming, with a fan magazine featuring Burns draped over their torsos. Clearly, racy, risqué, and shocking images comprised part of the dream of Hollywood for some in the audience.

Then, as now, the movie studios pushed the envelope of culturally acceptable images to generate more attention and business. Movie makers, along with the Hollywood novelists and newspaper writers, used the images as a way to entertain but also to describe and explain their Hollywood world. Together, these groups' use of Hollywood players helped forge the mystique of Hollywood's locations and the movie capital in general.

Notes

1. Jack Lord and Lloyd Hoff, *How to Sin In Hollywood* (Hollywood, CA: n.p., 1940), 39.

2. Sharon R. Ullman, *Sex Seen: Emergence of Modern Sexuality in America* (Berkeley: University of California Press, 1997); Ann Douglas, *Terrible Honesty: Mongrel Manhattan in the 1920s* (New York: Farrar, Straus and Giroux, 1995); Vern L. Bullough, *Science In the Bedroom: A History of Sex Research* (New York: Basic Books, 1994); Lynn Duminel, *The Modern Temper: American Culture in the 1920s* (New York: Farrar, Straus and Giroux, 1995); Richard de Cordova, *Picture Personalities: The Emergence of the Star System in America* (Urbana: University of Illinois Press, 1990), 140—43; Joshua Gamson, *Claims to Fame: Celebrity in Contemporary America* (Berkeley: University of California Press, 1994), 35, 66–68.

3. Edward Alwood, *Straight News: Gays, Lesbians and the News Media* (New York: Columbia University Press, 1996); Simon Michael Bessie, *Jazz Journalism: The Story of the Tabloid Newspaper* (New York: E. P. Dutton., 1938); James Parris Springer, "Hollywood Fictions: The Cultural Construction of Hollywood In American Literature, 1916–1939" (PhD diss., University of Iowa, 1994); Anthony Slide, *The Hollywood Novel* (Jefferson, NC: McFarland, 1995); Christopher Ames , *Movies About the Movies: Hollywood Reflected* (Lexington: University of Kentucky Press, 1997).

4. Brett Beemyn, ed., *Creating a Place For Ourselves: Lesbian, Gay, and Bisexual Community Histories* (New York: Routledge, 1997); George Chauncey, *Gay New York: Gender, Urban Culture and the Making of the Gay Male World, 1890–1940* (New York:

Basic Books, 1994); Kevin J. Mumford, *Interzones: Black/White Sex Districts in New York and Chicago in the Early Twentieth Century* (New York: Columbia University Press, 1997); Judith Schwarz, *The Radical Feminist of Heterodoxy: Greenwich Village, 1912–1940* (Norwich, VT: New Victoria Publishers, 1986); Elisabeth Lapovsky Kennedy and Madeline D. Davis, *Boots of Leather, Slippers of Gold: The History of a Lesbian Community* (New York: Routledge, 1993). The Club International operated in the western section of Hollywood. Other nightspots catering to this clientele appeared within Los Angeles's Twelfth District, an area northwest of downtown that included portions of the Colegrove, Edendale, and Wilshire-Pico and contained mostly middle- and working-class housing. For references to the bars see *Los Angeles Times*, May 3, 1933, sec. 2; May 4, 1933, sec. 2; *Los Angeles Evening Herald and Express*, September 11, 1935, sec. B. For information about the area of Los Angeles see *Sandborn Fire Insurance Maps of Los Angeles, 1919–1950*, and Eshref Shevky and Marilyn Williams, *The Social Areas of Los Angeles: Analysis and Typology* (Berkeley: University of California Press, 1949), 68–89, appendixes C–E.

5. Thomas A. Bolze, "Female Impersonation in the United States, 1900–1970" (PhD diss., State University of New York at Buffalo, 1994), 162–63; Chauncey, 333–54. As George Chauncey concluded, the visibility of homosexuals in the public sphere, where they were perceived as a threat to the gender and sexual arrangements already in crisis because of the Great Depression, proved so powerful that even the *representation* of homosexuals disappeared from many media forms.

6. Nancy Cott, *The Grounding of Modern Feminism* (New Haven: Yale University Press, 1987), 155–65; Mary Ryan, "The Projection of a New Womanhood: Movie Moderns in the 1920s," in *Decades of Discontent: The Women's Movement, 1920–1940* (Westport, CT: Greenwood Press, 1983). Depictions of New Women in mass culture, such as Hollywood movies, showed them desiring to escape work and winning retirement through the prompting of love and trusting submission to her man. The idea for a contestation of stories forming lesbian identities and media representations of the "mannish lesbian," appeared in Lisa Duggan, "The Trials of Alice Mitchell: Sensationalism, Sexology, and the Lesbian Subject in Turn-of-the-Century America," *Signs: Journal of Women in Culture and Society* 18 (1993): 792–94.

7. Kathy Peiss, Christina Simmons, and Robert A. Padgug, eds., *Passion & Power: Sexuality in History* (Philadelphia: Temple University Press, 1989), 159–61.

8. These topics included the seduction in Upton Sinclair's *Oil!* and the rape and voyeurism in William Faulkner's *Sanctuary*. In 1929, the New York Special Sessions Court overturned a lower court ruling that Radclyffe Hall's *The Well of Loneliness* was obscene because it "idealized and extolled perversion." Over 100,000 copies of the book sold between the decision in April and the beginning of 1930. The decision offered the publishing world the ability to print books with homosexuality as a theme. Felice Flanery Lewis, *Literature, Obscenity and Law* (Carbondale: Southern Illinois University Press, 1976), 109–11; Jeannette Foster, *Sex Variant Women in Literature* (New York: Vantage Press, 1956); Roger Austen, *Playing the Game: The*

Homosexual Novel In America (Indianapolis: Bobbs-Merrill, 1977), 20–30, 69–72; Lillian Faderman, *Odd Girls and Twilight Lovers: History of Lesbian Life in Twentieth-Century America* (New York: Columbia University Press, 1991), 65, 100–102.

9. Janet Steiger, *Bad Women: Regulating Sexuality in Early American Cinema* (Minneapolis: University of Minnesota Press, 1995); Lea Jacobs, *The Wages of Sin: Censorship and the Fallen Woman Film, 1928–1942* (Madison: University of Wisconsin Press, 1991).

10. Vito Russo, *The Celluloid Closet: Homosexuality in the Movies* (New York: Harper & Row, 1981); Andrea Weiss, *Vampires and Violets: Lesbians in Film* (New York: Penguin Books, 1993). Scholar David Lugowski argues that homosexual representations in motion pictures during the Great Depression were linked to other groups considered disreputable and otherwise socially outcast. David Lugowski, "Queering the (New) Deal: Lesbian and Gay Representation and the Depression-Era Cultural Politics of Hollywood's Production Code," *Cinema Journal* 38 (1999), 3–35.

11. More recently, works have noted that publicity on particular stars, such as Marlene Dietrich and Clark Gable, suggested that nonconformist behavior might account for some of their popularity. Hollywood players included a wide array of movie industry workers who found Hollywood filled with places and opportunities to act outside conventions. Patty Fox, *Star Style: Hollywood Legends as Fashion Icons* (Los Angeles: Angel City Press, 1995); Samantha Barbas, *Movie Crazy: Fans, Stars and the Cult of Celebrity* (New York: Palgrave, 2001), 150–56.

12. Kevin Starr, *Material Dreams: Southern California through the 1920s* (New York: Oxford University Press, 1990), 94, 290–340; Leo Rosten, *Hollywood: The Movie Colony—The Moviemakers* (New York: Harcourt, Brace & Co., 1941), 5, 371; Edwin O. Palmer, *History of Hollywood* (New York: Garland Publishing, 1938), 236; Neal Gabler, *An Empire of Their Own: How the Jews Invented Hollywood* (New York: Crown, 1988), 36–42, 63–64, 104–54; *Los Angeles City Directory*, 1927, 2330–35; 1933, 2637–43; *Sanborn Fire Insurance Maps of Los Angeles, 1919–1950*; David Ehrenstein, interviewed by author, West Hollywood, California, January 15, 2000.

13. Margaret Tante Burk, *Are the Stars Out Tonight: The Story of the Famous Ambassador and Coconut Grove* (Los Angeles: Round Table West, 1980), 25–39; Robert S. Sennett, *Hollywood Hoopla: Creating Stars and Selling Movies in the Golden Age of Hollywood* (New York: Watson-Guptill Publications, 1998), 86–89; Jim Heimann, *Out with the Stars: Hollywood Nightlife in the Golden Era* (New York: Abbeville Press, 1985), 23–37; Anthony Slide, "The Regulars" article in the Hollywood Community MFL, NC 2812 folder, New York Public Library (NYPL); unidentified clipping, Patsy Kelly folder, NYPL.

14. Mildred Adams, "The City of Angels Enters Its Heaven," *New York Times*, August 3, 1930, sec. 5.

15. Untitled article in Cinema: Hollywood folder MWEZ, 14, 280 at NYPL; Christopher Finch and Linda Rosenkrantz, *Gone Hollywood* (Garden City, NY: Doubleday, 1979), 215–19; "Protest West Hollywood's Alleged Vice," *Los Angeles Evening Herald*,

June 20, 1933, sec. B; Hedda Hopper, "Hedda Hopper's Hollywood," *Los Angeles Times*, December 11, 1939, sec. 2; Slide, "The Regulars," Heimann, *Out with the Stars*, 43–47; Sennett, *Hollywood Hoopla*, 86–91.

16. "The big men came in [the Derby] and casually nodded to unimportant folk. In-betweeners rated a quick smile and a vague, 'H'yuh.' Top notchers received an enthusiastic back slapping, 'Old boy-old-boy!'" Jimmy Fiddler, "Jimmy Fiddler in Hollywood," *Los Angeles Times*, May 29, 1939, sec. 2; Heimann, *Out with the Stars*, 44–49.

17. *What Price Hollywood?* directed by George Cukor (1932, RKO).

18. Quoted in Rudy Behlmer, Memo to David O. Selznick (New York: Avon Books, 1972), 132. See also Irene Mayer Selznick, *A Private View* (New York: Alfred A. Knopf, 1983), 168–72.

19. The teaser campaign of what was happening behind the picture studios proved alluring to customers. Eastern, Midwestern, and far Western cities provided strong box office returns. However, it did poorly in southern cities like Louisville and Birmingham. *Motion Picture Herald*, June 18, 1932, 35; *Film Daily*, June 22, 1932; *Variety*, June 28, 1932; July 12, 1932; July 19, 1932; July 26, 1932; August 16, 1932.

20. Herbert Cruikshank, "Director Dorothy: The One Woman Behind the Stars," *Motion Picture Classic* 30, (September 1929): 76; *Los Angeles Times*, September 18, 1927, sec. 3; February 9, 1936, sec. 3; June 9, 1935, sec. 3; August 16, 1936, sec. 3; *Los Angeles Evening Herald*, November 15, 1932 sec. B.

21. Patricia Meyer Spacks, *Gossip* (New York: Alfred A. Knopf, 1985), 3–22; Jack Levin and Arnold Arluke, *Gossip: The Inside Scoop* (New York: Plenum, 1987), 7–30; Richard Schickel, *Intimate Strangers: The Culture of Celebrity* (Garden City, NY: Doubleday, 1985).

22. Grace Kingsley, "Hobnobbing in Hollywood," *Los Angeles Times*, January 2, 1933, sec. 2; January 25, 1933, sec. 2. As the contracts of both director Josef von Sternberg and Dietrich approached their end, most of the studio's executives wanted to break up this pairing. Dietrich's last motion picture in 1932, *Blonde Venus*, earned unenthusiastic reviews and lackluster box office returns. The top executives released von Sternberg and strove to get Dietrich into another picture before her contract expired. Dietrich rebelled over von Sternberg's absence and spoke of returning to Germany, but Paramount sued the star for irreparable loss due to its inability to proceed with filming of *The Song of Songs*. The star agreed to act in the motion picture two days later and received a new five-year contract. Donald Spoto, *The Blue Angel: The Life of Marlene Dietrich* (New York: Doubleday, 1992), 100–102.

23. Grace Kingsley, "Hobnobbing in Hollywood," *Los Angeles Evening Herald and Express*, January 5, 1933, sec. B.

24. Harrison Carroll, "Stars, Design Advocate Figure to Match Styles," *Los Angeles Times*, January 6, 1933.

25. Jimmy Starr, "Football Season Past, Film Folk Turn Toward Polo," *Los Angeles Evening Herald and Express*, March 22, 1933, sec. B.

26. Finch and Rosenkrantz, *Gone Hollywood*, 273.

27. Paramount Collection, Press Sheets, August 1, 1933–July 31, 1934. Academy of Motion Picture Arts and Sciences, (AMPAS); Rachel Bowlby, *Just Looking: Consumer Culture in Dreiser, Gissing and Zola* (New York: Methuen, 1985), 10–13. Quoted material from Edward Schallert, "Warblers Ripe for Comeback," *Los Angeles Times*, February 1, 1933, sec. 2.

28. Grace Kingsley, "Hobnobbing in Hollywood," *Los Angeles Times*, January 25, 1933, sec. 2.

29. Rebecca Bell-Metereau, *Hollywood Androgyny* (New York: Columbia University Press, 1985), 103–5; Josef von Sternberg, *Fun In a Chinese Laundry* (New York: MacMillan, 1965), 247; Fox, *Star Style*, 52.

30. The song in its entirety follows: "When beautiful Lillian Russell put on a great big bustle she glorified the backbone of a Nation! I wore it! I wore it! And made the world adore it! It started the first inflation. When Madame Sara Bernhardt wore the Hobble skirt I was the very first to Hobble on Broadway. I've always had a passion to wear the latest fashion. That's why I have to look like this today." Chorus: "I'm one of the boys, just one of the boys. I go the tailor that Marlene employs. No dresses from France are so modern as these, And under my Pants are BVD's. I'm one of the boys, girls, I'm one of the boys. I handle a big cigar with manly poise. Once I was maternal. Now they call me Colonel. I'm one of the boys, one of the boys." Second Refrain: "I'm one of the boys, just one of the boys. I've got to go in for things a man enjoys. Men who bought me candy said 'How sweet you are.' Now I take my brandy at the bar. Dice, cards, and tobacco are my favorite toys. People ask me 'Dearie ain't you Wallace Beery?' I'm one of the boys, one of the boys." *Hollywood Party MPP*, AMPAS. Letter from James Wingate to E. J. Mannix, June 23, 1933, *Hollywood Party MPP*, AMPAS.

31. "Hollywood Tourists Accommodated," *New York Times*, March 22, 1936, sec. 9.

32. *Variety* predicted that the craze in Hollywood would end in 1933. *Variety*, November 21, 1933, 59. Historian George Chauncey also believes that most of the spark in the pansy craze diminished with the passing of the ordinance law barring cross dressing in local night clubs and bars in 1933, although he observes that the craze continued for two more years before either the discovery or enforcement of the ordinance led to the demise of the clubs. Chauncey, *Gay New York*, 321.

33. *Los Angeles City Directory*, 1927, 2330–35; 1933, 2637–43; *Insurance Maps of Los Angeles, 1919–1950*, vol. 20.

34. Gavin Lambert, *Nazimova: A Biography* (New York: Alfred A. Knopf, 1997), 11, 178–92. See also Rosten, *Hollywood: The Movie Colony—The Moviemakers*, 5, 371; Palmer, *History of Hollywood*, 236; Gabler, *An Empire of Their Own*, 36–42, 63–64, 104–54.

35. Herbert Howe, "A Misunderstood Woman: She's Addressed as Madame Nazimova, but One Thinks of Her as Naz," *Photoplay* (April, 1922), 19.

36. Ibid, 24–25.

37. Quote comes from an unidentified clipping in Alla Nazimova file, Lesbian Her-story Archives, Brooklyn, New York; Grace Kingsley, "Flashes," *Los Angeles Times*, April 20, 1921, sec.3; July 18, 1920, sec.3; Lambert, *Nazimova: A Biography*, 220–22.

38. Quote comes from an unidentified clipping in Alla Nazimova file; Anne Frior Scott, *Natural Allies: Women's Associations in American History* (Urbana: University of Illinois Press, 1991), 141–50; Cott, *Grounding of Modern Feminism*, 197–201. Feminist advocates offered compromise solutions about motherhood, which did not fully offset the professional and salary risks and other issues that this path entailed. Most career advocates supported the gender norms of wife and mother, and these advocates viewed women's jobs as acceptable when this work aimed to improve family life. Most creative women argued that being a mother helped their creative energy and provided grist for their mill.

39. Carroll Smith-Rosenberg, "Discourses of Sexuality and Subjectivity: The New Woman, 1870–1936," in *Hidden From History: Reclaiming the Gay and Lesbian Past* (New York: North American Library, 1989), 276–80; Norma Fain Pratt, "Culture and Radical Politics: Yiddish Women Writers in American, 1890–1940," in *Decades of Discontent*, 142–44.

40. "How Twelve Famous Women Scenario Writers Succeeded," *Photoplay* (August, 1923), 31; F. Scott Fitzgerald, *The Last Tycoon* (New York: Charles Scribner's Sons, 1941), 36.

41. "Woman Lived as Man, Wed to One of Her Sex," *New York Times*, May 4, 1929; "Writer Blamed Pity for Affair," *Los Angeles Times*, May 4, 1929, sec. 2; "Dying 'Man' Proves Woman," *Los Angeles Times*, May 3, 1929; "Tell Mother Romance with Woman Poser," *Los Angeles Evening Herald*, May 4, 1929, sec. A.

42. "Writer Blamed Pity for Affair," *Los Angeles Times*; "Bare Loves of 'Man' Found to be Woman," *Los Angeles Evening Herald*, May 3, 1929, sec. A; *American Film Institute Catalog of Motion Pictures produced in the United States, 1931–1940*, Patricia King Hanson, exec. ed., (Berkeley: University of California Press, 1993), 1003.

43. Mercedes de Acosta, *Here Lies The Heart* (New York: Reynal, 1960); 212–27, 240–45, 316–18; Axel Madsen, *Forbidden Lovers: Hollywood's Greatest Secret—Female Stars Who Loved Other Women* (New York: Carol Publishing Group, 1996), 9, 21–26, 66–79; Mia Riva, *Marlene Dietrich* (New York: Alfred A. Knopf, 1993).

44. Alma Whitaker, "Change Her Name? Well, Mercedes Just Refuses," *Los Angeles Times*, December 27, 1931, sec. 3.

45. Whitaker, "Change Her Name?"

46. Wendy Holliday, "Hollywood's Modern Women: Screenwriting, Work Culture and Feminism, 1910–1940" (PhD diss., New York University, 1995), 330–31.

47. Both quotes from Whitaker, "Change Her Name?"

48. *Los Angeles Times*, December 27, 1931, sec. 3. As a gender role, the position of mother dramatically influenced the opportunities that women have had to enter the cultural, political, and social worlds in the United States. During this era opponents of

women's involvement in these worlds used motherhood to deny women the opportunity to enter those realms. As noted earlier, an ideology of motherhood enabled some women to enter these worlds during the Progressive era, if their activities stayed within those areas where the ideology could justify women's involvement. Susan Ware, *Holding Their Own: American Women in the 1930s* (Boston: Twayne Publications, 1982).

49. Richard Koszarski, *An Evening's Entertainment: The Age of the Silent Feature Picture, 1915–1928* (New York: Charles Scribner's Sons, 1990); quoted material from Duncan Aikman, "Hollywood Assumes the Grand Manner," *New York Times*, March 8, 1931, sec. 5.

50. Gary Alan Fine, "Scandal, Social Conditions, and the Creation of Public Attention: Fatty Arbuckle and the 'Problem of Hollywood,'" *Social Problems* 44, no. 3 (August 1997), 297–317.

51. Nina Putnam, *Laughter Limited* (New York: George Duran, 1922), 115–23.

52. D.L.M., review of *Laughter Limited*, by Nina Putnam, *Boston Evening Transcript*, November 4, 1922, sec. 5; *Springfield Republican*, October 29, 1922.

53. Paul Bauer and Mark Dawidziak, *Jim Tully: American Writer, Irish Rover, Hollywood Brawler* (Kent, OH: Kent State University Press, 2011); Charles Willeford, "Jim Tully: Holistic Barbarian," in *Writing and Other Blood Sports* (Tucson, AZ: Dennis McMillan, 2000); "Miss Millay's 'Wayfarer' and Other Works of Fiction," *New York Times*, September 19, 1926.

54. Jim Tully, *Jarnegan* (New York: Albert and Charles Boni, 1926), 259.

55. Readers recognized the petting party as a reality in their lives. The mid-1920s Lynds study of Middletown, Indiana, revealed that many high school boys and girls had been to these affairs and engaged in kissing and light petting. Scholar Paula Fass observed that many college women of the era had this experience also. Their peers, particularly among women, used social pressure to place limits on how "far" the sexual activities would go, even with the man that they intended to marry. Frederick Lewis Allen, *Only Yesterday: An Informal History of the 1920s* (New York: Blue Ribbon Books, 1931); Paula S. Fass, *The Damned and the Beautiful: American Youth in the 1920s* (New York: Oxford University Press, 1979).

56. "Miss Millay's 'Wayfarer' and Other Works of Fiction," *New York Times*, September 19, 1926, sec.5; Will Cuppy, "A Roughneck in Art," *New York Herald Tribune*, September 19, 1926, sec. 7; W.B. "Jim Tully and 'Jarnegan,'" *Boston Evening Transcript*, October 20, 1926, sec. 5.

57. Edwin Schallert, "Star Invasion: Stars New Boom at Malibu," *Los Angeles Times*, June 4, 1933, sec. 2. At the time of the newspaper article the owners in Malibu Beach were directors John Stahl, David Butler, William Le Baron, and Frank Capra, actors Alexander Kirkland, George Raft, Norman Foster, Stephen Gooson, and studio executives Jack Warner and Bud Schulberg.

58. "Movie 'Celebs' Show Off At a Premiere and Party for Marie Antoinette," *Life*, July 25, 1938, 44, in Premieres and Previews File, Academy of Motion Picture Arts and Sciences.

59. Ibid.; Ephraim Katz, *The Film Encyclopedia* (New York: G. P. Putnam's Sons, 1979), 730–31. Finch and Rosenkrantz, *Gone Hollywood*, 234–35; William Mann, *Wisecracker: The Life and Times of William Haines, Hollywood's First Openly Gay Star* (New York: Viking, 1998), 219–21; Barbas, *Movie Crazy*, 151–54; Edward Doherty, "Can the Gable-Lombard Love Story have a Happy Ending?" in *Photoplay Treasury*, ed. Barbara Gelman (New York: Crown Publishers, 1972).

60. "Pajama Charge Denied by Actress," *Los Angeles Evening Herald*, November 22, 1920, sec. B; Isabel Ross, *Taste in America: An Illustrated History of the Evolution of Architecture, Furnishings, Fashions, and Customs of the American People* (New York: Thomas Y. Cromwell Co., 1967), 180—82; *Modern Screen*, March 1931, cited in Finch and Rosenkrantz, *Gone Hollywood*, 91.

61. *Bombshell* (MGM, 1933); Katz, *The Film Encyclopedia.*

62. Mordaunt Hall, "The Screen," *New York Times*, October 21, 1933; Mordaunt Hall, "Passing Broadway Pictures," October 29, 1933, sec.10; Rush, "Bombshell," *Variety*, October 17, 1933; October 24, 1933; October 31, 1933 through December 26, 1933.

63. Thomas Cripps, *Hollywood's High Noon: Moviemaking and Society before Television* (Baltimore: Johns Hopkins University, 1997); *Los Angeles Herald Examiner*, January 17, 1940; "Application of Julian Eltinge to operate as a female impersonator at the *Hollywood Rendezvous*," January 16, 1940, *The Official Minutes of The Board of Police Commissioners of the City of Los Angeles*, January 2, 1940, to June 28, 1940. See Chauncey and Kennedy and Davis for more explanation of this change in cultural perception.

64. Ann Bell, *Lady's Lady* (New York: House of Field, 1940), 88.

CHAPTER 4

Saying "Nothin'"

Pachucas and the Languages of Resistance

CATHERINE S. RAMÍREZ

On June 9 and 10, 1943, in the midst of the Zoot Suit Riots, Los Angeles newspapers announced the arrest of a "pachuco woman." According to the press, twenty-two-year-old Amelia Venegas, mother of a toddler and wife of a sailor, had incited violence by urging a gang of pachucos to attack sheriff's deputies in her East Los Angeles neighborhood. "I no like thees daputy sheriffs [*sic*]," the *Herald-Express* quoted her. Additionally, newspapers reported that she attempted to smuggle a pair of brass knuckles to "zoot suit hoodlums" to assist them in their street brawls with sailors. Venegas was arrested and jailed for disturbing the peace.[1]

Although newspaper photographs do not show her wearing a "finger-tip" coat or short, full skirt—identifying features of the pachuca look in wartime Los Angeles—Venegas was nonetheless described as a "lady zoot suiter, or at least a sympathizer with the zoot suit fraternity."[2] As various scholars have shown, the zoot suit, which generally consisted of a long coat and skirt or pair of billowing trousers, signified difference and defiance in the United States during World War II, a moment of heightened jingoism, xenophobia, and concern over shifting gender roles.[3] Both the ensemble and, more often than not, its Mexican-American wearer were deemed unpatriotic and un-American and were even directly linked to the Axis. In Venegas's case, the incorrect grammar and caricature Mexican accent attributed to her emphasized that her transgression was two-fold: she was not only un-American but unladylike as well.

Many studies of *pachuquismo*—the Mexican-American pachuca/o subculture—have stressed the symbolic economy of style: clothes, hair, and, to a lesser extent, makeup.[4] This essay seeks to add to this exciting body of work by focusing on another important—albeit literally unspectacular—stylistic element of wartime *pachuquismo*: language and speech. Like their African-American counterparts who spoke jive, many pachucas and pachucos (that is, Mexican-American zooters) spoke pachuco slang (also known as *caló*). Additionally, many used *pochismos* (lexical borrowings) and a working-class-inflected form of American English. During the Chicano movement of the 1960s, 1970s, and early 1980s, these linguistic varieties, like zoot suits, became signs both of difference and of opposition for a number of Chicana and Chicano writers. They signified a refusal to conform to the status quo and a distinctly racialized, working-class, urban youth style. In short, many of the utterances of Mexican-American zooters came to signify resistance, style, and style as resistance.

The concept of resistance has had an indelible effect on the study of popular culture in the United States as well as on Chicano studies (and cultural and ethnic studies more broadly). Drawing from James C. Scott's metaphor of the "hidden transcript," Robin D. G. Kelley, for example, argues that the "veiled social and cultural worlds of oppressed people frequently surface in everyday forms of resistance—theft, footdragging, the destruction of property."[5] Within African-American and Chicano studies, the zoot subculture of the World War II period is often looked to as an example of a "hidden transcript." As Kelley notes, "The language and culture of zoot suiters represented a subversive refusal to be subservient."[6]

By focusing on women speakers of pachuco slang, this essay explores the relationship of resistance—what Kelley describes as the "subversive refusal to be subservient"—to gender and style, specifically coolness and hipness. "Coolness" refers to self-control; "hipness" to knowledge and sophistication. Both terms connote style and, as I argue below, social marginalization. This essay examines the gendering of Chicano resistance and style and Chicano resistance *as* style. It asks, "What is the gender of Chicano resistance and does Chicanas' resistance differ from that of Chicanos?" In addressing these questions, I draw upon an eclectic array of sources, including a poem, short story, *corrido* (ballad), trial transcript, and play, to better understand the linguistic varieties of pachucos and pachucas in the 1940s—namely, *caló*, *pochismos*, and nonstandard American English—and the ways in which their utterances were recuperated by a later generation of Chicana and Chicano cultural workers. I argue that where male speakers of pachuco slang have been upheld as icons of resistance and cultural affirmation, female, Mexican-American speakers have faced heavier consequences. Like Amelia Venegas, they have been mocked, punished, or silenced for failing to reproduce the ideal subjects of U.S. national identity (the loyal, white, Anglophone citizen), of an oppositional Chicano cultural identity (the pachuco), and of normative femininity (the "lady").

Because recovering Chicanas' past use of pachuco slang—what the late feminist sociolinguist D. Letticia Galindo termed a "taboo language" for women and girls—poses particular challenges, this essay also emphasizes silence.[7] In exploring the meanings and uses of silence for those who called themselves and were called pachucas, I argue that Chicanas' silence can be and has been as oppositional, rich, and complex as their male counterparts' speech. My hope is that this study will provide us with a glimpse (or echo) of the voices and silence of the pachucas of the 1940s and thus contribute to zoot studies and feminist scholarship on the linguistic varieties and practices of Chicana homegirls in the late twentieth and early twenty-first centuries.[8] Finally, I hope that my work not only complicates conventional notions of Chicano defiance and style as it exposes their masculinist and heterosexist underpinnings, but that it also amplifies the less audible forms of Chicana resistance.

"Double Talk" and Disloyalty

In addition to scrutinizing pachucos' and pachucas' hair and clothes, law enforcement officers, newspapers, and social scientists demonstrated a concern with pachuco slang beginning in the early 1940s. Described both as a "pidgin dialect" and "creole language," pachuco slang draws from Spanish, English, *pochismos*, and *caló*.[9] (Although *caló* is one component of pachuco slang, the two terms are often used interchangeably.) Contrary to claims that it is distinctly and exclusively Mexican American, *caló* is a product of the Old and New Worlds, as it borrows from indigenous American languages, such as Nahuatl, and from *zincaló*, the idiom of the Spanish gypsies. For centuries, it has been associated with the underclass, with "the criminal, the poor, and the uneducated."[10] In particular, it has been associated with the Tirilis, a subgroup of Mexicans and Mexican Americans who reputedly trafficked in sex and drugs in and around El Paso-Juárez in the early part of the twentieth century.[11]

In general, social scientific studies of pachuco slang have emphasized criminality. For this reason, it has been labeled an argot, "a secret language or conventional slang peculiar to a group of thieves, tramps or vagabonds."[12] Yet, as Galindo cautions, "early research conducted by Anglo social scientists" tended to be more alarmist than "ethnosensitive," as evidenced, for example, by the title of Lurline Coltharp's 1965 study *The Tongue of the Tirilones: A Linguistic Study of a Criminal Argot*.[13] Likewise, articles on pachucas and pachucos (and Mexican-American youth in general) that appeared in Angeleno newspapers during the early 1940s highlighted sex, drugs, and violence. For example, a July 1944 *Los Angeles Times* story that purported to expose the sinister pachuco underworld reported, "Gang members speak a strange argot unintelligible to the uninitiated." The paper translated several supposedly exemplary words from pachuco slang into English, such as *yisca* (marijuana), *la jefe* (the leader of a local gang), and *volte* (jail).[14]

In fact, for many Mexican-American youths of the 1940s, pachuco slang was "hep" and street smart and nothing more. Yet, more than merely pointing to a generation gap, *caló* words, such as *chale* (no) and *orale* (right on, attention), accentuated what some contemporary observers perceived as more deep-seated and troubling differences. An August 1942 story in the Spanish-language newspaper *La Opinión*, for instance, dismissed pachuco slang as a combination of " *pochismos y jerga*" (*pocho*-isms and slang) and lamented that its speakers were neither truly Mexican nor full-fledged Americans.[15] A *pochismo* is a lexical borrowing or loan word that combines English and Spanish, such as *marketa* (instead of *mercado*) for market.[16] Similarly, a *pocha* or *pocho* is an Americanized Mexican or Mexicanized American. Just as *pochismos* have been dismissed as "a tragic sign of language decadence," the invective *pocha/o* originally signified cultural and linguistic degradation, retardation, and lack.[17] In the words of one scholar, *pochos* "did not do a good enough job imitating the Yankee."[18]

Pochos and *pochas* not only did a poor job at imitating Yankees, they also failed to mimic Mexicans adequately. Indeed, many Mexicans have used the term to chastise and deride Mexican Americans, especially those who appeared to have "ruined their Spanish without ever quite learning English."[19] The second-generation pachucas and pachucos of the 1940s have been identified as the first *pochas* and *pochos*, for they lived in two worlds at once: "the Anglo American and the Mexican American barrio."[20] Bilingual and bicultural, many young Mexican Americans in the 1940s were the children of immigrants who came to the United States in an effort to flee the social, political, and economic turbulence of the Mexican Revolution and to work in a rapidly industrializing U.S. Southwest and Midwest during the early twentieth century. Many were the first in their families to be born or reared in an urban setting, to speak English, and to attend school for an extended period of time. However, despite their status as U.S. citizens, they were denied the rights and privileges of full citizenship, as evidenced, for example, by de jure and de facto racial segregation throughout the Southwest. At the same time, they were expected to assimilate and all too frequently faced corporal punishment for speaking Spanish in school. What's more, many came of age in the widespread poverty and nativist (specifically, anti-Mexican) sentiment of the Great Depression.

For several contemporary observers on both sides of the U.S.-Mexico border, pachucos and pachucas constituted a "lost generation."[21] They were rejected by white, middle-class America, but they also appeared to have renounced all things Mexican, including their own parents. Consequently, they were pitied or ridiculed as cultural orphans. After spending two years in Los Angeles shortly after World War II, Octavio Paz concluded that the pachuco had "lost his whole inheritance: language, religion, customs, beliefs."[22] In other words, he was a cultural bastard. Even the word *pachuco* was of "uncertain derivation," the Mexican writer and statesman pointed out.[23] Neither this nor that, pachucas and pachucos appeared to be more cultural void than cultural hybrid. Their ability to speak English, Spanish, and pachuco slang, to code-switch, and to invent neologisms were seen not as signs of a creative and rich bi- or multilingualism but as an utter lack of language.

Above all, pachuco slang was regarded as a mark of disloyalty and lapse in "identical equivalence."[24] That is, it supposedly indicated a failure to reproduce an authentic or legitimate national identity (such as Americanness or Mexicanness). During World War II, pachuco slang was deemed evidence of a refusal or inability to conform—to assimilate, in other words—and cast doubt on its speakers' allegiance to the United States, rather than signaling an alternative form of Americanness. Indeed, since the earliest days of the Republic, fluency in English has been regarded as a salient marker of American identity.[25] During the Zoot Suit Riots, stories in the Angeleno press about an alleged Axis plot to foment unrest on the home front underscored the commensurability of standard, unaccented English and authentic Americanness. As civic leaders publicly speculated that Axis agents had instigated the riots by infiltrating the city's barrios and prompting young Mexican Americans to attack white servicemen, newspapers reported that "an enemy agent"—identified as such because he spoke "broken English"—had been spotted in Watts.[26] In the midst of this paranoia and xenophobia, the so-called "double talk" of pachucos and pachucas did little to affirm their Americanness.[27]

"Dude Talk" and the Birth of Cool

Long before the (white) "bad boy" emerged in Cold War America (for example, Holden Caulfield, Elvis Presley, James Dean), young, American men of color—in particular, African Americans and Mexican Americans—came to represent youthful rebellion.[28] Much like black jive before it, which jazz vocalist Cab Calloway described as "Negro slang, the super-hip language of the times," pachuco slang helped to produce and express a dissident, working-class masculinity in the United States beginning in the early 1940s.[29] At times, this masculinity was the antithesis of socially sanctioned (specifically white and middle-class) masculinities as it privileged street smarts over formal education and found expression by reversing the signifiers and referents of standard American English (for example, "bad" became good).

For some social scientists, black jive and pachuco slang were more than just colloquial speech; they were evidence of a disturbing insubordination on the part of their speakers. In the wake of the 1943 Harlem riot, psychologists Kenneth Clark and James Barker fretted that the African-American zooter's "habitual, seemingly deliberate, disregard of . . . the simple rules of grammar in his everyday speech" indicated a "generalized defiance of the larger society."[30] Twenty years later, during the youth movement of the late 1960s, *caló* was linked to rage: it was described as "a 'snarl' language" that reflected "an uncompromising attitude of anger, sarcasm, cynicism, and undifferentiated rebellion."[31] Of particular concern to both generations of scholars was zooters' "excessive use of profanity in ordinary conversation."[32] In a 1967 essay on *caló*, George Alvarez insisted that the "expletives *chinga* and *pinchi*, which are analogous to the English word 'damn,'" could be found "in almost every *caló* utterance."[33] And recalling his days as a young hustler, Malcolm X claimed, "Every word I spoke was hip or profane."[34]

By the late 1960s, the pachuco was more than an avatar of youthful rebellion. Like Malcolm X, he became a symbol of racial or ethnic pride as movement-era Chicano writers and artists, among them José Montoya, embraced him as a symbol of cultural affirmation and resistance. Montoya's 1970 poem "El Louie," perhaps one of the most scrutinized Chicano literary works, recounts the life and times of Louie Rodríguez, a cool, charismatic, and doomed pachuco from the small town of Fowler in California's rural San Joaquin Valley.[35] Written in pachuco slang, the poem points to the beauty and elegance of the vernacular and vulgar (that is, the common and rough). The narrator concedes that

> Fowler no era nada como [Fowler was nothing like]
> Los, o'l E.P.T. Fresno's [L.A. or El Paso]
> westside was as close as
> we ever got to the big time.[36]

But Louie exudes big-city flair nonetheless. He wears tailor-made zoot suits and renames himself "Blackie," "Little Louie," and "Diamonds."[37] A local celebrity of sorts, he is famous throughout the small towns of central California, such as Selma and Gilroy, and his panache is on par with that of a movie star: "melodramatic music, like in the / mono (movies)," seems to accompany him as he swaggers into the Palomar dance hall, Nesei's pool parlor, or a parking lot fight.[38] And when he "sport[s] a dark topcoat" in San Jose, the metropolis, he "play[s] in his fantasy / the role of Bogart, Cagney / or Raft."[39] Tragically, "booze y la vida dura (and the hard life)" catch up with Louie and he dies alone in a rented room, in all likelihood of a heroin overdose.[40] The narrator laments his death as an "insult" and "cruel hoax," yet speculates that it was "perhaps like in a / Bogart movie"[41] and maintains that he had "class to the end."[42] Even in death, Louie manages to evoke Hollywood glamour.

Contrast the pachuco's portrayal in "El Louie," a cultural product of the Chicano and youth movements of the second half of the twentieth century, with his unambiguous denigration in Mario Suárez's 1947 short story "Kid Zopilote." After Pepe García, the protagonist, spends a summer in Los Angeles and returns to his hometown of Tucson, he not only looks different (now that he wears a zoot suit and combs his hair in a ducktail), but "[h]is language had changed quite a bit, too."[43] Having picked up *pochismos* in "Los Angeles, *Califo* (California)," Pepe tells his mother, "Ma, I will *returniar* (return) in a little while" every time he leaves the house.[44] When he comes back, he reports, "Ma, I was *watchiando* (watching) a good movie, that is why I am a little bit late."[45] In the end, Pepe and Tucson's other pachucos are punished for their big city airs when they are beaten by a group of respectable Mexican Americans, then thrown into jail, where their zoot suits are destroyed and their hair is cut. Upon their release, "[t]hey crept home along alleys, like shorn dogs with their tails between their legs, lest people should see them."[46]

While "Kid Zopilote" expresses disdain for the pachuco, "El Louie" redeems him as the apotheosis of Chicano style. And where Pepe García, an emasculated dandy, is embarrassed by his square appearance and shuns attention after his hair is shorn, Louie Rodriguez epitomizes macho style and flourishes in the limelight. Wearing "buenas garras (cool threads)," he cruises around town in a "48 Fleetline, two-tone."[47] And if Pepe is a ridiculous *pocho*, then Louie exemplifies seamless cultural hybridity: he dances both "el boogie" and "los mambos."[48] Furthermore, he does not want for "rucas (chicks)—como la Mary y / la Helen."[49] Pepe, meanwhile, has a hard time getting a girl to dance with him: "When he went to the Tira-Chancla Dance Hall very few of the girls consented to dance with him. When they did, it was out of compassion."[50] Adding injury to insult, Pepe is beaten by a group of squares and is further humiliated by the police. In contrast, Louie, a decorated Korean War veteran, demonstrates that he is a "soldado de / levita con huevos (a very ballsy soldier)" as he moves between the battlefield and street brawl.[51] With a "smile as deadly as his vaisas"—that is, with a smile as deadly as his hands—he embodies masculine power, in the forms of both charm and violence.[52]

Since its initial publication in 1970, "El Louie" has been upheld as an exemplar of pachuco poetry (and Chicano literature in general) because of both its content and form.[53] As literary critic Alfred Arteaga asserts, its language "matches its content: the verse is as thoroughly Chicano as is Louie's life."[54] Yet, how "thoroughly Chicano"—or Chican *a*—is "El Louie" when it is written in pachuco slang, a linguistic variety that has been designated male and masculine? Like black jive, pachuco slang's origins are in activities and realms generally associated with men and masculinity, such as the criminal underworld, androcentric jazz subculture, and working class, which, in and of itself, is often configured as male and masculine.[55] Consequently, it has been widely regarded as a "male-dominated, intragroup form of communication."[56] As one of Galindo's informants put it, it is "dude talk."[57]

For some movement-era Chicanos, many of whom were Baby Boomers who prized youthful rebellion and defied authority by protesting the Vietnam War, boycotting agribusiness, and participating in school walkouts, the pachucos of the previous generation were "*vatos de huevos* (ballsy guys)" and "*vatos firmes* (stoic or steadfast guys)"—two of "the most complimentary terms in the *caló* vocabulary," according to one scholar—because they articulated a distinct and dissident cultural identity in the face of denigration, assimilation, and erasure.[58] In other words, pachucos were hip and cool, terms that connote self-conscious social marginalization, resistance, and/or transgression.[59] The latter refers to an affected affectlessness, to emotional self-control and relaxation. The former originally meant "wise" or "sophisticated" and could signify worldliness in general and knowledge of the underworld in particular. While the concept of "cool" pointed to the masculine ideal of emotional detachment, "hip" was the antonym of innocent, a characteristic ascribed to both children and the ideal (that is, virgin) bride.

Just as "real" (white, middle-class, Anglophone) Americanness has been linked to mimesis and assimilation, U.S. racial and ethnic minority identities have been and still are associated with authenticity and fidelity—in other words, with "keeping it real." The link between language and "realness" is evident in Malcolm X's 1964 *Autobiography*. In a refreshing reading of this work, María Josefina Saldaña-Portillo argues that Malcolm X revels in his ability to speak jive, contrary to claims that he appeared to dismiss his hustling days as "a destructive detour on the road to self-consciousness and political enlightenment."[60] Indeed, he opens the chapter marking his transition from country bumpkin to urban hipster with an entire paragraph in it "just to display a bit more of the slang that was used by everyone I respected as 'hip' in those days."[61] Furthermore, he reveals great pride in his command of the vernacular, for his fluency supposedly indicated that he was closer to and, therefore, the most appropriate leader of "the ghetto black people."[62] He recounts translating jive for a putative black leader who, after being approached by a "Harlem hustler. . . . look[ed] as if he'd just heard Sanskrit."[63] In this recollection, Malcolm distinguishes the confused "downtown 'leader'" from the slick "Harlem hustler," both of whom serve as respective metonyms for "'middle class' Negro[es]" and "ghetto blacks."[64] For Malcolm, black jive, the language of poor, urban blacks, functioned as a cultural identity marker, as a sign of authentic blackness; while standard American English, the language of middle-class blacks who lived and worked outside the ghetto (e.g., "downtown"), smacked of selling out.

Malcolm's observations concerning the chasm between the real and the fake point to another set of binary oppositions: the hipster and the square, and, by extension, masculinity and femininity. A "fake" black man or "wannabe" white man, the figure of the Uncle Tom has been linked to "passivity, obedience, docility, accommodation, and submissiveness"—characteristics that are frequently associated with women and femininity.[65] As a Tom, the "downtown 'leader'" Malcolm encounters is helpless (i.e., feminine). He must rely on Malcolm to translate for him. In addition, he is a square, for he is not "hep to the jive" (i.e., he does not understand jive, nor is he worldly or aware). As Norman Mailer has posited, if one is not hip, then "one is Square."[66] Similarly, in pachuco slang, "there is no grey area between an *escuadra* (square) and a vato loco."[67] In other words, if one is not hip, then one is square, and if one is square, then one is not a *vato loco*, a highly gendered term comparable to today's "dawg" (as opposed to "bitch"), (male) "gangsta," and, in its most general sense, "dude" or "guy." Thus, if one is not hip, then one is not a guy, and, according to the logic of the sex/gender binary, if one is not a guy, then one is female or feminine.

Yet, coolness—in particular, black and brown coolness—is not just coded masculine; it is also often coded heterosexual. Its opposite, uncoolness, has been equated with social incompetence and physical impairment, with being "lame" and "a sissy."[68] Likewise, *puto* (homosexual) and *culero* (coward) have been identified as the "most derogatory" terms in *caló*.[69] Both invectives are homophobic and denote anal sex: *culero* derives from *culo*, which is the equivalent of "ass" in American English; while *puto* refers to a male homosexual and "speak[s] to the passive sexual role taken by . . . men . . . in the homosexual act."[70] The latter is related to the word *puta*, which means female prostitute. As Tomás Almaguer observes, "It is significant that the cultural equation made between the feminine, anal-receptive homosexual man and the most culturally-stigmatized female in Mexican society (the whore) share a common semantic base."[71]

Instead of being celebrated as cool or hip, Chicana speakers of pachuco slang have been branded *putas*.[72] In addition, they have been dismissed as *cantineras* (barflies, drunks) and gang members' girlfriends.[73] In other words, they are ancillary. As John Leland points out in his history of hipness, women are generally not recognized as hipsters per se, but as (male) hipsters' auxiliaries, "either the apron strings from which male hipness takes flight or the enticements it consumes along the road."[74] The hipster flees his reproving mother to enjoy whores and other good-time girls. Indeed, according to Susan Fraiman, the figure of mother is the antithesis of cool.[75] To maintain hipness, the hipster must forsake her, his wife, and his children. In short, he must distance himself from domesticity and socially sanctioned femininity.

Pachuco slang's ban from the Mexican-American domestic sphere and its incommensurability with socially sanctioned femininity are apparent in *Hoyt Street*, Mary Helen Ponce's 1993 autobiography. Ponce, who grew up in Southern California's San Fernando Valley during the 1940s and 1950s, recounts that when a friend inadvertently responded to her grandmother in *caló*, the girl was promptly sent to her room "to escape being slapped by her older brother, who allowed no disrespect for his grandma."[76] The concept of *respeto* (respect) within and toward the biological family also resonates in Galindo's 1992 study of Tejanas and pachuco slang. A number of her interviewees claimed that they would not use pachuco slang in the presence of their fathers out of *respeto*.[77] And one reported that, while her brothers could speak pachuco slang among themselves, they were not allowed to speak it to their parents. "If the girls used it, we were reprimanded. Especially by my mother; she wouldn't tolerate it."[78]

According to Galindo, pachuco slang is a "'taboo language' for women and girls."[79] Many have been prohibited from speaking it and some have even actively distanced themselves from it lest they be labeled the sort of woman who deviates from the home, such as a *puta* or *cantinera*. For instance, in her 1965 study of the Tirilis, Coltharp maintained that many of the young women she encountered understood *caló*, but were "horrified" when she attempted to enlist their aid as translators.[80] She concluded that no law-abiding woman "would admit that she even understood one word of the language."[81]

As the language of the outlaw, rebel, and hipster, pachuco slang is masculine. Since the early 1940s, it has provided young, working-class, Mexican-American men with a means—literally, a vocabulary—"to prove their manhood and vent their frustrations."[82] In short, pachuco slang has allowed men to oppose the status quo. Like black jive, it has helped them to produce and shape a distinctly raced and classed masculinity and, thus, to challenge dominant (i.e., white and middle-class) definitions of manhood. Yet, unlike black jive, much of which has been incorporated into standard American English, pachuco slang has remained relatively insular, thus making it all the more distinct and dissonant. Additionally, its connections to Spanish and *caló* render it more alien and, therefore, more threatening to a white and Anglophone American identity. In speaking it, young Mexican-American men have become icons of un-Americanness, resistance, and style, from the *chukos suaves* of the 1940s to the *vatos locos* of the post-war period and the dawgs of the present.

Yet, what happened when young, Mexican-American women spoke pachuco slang during the 1940s? And what or whom did they resist by speaking it, along with nonstandard forms of English and Spanish, at a moment not only of increased social and cultural homogenization but of changing expectations of women, especially outside the home? To address these questions, I juxtapose three cultural artifacts in the following sections: a *corrido*,

People v. Zammora (the Sleepy Lagoon trial transcript), and Luis Valdez's play *Zoot Suit*. Together, these texts show that Chicanas who spoke pachuco slang rejected not only white Americanness and middle-class comportment but normative gender as well. They failed to imitate white, Anglophone Americans and respectable ladies alike but were still not homologous with their male counterparts, pachucos. And while the pachuco would come to embody an idealized Chicano masculinity and subjectivity during the Chicano movement, the "tough-tongued" pachuca would be ignored or maligned.[83]

"El Bracero y la Pachuca"

The pachuco's transformation from effete social pariah (for example, Pepe García) to macho cultural hero and icon (for example, Louie Rodríguez) in movement-era Chicano cultural production is probably most apparent in *Zoot Suit*. With the play's premier in 1978, interest in pachuco slang appeared to re-surge among Chicanos. Throughout the late 1970s and early 1980s, advertisements for the *Dictionary of Pachuco Slang*, which guaranteed to make its reader "the baddest vato en tu barrio (dude in your neighborhood)," appeared in *LowRider* magazine. Nostalgia for the 1940s was also evident in 1940s-themed fundraiser dances sponsored by the magazine. Advertisements called on attendees to wear zoot suits and promised an evening of not only disco, but "boogie woogie" and "big bands" as well.[84]

Zoot Suit featured "boogie woogie-influenced Pachuco songs" by Lalo Guerrero, who, along with other Mexican-American musicians of the 1940s and 1950s, such as Don Tosti (*né* Edmundo Martínez Tostado), is responsible in great part for helping to preserve contemporary pachuco slang. Because of these musicians' efforts, pachuco slang of the 1940s and 1950s has been recorded not only in anthropological, sociolinguistic, and literary works but in popular music as well.[85] While most songs in pachuco slang were sung by men, the *corrido* "El Bracero y La Pachuca" is extraordinary because it prominently features a female vocalist.[86]

"El Bracero y La Pachuca" was written by Miguel Salas and recorded in 1948 in Los Angeles by Dueto Taxco and Mariachi Los Caporales del Norte. Its lyrics, sung by a man and woman identified collectively as Dueto Taxco, are in a combination of Spanish and pachuco slang and recount the unlikely union of a mellifluous Mexican bracero and pachuco-slang-speaking pachuca who meet at a dance. Using proper Spanish, the bracero attempts to woo the pachuca with poetry. When she responds, both he and the listener learn that she is an uncouth *pocha* who does not understand or appreciate the beauty of her suitor's words. She tells him, "Ya tíreme bute chancla / traserito sin sabor, / ya me esta cayendo sura (Cut it out and let's dance / you're so square that /

you're getting on my nerves)."[87] Then, in her solo, she matches the bracero's poem with one attributed to the "Tírilí" (reefer man):

Nel ese, ya parale con sus palabras
del alta que por derecho me aguitan ese,
mejor pongase muy alalva con
un pistazo de aquella, y un frajito
del fuerte pa' despues poder borrar. Ja. . . .

[Slow down, man,
cut out that high-toned
poetry jazz, you're really bringing me down.
You better have a drink and get with it,
and then smoke a joint to mellow out. Ha![88]]

Whereas the bracero's poem speaks of "rosas encarnadas . . . con sus lindas aromas (red roses with their beautiful perfume)," the pachuca's is about boozing it up and smoking dope. And while the bracero implores the pachuca to love him "porque te quiero . . . porque te adoro (because I love you . . . because I adore you)," the pachuca demands that he cut the crap and simmer down. Apparently, he does as he is told, for in the final stanza, we learn that our hero and heroine dance the night away and are married the next morning.

As is often the case in romance, opposites attract; the bracero and pachuca are drawn to one another precisely because "eran muy diferentes (they were very different)." In addition to contrasting proper Spanish and pachuco slang, "El Bracero y La Pachuca" juxtaposes *lo mexicano y la pocha* (the Mexican and the *pocha*), the country and the city, and high and low cultures. Despite his association with agricultural labor, the bracero exemplifies high culture and politesse. Using especially flowery Spanish and hyperbolically correct diction, he addresses the pachuca as "mujer del alma mía (woman of my soul)" and "linda princesa encantada (beautiful enchanted princess)" as he recites poetry to her. In contrast, the pachuca speaks with the "whining nasal quality" and "sing-song" rhythm often attributed to pachuco slang, addresses the bracero as "ese (dude/man)," rejects his "palabras del alta (lofty speech)," and does not hide the fact that he bothers her.[89] If "toughness" in language is associated with "manliness" and "working-class culture" and "[f]emaleness . . . with respectability, gentility, and high culture," then "El Bracero y La Pachuca" reverses gender stereotypes (even if it does offer a hackneyed tale of heterosexual romance).[90] The ballad's respectable and genteel bracero represents high culture with his proper, perfectly enunciated Spanish poetry. As such, he is feminine. Meanwhile, the slang-speaking pachuca is a coarse philistine and, therefore, a traitor: as a boorish woman who speaks pachuco slang, she assumes a masculine position and, thus, betrays gender norms.[91]

People v. Zammora

The betrayal of normative (that is, white, middle-class) Americanness and femininity via speech is also evident in *People v. Zammora*, the Sleepy Lagoon trial transcript. It is especially apparent in testimony by Bertha Aguilar, a fourteen-year-old girl from the 38th Street neighborhood who was involved in what came to be known as the Sleepy Lagoon incident. This event took place in Los Angeles on the night of August 1 and in the early-morning hours of August 2, 1942, and it involved at least two fights: the first at a swimming hole known as Sleepy Lagoon and the second at a party at the home of the Delgadillo family at nearby Williams Ranch. After the second fight, the body of twenty-two-year-old José Díaz was found on the ground outside the Delgadillos' house. Díaz had suffered a massive blow to the head and was transported to a hospital, where he died without regaining consciousness. The police began to arrest suspects in what they determined was a murder case on August 3, the Grand Jury hearing began the following day, and the criminal trial opened on October 13. It ended three months later on January 15, 1943, with the conviction of the twenty-two defendants, all of whom were male. In October 1944, their conviction was overturned and they were released from prison.[92]

Along with several other girls and young women, whom court documents refer to as the defendants' "girl companions" (i.e., friends, neighbors, girlfriends), Aguilar was incarcerated at the Ventura School for Girls, a reformatory, and was forced to testify before the Los Angeles County Grand Jury and in *People v. Zammora* in connection with the death of José Díaz.[93] Although we do not know whether they ever called themselves pachucas, these girls and young women were labeled such by the mainstream Angeleno press. And just as the prosecution drew attention to the defendants' zoot suit suits and long hair, which were widely regarded as hallmarks of juvenile delinquency, it also pointed to the coats, coiffures, and black dresses that their "girl companions" had donned the night of August 1, 1942.[94] Not surprisingly, by the time the defendants were convicted of conspiracy to murder in January 1943, *People v. Zammora* was known as the "'zoot suit' murder case."[95]

In court, Aguilar reported that, immediately after crashing the Delgadillos' party, she entered a fight when she saw that a group of approximately five women had attacked her friend Delia Parra. She stated that, initially, "I didn't do nothing. I didn't want to do nothing, but when I seen the girl, you know, put up the bottle to hit Delia, I ran towards her."[96] Consequently, Aguilar was struck in the leg with the bottle and was left with scars. During cross-examination, defense attorney Anna Zacsek asked to see the scars and both the defense and prosecution suggested that "the young lady step along the jury rail and hold that leg up so that the jury [might] see it."[97] Aguilar complied. When Deputy District Attorney John Barnes noted that the scars did not appear to be anything more than mere scratches, Aguilar retorted defensively, "Well, they sure were."[98]

Even though she was described as a "young lady," both the content of her words and her words themselves—combined with the manner in which her statements were recorded by the court—suggest that Aguilar was not quite a "lady." In the 1942 edition of *Etiquette: The Blue Book of Social Usage*, Emily Post insisted that the "oft-heard expression, 'You know she is a lady as soon as she opens her mouth,' is not an exaggeration."[99] The arbiter of social manners and good taste instructed would-be ladies "how to cultivate an agreeable speech."[100] She implored them not to mumble, but bemoaned the loud and shrill voice as "extremely bad form."[101] Additionally, Post advised her readers, especially those who wished to climb the social ladder, to avoid incorrect grammar (in particular, phrases such as "I seen it") and "the vernacular of today."[102] While she stressed that there was no place for "course or profane slang" in a lady's vocabulary, she deemed "certain words and phrases in common use," such as "swell," "O.K.," and "you betcha," acceptable, even though they interfered with "perfect diction."[103]

Regardless of how seriously its readers heeded its advice and admonitions, Post's *Etiquette* points to the intersection of language, gender, and class. It shows women—in particular, those with middle-class aspirations—how to reproduce or perform a certain kind of femininity ("ladyness") via language.[104] Decades later, feminist sociolinguist Robin Lakoff would scrutinize the role language plays in the production of gender in her groundbreaking *Language and Women's Place*. According to Lakoff, women—specifically, white, middle-class, American women—speak and, more important, are supposed to speak "women's language," which is characterized by "hypercorrect grammar" and "superpolite forms."[105] Of course, not all women speak "women's language," and not all speakers of "women's language" are white, middle-class women. Indeed, since its initial publication in 1975, Lakoff's study has received much warranted criticism—in particular, for positing the a priori existence of a universal, timeless, and homogeneous feminine identity projected or displayed by language. At the same time, *Language and Woman's Place*, like Post's *Etiquette*, points to a range of femininities (that is, to different ways in which to enact femininity or womanness). It exposes the constructedness of gender, race, and class and shows the ways in which these social categories and relations come into being via language.

Throughout *People v. Zammora*, Anna Zacsek, the only female attorney in the courtroom (and, coincidentally, a former professional actress), clearly spoke Post's "agreeable speech" and Lakoff's "women's language."[106] By and large, she used correct grammar and was respectful, even when she took issue with Judge Charles Fricke or one of the prosecutors. Indeed, at times, she was cloyingly polite. For example, when Judge Fricke complained that fifteen-year-old witness Juanita Gonzáles was inaudible because she repeatedly turned her head away from the microphone while testifying in the witness stand, Zacsek instructed her, "Will you please be a good girl and take this microphone in your hand—you have talked on telephones, haven't you, Juanita?"[107] Underscoring her own femininity, the defense attorney assumed a maternal role in the courtroom and claimed that she was "just old enough to know how to handle children" such as the uncooperative Gonzáles.[108]

In contrast, most of the young, Spanish-surnamed female witnesses, including Gonzáles, were neither grammatically correct nor polite. Many sprinkled their sentences with double negatives and the contraction *ain't* and defied Emily Post with their improper use of the verb *seen*. For example, when Deputy District Attorney Clyde C. Shoemaker asked Aguilar how many cars she saw at Williams Ranch the night of the fight, she replied, "I *seen* about two."[109] Furthermore, the court reporter indicated that Aguilar used improper or incorrect diction by recording her use of the words *nothing* and *going* as *nothin'* and *goin'.* In this instance, Shoemaker asked her if she was with defendant Henry Leyvas on the night of August 1, 1942. Aguilar impatiently reminded him,

> I said I wasn't going to say *nothin'*. Don't ask me no more things. You can punish me—
> Mr. Shoemaker: We ask you to answer that question, Bertha.
> A: I ain't *goin'* to answer it.[110]

Because there is no audio recording of her testimony, whether or not Aguilar actually stated "nothin'" and "goin'" (as opposed to *nothing* and *going*) is unclear. Regardless, to my knowledge, this is the only instance in the entire trial transcript (which is thousands of pages in length) in which the court reporter truncated a speaker's words. By doing so, he rendered Aguilar's utterance a slang locution and expression of improper or incorrect diction and, in effect, masculinized her words.[111] What's more, just as a caricature Mexican accent was attributed to Amelia Venegas by the *Los Angeles Herald-Express* during the Zoot Suit Riots, attention was drawn to Aguilar's "slight accent" in the courtroom.[112] By using incorrect grammar and allegedly substandard diction, she appeared both unladylike and un-American.

Although we do not know if Aguilar had an accent or if she really dropped the *g* in *nothing*, her speech clearly was not polite or indirect, two characteristics of "women's language," according to Lakoff. The following exchange between her and Shoemaker further illustrates her candor and tenacity:

> Q [by Shoemaker]: Now state whether or not at the time you testified before the Grand Jury, on August 4, which was three days after [the Sleepy Lagoon incident], that your memory was better on the subject than it is today. What is your answer, Bertha? Talk right into the microphone.
> A [by Aguilar]: I am not going to say nothing. I told you all I wasn't going to say nothing.
> Q: Will you answer that question?
> A: No.
> Q: The question is, whether your memory was better when you testified before the Grand Jury than it is today. Will you answer that? What is your answer? What is your answer, Bertha? Will you answer the question?
> Q: You don't have to holler at people. I am right here.
> A: I am not hollering at you.
> Q: You sure are.
> A: I am just talking in an ordinary tone of voice.
> The Court: Answer the question, Bertha. You are just wasting time. Will you answer the question?
> A: No, I won't.
> Mr. Shoemaker: Will your Honor direct the witness to answer the question, please?
> The Court: Answer the question, Bertha. There is no reason why you cannot answer that question.
> (No response.)[113]

Instead of cultivating "agreeable speech" by using a "pleasing voice," "hypercorrect grammar," and "superpolite forms," Aguilar displayed and then boasted about injuries she claimed to have sustained in a fight. (As Galindo has noted, boasting, also known as *cábula* or *vacilada* in pachuco slang, "is generally confined to male speech behavior.")[114] Furthermore, the bold teenager repeatedly and adamantly refused to cooperate with authorities; ordered the deputy district attorney to refrain from asking her any more questions; indicated that she was willing to face punishment rather than yield to his demands; reprimanded him for "hollering" at her; openly disagreed with him; and, finally, refused to speak. It should come as no surprise that she was held in contempt of court for refusing to answer the prosecution's questions.[115] However, she was purged of it after offering the judge what was described as a "rare smile."[116] That is, she was rewarded after behaving as a lady should.

By saying "nothing" (or "nothin'") rather than "anything," Aguilar demonstrated a disregard for (or unawareness of) the rules of grammar. And by saying nothing (that is, by refusing to speak), she flouted the authority of the state, as represented by the deputy district attorney and judge. As historian Eduardo Obregón Pagán observes, "Most of the girls [forced to testify against their male companions] refused to implicate the boys and subverted the trial proceedings or defied the court outright."[117] Aguilar further disobeyed and hamstrung the prosecution by playing the role of good subject and claiming to have forgotten what happened the night she and her friends crashed the Delgadillos' party. Even after Shoemaker attempted to "refresh" her memory by citing her August 1942 Grand Jury testimony (taken just days after José Díaz's death), she insisted that she was unable to remember what happened. "I don't remember nothing," she stated. "When I went to Ventura they told me to forget everything."[118] Similarly, during cross-examination, Juanita Gonzáles reported that when she entered "Juvenile," she was instructed "to forget all this as quickly as possible."[119] The two teenage girls continued to stymie the prosecution by refusing to say anything lest they incriminate themselves. For instance, when Shoemaker asked Gonzáles on what grounds she refused to testify, she responded, "On the grounds you may charge me for the murder of Joe Diaz, like you done to the boys."[120] Aguilar offered a more curt reply when asked why she would not answer one of the prosecutor's questions: "I don't know, but I ain't going to answer it that's all."[121] Others refused to cooperate by not speaking clearly (and thus they broke yet another one of Post's rules of feminine speech). Eighteen-year-old Dora Baca, for example, claimed to suffer from a sore throat when both the prosecution and defense complained that she was inaudible on the witness stand.[122]

In "Life and Language in Court," Lakoff argues that, while "the giver of information" (the speaker) usually holds power in everyday speech, in court, "the giver of information" (the witness) does not control topics for discussion "or their interpretation and has no say over when the conversation begins and ends. The witness is generally a neophyte in the courtroom; the lawyer, a polished professional . . . the attorneys are running the show."[123] Undeniably, Aguilar and the other teenage girls and young women who found themselves reluctant witnesses in *People v. Zammora* were neophytes in the courtroom vis-à-vis the judge, lawyers, court reporters, bailiffs, and others. Yet, as Kelley reminds us, "One also finds the hidden transcript emerging 'onstage' in spaces controlled by the powerful, though almost always in disguised forms."[124] Despite her youth and inexperience, Aguilar showed remarkable bravery and resolution in the witness stand. Within her words (and lack thereof) we find a "hidden transcript" in the form of defiance, evasion, and refusal. At times, her resistance is overt (for example, when she reprimands Shoemaker for "hollering" at her). At others, it is less easily recognized—for example, when she claims to have forgotten the ill-fated events of August 1 and 2, 1942, and in instances when she refuses to speak at all, which the transcript notes as "(No response.)" Aguilar's strategic use of silence reveals that the absence of words "has its own contours, its own texture."[125] It compels us to rethink resistance and to recognize the many contradictory forms it may take, especially for working-class, Mexican-American girls and women. Her refusal to speak shows us that, like the creative wordplay of young Mexican-American men, silence, too, can express opposition, especially when it comes from someone whose speech is overdetermined by the fact that she has already been spoken for and about.

Indeed, Aguilar's life has been marked by silence. She passed away in 1999 and, beyond her family and close friends, very little is known about her.[126] According to a friend who grew up with her, she was "very strong and defiant."[127] As a girl, she "was a pachuca who hung around the neighborhood," and as an adult, she associated with the Brown Berets.[128] Yet, unlike the male defendants in *People v. Zammora*—in particular, Henry Leyvas—Aguilar's participation in the Sleepy Lagoon incident and subsequent trial was not celebrated or valorized in *Zoot Suit.*

Zoot Suit

When *Zoot Suit*, a play about the Sleepy Lagoon incident and Zoot Suit Riots, opens, the audience is told that it is about to see a "construct of fact and fantasy."[129] In writing the play, Valdez drew directly from contemporary Angeleno newspapers and *People v. Zammora* and based many of the characters on real men and women. For example, Hank Reyna, the protagonist, is based on defendant Henry Leyvas; Hank's sweetheart, Della Barrios, is based on Henry Leyvas's girlfriend Dora Baca; and the loud, foul-mouthed pachuca Bertha Villarreal is, in all likelihood, based on Bertha Aguilar.

Bertha Villarreal is by no means a major character in *Zoot Suit*. However, she plays an important role, especially in relation to Della. Bertha first appears in scene seven, "The Saturday Night Dance," where she encounters her ex-boyfriend Hank dancing with Della. After Hank rejects her advances, she dismisses Della as his "new huisa (broad)" and "little fly chick."[130] Hank then tells his ex-girlfriend to "beat it," to which she retorts, "Beat it yourself. Mira (Look). You got no hold on me, cabrón (stupid). Not anymore. I'm free as a bird."[131] In addition to using pachuco slang, incorrect grammar, and profanity, Bertha revels in violence. Anticipating bloodshed, she excitedly exclaims "ALLRIGHT!" when a fight breaks out between Hank's younger brother and the leader of the rival Downey gang.[132] As the Downey gang retreats, she shouts at them, " *¡Chinga tu madre!* (Fuck your mother!)" and insists that she "could have beat the shit out of those two rucas (chicks)."[133]

Although Valdez describes her as "cool and tough," Bertha is actually quite loud and animated. [134] As film critic Rosa Linda Fregoso observes, she shows lust, exhilaration, and anger, and thus is ridiculed "as exaggerated and hyper-sexed."[135] In contrast, the character of El Pachuco, Hank's alter ego, always plays it cool. When Hank begins to worry about the fact that he is the prime suspect in the Sleepy Lagoon murder case, El Pachuco demands that he "[h]ang tough" and "[s]top going soft."[136] Indeed, El Pachuco keeps cool even as he is stripped to a mere loincloth and beaten by a group of white sailors during the Zoot Suit Riots. In Valdez's words, he exits this scene "slowly . . . with powerful calm. [137]

As a number of feminist scholars, including Fregoso, have shown, the female, Mexican-American characters in *Zoot Suit* fall into two categories: "the virgin or the whore, the long-suffering mother or the 'cheap broad.'"[138] Della, Hank's loyal girlfriend, is the virgin; in the 1981 film version of the play, she is described as "very pretty," "very young," and "innocent."[139] Although her strict father does not approve of her relationship with Hank, she promises to marry him upon his return from the war. When he ends up in jail rather than in the Navy and she is sent to the Ventura School for Girls, he is her "only hope."[140] All the while, Hank two-times her, even though he concedes that Della "did a year in Ventura" and "stood up for me when it counted."[141] Furthermore, unlike Bertha, Della mostly speaks grammatically correct English and does not wear a zoot suit. (Interestingly, only at the end of the play, after she has done time at Ventura, does she curse or insert some pachuco slang into her sentences.) In summary, she is not a pachuca. As Hank's mother observes, she does not look "[l]ike a *puta* . . . I mean, a pachuca."[142]

Bertha Villarreal, on the other hand, is both pachuca and *puta*. In the film, Della wears saddle shoes and modest dresses, including a jumper reminiscent of a Catholic school uniform; Bertha, meanwhile, shows leg and cleavage. Moreover, Hank's father describes her as "the one with the tattoo," a sign that she is a real or "hardcore" pachuca and quite possibly a gang member.[143] Yet, even though she is Della's antithesis, the two young women have one thing in common: both are uncool. Bertha acts the fool at the Saturday night dance, while Della loses her cool in the courtroom when she is forced to testify against Hank. During examination, she, like the real Bertha Aguilar, shows defiance and refuses to answer some questions. Ultimately, however, she cracks under pressure; she fails to hang tough and goes soft.

Although *Zoot Suit* earned much critical praise, it was not well received by some of the real-life men and women who took part in and were affected by the Sleepy Lagoon incident and trial. As defense attorney George Shibley (portrayed by the character of George Shearer) complained, the play "perpetuate[d] some seriously damaging distortions of the Sleepy Lagoon murder case."[144] In 1979, one year after *Zoot Suit* opened in Los Angeles, several of the former defendants filed a $2.5 million lawsuit against Valdez, charging "invasion of privacy and intentional and negligent infliction of emotional distress." "That event ruined my life," Gus Zamora (after whom *People v. Zammora* was named) lamented.[145] Decades later, he was still haunted by the Sleepy Lagoon incident and its aftermath and claimed that the play had opened up old wounds.

One reason that it has been difficult for me to acquire information about Aguilar's life from her close friends and family (and that I do not identify those interviewees who did talk to me) is that some were "shocked" and "insulted" by her portrayal as Bertha Villarreal in *Zoot Suit* and are thus loath to talk to an academic writing about this play.[146] Whereas the Sleepy Lagoon trial transcript shows us that Bertha Aguilar was extraordinarily courageous, self-possessed, clever, and articulate, *Zoot Suit* reduces her to a boisterous buffoon and "cheap broad" through the character of Bertha Villarreal. Because it restricts Mexican-American women's roles to the virgin-whore dyad, the play erases the complexity of a pachuca's words and deeds. Instead, like much of the early, alarmist scholarship on women speakers of pachuco slang, *Zoot Suit* fails to appreciate Chicanas' complex relationship to coolness and hipness and misrecognizes the ways in which they have expressed resistance via both language and silence. Ultimately, it renders their artful and oppositional use and rejection of words a condemnation and mockery.

Taming a Wild Tongue

In chapter 5 of *Borderlands/La Frontera*, "How to Tame a Wild Tongue," Gloria Anzaldúa confronts the "linguistic terrorism" that Chicanos and Chicanas have endured.[147] In addition to being robbed of Spanish and told that we do not speak it or English well enough, Chicanas in particular have had to overcome a "tradition of silence."[148] Anzaldúa enumerates some of the labels applied to women who talk too much or too loudly: *hocicona* (big mouth), *repelona* (whiner), *chismosa* (gossip). "In my culture they are all words that are derogatory if applied to women," she observes, adding, "I've never heard them applied to men."[149]

Bertha Aguilar's working-class and *pocha* tongue was tamed twice: first, by the state, which found her threatening enough to incarcerate her at the Ventura School for Girls, then by *Zoot Suit*, which transforms her into the *hocicona* Bertha Villarreal. As Lakoff points out, the "young girl" who refuses to speak women's language "is exceedingly brave—in fact, reckless," for there are consequences for not "talk[ing] like a lady."[150] At the same time, she reminds us, those women who do speak women's language also pay a high price: they (we) are deemed stupid, frivolous, and, I would add, easily manipulated (that is, pushovers). In short, "a woman is damned if she does and damned if she doesn't."[151] Yet, if Lakoff's universal female subject (the white, middle-class, American woman) faces a double bind, then Chicanas face a triple one. Those who "keep it real" by speaking pachuco slang—who remain faithful to an oppositional cultural identity—betray gender norms. And those who adhere to normative definitions of female and feminine decency by speaking Lakoff's women's language betray the Chicano culture of oppositionality and are white-washed. In either case, they (we) are branded traitors.

Undeniably, *Zoot Suit*, which is still performed and screened across the United States, has proven itself an effective tool for generating discussion on the Sleepy Lagoon trial, Zoot Suit Riots, and Mexican-American zoot subculture of the World War II period. In my research, I have also found it to be valuable in my interviews with Mexican-American women who came of age in Los Angeles during the 1930s and 1940s. Initially, many of these women were reluctant to talk to me about the zoot subculture of their youth and vehemently denied that they were or even knew pachucas (for reasons that I hope this essay makes apparent). However, when our conversations turned to *Zoot Suit*, which nearly all of my interviewees had seen, some waxed nostalgic about wearing "drapes" and teasing their hair into "rats" as teenagers. One even reminisced in pachuco slang. I find it sadly ironic that a cultural product that exposes the power of art to shape historical perspective and the promises and pitfalls of oral history also warps the words of its primary pachuca character—and eventually silences her.

While *Zoot Suit* continues to receive much well deserved attention from scholars in Chicano studies, it, fortunately, does not have the final say when it comes to Chicana speakers of pachuco slang. Literary works by Chicana feminist writers, such as Cherríe Moraga and Evangelina Vigil, offer more complex and nuanced portrayals of women speakers of pachuco slang, including pachucas. Within the multidisciplinary field of Chicano studies, these texts merit additional scrutiny, for they add to our conversations on *pachuquismo* and can assist us in recognizing and understanding the multiple, often contradictory languages of Chicana and Chicano resistance.[152]

Notes

1. Quotations in this paragraph are from "Policeman Is Ambushed, Run Over by Zoot Auto," *Los Angeles Evening Herald-Express*, sec. A1 and sec. A6, June 10, 1943. For more accounts of the arrest of Amelia Venegas, see "Zoot Suit Hunt On in Suburbs as Navy Clamps Ban on L.A," *Los Angeles Examiner*, 1, June 9, 1943; "6-Day Zoot War Hospitalizes 112," *Los Angeles Daily News*, 1, June 10, 1943; "U.S., Warren Act on

Zoot Suits, New Outbreak of Gang Rioting," *Los Angeles Examiner*, 1, June 10, 1943; and "Brass Knuckles Found on Woman 'Zoot Suiter,'" *Los Angeles Times*, sec. IA, June 10, 1943.

The Zoot Suit Riots, which occurred in Los Angeles during the first weeks of June 1943, were marked by clashes between white servicemen and young Mexican Americans, some of whom were pachucos or zooters. When servicemen apprehended those wearing zoot suits, they usually beat them; some defrocked their victims, cut their relatively long ducktails, and destroyed their clothing. Although the riots are generally associated with Mexican Americans, Angelenos of various races and ethnicities were involved, whether or not they wore zoot suits. For more information regarding the Zoot Suit Riots, see Luis Alvarez, "The Power of the Zoot: Race, Community, and Resistance in American Youth Culture, 1940–1945" (PhD diss., University of Texas at Austin, 2001); Luis Alvarez, "Zoot Violence on the Home Front: Race, Riots, and Youth Culture during World War II," in *Mexican Americans and World War II*, ed. Maggie Rivas-Rodríguez (Austin: University of Texas Press, 2005), 141–75; Edward J. Escobar, *Race, Police, and the Making of a Political Identity* (Berkeley: University of California Press, 1999); George Lipsitz, *Rainbow at Midnight: Labor and Culture in the 1940s* (Urbana: University of Illinois Press, 1994); Maurico Mazón, *The Zoot-Suit Riots: The Psychology of Symbolic Annihilation* (Austin: University of Texas Press, 1984); Eduardo Obregón Pagán, *Murder at the Sleepy Lagoon: Zoot Suits, Race, and Riot in Wartime L.A.* (Chapel Hill: University of North Carolina Press, 2003); and Joseph Tovares, *The American Experience: Zoot Suit Riots* (Boston: WGBH Educational Foundation, 2001).

2. "Brass Knuckles Found on Woman 'Zoot Suiter,'" sec. IA. For photographs of Venegas, see page 3 of the June 10, 1943, *Los Angeles Daily News*; page 8 of the June 8, 1943, *Los Angeles Examiner*; page A1 of the June 10, 1943, *Los Angeles Evening Herald-Express*; and page A of the June 10, 1943, *Los Angeles Times*.

3. In wartime Los Angeles, the zoot suit was the most prominent hallmark of wartime *pachuquismo*, the pachuca/o subculture. For young Mexican-American women, the zoot look generally consisted of a long, broad-shouldered "finger-tip" coat or sweater, a knee-length (and therefore relatively short) pleated skirt, fishnet stockings or bobby socks pulled up the calves, and platform heels, saddle shoes, or *huarache* sandals. Many pachucas also wore dark lipstick and used "rats" (foam inserts) to lift their hair into a high bouffant. For extra panache, a number lightened their hair with peroxide and some sported the masculine version of the zoot suit. Also known as "drapes" or *el tacuche*, this consisted of the "finger-tip" coat, which sometimes extended to the knee, and a pair of puffy "Punjab" pants that tapered at the ankle. Some Mexican-American male zooters added a long watch chain, a hat (known as a *tando*), or both to the ensemble, but many abandoned the hat in favor of combing their relatively long hair into a pompadour on top and what was known as an "Argentine ducktail" or "duck's ass" ("D.A.") in back. *Calcos* or thick-soled shoes often punctuated the look.

For a partial list of scholarly works on Mexican-American zooters during World War II, see endnote 1. Also see Elizabeth Escobedo, "Mexican American Home Front: The Politics of Gender, Culture and Community in World War II Los Angeles" (PhD diss., University of Washington, 2004); and Catherine S. Ramírez, "Crimes of Fashion: The Pachuca and Chicana Style Politics," *Meridians* 2, no. 2 (2002): 1–35.

4. In addition to zoot suits, pompadours, and red lipstick, other defining features of wartime *pachuquismo* included pachuco slang or *caló*, jazz, and, in some instances, youth gangs and crime. Regarding the subculture's symbolic economy of style, see L. Alvarez, "The Power of the Zoot"; L. Alvarez, "Zoot Violence on the Home Front"; Escobedo, "Mexican American Home Front"; Rosa Linda Fregoso, "Homegirls, *Cholas*, and *Pachucas* in Cinema: Taking Over the Public Sphere," *California History* 74, no. 3 (1995): 316–27; Fregoso, "Re-Imagining Chicana Urban Identities in the Public Sphere, *Cool Chuca Style*," in *Between Women and Nation: Nationalisms, Transnational Feminisms, and the State*, ed. Caren Kaplan, Norma Alarcón, and Minoo Moalle (Durham: Duke University Press, 1999), 72–91; Curtis Márez, "Brown: The Politics of Working-Class Chicano Style," *Social Text* 48, vol. 14, no. 3 (1996): 109–32; Mazón, *The Zoot Suit Riots*; Pagán, *Murder at the Sleepy Lagoon*; and Ramírez, "Crimes of Fashion."

For discussions of the wartime African-American zoot subculture, see Steve Chibnall, "Whistle and Zoot: The Changing Meaning of a Suit of Clothes," *History Workshop Journal* 20 (1985): 56–81; Stuart Cosgrove, "The Zoot Suit and Style Warfare," *History Workshop Journal* 18 (1984): 77–91; Douglas Henry Daniels, "Los Angeles Zoot: Race 'Riot,' the Pachuco, and Black Music Culture," *Journal of African American History* 87 (2002): 98–118; Robin D. G. Kelley, *Race Rebels: Culture, Politics, and the Black Working Class* (New York: The Free Press, 1994); Bruce M. Tyler, "Black Jive and White Repression," *The Journal of Ethnic Studies* 16, no. 4 (1989): 31–66; and Shane White and Graham White, *Stylin': African American Expressive Culture from Its Beginnings to the Zoot Suit* (Ithaca, NY: Cornell University Press, 1998).

5. James C. Scott, *Domination and the Arts of Resistance: Hidden Transcripts* (New Haven: Yale University Press, 1990). The quotation is from Kelley, *Race Rebels*, 8.

6. Kelley, *Race Rebels*, 166.

7. D. Letticia Galindo, "Dispelling the Male-Only Myth: Chicanas and Calo," *The Bilingual Review/La Revista Bilingüe* 17, no. 1 (1992): 19.

8. See, for example, Julie Bettie, *Women without Class: Girls, Race, and Identity* (Berkeley: University of California Press, 2003); María Herrera-Sobek,"The Street Scene: Metaphoric Strategies in Two Contemporary Chicana Poets," in *Chicana (W)rites: On Word and Film*, ed. María Herrera-Sobek and Helena María Viramontes (Berkeley: Third Woman Press, 1995), 147–69; Norma Mendoza-Denton,"Language Attitudes and Gang Affiliation among California Latina Girls," in *Cultural Performances: Proceedings of the Third Berkeley Women and Language Conference*, ed. Mary Bucholtz, A. C. Liang, Laurel A. Sutton, and Caitlin Hines (Berkeley: Berkeley Women and Language Group, University of California, 1994), 478–86; Mendoza-Denton,

"'Muy Macha': Gender and Ideology in Gang-Girls' Discourse about Makeup," *Ethnos* 61, nos. 1–2 (1996): 47–63; Mendoza-Denton, "Fighting Words: Latina Girls, Gangs, and Language Attitudes," in *Speaking Chicana: Voice, Power, and Identity*, ed. D. Letticia Galindo and María Dolores Gonzáles (Tucson: University of Arizona Press, 1999), 39–56; Mendoza-Denton, "Turn-Initial *No*: Collaborative Opposition among Latina Adolescents," in *Reinventing Identities: The Gendered Self in Discourse*, ed. Mary Bucholtz, A. C. Liang, and Laurel A. Sutton (New York: Oxford University Press, 1999), 273–92; Mendoza-Denton, "The Anguish of Normative Gender: Sociolinguistic Studies among U.S. Latinas," in *Language and Woman's Place: Text and Commentaries*, ed. Mary Bucholtz (New York: Oxford University Press, 2004), 260–68; Marie "Keta" Miranda, *Homegirls in the Public Sphere* (Austin: University of Texas Press, 2003); and Amy Schalet, Geoffrey Hunt, and Karen Joe-Laidler, "Respectability and Autonomy: The Articulation and Meaning of Sexuality among the Girls in the Gang," *Journal of Contemporary Ethnography* 32, no. 1 (2003): 108–43.

9. My discussion of pachuco slang, *caló*, and tirili/tirilongo is indebted to the following works: George R. Alvarez, "Calo: The 'Other' Spanish," *ETC: A Review of General Semantics* 24, no. 1 (1967): 7–13; George Carpenter Barker, *Pachuco: An American-Spanish Argot and Its Social Functions in Tucson, Arizona* (Tucson: University of Arizona Press, 1950); Susan Berk-Seligson, "A Sociolinguistic View of the Mexican-American Speech Community," *Latin American Research Review* 15, no. 2 (1980): 65–110; Haldeen Braddy, "The *Pachucos* and Their Argot," *Southern Folklore Quarterly* 24, no. 4 (1960): 255–71; Lurline Coltharp, *The Tongue of the Tirilones: A Linguistic Study of a Criminal Argot* (Tuscaloosa: University of Alabama Press, 1965); Coltharp, "Invitation to the Dance: Spanish in the El Paso Underworld," in *Texas Studies in Bilingualism: Spanish, French, German, Czech, Polish, Serbian, and Norwegian in the Southwest*, ed. Glenn G. Gilbert (Berlin: Walter de Gruyter, 1970), 7–17; Dagoberto Fuentes and José A. López, *Barrio Language Dictionary: First Dictionary of Caló* (La Puente, CA: Sunburst Enterprises, 1974); Alfred Bruce Gaarder, "Notes on Some Spanish Terms in the Southwest," *Hispania* 27, no. 3 (1944): 330–34; Galindo, "Perceptions of Pachuquismo and Use of Calo/Pachuco Spanish by Various Chicana Women," *La Red/The Net*, no. 48 (1981): 2, 10; Galindo, "Dispelling the Male-Only Myth"; Galindo, "The Language of Gangs, Drugs, and Prison Life among Chicanas," *Latino Studies Journal* 4, no. 3 (1993): 23–43; Galindo, "Capturing Chicano Voices: An Interdisciplinary Approach," in *Cultural* Performances, 220–31; Galindo, "Caló and Taboo Language Use among Chicanas: A Description of Linguistic Appropriation and Innovation," in *Speaking Chicana*, 175–93; Rafael Jesus González, "Pachuco: The Birth of a Creole Language," *Arizona Quarterly* 23, no. 4 (1967): 343–56; George K. Green, "Calo, Pachuco, and Lunfardo: Certain Homogeneous Tendencies in Vernacular Spanish," in *Research Issues and Problems in United States Spanish: Latin American and Southwestern Varieties*, ed. Jacob L. Ornstein-Galicia, George K. Green, and Dennis J. Bixler-Márquez (Brownsville, TX: Pan American University, 1988), 243–49; Beatrice Griffith, "The Pachuco Patois," *Common Ground* 7, no. 4 (1947):

77–84; Eduardo Hernández-Chávez, Andrew D. Cohen, and Anthony F. Beltramo, *El Lenguaje de los Chicanos: Regional and Social Characteristics Used by Mexican Americans* (Arlington, VA: Center for Applied Linguistics, 1975); Francisco G. Hinojos, "Notes on the Pachuco: Stereotypes, History and Dialect," *Atisbos: Journal of Chicano Research* (Summer 1975): 53–65; Linda Fine Katz, "The Evolution of the Pachuco Language and Culture" (MA thesis, University of California, Los Angeles, 1974); Mazón, *The Zoot Suit Riots*; Jacob Ornstein-Galicia, "Chicano Caló: Description and Review of a Border Variety," *Hispanic Journal of Behavioral Sciences* 9, no. 4 (1987): 359–73; Adolfo Ortega, *Caló Tapestry* (Berkeley: Editorial Justa Publications, 1977); Pagán, *Murder at the Sleepy Lagoon*; Harry Polkinhorn, Alfredo Velasco, and Malcolm Lambert, *El libro de caló: The Dictionary of Chicano Slang* (Oakland, CA: Floricanto Press, 1986); Jay B. Rosensweig, *Caló: Gutter Spanish* (New York: E. P. Dutton, 1973); Rosaura Sánchez,"Chicano Spanish:Varieties, Styles and Functions," in *Chicano Speech in the Bilingual Classroom*, ed. Dennis J. Bixler-Márquez and Jacob Ornstein-Galicia (New York: Peter Lang, 1988), 55–68; and Sánchez, *Chicano Discourse: Socio-historic Perspectives* (Houston: Arte Público Press, 1994).

10. Mazón, *The Zoot-Suit Riots*, 3.

11. Pagán, *Murder at the Sleepy Lagoon*, 37.

12. Barker, *Pachuco*, 13.

13. Galindo, "Dispelling the Male-Only Myth," 5.

14. "Youthful Gang Secrets Exposed," *Los Angeles Times*, Part II, 1, July 16, 1944.

15. Carlos Amezcua, "Origenes de 'Pachucos' y 'Malinches,'" *La Opinión*, 2, August 26, 1942.

16. Galindo, "Capturing Chicana Voices," 221; Sánchez, *Chicano Discourse*, 127. According to Galindo, "Lexical borrowings from English are morphosyntactically and phonologically adapted to Spanish; for example, *troca* is adapted from truck." See Galindo, "Capturing Chicana Voices," 221.

17. Sánchez, *Chicano Discourse*, 127.

18. Braddy, "The *Pachucos* and Their Argot," 261.

19. "Authentic Pachuco," *Time*, July 10, 1944, 72.

20. Julian Nava, *¡Viva La Raza! Readings on Mexican Americans* (New York: D. Van Nostrand, 1973), 150.

21. Wallace Stegner, *One Nation* (Boston: Houghton Mifflin Company, 1945), 117.

22. Octavio Paz, *The Labyrinth of Solitude: Life and Thought in Mexico*, trans. Lysander Kemp (New York: Grove Press, 1961), 15.

23. Ibid., 14.

24. Lisa Lowe, *Immigrant Acts: On Asian American Cultural Politics* (Durham: Duke University Press, 1996), 130.

25. Regarding the relationship of English to Americanness, see Benjamin Franklin, *The Autobiography and Other Writings on Politics, Economics, and Virtue*, ed. Alan Houston (Cambridge: Cambridge University Press, 2004). Also see Samuel P.

Huntington, *Who Are We? The Challenges to America's Identity* (New York: Simon and Schuster, 2004).

26. See "Watts Pastor Blames Riots on Fifth Column," *Los Angeles Times*, A, June 11, 1943; and "Pastor Blames Fifth Column," *Los Angeles Examiner*, 12, June 11, 1943.

27. "Web of 'Zoot Suit' Gangs Spreads Over Entire L.A. Area," *Los Angeles Herald-Express*, 1, June 8, 1943.

28. For a discussion of the Cold War–era "bad boy," see Leerom Medovoi, *Rebels: Youth and the Cold War Origins of Identity* (Durham: Duke University Press, 2005).

29. Cab Calloway, *Of Minnie the Moocher and Me* (New York: Thomas Y. Crowell Company, 1976),182

30. Kenneth B. Clark and James Barker, "The Zoot Effect in Personality: A Race Riot Participant," *Journal of Abnormal and Social Psychology* 40, no. 2 (1945): 147.

31. G. Alvarez, "Calo," 9.

32. Clark and Barker, "The Zoot Effect in Personality," 147.

33. G. Alvarez, "Calo," 9.

34. Malcolm X, *The Autobiography of Malcolm X* (New York: Ballantine, 1964), 134.

35. "El Louie" was first published in 1970 in *Rascatripas*. I quote from the following version: Jose Montoya, "El Louie," in *Literatura Chicana: texto y contexto*, ed. Antonia Castañeda Shular, Tomás Ybarra-Frausto, and Joseph Sommers (Englewood Cliffs, NJ: Prentice-Hall, 1972), 173–78.

36. Montoya, "El Louie," 174. Unless otherwise indicated, all translations of "El Louie" are my own.

37. Ibid., 175.

38. Ibid.

39. Ibid., 174.

40. Ibid.

41. Ibid., 176.

42. Ibid., 174.

43. Mario Suárez, "Kid Zopilote," *Arizona Quarterly* 3, no. 2 (1947): 131.

44. Ibid.

45. Ibid.

46. Ibid., 136.

47. Montoya, "El Louie," 174.

48. Ibid.

49. Ibid.

50. Suárez, "Kid Zopilote," 131.

51. Montoya, "El Louie," 175.

52. Ibid.

53. See, for example, Juan Bruce-Novoa, *Chicano Authors: Inquiry by Interview* (Austin: University of Texas Press, 1980), 115; Bruce-Novoa, *Chicano Poetry: A Response to Chaos* (Austin: University of Texas Press, 1982), 16; and Bernice

Zamora, "Mythopoeia of Chicano Poetry: An Introduction to Cultural Archetypes" (PhD diss., Stanford University, 1986), 167.

54. Alfred Arteaga, *Chicano Poetics: Heterotexts and Hybridities* (New York: Cambridge University Press, 1997), 68.

55. Bettie, *Women without Class*, 34; Barbara Ehrenreich, *Fear of Falling: The Inner Life of the Middle Class* (New York: Pantheon Books, 1989), 109.

56. Galindo, "Dispelling the Male-Only Myth," 6.

57. Galindo, "The Language of Gangs, Drugs, and Prison Life among Chicanas," 33.

58. G. Alvarez, "Calo," 12.

59. In defining "cool" and "hip," I draw from the following: Calloway, *Of Minnie the Moocher and Me*; Susan Fraiman, *Cool Men and the Second Sex* (New York: Columbia University Press, 2003); Thomas Frank, *The Conquest of Cool: Business Culture, Counterculture, and the Rise of Hip Consumerism* (Chicago: University of Chicago Press, 1997); Hyman E. Golden, Frank O'Leary, and Morris Lipsius, *Dictionary of American Underworld Lingo* (New York: Twayne Publishers, 1950); John Leland, *Hip: The History* (New York: HarperCollins, 2004); Lewis MacAdams, *Birth of the Cool: Beat, Bebop, and the American Avant-Garde* (New York: The Free Press, 2001); Norman Mailer, "The White Negro," in *Keeping Time: Readings in Jazz History*, ed. Robert Walser (New York: Oxford University Press, 1999), 242–46; Richard Majors and Janice Mancini Bilson, *Cool Pose: The Dilemmas of Black Manhood in America* (New York: Lexington Books, 1992); Medovoi, *Rebels*; Milton "Mezz" Mezzrow and Bernard Wolfe, *Really the Blues* (New York: Random House, 1946); Dick Poutain and David Robins, *Cool Rules: Anatomy of an Attitude* (London: Reaktion Books, 2000); Peter N. Stearns, *American Cool: Constructing a Twentieth-Century Emotional Style* (New York: New York University Press, 1994); and Robert Farris Thompson, "An Aesthetic of the Cool," *African Arts* 7, no. 1 (1973): 40–91.

60. María Josefina Saldaña-Portillo, *The Revolutionary Imagination in the Americas and the Age of Development* (Durham: Duke University Press, 2003). The quote is from Kelley, *Race Rebels*, 162.

61. Malcolm X, *The Autobiography of Malcolm X*, 56.

62. Ibid., 310.

63. Ibid.

64. Ibid.

65. Majors and Billson, *Cool Pose*, 7.

66. Mailer, "The White Negro," 243.

67. G. Alvarez, "Calo," 9.

68. Majors and Billson, *Cool Pose*, 83. I recall that when I was in high school and college in the 1980s and early 1990s, "gay" was synonymous with uncool: regardless of sex or sexual orientation, a person was "gay" if she or he removed the mask of coolness and showed excessive emotion—in particular, excitement, sadness, or fear. For a brief discussion of gay cool, see Leland, *Hip*.

69. G. Alvarez, "Calo," 12.

70. Tomás Almaguer, "Chicano Men: A Cartography of Homosexual Identity and Behavior," *Differences* 3, no. 2 (1991): 82.

71. Ibid.

72. Berk-Seligson, "A Sociolinguistic View of the Mexican-American Speech Community," 94; Coltharp, "Invitation to the Dance," 7.

73. Coltharp, *The Tongue of the Tirilones*, 32.

74. Leland, *Hip*, 241.

75. Fraiman, *Cool Men and the Second Sex*.

76. Mary Helen Ponce, *Hoyt Street: An Autobiography* (Albuquerque: University of New Mexico Press, 1993), 167.

77. Galindo, "Dispelling the Male-Only Myth," 20.

78. Ibid., 19.

79. Ibid.

80. Coltharp, *The Tongue of the Tirilones*, 32.

81. Ibid.

82. Galindo, "Dispelling the Male-Only Myth," 19.

83. Chuy Varela, "Pachuco Boogie," liner notes for *Pachuco Boogie, featuring Don Tosti* (El Cerrito, CA: Arhoolie Productions, 2002), 11.

84. The advertisement for the *Dictionary of Pachuco Slang* may be found in *LowRider* 2, no. 2 (November 1978), page number unknown. Regarding the 1940s-themed fundraiser dances, see *LowRider* 1, no. 11 (August 1978), 39; and *LowRider* 2, no. 2 (November 1978), page number unknown.

85. For transcriptions of conversations in pachuco slang, see Barker, "Pachuco"; Coltharp, "Invitation to the Dance"; Gaarder, "Notes on Some Spanish Terms in the Southwest"; Galindo, "The Language of Gangs, Drugs, and Prison Life among Chicanas"; Sánchez, "Chicano Spanish"; and Sánchez, *Chicano Discourse*. Coltharp's "Invitation to the Dance" and Galindo's "The Language of Gangs, Drugs, and Prison Life among Chicanas" feature women speaking pachuco slang. Barker's audio recording of a conversation between two men speaking pachuco slang may be found at the University of Arizona Library, Department of Special Collections, Southwest Folklore Center Manuscript Collection (SWF 009, items 85.2/C.1 and 85.2/R.1). I am grateful to Veronica Reyes and Scott Cossel of the University of Arizona library for providing me with access to it.

86. Songs that feature pachuco slang by Lalo Guerrero and Don Tosti's Pachuco Boogie Boys, as well as other artists, may be found on *Pachuco Boogie*. "El Bracero y La Pachuca" is also on this album. I thank Anthony Macias for bringing it to my attention.

87. Translated by Don Tosti, Chuy Varela, and Zac Salem, liner notes for *Pachuco Boogie*, 21.

88. Translated by Tosti, Varela, and Salem, liner notes for *Pachuco Boogie*, 22.

89. Katz, "The Evolution of the Pachuco Language and Culture," 55.

90. Susan Gal, "Language, Gender, and Power: An Anthropological Review," in *Gender Articulated: Language and the Socially Constructed Self*, ed. Kira Hall and Mary Bucholtz (New York: Routledge, 1995), 173.

91. For a discussion of the theme of women and betrayal in *corridos*, see María Herrera-Sobek, *The Mexican Corrido: A Feminist Analysis* (Bloomington: Indiana University Press, 1993); and María Herrera-Sobek,"The Treacherous Woman Archetype: A Structuring Agent in the Corrido," *Aztlán* 13, nos. 1–2 (1982): 135–48.

92. For more information regarding the Sleepy Lagoon case and trial, see Frank P. Barajas, "The Defense Committees of Sleepy Lagoon: A Convergent Struggle against Facism, 1942–1944," *Aztlán* 31, no. 1 (2006): 33–62; Escobar, *Race, Police, and the Making of a Political Identity*; Escobedo,"Mexican American Home Front"; Alice McGrath, with Michael Balter, *The Education of Alice McGrath* (Los Angeles: Oral History Program, University of California, Los Angeles, 1987); Pagán, *Murder at the Sleepy Lagoon*; and Tovares, *The American Experience.*

93. During *People v. Zammora*, thirty-nine witnesses were called by the prosecution and twenty-two by the defense (certain individuals were called as witnesses by both parties). The "girl companions" who were called as the prosecution's witnesses were Bertha Aguilar, Dora Barrios, Ann Kalustian, Betty Nuñez Zeiss, Josephine Gonzáles, and her sister Juanita Gonzáles. Dora Baca and Lorena Encinas were called as the defense's witnesses. Frances Silva was also held by the police as a suspect in José Diaz's murder and testified before the Grand Jury in August 1942. However, unlike the others, she was not a witness in the trial. See *People v. Zammora, et al.*, Superior Court in the District Court of Appeal of the State of California, Second Appellate District (Sleepy Lagoon Defense Committee Collection, Collection 107, Department of Special Collections, Charles E. Young Research Library, University of California, Los Angeles). The list of witnesses may be found in box 7, volume 1. Regarding the incarceration of some of the girls and young women at the Ventura School for Girls, see Escobedo, "Mexican American Home Front"; and McGrath, *The Education of Alice McGrath*.

94. References to the young women's hair and clothing may be found on the following pages of the court transcript: 1336, 1345, 3720, and 3722.

95. "Jury's Gang-Case Verdict Disproves 'Persecution,'" *Los Angeles Times*, page number unavailable, January 14, 1943.

96. Testimony of Bertha Aguilar, court transcript, 1324.

97. Court transcript, 1318–19.

98. Ibid., 1319.

99. Emily Post, *Etiquette: The Blue Book of Social Usage* (New York: Funk and Wagnalls, 1942), 97.

100. Ibid.

101. Ibid., 98.

102. Ibid., 86.

103. Ibid., 92.

104. Here, "perform" refers to the repetition and disruption of symbolic categories. See Judith Butler, *Gender Trouble: Feminism and the Subversion of Identity* (New York: Routledge, 1990); and Butler, "Critically Queer," *Bodies That Matter: On the Discursive Limits of "Sex"* (New York: Routledge, 1993). Also see Homi K. Bhabha "Disemminations," *The Location of Culture* (New York: Routledge, 1994).

105. Robin Tolmach Lakoff, *Language and Woman's Place: Text and Commentaries*, ed. Mary Bucholtz (New York: Oxford University Press, 2004), 80.

106. According to Pagán, Zacsek (a.k.a. Olga Grey) had a supporting role in *Birth of a Nation* and "relied on her dramatic talents and personal flair" in the courtroom. See Pagán, *Murder at the Sleepy Lagoon*, 77.

107. Court transcript, 297.

108. Ibid., 298.

109. Testimony of Bertha Aguilar, court transcript, 1235(italics added). Other instances in which the young women used incorrect grammar may be found on the following pages of *People v. Zammora*: 207, 218, 300, 403, 770, 1046, 1088, 1099, 1106, 1141, 1142, 1153, 1180, 1185, 1192, 1198, 1201, 1204, 1212–13, 1215, 1231, 1324, 1394, 1420, 1437, and 4509. Incidentally, each teenage girl had attended school up to the proper grade according to her age.

110. Testimony of Bertha Aguilar, court transcript, 1215 (italics added).

111. Lakoff adds that the omission of the final *g* in the gerund form is generally associated with boys. See Lakoff, *Language and Woman's Place*, 80.

112. Court transcript, 1173.

113. Testimony of Bertha Aguilar, court transcript, 1212–13.

114. Galindo, "The Language of Gangs, Drugs, and Prison Life among Chicanas," 32.

115. Court transcript, 1202.

116. Ibid., 1273–74.

117. Pagán, *Murder at the Sleepy Lagoon*, 82.

118. Testimony of Bertha Aguilar, court transcript, 1212.

119. Testimony of Juanita Gonzáles, court transcript, 1043. Other examples of the young women's "forgetfulness" may be found on the following pages: 263–66, 274–79, 454, 851, 854, 917, 1023, 1026, 1095, 1107, 1204, 1211, 1222–23, 1229, and 1437–39.

120. Testimony of Juanita Gonzáles, court transcript, 207.

121. Testimony of Bertha Aguilar, court transcript, 1201–02. See pages 225, 233, 767, 787, 1095, 1182, 1185–1189, 1192–95, 1197, 1199, 1204, 1211–13, 1229, 1233, 1238, 1354, 1386, 1396, and 1437–40 for other instances in which the young women refused to testify or to cooperate while in court.

122. Testimony of Dora Baca, court transcript, 4550. There are numerous complaints from the judge and lawyers about the female witnesses' inaudibility. See, for example, the following pages: 234, 258, 296–97, 403, 410, 449, 521, 527, 678, 1084, 1271, 1457, 4496, and 5483.

123. Robin Tolmach Lakoff, *Talking Power: The Politics of Language in Our Lives* (New York: Basic Books, 1990), 90–91.

124. Kelley, *Race Rebels*, 8.

125. Yolanda Chávez Leyva, "Listening to the Silences in Latina/Chicana Lesbian History," in *Living Chicana Theory*, ed. Carla Trujillo (Berkeley: Third Woman Press, 1998), 432.

126. For a brief, albeit vivid, discussion of Aguilar's sentence at the Ventura School for Girls, see Escobedo, "Mexican American Home Front," 68–69.

127. For reasons I explain below, I cannot disclose the identity of this speaker. Suffice it to say that my interview with this person, whom I shall call unidentified interviewee #1, was conducted by telephone on February 19, 2005.

128. Ibid.

129. Luis Valdez, Zoot Suit *and Other Plays* (Houston: Arte Público Press, 1992), 25.

130. Valdez, Zoot Suit *and Other Plays*, 43.

131. Ibid.

132. Ibid., 46.

133. Ibid.

134. Ibid., 44.

135. Fregoso, "Re-Imagining Chicana Urban Identities in the Public Sphere, *Cool Chuca Style*," 84.

136. Valdez, Zoot Suit *and Other Plays*, 51.

137. Ibid., 81.

138. Yolanda Broyles-González, *El Teatro Campesino: Theater in the Chicano Movement* (Austin: University of Texas Press, 1994), 203. Other feminist critiques of *Zoot Suit* may be found in Fregoso, *The Bronze Screen: Chicana and Chicano Film Culture* (Minneapolis: University of Minnesota Press, 1993); Fregoso, "Homegirls, *Cholas*, and *Pachucas* in Cinema"; Fregoso, "Re-Imagining Chicana Urban Identities in the Public Sphere, *Cool Chuca Style*"; and Yvonne Yarbro-Bejarano, "The Female Subject in Chicano Theatre: Sexuality, 'Race,' and Class," *Theatre Journal* 38, no. 4 (1986): 389–407.

139. Valdez, *Zoot Suit* (Universal Pictures, 1981).

140. Valdez, Zoot Suit *and Other Plays*, 90.

141. Ibid.

142. Valdez, Zoot Suit *and Other Plays*, 35.

143. Ibid.

144. George Shibley, "Sleepy Lagoon: The True Story," *New West*, January 15, 1979, 88 (box 3, folder 27, Alice G. McGrath Collection, Collection 1490, Department of Special Collections, Charles E. Young Research Library, University of California, Los Angeles).

145. See "Suit Filed Against 'Zoot Suit' Producers," *Los Angeles Times*, Part IV, 34, November 23, 1979 (box 24, "Zoot Suit Murders/Sanchez" folder, Carey McWilliams Collection, Collection 1390, Department of Special Collections, Charles E. Young Research Library, University of California, Los Angeles).

146. Telephone interview with unidentified interviewee #2 (November 20, 2004).

147. Gloria Anzaldúa, *Borderlands/La Frontera: The New Mestiza* (San Francisco: Aunt Lute, 1987), 58.

148. Ibid., 54.

149. Ibid.

150. Lakoff, *Language and Woman's Place*, 84.

151. Ibid., 85.

152. See Cherríe Moraga, "Later, She Met Joyce," *Loving in the War Years: Lo que nunca pasó por los labios* (Boston: South End Press, 1983); Moraga, *Giving Up the Ghost* (Albuquerque: West End Press, 1986); and Evangelina Vigil, *Thirty an' Seen a Lot* (Berkeley: Third Woman Press, 1982). See also Herrera-Sobek, "The Street Scene," for an insightful analysis of Vigil's poetry. I discuss Moraga's and Vigil's works in more detail in *The Woman in the Zoot Suit: Gender, Nationalism, and the Cultural Politics of Memory* (Durham, NC: Duke University Press, 2009).

PART II

Colonized Places

The three articles in this section examine colonialism in the post-conquest West, tracing the incorporation of Indigenous lands into the nation and the subjection of Indigenous people to the colonial state. They explore how colonizers acquired and consolidated their control of land and people, and how the colonized accommodated to and resisted that power. One theme of the articles is how imaginary Wests served the colonial project. When colonizers imagined the Wests of the past, they naturalized the conquest by developing nostalgic narratives that sought to legitimate and minimize the violence of conquest. These western imaginaries helped develop and maintain regional tourism that relied on Indians, Mexicans, and Mexican Americans as colorful, colonial attractions. A second theme of these articles is how Indigenous women challenged colonization, including its imaginaries, by constructing for themselves places that offered some personal autonomy and identities of their own choosing.

The point of departure for Yolanda Venegas in "The Erotics of Racialization: Gender and Sexuality in the Making of California" and Laura Jane Moore in "Elle Meets the President: Weaving Navajo Culture and Commerce in the Southwestern Tourist Industry" is the completion of transcontinental railroads in the late nineteenth century, which encouraged enterprising Euro-Americans to develop western tourism by promoting the allure of imaginary Wests. For both Venegas and Moore, Euro-Americans developed the Far West as "America's Orient," a term that acknowledges their debt to Edward Said, a founder of the field of postcolonial studies, who, crucially for us, documented the relationship between colonialism and "imaginative geography." Since Said's *Orientalism* appeared in the late 1970s, geographers and others have further explored the spatial dimensions of colonialism as invention and reality. When Venegas and

Moore contend in this volume that colonizers transformed California and New Mexico into "America's Orient," a place for moderns to view the primitives, whether Indigenous, Spanish, or Mexican, they build on foundations laid by Said's exploration of the "invention" of the "Orient." In the nineteenth century, Europeans and Euro-Americans, at home and abroad, developed a constellation of ideas about the superiority and rightful dominance of the "West" and the inferiority and deserved subordination of the "Orient"—the Middle East and Asia. Said terms this body of thought "Orientalism," and he shows how Western nations deployed their military, political, economic, and cultural power to impose these ideas on subject populations, making them seem real to colonized and colonizer alike. When American tourists came west on the trains, they were already well versed in Orientalist thinking. They knew they would see savages or primitives because they were already equipped with colonial narratives that had told them so.[1]

Part of the appeal of the imaginary Wests for Euro-American tourists derived from their complex relationship with modernity. They embraced modern civilization, including the conquest of Indigenous peoples and the incorporation of the West into the industrialized nation. At the same time, however, white tourists worried that modernity, with its railroads, telegraph lines, and growing cities, was crushing the West and, with it, American democracy. Colonizers assuaged these fears by touring an imaginary West, a frontier of nostalgia where they could encounter Native peoples who, as primitives, clung to values and practiced skills the colonizers prized, but feared were lost in modern America. As Moore writes, white tourists stopped in early twentieth-century Albuquerque to see Indigenous artisans producing traditional crafts, which the tourists valued as antidotes to the mass-produced items of the modern world.

But the colonizers who mourned the loss of Indigenous lifeways nevertheless concluded their nostalgic narratives by asserting that Indians "inevitably" lost to the forces of modernity. In so doing, they minimized their responsibility for the lives, cultures, and places that the conquest had destroyed, from which destruction they had benefited. In late nineteenth-century California, as Yolanda Venegas explains, Euro-Americans began restoring crumbling Spanish missions built in the previous century as a way of developing and preserving collective memories about a pious, pastoral way of life they believed could not survive in a society of hardworking Yankee capitalists. For the colonizers, the imaginary West of "Spanish" California helped to legitimate conquest and to evoke a past that served as a soothing counter to the destabilizing forces of modernity.

Through a discussion of Helen Hunt Jackson's popular novel *Ramona*, published in 1884 to protest American treatment of the California Indigenous peoples, Venegas considers how bodies imagined by colonizers embodied their beliefs about racialized conquest. In *Ramona*, Jackson portrays the near decimation of California's Indigenous peoples as tragic, and she condemns the American ideology of Manifest Destiny that supported this bloody conquest. But she also represents Indians as primitives so tied to the past that they cannot survive in Anglo California. Jackson is similarly critical of the effect of Manifest Destiny on the "Spanish" landed elite and Mexican workers, yet she depicts these people as also unable to flourish in a modern Anglo nation. Thus, as Venegas demonstrates, although Jackson's novel begins as a protest against racial injustice, it ends as a justification for the conquest of California and the subsequent racialized subordination of the conquered. Jackson conveys the seeming inevitability of this story in large part by representing bodies of Indians, Mexicans, and Spaniards as racialized, often sexualized, and always inferior.

In the last article in this section, "Working on the Domestic Frontier: American Indian Domestic Servants in White Women's Households in the San Francisco Bay Area, 1920–1940," Margaret D. Jacobs examines a very different imaginary West from those of Venegas and Moore. Jacobs describes how colonial networks, developed as part of federal Indian policies, transformed the houses of white, middle-class women in the San Francisco Bay Area into a "domestic frontier." The outing system sent Indian women to work as domestic servants in white homes. Agents of the Office of Indian Affairs (now Bureau of Indian Affairs) in the late nineteenth and early twentieth centuries developed this system in tandem with the boarding schools to transform the children of defeated savages into civilized beings. Firm in their belief in the "home" as the crucible of civilization, Euro-Americans saw such placements as the last step in colonizing Indian women. Posted to this "domestic frontier," Indian women would lose their identity as Indians and become fully "civilized," or modern. The reality of the outing system proved quite different from the imagined scenario. Jacobs shows that Indigenous servants did not simply acquiesce to assimilation. Instead, white mistresses and Native servants negotiated conditions of employment, which is to say their understandings of class, citizenship, gender, and race within a place created and sustained by colonialism.

In the Wests imagined by colonizers, as described by Venegas, Moore, and Jacobs, Indians happily accept their defeat, a fate that includes temporary employment in the tourist industry, followed by their disappearance as a people, perhaps through assimilation programs. But Moore and Jacobs also depict entirely different Wests, places where Native women contested colonialism. Moore writes about Elle of Ganado, or Asdzaa Lichii' (Red Woman), who lived the real and complicated life of a Diné woman in a post-conquest world. She was employed by the Fred Harvey Company, a corporation dedicated to promoting tourism of the Southwest, which built restaurants and hotels at train stations and staged performances of "authentic" Indian life at trackside. Elle and her family earned their livelihoods by participating in these re-creations of

Indian life as imagined by Euro-Americans. But as a paid performer of Native authenticity, she was hardly passive, negotiating with the company about the terms of her employment—she demonstrated weaving—and using her wages to sustain her life as a Navajo. Elle moved regularly between Albuquerque, where she performed as a Native American, and her Diné home in Ganado, Arizona. Neither a colonial subject nor a pre-contact Navajo, she embodied an identity that, however contingent, conflicted, and contested, was of her own making.

The young Indian women placed by the outing system into the homes of white matrons in the Bay Area also strove to make their own decisions despite federal oversight and regulation and the demands of their employers. They protested poor working conditions and unfair wage practices, insisted on returning to their home reservations to participate in their communities' annual subsistence cycle, and pursued the pleasures (and dangers) of modern urban sexuality. Both Moore and Jacobs demonstrate that Native women exercised agency, but were not free agents. To use Jacobs's term, they contested "colonial scripts."

The articles in "Colonized Places" thus juxtapose the work of colonization as imagined by its beneficiaries with the actual process on the ground. They contrast imagined places—whether "Spanish California" or the "home"—with actual sites of encounter between colonizer and colonized as mediated by the imaginaries. In the articles by Venegas and Moore, we see how the iron networks of the railroads, visible forces of modernization, enabled the development of modern tourism that, in turn, sparked and relied on the development of western imaginaries. Euro-Americans who rode west by rail in modern comfort saw the "authentic" Indian villages constructed at depots and restored California missions as nostalgic celebrations of colonialism. Jacobs explores the centrality of the culturally freighted spatial trope of "home" to the colonial project, as manifested in federal Indian policy during the Era of Assimilation. Equally important, Moore and Jacobs help us gauge, at least to some extent, Indigenous women's experiences within colonialism, how they shaped their roles within the tourist industry and as domestic servants. Colonialism constituted many places in the modern West, but Indigenous women nevertheless found ways to construct alternate places and identities.

Notes

1. Edward W. Said, *Orientalism* (New York: Random House, 1978), 1–28, 71–73. A good, recent study of the imaginative geography of colonialism is Derek Gregory, "Between the Book and the Lamp: Imaginative Geographies of Egypt, 1849–1850," *Transactions of the Institute of British Geographers*, New Series 20, no. 1 (1995): 29–57.

CHAPTER 5

The Erotics of Racialization

Gender and Sexuality in the Making of California

YOLANDA VENEGAS

> *Indigenous people understand that there is no difference between the telling and the material. They understand how we all, in fact, live inside and through the narratives we tell and that the importance in telling stories is inseparable from the identity, community, and history they compose and the spiritual, economic and political realities on which they depend and which they subvert or preserve.*
>
> —joannemariebarker and Teresia Teaiwa, "Native InFormation"[1]

The metaphoric use of the female body in white men's conquests and wars is a global phenomenon as old as Portuguese navigation. Women as symbols—particularly women as sex objects—have been a cornerstone of Orientalist ideology and, hence, essential to the entire colonial undertaking.[2] In the Americas, sixteenth-century engravings depicting the encounter between the Old World and the New represented the recently "discovered" continent, "America," as a naked woman awakened from savagery by a European man with cross and compass in hand. In this dichotomous portrayal of New World savagery and European civilization, the lascivious image of America alluded to the voracious and erotic Amerindian women pervasive in New World accounts. With the invention of the printing press in the sixteenth century, these feminized representations of the New World became widely available.[3] Significantly, the sexualized representations of Amerindian women were an integral part of the very first writings introducing the newly discovered world and its Others to Europeans.

The symbolic use of women in colonization projects involves imagining the land about to be colonized as female and repeatedly constructing Native women in ways that justify not only the violence and the destruction of the conquest but also the subsequent marginalization of the colonized. For example, in the Southwest, the U.S. invasion in the early 1800s was a gendered enterprise in which "Spanish" women symbolized the desirable part of the country about to be conquered, and dichotomous constructs of morally and racially inferior Mexicanos justified expansion and war.[4] In *Presidarias y Pobladoras: Spanish-Mexican Women in Frontier Monterey, Alta California, 1770–1821*, Antonia Castañeda examines the narratives of the first Euro-Americans to write about California; she finds that negative stereotypes of Native women and lower-class Mexicanas combined with romanticized stereotypes of upper-class Spanish women constituted a politics of sex central to the ideology of Manifest Destiny.[5] In the context of emerging Social Darwinism, the denigrating portrayals of Native and Mexicana women served the inaccurate judgment of the character of Southwestern peoples. Meanwhile, upper-class Californianas became highly sexualized targets of Euro-American chivalric missions that were used to justify territorial conquest and war.[6] Yet how did the symbolic use of Native, Mexicana, and Californiana women evolve from the period of western territorial conquest to the turn of the twentieth century, when racialization processes began to be justified and legitimated through romance and nostalgia? Indeed, how did the politics of sex essential to the ideology of Manifest Destiny evolve to better serve the hegemonic needs of a newly racialized California?

This essay traces the symbolic use of Southwestern women in California's popular culture from the early 1800s to the turn of the twentieth century. In the late 1800s, as the United States shifted its imperial gaze abroad, the Spanish-heritage movement emerged as a regional manifestation of much broader national movements to secure hegemonic dominance at home. My discussion of the movement's most important novel, *Ramona*, and of other cultural manifestations promoting the state's Spanish heritage shows how the discursive dimensions of the racial order emerging in late nineteenth-century California were grounded in a gendered and sexually charged Manifest Destiny ideology regenerated through the romanticization of the state's Spanish past.

The "Orient" of the United States

The late 1800s marked the beginning of massive cultural movements to remember, recover, romanticize, and celebrate the cultures of the newly conquered peoples. Frederick Jackson Turner's "The Significance of the Frontier in American History," a presidential address delivered to the American Historical

Association, was presented at a conference organized in conjunction with the 1893 Columbian Centennial Exposition in Chicago at which, as Shari Huhndorf has pointed out, "the nation celebrated a particular vision of its origins begun in a racial conquest when Columbus first arrived in the Americas just over 400 years earlier."[7] Thus, with the United States' shift to territorial conquest abroad came a nationwide movement to secure hegemonic dominance of the conquered territories at home through the use of romance and nostalgia. The use of sentimental discourses to justify Manifest Destiny and to reaffirm and consolidate Euro-American dominance was a domestic version of what Renato Rosaldo termed "imperialist nostalgia"--a type of nostalgia that accompanies a particular sense of mission, a "white man's burden," in which "a person kills somebody and then mourns his or her victim."[8] Since the late 1800s this has been a useful means for the agents of destruction, at home and abroad, to secure the appearance of their own innocence.

In *Going Native*, Huhndorf describes how, especially after the end of the U.S.-Indian wars marked by the Wounded Knee Massacre of 1890 (when the Native American population of the United States was close to its nadir of 250,000 reached in 1900), the conquering culture began a feverish appropriation of Native symbols and myths to redefine itself in nationalistic terms. By refiguring the history of conquest, this attempt to remember Native America, now redefined as white America's past, helped create a new model of "Americanness" that privileged the Euro-American middle classes when the nation was fractured by turn-of-the-century labor disputes, waves of immigration, and the divisive aftermath of the Civil War.[9] While the nation as a whole turned to Native America to redefine itself, during the same period in California, the "vanishing past" that preoccupied historians, ethnographers, and a host of enthusiastic businessmen was the state's Spanish heritage, now ironically claimed by the group that had so recently dispossessed the Californios.

The nationwide move by the conquering culture to reimagine its objects of conquest and thus reconstitute a raced and gendered sense of national identity assumed various forms in different regions. The tendency to silence specific regional genocidal histories and the marginalization processes that took place after the Euro-American invasion remained uniform, however. As Jimmie Durham points out, since its inception the United States has nurtured a nostalgia for America's "loss of innocence," for a past when America was "truly good."[10] This nostalgia stems not from an invented perception of guilt but rather from concrete histories of genocide and displacement. America's narrative about itself has its operational center in a hidden history of its relationship with American Indians. In California, the Spanish-heritage fantasy is the regional form of this centuries-old denial, and it reflects the particularly violent history of the region.

Gente de Razón and Indios in the Making of Californio Identity

When Euro-Americans began their zealous appropriation of the Spanish heritage, they were continuing a racial project begun by the first wave of colonizers a century earlier.[11] Although the idea that California's first settlers were Spanish continues to permeate popular culture, few Spaniards made their way to California. In fact, as Carey McWilliams, Douglas Monroy, and others point out, the majority of settlers during the colonial period were not Spanish but mestizos of Mexican and Indigenous descent.[12] Lisbeth Haas notes that the settlers who came to California and other parts of the Spanish frontier came from places with a high degree of racial mixing, such as Baja California and Sinaloa.[13] The multiethnic composition of these colonists included mestizos, acculturated Indigenous people from other parts of the Spanish frontier, mulattos, blacks, and a small number of Spanish-descent individuals. California's Native population, which constituted most of the labor force during California's "Spanish" days, also added significantly to the ethnic diversity of the region. Given the mestizaje of the settlers, the opposition between *gente de razón* and local Indians (between the "bearers of civilization, those endowed with reason," and the "heathen/uncivilized") became an important means through which the new landed elite forged a collective Californio identity.

The distinction between Indians and *gente de razón* became increasingly important for Californios after Mexico gained independence from Spain (1821). The Californios were new elite, retired military men, or children of soldiers who only recently had come to control the economic and social institutions of Alta California. After Mexican independence, as questions of what freedom meant, who would own mission lands, and who would control the labor of Indigenous people emerged, the category of *gente de razón* was used to severely limit the conditions of freedom and land rights for Native Californians.[14] In her analysis of the construction of Californio identity, in the testimonies of Californios collected by Hubert H. Bancroft, Rosaura Sánchez noted that the distinction between Indian and non-Indian was the linchpin around which discourses of collective identity were articulated.[15] Although in Spanish America legal, social, and economic stratification was organized around the caste system—a system that categorized people by their purported racial heritage—in California there was a shift from caste distinctions based on race, color, and ancestry to *gente de razón*, a category defined on the basis of culture. Discourses of caste continued to be important in colonial California, for notions of *pureza de sangre*—purity of blood—continued to hold sway and fair skin was highly valued; yet the heterogeneity of the population made caste distinctions inoperative.[16] Instead, Californio identity focused on the perceived insurmountable cultural, linguistic, and ethnic differences between *gente de razón* and Indians.

Californio identity was thus forged through what Étienne Balibar has called "culturalist" racism in which culture functions like nature to explain, naturalize, and legitimize racist conduct.[17] For the Californio *gente de razón*, the claim to Spanish heritage and Spanish culture became a way to mask their mestizo heritage, justify the racism of extermination, and legitimize the exploitation of the Indians on the basis of their superiority. Ironically, within the same century, the Californio elite would themselves be subjected to Manifest Destiny's overt racism and its regenerated varieties.[18]

The Spanish-Heritage Movement

After the 1870s, when Euro-Americans had consolidated political and economic control of the state, the myth about California's Spanish origins became part of a larger Spanish-heritage movement. In this movement newly established romance writers, painters, capitalist developers, and local civic and historical organizations collaborated to hispanicize California. The population that came to settle California after the U.S. takeover included a diverse group of foreign and native-born German, Irish, French, English, Italian, and other Euro-Americans. As they came in contact with Mexicanos, Chinese, and other ethnic groups in California, Euro-Americans came to use the collective designation "white" to overshadow their own diversity. At the same time, however, Euro-Americans appropriated the notion that California's "original" inhabitants were "pure-blooded" Spaniards, because it provided a needed racial and social history.[19] For uprooted Euro-American settlers, the Spanish-heritage myth provided an epic antiquity, a California Plymouth Rock as ancient (and pure-blooded European) as the nation's traditional cultural centers in Boston and New York.[20] The Spanish-heritage myth also became a way to manage and account for the undeniable Mexicana/o presence throughout California—a presence that was crucial to California's economic development. In other words, California's "pure-blooded" Spanish heritage, complete with its missions, pious priests, and "humble Indians," provided Euro-Americans with antiquity and a sense of stability in a newly racialized California.

Euro-Americans had not always thought favorably of California's Spanish heritage. During the period before and immediately after the U.S. invasion of the Southwest (1846—48), foreigners arriving in California viewed the Californios' claim to European ancestry with derision, describing them in highly racialized ways. The writings of the first Euro-Americans describing California and its inhabitants were integral to the ideology of Manifest Destiny. In 1844, Thomas Jefferson Farnham described the Californios as "an imbecile, pusillanimous race of men, and unfit to control the destinies of that beautiful country."[21] In the first half of the nineteenth century, images of the Spanish dons as lazy, indolent, and ultimately unworthy of their land and their women served to prepare the ideological ground for the subsequent territorial conquest. Immediately after the U.S. conquest (after 1848) a movement began to eradicate all "Spanish" dwellings, civic buildings, and urban structures.[22] The process of consolidating Euro-American hegemonic control included ridding California of its "backward" culture and institutions. As Sánchez and Castañeda observe, the notion that mismanaged land awaited Euro-American improvement was a primary component of the ideology of Manifest Destiny.[23] This negative attitude toward the state's Spanish heritage began to change dramatically after 1869, when the transcontinental railroad made the Southwest the "Orient" of the United States. Soon California's Spanish heritage became a tourist attraction.[24] By the late 1800s, East Coast tourists, whose middle-class status precluded travel to Africa or Asia, could temporarily escape the growing pressures of industrialization by experiencing exotic people and cultures within the borders of the United States. The influx of tourists constituted a final step in the Euro-American domination of the region.

As a result of the Spanish-heritage movement, California now has more statues of Spanish "explorers" than any other Southwestern state. Many of the public parks dotting the Pacific Coast boast statues or plaques guiding one's gaze from the vast Pacific Ocean to the brush-lined hillsides, thus evoking European discoveries of uninhabited lands. Despite decades of wide-ranging Chicana/o and Native challenges to the state's Eurocentric history, strategically placed "historic sites" combined with Spanish-heritage cultural events (such as the many annual "Old Spanish Days" fiestas held statewide) continually reinscribe the nineteenth-century Spanish-heritage myth and its implicit forms of gendered racism.

In the Tracks of *Ramona*

The Spanish-heritage movement was, above all, a synthesis of Euro-American invaders' ideologies that created a myth, which in time became the basis for California's unique identity and its textbook history. A curious conglomeration of East Coast intellectuals—including novelist Helen Hunt Jackson, painter Charles Christian Nahl, historian Hubert H. Bancroft, and Southwest promoter Charles Fletcher Lummis—participated in the creation of the Spanish-heritage myth. Varied cultural expressions of the Spanish-heritage myth fulfilled the ideological needs of newly established Euro-American Californians in several ways: they concealed the state's violent origins, legitimized Manifest Destiny by asserting white supremacy (and thereby assuaging white guilt where the effects of Manifest Destiny were blatantly obvious), and justified emerging racialization processes that placed the "conquered" population at the bottom of the socioeconomic scale. Integral to this process was an erotics of racialization that redeployed age-old images of exotic Native maidens ("squaws"), Californianas of "pure Spanish" blood, and lowly Mexicanas within the emergent rhetoric of romance and nostalgia.

Literature presenting romantic versions of California before annexation was key in the creation of the Spanish-heritage movement. In fact, novels and short stories celebrating the missions and California's pastoral days became a distinct genre after the 1880s. Euro-American writers, such as Bret Harte, George Wharton James, and, most prominently, Helen Hunt Jackson, produced novels that became integral to the creation of California's fantasy heritage. Of these novels, Jackson's *Ramona* (1884) was the first and quickly became the most important.[25] According to Richard Griswold del Castillo, the novel eventually went through 135 editions, was published in many European languages, and was adapted for at least four movies and numerous plays.[26]

Ramona tells the story of a half-Indian, half-white orphan adopted by the Morenos, a "Spanish" Californio family. Ramona, a dark-haired beauty with steel-blue eyes, falls in love with Alessandro Assis, a Luiseño laborer hired by the Morenos.[27] The novel is set in southern California during the late 1800s, a period of dramatic sociopolitical transformation in the area. As the love story of Ramona and Alessandro unfolds, readers consume Jackson's highly romanticized version of the golden days of the Californio ranches and missions.

The first part of the novel creates a romantic version of bygone Californio rancher days as it narrates the dispossession of Californios by "American hounds." The Moreno ranch house, "one of the best specimens to be found in California,"[28] provides a backdrop for the soon-to-be-gone ranchero days. The book's early passages are filled with descriptions of the pious nature of the family matriarch Señora Moreno and her obedient son Felipe who struggle to maintain their land and way of life. During General Moreno's heyday, readers are told, "It had been a free-handed boast of his that never less than fifty persons, men, women and children were fed within his gates each day."[29] These descriptions of a "picturesque life, with more sentiment and gayety . . . than will ever be seen again" are interspersed with specific details about how the Moreno family lost their land grant, which at one time encompassed "a radius of forty miles."[30] After the surrender of California, the United States Land Commission "undertook to sift and adjust Mexican land titles; and that was the way it had come about that the Señora Moreno now called herself a poor woman. Tract after tract, her lands had been taken away from her." This was the reason Señora Moreno believed Euro-American settlers were "thieves" and "hounds."[31] In *Ramona* Californians bear the brunt of Mexico's surrender; they lose everything. Still, Señora Moreno manages to hold onto enough wealth to have her own river, meadows, and orchards.

Soon after the novel's beginning, the star-crossed lovers, Ramona and Alessandro, declare their feelings for each other. This presents them with a series of obstacles rooted in sociopolitical problems. First, the lovers face the opposition of Señora Moreno, who cannot accept her adopted daughter's love for an Indian. When Ramona tells her stepmother she intends to marry Alessandro, Señora Moreno responds, "'You marry an Indian? Never! Are you mad?'"[32] She thus articulates the widespread disdain for Native peoples in Californio society. Ramona eventually defies Señora Moreno's authority by running away with Alessandro. The young couple thereafter experience a series of tragedies that mirror the annihilation of southern California's Native communities as a result of nineteenth-century Euro-American settlement.

The first of these tragedies, and the one that initially compels Alessandro to leave the Moreno household, is the death of his father. After a long absence during which Ramona believes Alessandro is dead, her beloved returns from his village in Temecula and tells her about a violent raid. Armed Americans arrived at his village, announced to residents that they had won a suit in San Francisco over their land, and at gunpoint evicted a village full of men, women, and children. Alessandro's father was dragged out of his home after refusing to leave, and when Alessandro arrived, he found his father sitting on the ground, no longer cognizant, with their belongings piled up around him. The fierceness of the raid had driven Alessandro's father mad. Despite the fact that Alessandro is left homeless after the devastation of Temecula, Ramona flees the Moreno home to live with him in the neighboring village of San Pasquale. Ramona and Alessandro build a home and live happily in San Pasquale, but their stay is short lived. Less than two years after Ramona and Alessandro establish themselves and begin to farm, Euro-American settlers begin to stake claims on the San Pasquale village lands. Although the village leader, Ysidro, has a land title from the Mexican government, the San Pasquale valley is declared property of the U.S. government and put on the market. The couple soon find themselves homeless. Alessandro bargains with the land's new owner for his own horse and wagon. Tragedy continues to follow the couple, leading eventually to Alessandro's madness and death. Ramona and her new daughter are saved from further despair by Felipe Moreno, who takes them back to the Moreno estate. In the end, Felipe also finds the methods, aims, and standards of the incoming Euro-Americans odious. He feels isolated in a country where even the Spanish language is being lost. The novel ends with Ramona and Felipe leaving California to start a new life in Mexico City.

Helen Hunt Jackson was clear about her strategy in *Ramona*. Before writing her novel, she had served as Indian commissioner in California and had tried to influence national sentiment about the plight of Native Americans by writing *A Century of Dishonor* (1881), a controversial history of U.S. treatment of Native people. This effort to affect the American people's conscience failed, so Jackson turned to writing a sugarcoated vehicle for her message and appropriated the increasingly popular genre of historical romance to do so. In his discussion of *Ramona*, Kevin Starr notes that popular audiences generally missed the novel's political message and focused instead on the romantic presentations of California's pastoral days. Starr attributes the paradox of a politically charged novel being turned into a founding fable for the state's Spanish-heritage myth to a process of appropriation as corrective. According to Starr, *Ramona* effectively made the mission era part of American history.[33] The novel atoned for Spanish California by documenting what had been done, while simultaneously making the Spanish past available for the purposes of Euro-American settlers seeking to bolster the class and racial hierarchies of their own society. David Hurst Thomas, on the other hand, attributes *Ramona's* failure to influence reform as the result of timing. According to Thomas, although Jackson intended to write "a story that would do for the Indians a thousandth part that *Uncle Tom's Cabin* did for the Negro," *Ramona's* timing was off.[34] Americans were ready to hear about slavery in *Uncle Tom's Cabin*; the issue had in fact been festering for a century. However, *Ramona's* indictment of the U.S. government's unacknowledged treatment of Native America was denounced as falsehood. Thomas's assertion that America was not ready in 1884 to reckon with the unjust treatment of Native people makes sense, particularly when we consider that the United States still denies the Native American holocaust that marks its beginning.[35] Yet, as Thomas and Starr point out, Ramona triumphed as a regional romance central to the state's Spanish-heritage myth.

Ramona's paradox—how a novel aimed at raising American consciousness regarding the devastation of Native communities became instead propaganda in the creation of the state's fantasy heritage—can be understood in part by examining how the novel explicitly indicts the effects of Manifest Destiny while implicitly legitimizing them. For example, although the novel narrates the fate of Native California resulting from Euro-American settlement through the series of tragedies endured by Ramona and Alessandro, it also silences the devastation of Native communities during the mission period by presenting a romanticized version of colonization in which benevolent Franciscan friars brought enlightenment to welcoming Natives.

According to *Ramona's* romantic version of the missions, pious Franciscan padres, at great sacrifice to themselves, dedicated their lives to the altruistic goal of bringing civilization to welcoming Natives. In *Ramona's* version of history, California's Indigenous people lived peacefully in the missions. There was, readers are told, "a deep-seated attachment on the part of the Indians and the older Mexican families in the country to the Franciscan Order."[36] During the process of colonization, they were baptized, they acquired agricultural skills, they learned how to produce a wide variety of products, and they generally benefited from the civilizing efforts of the Catholic Church. Father Junípero Serra, who led the missionaries into California, is remembered with nostalgia as the "master in this land," a man who past eighty years old, walked from San Diego to Monterey, with "a running ulcer in one of his legs."[37] With deep sentimentality, readers are told how Father Serra began his work, "he went up and down for those first terrible weeks, nursing the sick, praying with the dying, and burying the dead, from the pestilence-stricken Mexican ships lying in the harbor."[38] Not mentioned at all in this romantic description of the establishment of the first mission is the fact that Native deaths throughout the colonization process were caused by European diseases and unbearable living conditions at the prison-like missions.[39] The reader's attention is instead selectively focused on "a pile of crumbling ruins" and "a few old olive-trees and palms," the only traces of Serra's "heroic labors and hard-won success."[40] Yet the main representative of *Ramona's* romantic Catholicism is Father Salvierderra, who had lost not only his health but also his heart after secularization when he witnessed "the Indian converts disappearing, driven back to their original wildernesses, the last traces of the noble work of his order being rapidly swept away."[41] And finally, readers are told that during General Moreno's time, Sundays at the Moreno ranch were a scene to behold, like the scenes at the missions: "Hundreds of Indians living within its borders . . . the chapel full of kneeling men and women; those who could not find room inside kneeling on the garden walks outside; Father Salvierderra, in gorgeous vestments, coming, at close of the services, slowly down the aisle, the close-packed rows of worshippers parting to right and left to let him through, all looking up eagerly for his blessing."[42] These examples illustrate a basic assumption, one that was widely propagated by Californios and generations of clerical historians, such as Zephyrin Engelhardt and Maynard Geiger, that the missionization process brought enlightenment to Native people.

The fact that the presidio compound and the mission complex during the colonial period were integral components of a feudal-like forced labor system is imperceptible in *Ramona's* nostalgic presentation of missionization. The system in which Señora Moreno spent her "gleeful youth" was actually a system adapted from the corporate Indigenous community in central Mexico, in which Franciscans subsidized the military by providing the food and other supplies needed during the colonization effort.[43] Native Californians steadfastly resisted colonization through resistance strategies, such as labor strikes, subversion of agricultural production, escape from the missions during the colonial period, and through raids and war after secularization, when Euro-Americans increasingly joined Californios in the intrusion of Native lands and the exploitation of Native people.[44] Native women played a pivotal role in resistance activities. They faced the tyranny of the church and state with powerful ideologies "derived from a non-Western religious-political system of power in which women were central to the ritual and spiritual life of the tribe." For example, in 1785, Toypurina, a medicine woman from the vicinity of San Gabriel Mission, organized a religious-political movement that confirmed the power of female deities and visionaries to resist colonial domination.[45]

Ramona's presentation of the primary Native characters also reasserts the dichotomy of savage and civilized, thereby naturalizing the disappearance of Native communities due to Manifest Destiny. Alessandro's fate shows that in the end only the "civilized" Euro-Americans triumph. Euro-American readers might have been sympathetic toward the poor Indian Alessandro, yet surely they were not surprised by his death. After all, the distinction between savagery and civilization was fundamental not only in constructing Californio identity but also in the American imagination.[46] At first glance, Alessandro is represented as handsome, honest, peaceful, and industrious; not all Luiseños are treated so favorably. Alessandro is exceptional among his race. At times though, Alessandro's inferiority is clear. He remains a servant for the Morenos, an "appropriate" occupation for an Indian, and he acts in simple, childlike ways. When Alessandro first sees Ramona, he is so overwhelmed that he cannot understand what is happening to him because, after all, he was not "what the world calls a civilized man."[47] If he had been civilized, he would have been able to analyze and reflect, but "he had to bring to bear on his present situation only simple, primitive, uneducated instincts and impulses."[48] Throughout the novel, he remains "the gentle Alessandro, only an Indian."[49] Although the reader is compelled to feel sympathy for Alessandro, he is clearly "othered." Significantly, in the end, Alessandro and his father go insane and die. In an ideologically constructed world of progress the two Native characters are depicted as unfit for the modern world, inevitable victims of Manifest Destiny. Euro-Americans who read *Ramona* could thus acknowledge the destructive effects of their settlement, yet they did not need to feel guilty, since by 1850 the idea that Native people were doomed to extinction was firmly in place.[50]

Examining the novel's regeneration of Manifest Destiny's raced politics of sex shows there is really no paradox to the novel's regional triumph: *Ramona* followed a long tradition of appealing to an American libido hungry for exotic Native maidens to justify violence and racial domination. Throughout the novel readers (who may still have felt ambivalent about California Indians) are lured with familiar and at times exhilarating constructs of Southwestern women. Images of exotic Native women and the binary constructions of

Californianas, Mexicanas, and Indian "squaws" central to the ideology used to justify western expansion and the U.S. conquest of California from 1846 to 1848 are regenerated in *Ramona*. As the story begins, readers learn that Señora Moreno "was of the past," while "Ramona was of the present. For one eye that could see the significant, at times solemn, beauty of the Señora's pale and shadowed countenance, there were a hundred that flashed with eager pleasure at the barest glimpse of Ramona's face."[51] Significantly, although during the early to mid-1800s the revolution in scientific thinking about race would have made the idea of a desirable half-Indian, half-white woman unimaginable, *Ramona* highlights the heroine's mixed-blood heritage and makes it the focal point of her exotic beauty. Ramona's mixed-blood heritage made her, "to the world at large, a far more important person than the Señora herself."[52] All men who saw her, even the devout Father Salvierderra, were stirred for "a man must be dead not to thrill" at Ramona's beauty. "She had just enough of olive tint in her complexion to underlie and enrich her skin without making it swarthy. Her hair was like her Indian mother's, heavy and black, *but* her eyes were like her father's, steel-blue."[53] When Alessandro catches his first glimpse of Ramona, she is by the brook: "Her hair in disorder, her sleeves pinned loosely on her shoulders, her whole face aglow with the earnestness of her task, she bent low over the stones, rinsing the altarcloth up and down in the water, anxiously scanning it, then plunging it in again. . . . The sunset beams played around her hair like a halo; the whole place was aglow with red light, and her face was kindled into transcendent beauty."[54]

By having readers gaze at Ramona's exotic beauty through Alessandro's eyes and otherwise exoticizing Ramona's Indianness, Jackson tapped into an old tradition. As Richard Hill notes, the first Europeans reporting on the "New World" created an image of Indians that was exotic, erotic, and dangerous.[55] Hill traces the "sexual savage" imagery from 1492 to the era of western expansion, when Euro-American voyeurism—watching Native women bathing and playing together—had remarkable appeal. Images of beautiful Indian princesses fueled the sexual fantasies of white men, while Indian men were seen as savages who had to be tamed or destroyed. In a culture founded on a tradition of conquest, sexy Indian women symbolized the spoils of victory, while savage Indian men (ready to kidnap helpless white women for their carnal pleasures) came to be seen as a threat to the well-being and success of Euro-Americans. Since Indian men were considered uncivilized, un-Christian, dangerous, and incapable of becoming good slaves, Native genocide by the hands of Europeans was justified.

Moreover, by exoticizing her Indianness and simultaneously hispanicizing Ramona, Jackson captivated readers with a turn-of-the-century Pocahontas. In her analysis of the "Pocahontas perplex," Rayna Green finds that the image of the exotic Indian Princess has had a defining impact on the American nation-making process. The image of Pocahontas, the beautiful Indian Princess ready to save, serve, and, if necessary, die for white men, appeared in the first writings attempting to forge a unique American identity distinct from Europe. In hispanicizing Ramona, Jackson proves that indeed both the "civilized" Indian Princess and her double the Indian "squaw" "wait to be resurrected when our anxieties about who we are make us recall her from her woodland retreat."[56] In fact, as the following discussion will show, the "good" Indian Princess and the "bad" Indian squaw are summoned to resolve not only who "we" (Americans) are but also what "we" have done and where "we" are going.

Despite Ramona's Indian blood, Jackson constructs her culturally as a fully assimilated Spanish señorita. As a proper "Spanish" señorita she had attended private Catholic school in Los Angeles and learned all the skills characteristic of a refined señorita: embroidery, weaving, and painting. Even after she leaves her adopted Spanish family and goes Native with her love, Alessandro, she acts according to her Spanish upbringing. She decorates their two-room house with an altar and Catholic saints and demands that Alessandro build a wide veranda in front of their new home, because she cannot do without it. Readers learn that Ramona's house was different from the houses in the rest of the Indian village: "it looked like a palace to the San Pasquale people."[57] At the request of Ramona who remained a fervent Catholic, Alessandro had procured a Madonna statuette and built a special niche in their new home for it. Below the niche, Ramona "hung her gold rosary and the ivory Christ"[58] so that eventually the niche became like a village shrine. The women in the different Native villages they lived in loved Ramona because she was so fine and so different—meaning civilized—"she had been like a sort of missionary in the valley ever since she came."[59]

Jackson's ranking of civilized ways above California's Indigenous lifeways is not surprising. One year before she wrote *Ramona*, she served as commissioner of Indian Affairs, assigned to report on the conditions of California Indians. In her report to President Chester Arthur and Congress, she recommended, among other things, the establishment of more schools in California's Native communities to assist the assimilation process. At a time when the idea that the solution to "the Indian problem" was extermination, her call for assimilation was progressive. By hispanicizing Ramona and placing civilized ways above those of California's Indigenous women, the novel reasserts a racial hierarchy that once again naturalizes the effects of Manifest Destiny—in particular, the Native genocide the "settlement" of California required.

Although *Ramona* presents a plea for California's Indigenous population, the novel continues the repression of the "non-civilized" Native woman in other important ways.[60] For example, Ramona's Native mother is completely silenced. Readers never learn what happened to her after her white husband took Ramona from her to give her to Señora Gonzaga. Was Ramona's mother alive at that point? Did she agree to give her daughter away? Despite the fact that Ramona asks, "Who was my mother?" "Is my mother alive? Where does she live?" we never hear of the mother's feelings, experience, and historicity.[61] She remains a nameless, silenced "squaw" until the end. All we are ever told is that she is "a squaw with several Indian children"—a fact suggesting a promiscuous nature.[62] The silence surrounding Ramona's mother haunts the story from beginning to end. It is highlighted every time Ramona asks questions about her mother. This glaring silence discloses that neither Ramona nor her mother are the subjects of *Ramona's* story; they are merely sites on which to make an explicit plea for the Indian cause through a nostalgic tale of California's rancho days, while implicitly justifying the effects of Manifest Destiny and reasserting its racialized tenants through the symbolic use of Native women. Reading *Ramona* against the grain of an ideology ostensibly about California's Native people reveals that Ramona and her mother are like the sati in colonial Indian debates of women, "neither subject, nor object, but ground" on which to launch a redeeming plea for California's Indigenous population.[63]

If in constructing Ramona as a thrilling hybrid beauty, fully assimilated as a proper Spanish señorita, *Ramona* continues to fuel sexual stereotypes of Indians as it reinscribes a racial hierarchy that places the Spanish Californianas above Mexicanas and Native women, the respective places of each of these groups in Californio society is clearly elaborated through Señora Moreno and the rest of the women populating the pages of *Ramona*. Señora Moreno's heritage as a pure-blooded Spaniard is established soon after *Ramona* begins. As readers move through the Moreno adobe house with its "delightsome" arched veranda, the señora wonders why it is that she is so compelled by the smell of the musk in the "great red water-jars, hand-made by the Indians." Father Salvierderra who has just arrived clarifies for her, "'It is in your blood Señora, . . . When I was last in your father's house in Seville, your mother sent for me to her room, and under her window was a stone balcony full of growing musk.'"[64] "Through wars, insurrections, revolutions, downfalls, Spanish, Mexican, civil, ecclesiastical, [Señora Moreno's] standpoint, her poise, remained the same." As depicted by Jackson, "she simply grew more and more proudly, passionately, a Spaniard and a Moreno; more and more staunchly and fierily a Catholic, and a lover of the Franciscans."[65]

This construct of the Spanish Señora Moreno regenerates the Californio racial fantasy about California's origins. By constructing Señora Moreno as a pure-blooded Spaniard and reaffirming the dichotomy between Spanish women and inferior Mexicanas, *Ramona* rearticulates colonial California's racial hierarchies in a veil of romance and nostalgia.

In contrast to the pure-blooded Señora Moreno are the Mexican maids: Margarita; her mother, "old Marda the cook"; Anita; and María. Of these maids, the saucy Margarita, "the youngest and prettiest of the maids," has the most prominent role in *Ramona*.[66] As the romantic picture of the typical Spanish rancho begins to emerge from the first pages of *Ramona*, readers learn that there is "no running away from work on the part of the maids, thus close to the eye of the Señora." Once the distinction between the proud Spanish Señora Moreno and the subservient Mexican maids is established, the racialized division of labor is romanticized: "and if they had known long [how] picturesque they looked there, kneeling on the grass, lifting the dripping linen out of the water, rubbing it back and forth on the stones, sousing it, wringing it, splashing the clear water in each other's faces, they would have been content to stay at the washing day in and day out, for there was always somebody to look on from above."[67] Thus even before readers are introduced to the story's heroine, Ramona, they already know the place of the "Spanish" Californiana and the Mexicana in the soon-to-be-gone Californio society. Prospective Euro-American settlers sympathetic to the Indian cause could thus imagine themselves watching over their own Mexican maids from the veranda. If in the literature of the Manifest Destiny period constructs of Mexicanas as morally and racially inferior justified the 1846 to 1848 conquest and war, the redeployment of these constructs in *Ramona* reasserts a racial hierarchy that justifies the position of Mexican-descent women as domestic workers in the state's emerging racialized labor force. As Mary Romero has documented, after the U.S.-Mexican War of 1846—48, a pattern of occupational stratification emerged throughout the Southwest, placing Mexicanas in domestic-service jobs with virtually no opportunity for upward mobility.[68] The patterns of ethnic and sexual stratification in domestic labor and other service industries that characterize California's economy today were established at the beginning of the twentieth century.[69]

Ramona's personal maid, Margarita, was "most beloved by Ramona." Yet although they have grown up together and are "more like friends than like mistress and maid,"[70] they become bitter enemies when they begin to compete for Alessandro's attention. The rivalry between Ramona and Margarita over Alessandro discloses the Mexican maid's inferior morality. The distinction between the promiscuous Margarita and the morally reserved Ramona (who, despite her Indian mother, was raised as a Spanish señorita) becomes clear as the two secretly set out to gain Alessandro's love. While Ramona is reserved, either unconscious of or unwilling to admit her attraction to Alessandro, Margarita proceeds confidently, fully aware of her desired goal, because "truth being told, it must be admitted, [she] did indeed know a great deal about the way it is with men."[71] In contrast, Ramona's "mind was not like Margarita's, full of fancies bred of freedom in intercourse with men."[72]

In *Ramona's* negative construct of Margarita, the saucy maid, turn-of-the-century readers found a stereotype familiar to them since the early 1800s. Images of Mexicanas such as *Ramona*'s Margarita as immoral and sexually and racially impure were the grist of popular fiction, newspapers, and the first histories of California.[73] Yet the critical difference between the lowly Mexicana as described by early Euro-American writers and *Ramona*'s Margarita is that she has changed occupations from gold-mine prostitute to promiscuous Californio ranch maid. Significantly, at the novel's end the only people of color left in Jackson's turn-of-the-century California are the Mexicano laborers, and Mexicana maids.

Ramona's characterization of Californio men provided further justification for the ensuing racialization processes. Although the novel explicitly condemns the dispossession of Californios, the racialized characterizations of their society implicitly justified Euro-American settlement and doomed the inferior Californios to permanent subordination. The representations of Californios regrettably leave the reader with a sense that Californios were surely unable to develop the land to its full potential. In this sense, the novel mirrors travel literature of the early 1800s by reintroducing negative characterizations of Californios as it romanticizes California history with elaborate descriptions of quaint adobes, desolate padres, and fertile orchards. Richard Henry Dana, for example, wrote, "The Californians are an idle, thriftless people, and can make nothing of themselves."[74] In *Ramona*, echoes of these very same stereotypes of idle, illiterate, semi-savage Mexicans, become a hidden text shrouded in romance and nostalgia. Here, however, they are set in a Pacific arcadia yearning for the bygone days of the Californio ranchos—they are still idle, yet their setting is much more pleasant—thus positioning California as an object of desire for Euro-American readers. Instead of the blatant racism of earlier texts, *Ramona's* method is obscure. For example, the Moreno family ranch house is described as "one of the best specimens to be found in California of the representative house of the half barbaric, half elegant, wholly generous and freehanded life led there by Mexican men and women of degree in the early part of this century."[75] Once the reader enters the house (of the "half barbaric, half elegant" Mexican), she can envision the head herder, Juan, sitting under the sunny veranda, "where it had been for twenty odd years his habit to sit on the long bench and smoke his pipe,"[76] and where "whoever came, spent all of his time, when not eating, sleeping, or walking over the place, sitting with the Señora on the sunny veranda."[77] Given these representations how could readers imagine Californios (or anyone of Mexicano descent, for that matter) doing anything else but manual labor in the new society? By the end of the century, the racialization of the workforce in California had secured the Mexican male population at the bottom of the occupational ladder. For example, by 1900, 77.3 percent of Mexicano workers in Ventura County composed the lowest levels of the working class.[78] California historian Albert Camarillo similarly found that by 1929, Mexicanos comprised 80 percent of the agribusiness workforce, as well as the majority of construction laborers for California's development boom.[79] Thus, the discursive dimensions of the new racial order emerging in late nineteenth-century California, as described by Mary Romero, Tomás Almaguer, and Albert Camarillo, included a gendered and sexually charged Manifest Destiny ideology regenerated through sentimental yearning for the state's Spanish past.

The ideological project of *Ramona* to justify and regenerate Manifest Destiny, in large part through the erotics of racialization mapped out above, was not only supported but further developed by other cultural expressions forming part of the Spanish-heritage movement. A striking example is the case of popular painting in which racialized images of Californios supported the early nineteenth-century notion of Californio indolence. Although *Ramona* was an important act of symbolic expression affecting the imagination of Californians in the nineteenth century, painters, printmakers, and photographers provided the visuals for California's mythical heritage. Throughout the United States, popular journals, newspaper articles, postcards, railroad promotionals, calendars, and restaurant menus disseminated images of old California and its missions. The shift in attitude regarding Spanish culture and institutions noted in the writings about California manifested itself in such popular imagery.

Through the 1870s, representations of wild-eyed vaqueros, handsome bandidos, and scantily clad señoritas focused on the passionate energies of the inhabitants of Spanish California.[80] With the expansion of the railroad after 1869 and subsequent increased tourism, popular images of feisty, naughty "Hispanics" such as Joaquín Murrieta were transformed to show these same figures as now-calm vaqueros who simply while life away with a pipe in hand. This shifting image of vaqueros, from angry and dangerous to satisfied and passive, and the growing interest in a vanishing pastoral California lifestyle compelled painters such as Charles Christian Nahl and Alexander Harmer to turn to "Old Spanish Days" themes. These popular painters were often commissioned by railroad tycoons such as Leland Stanford and E. B. Crocker. One such example is *El Fandango*, produced in 1873 by Charles Christian Nahl for E. B. Crocker.

El Fandango is Nahl's depiction of a typical Spanish-style fiesta in old California. The once-rebel bandit Joaquín Murrieta, as painted by Nahl in 1868, appears in *El Fandango*. But here, in 1873, Murrieta is in the mood for a fiesta. In these celebratory renditions of California's pastoral days, the fact that so much of the imagery is grounded in the rhetoric of fandangos is important, because the emphasis on leisure reinforces the early 1800s notion of Californio indolence. In the first Euro-American travel writings about California, the fandango was a recurring trope that served to instill racialized characterizations of California's inhabitants in descriptions of Californio lifestyle. In an attempt to depict "life as it was" during the age of the great Californio ranchos, works such as *El Fandango* and those by Alexander Harmer, such as *Fiesta in Old California*, represent a notion of indolence and intellectual aridity that survives to this day. Visual representations of fandangos, vaqueros on horseback, and dancing señoritas (usually scantly dressed) tacitly create a Californio landscape devoid of intellectual production, political resistance, or transformative intervention in the emergent society.

Significantly, while the conquered Californio population dances away its time in the popular paintings of Charles Christian Nahl and others, Euro-Americans are shown reading and writing, even when confronted by the most adverse living conditions such as those in the California gold mines. Absent from all of these images are the writers, philosophers, and historians of the Mexican California period.[81] Faced with these images, how would the average museum-going American know that Californios had a vibrant intellectual community in which women figured centrally? More specifically, how would they know that while Nahl painted *El Fandango*, a Californiana named María Amparo Ruiz de Burton penned the first English language novel denouncing the machismo inherent in Euro-American capitalism and Californio patriarchy?[82]

Preserving Hegemony in the Age of Multiculturalism

The Spanish-heritage myth thrives in contemporary California largely because of Spanish historic preservation projects and Spanish-heritage cultural celebration events such as "Old Spanish Days" fiestas. In fact, institutionalization through these efforts was the primary way mythmakers reached the popular imagination of most Californians. A major figure in California's Spanish-heritage historic preservation movement was Charles Fletcher Lummis, author of *Some Strange Corners of Our Country* (1892) and *The Land of Poco Tiempo* (1893). Lummis, a Harvard-educated historian and archaeologist, became interested in the preservation of California's romantic past soon after moving to California in 1884. His promotional efforts were carried forth through his position as a writer for the *Los Angeles Times* and as the author and editor of various Southwestern publications, such as *Land of Sunshine*. In a gesture not unlike that described by Rosaldo as "humanitarian imperialism," Lummis and Tessa L. Kelso led California's movement to preserve the decaying California missions with the founding of the Landmarks Club in 1895 and the subsequent restoration of Mission San Fernando and other sites.[83]

In Los Angeles, the enthusiasm for historic preservation turned the efforts of the Landmarks Club into a statewide "landmarks" movement, which would eventually spread throughout the Southwest. Although historic preservation was the emphasis of the club until 1917, after this period the emphasis shifted from the preservation of the original mission buildings to the restoration of missions as historic sites used to fabricate the romanticized versions of the state's Spanish heritage.[84] The mission restoration project became a free-for-all restoration affair in which the most nostalgic versions of *Ramona's* world usually prevailed. For Euro-Americans involved in the promotion and preservation of California's Hispanic past, the effort became a way of life far beyond a simple embrace of bygone Spanish days. The newly established class of real estate developers, bankers, artists, and professional historians took every occasion to dress in the Spanish regalia of the dispossessed Californio population.

Programs restoring Spanish buildings were developed, and civic organizations mounted massive campaigns to preserve California's neglected past. Euro-Americans, with the help of the few remaining prominent Californios, founded organizations such as the Native Sons of Golden West (1887). In community after community, the first Spanish-heritage fiestas, which continue to this day, began to be organized. By the time the 1893 Columbian Exposition in Chicago took place, California had consolidated a unique regional identity, an official style based on the Spanish-heritage myth. The state's World's Fair Commission for this exposition selected for the California pavilion a building featuring different mission façades.[85]

Whose Past for Whom?

For many of us, California's "historic sites" are violent places: they continually reinforce a hegemonic version of history that denies the violence of California's origins even as it justifies the past and present effects of Manifest Destiny on Native and Mexican-descent people. Once a historic site is "preserved," it is used to bring "Spanish" history and its sexually and racially inflected representations of fandango-loving Californians to life through cultural celebrations such as Spanish fiestas.

Since 1926, Santa Barbara, California, has held its annual "Old Spanish Days Fiesta." In a 1997 interview, Father Virgil Cordano, a Santa Barbara Mission priest, proudly asserted that during the thirty-six years since he has served on the board for Santa Barbara's "Old Spanish Days Fiesta," the essence of fiesta, "to discover that which unites us," has endured.[86] The benevolent celebration of Santa Barbara's Spanish legend may thrill spectators with flamenco dances, Latin food, and events such as a "Run with the Bulls," but this annual celebration of things Spanish notably functions in conjunction with historic preservation sites by providing a stage to act out the Spanish-heritage mythology. Santa Barbara's current efforts to "appreciate" difference when presented in a dehistoricized celebratory manner create a mystified understanding of difference that, in the words of David Palumbo-Liu, "serves to restabilize the individual momentarily disoriented by the encounter with the Other."[87] The uncritical calls for understanding difference, or as Father Cordano put it, "for understanding that which unites us," have the very real effect of silencing the history that created the diversity in Santa Barbara in the first place, even as it conceals contemporary racial inequalities. The historical and material effects of the caste system imposed on California's Native communities during the colonial period and the subsequent dispossession of Californios by the heirs of Manifest Destiny are concealed by the focus on celebrating the plurality of cultures. The function of this type of cultural pluralism in the management of race is a depoliticized and dehistoricized idea of culture that creates an illusion of racial cooperation and harmony while concealing extant inequities.[88]

As more "historic sites" are reconstructed for visitors and school children to "step into living history," the question is this: Whose history are they "experiencing" as they are guided through the California missions, the flagpole in Monterey where U.S. troops made Manifest Destiny a reality, and so many other state-funded shrines to colonization and conquest? Given recent demographic trends, what will the focus of "preservation," "historic sites," and cultural heritage museums be in fifty years, when the majority of visiting tourists and school children will be second- and third-generation Latinos with strong ties to Indigenous cultures in Mexico and beyond?

Notes

1. joannemariebarker and Teresia Teaiwa, "Native InFormation," *Inscriptions* 7 (1994): 17–18.

2. Here I am referring to Edward Said's study of Orientalism as a discourse by which European culture was able to manage and produce the Orient during the post-Enlightenment period. See *Orientalism* (New York: Vintage Books, 1979). For discussions of the erotics of imperial conquest and the gendered dynamics of colonialism, see Ann McClintock, *Imperial Leather: Race, Gender, and Sexuality in the Colonial Contest* (New York: Routledge, 1995); and Cynthia Enloe, *Bananas, Beaches and Bases: Making Feminist Sense of International Politics* (Berkeley: University of California Press, 1990).

3. José Rabasa, *Inventing America: Spanish Historiography and the Formation of Eurocentrism* (Norman: University of Oklahoma Press, 1993), 23–48.

4. The Spanish designation is parenthetical, because as the following discussion makes clear, its meaning has historically been constructed in processes of racial and cultural differentiation.

5. Antonia I. Castañeda, "Presidarias y Pobladoras: Spanish-Mexican Women in Frontier Monterey, Alta California, 1770–1821" (PhD diss., Stanford University, 1990), 8–47.

6. Ibid., 14.

7. Shari Huhndorf, "Engendering Indians, Making Men: Race, Gender, and National Identity in Turn-of-the-Century American Culture" (Paper Presentation, annual Ford Foundation Conference, Irvine, CA, November 1998).

8. Renato Rosaldo, "Imperialist Nostalgia," *Representations* 26 (Spring 1989): 108.

9. Shari Huhndorf, "If Only I Were an Indian," in *Going Native: Indians in the American Cultural Imagination* (Ithaca: Cornell University Press, 2001), 1–78.

10. Jimmie Durham, "Cowboys and . . . Notes on Art, Literature, and American Indians in the Modern American Mind," in *The State of Native America, Genocide, Colonization and Resistance*, ed. Annette Jaimes (Boston: South End Press, 1992), 426.

11. A "racial project," as defined by Michael Omi and Howard Winant, is one that "creates or reproduces structures of domination based on essentialist categories of race. Such a definition recognizes the importance of locating racism within a fluid and contested history of racially based social structures and discourses." *Racial Formation in the United States: From the 1960s to the 1990s* (New York: Routledge Press, 1994), 71.

12. Carey McWilliams, *North from Mexico: The Spanish-Speaking People of the United States* (1949; reprint, New York: Greenwood Press, 1968), 44; Douglas Monroy, *Thrown Among Strangers: The Making of Mexican Culture in Frontier California* (Berkeley: University of California Press, 1990), 134.

13. Lisbeth Haas, *Conquests and Historical Identities in California, 1769–1936* (Berkeley: University of California Press, 1995), 29–38.

14. Ibid.

15. This is compelling if, in fact, Chicanas/os are to consider Californio collective consciousness a precursor to Aztlán.

16. Rosaura Sánchez, *Telling Identities: The Californio Testimonios* (Minneapolis: University of Minnesota Press, 1995), 56–58.

17. Ibid., 58.

18. The notion of regenerated racism is indebted to Richard Slotkin's study of the evolution of American attitudes and traditions that shape American culture. *Regeneration Through Violence: The Mythology of the American Frontier, 1600–1860* (Norman: University of Oklahoma Press, 2000).

19. Castañeda, "Presidarias y Pobladoras," 29.

20. James Rawls, "The California Mission as Symbol and Myth," *California History* 71, no. 3 (Fall 1992): 356.

21. Thomas Jefferson Farnham, *Travels in the Californias, and Scenes in the Pacific Ocean* (New York: Saxton and Miles, 1844), 139.

22. For a detailed account, see David Hurst Thomas, "Harvesting Ramona's Garden: Life in California's Mythical Mission Past," in *The Spanish Borderlands in Pan-American Perspective*, ed. David Hurst Thomas (Washington, DC: Smithsonian Institution Press, 1991), 119–56.

23. Sánchez, *Telling Identities*, ix–30; Castañeda, "Presidarias y Pobladoras," 1–47.

24. Leah Dilworth, *Imagining Indians in the Southwest: Persistent Visions of a Primitive Past* (Washington, DC: Smithsonian Institution Press, 1996), 4–7.

25. Several California historians have made this claim, including Carey McWilliams, *Southern California Country: An Island on the Land* (Santa Barbara: Peregine Smith, 1973), 70–83; and Kevin Starr, *Inventing the Dream: California Through the Progressive Era* (New York: Oxford University Press, 1985), 54–63.

26. Richard Griswold del Castillo, "The Del Valle Family and the Fantasy Heritage," *California History* 59 (Spring 1990): 3–4. Every spring, *Ramona*, the play established in the early 1900s, continues to draw large audiences to Hemet, California.

27. In *Ramona*, Luiseños are Native people from Temecula.

28. Helen Hunt Jackson, *Ramona* (New York: New American Library, 1988), 11.

29. Ibid., 7.

30. Ibid., 12.

31. Ibid.

32. Ibid., 129.

33. Starr, *Inventing the Dream*, 54–63.

34. Thomas, "Harvesting Ramona's Garden," 124.

35. See Ward Churchill, *A Little Matter of Genocide: Holocaust and Denial in the Americas 1492 to the Present* (San Francisco: City Lights Books, 1997).

36. Jackson, *Ramona*, 18.

37. Ibid., 39–40.

38. Ibid., 232.

39. See Sherburne F. Cook, *The Population of the California Indians, 1769–1970* (Berkeley: University of California Press, 1976); and Robert H. Jackson and Edward Castillo, *Indians, Franciscans, and Spanish Colonization: The Impact of the Mission System on California Indians* (Albuquerque: University of New Mexico Press, 1995).

40. Jackson, *Ramona*, 232.

41. Ibid., 35.

42. Ibid., 18.

43. Jackson and Castillo, *Indians, Franciscans, and Spanish Colonization*, 11–29.

44. See Monroy, *Thrown Among Strangers*, 91–96; Jackson and Castillo, *Indians, Franciscans, and Spanish Colonization*, 73–86; and Roberto Perez, "Indian Resistance Efforts in Southern California, 1769–1819: The Kumeyaay Rebellion and Other Key Events" (PhD diss., University of California, Riverside, 2001).

45. Antonia Castañeda, "Engendering the History of Alta California, 1769–1848: Gender, Sexuality, and the Family," in *Contested Eden: California Before the Gold Rush*, ed. Ramón Gutiérrez and Richard J. Orsi (Berkeley: University of California Press, 1998), 235–36.

46. Roy Harvey Pearce historicized the significance of this dichotomy in the American mind. See *Savagism and Civilization, A Study of the Indian and the American Mind* (Baltimore: Johns Hopkins Press, 1967).

47. Jackson, *Ramona*, 53.

48. Ibid., 54.

49. Ibid., 73.

50. James Rawls documents this phenomenon in his study. See *Indians of California: The Changing Image* (Norman: University of Oklahoma Press, 1984).

51. Jackson, *Ramona*, 23.

52. Ibid.

53. Ibid., 38; emphasis mine.

54. Ibid., 46–47.

55. Richard Hill, "Savage Splendor: Sex, Lies, and Stereotypes," *Turtle Quarterly* (Spring–Summer 1991): 14.

56. Rayna Green, "The Pocahontas Perplex: The Image of the Indian Woman in American Culture," *The Massachusetts Review* 16 (Autumn 1975): 701.

57. Jackson, *Ramona*, 250.

58. Ibid.

59. Ibid., 255.

60. Norma Alarcón, "Chicana Feminism: In the Tracks of 'the' Native Woman," *Cultural Studies* 4, no. 3 (October 1990): 248–56.

61. Jackson, *Ramona*, 132–33.

62. Ibid., 26.

63. Lata Mani, "Contentious Traditions: The Debate on Sati in Colonial India," in *Recasting Women: Essays in Indian Historiography*, ed. Kumkum Sangari and Sudesh Vaid (New Brunswick: Rutgers University Press, 1990), 118.

64. Jackson, *Ramona*, 15.

65. Ibid., 21.

66. Ibid., 6.

67. Ibid., 16.

68. Mary Romero, "Domestic Service and Women of Color in the United States," in *Maid in the U.S.A.* (New York: Routledge, 1992), 71–95.

69. For a recent analysis of how Latinas and African American women continue to face the greatest risk of poverty and low wages in a restructured U.S. economy, see Irene Browne, ed., *Latinas and African American Women at Work: Race, Gender, and Economic Inequality* (New York: Russell Sage Foundation, 1999).

70. Jackson, *Ramona*, 41.

71. Ibid., 80.

72. Ibid., 102.

73. Castañeda, "Presidarias y Pobladoras," 13–18.

74. Richard Henry Dana, *Two Years Before the Mast: A Personal Narrative of Life at Sea* (New York: World Publishing, 1946), 82.

75. Jackson, *Ramona*, 11.

76. Ibid., 5.

77. Ibid., 16–17.

78. Tomás Almaguer, *Racial Fault Lines: The Historical Origins of White Supremacy in California* (Berkeley: University of California Press, 1994), 102.

79. Albert Camarillo, *Chicanos in a Changing Society: From Mexican Pueblos to American Barrios in Santa Barbara and Southern California, 1848–1930* (Cambridge, MA: Harvard University Press, 1979), 154–68.

80. Claire Perry, "Spanish Arcadia," in *Pacific Arcadia: Images of California, 1600–1915* (New York: Oxford University Press, 1999), 135–62.

81. From Chicana/o literary history, we know that pre-1848 California was a vibrant intellectual community. See, for example, Sánchez, *Telling Identities*; and Genaro Padilla, *My History Not Yours: The Formation of Mexican American Autobiography* (Madison: University of Wisconsin Press, 1993).

82. María Amparo Ruiz de Burton, *The Squatter and the Don*, ed. Rosaura Sánchez and Beatrice Pita (Houston: Arte Público Press, 1992).

83. Rosaldo, "Imperialist Nostalgia," 112.

84. Thomas, "Harvesting Ramona's Garden," 133.

85. According to David Hurst Thomas, historic preservationists, artists, architects, and capitalist developers colluded to develop California's unique identity. One result of this collaboration was that within two decades mission revival style architecture became the hallmark of California architecture. See "Harvesting Ramona's Garden."

86. Father Virgil Cordano (Old Spanish Days Fiesta organizer), interviewed by the author, August 25, 1997.

87. David Palumbo-Liu, "Introduction," in *The Ethnic Canon: Histories, Institutions, and Interventions*, ed. David Palumbo-Liu (Minneapolis: University of Minnesota Press, 1995), 12.

88. Chandra Talpade Mohanty, "On Race and Voice: Challenges for Liberal Education in the 1990s," *Cultural Critique* 14 (Winter 1989–90): 185.

CHAPTER 6

Elle Meets the President

Weaving Navajo Culture and Commerce in the Southwestern Tourist Industry

LAURA JANE MOORE

During the spring of 1903, President Theodore Roosevelt included a two-hour stop in Albuquerque while on a speaking tour through the western territories. The Commercial Club of Albuquerque chose a Navajo woman, called Elle of Ganado, to weave a gift for the president—a textile rendition of his honorary Commercial Club membership card. Club members provided the design, which Elle wove quickly in hand-spun red, white, and blue yarn. During his tour of Albuquerque, Roosevelt visited the Commercial Club, where he received Elle's blanket, and he stopped by the Alvarado Hotel's Indian Building, where he met the weaver herself. An Albuquerque newspaper reported that upon meeting the weaver, the "president gave her a hearty shake and told her how much he appreciated her work. The little speech was interpreted and pleased the Indian woman beyond expression."[1]

Although her own thoughts were apparently "beyond expression," Elle's image spoke volumes to turn-of-the-century Americans, showing New Mexico as not only conquered but commercialized, safe for investment and safe for statehood. Indeed, Commercial Club members orchestrated this performance as part of a statehood campaign, a drive for integration into the social, economic, and political life of the United States, an effort that would not pay off for nearly ten more years. Elle and the president's meeting suggests ways in which race and gender, regional and national politics, culture and commerce interacted and were inextricably linked as the twentieth century began. The pivotal role that Elle played in Roosevelt's visit reveals that while we tend to think of women like Elle as marginalized historical figures, they were far from peripheral to the unfolding of twentieth-century American history. Not only can we better understand such women by placing them within the larger economic, cultural, and political context of their times, but we can better understand that context by putting a woman like Elle at its center.

Elle of Ganado, also called Asdzaa Lichii' (Red Woman) in Navajo, was born to the Black Sheep Clan and lived in the southern part of the Navajo Reservation near the Hubbell Trading Post in Ganado, Arizona. She might have been about fifty years old at the time she met Roosevelt, and she lived until 1924. At the suggestion of trader John Lorenzo Hubbell, she and her husband Tom began spending substantial periods of time in Albuquerque beginning in 1903 after the Fred Harvey Company opened its Indian Building as part of the Alvarado Hotel complex at the Santa Fe Railroad depot. Together with other Navajo and Pueblo families, they worked as arts and crafts demonstrators within the burgeoning southwestern tourist industry.[2]

Most scholarly literature on southwestern tourism examines the ironies and complexities of images of Indians portrayed as purely nonindustrial producers of "traditional" handcrafts, "outside history, outside industrial capitalism" that had begun to emerge at the turn of the century.[3] Elle's Commercial Club blanket, however, unabashedly declared the link between Indian art and turn-of-the-century capitalism. It is a reminder that those who worked as demonstrators were, like all Americans at the time, entering new kinds of economic relationships that would affect their work and their communities in profound ways. Beyond their ideological implications, then, these tourist sites were workplaces to which a number of Native Americans agreed to travel for extended periods of time. The sites were also cultural crossroads at which negotiations took place between employers and employees, between young corporate and rural America, between white men and Indian families, between metropolitan and peripheral economies. This essay explores the contours of these crossroads, the compromises demanded by and the benefits promised to various participants.[4]

The Fred Harvey Company, it has been said, "invented" the Southwest as "America's Orient." Fred Harvey was an English immigrant who opened his first restaurant along the Santa Fe Railroad line in 1876 in Topeka, Kansas. From there the company grew into the first chain of restaurants and of railroad hotels. Harvey built his company's reputation on the notion of civilizing rail travel to the West by selling good food served by respectable young, white, single women called "Harvey girls." Combining hot meals, Harvey girls, and Indian images in their advertising, the company presented the West as an exotic but accessible tourist paradise. By the time of Harvey's death in 1901, his empire consisted of twenty-six restaurants, sixteen hotels, and twenty dining cars.[5]

The Harvey Company went into the Indian art business at the instigation of Harvey's daughter, Minnie Harvey Huckel, an avid Indian art collector. In 1902 she suggested that a display of Indian art be included in Albuquerque's new Harvey hotel, the Alvarado. Her husband, J. F. Huckel, a New Yorker who had been in the publishing business and was now a Fred Harvey vice president, began to commute from Harvey headquarters in Kansas City to Albuquerque, where he created the Fred Harvey Indian Department. The Huckels' collaboration with Harvey employee Herman Schweizer ensured the success of this venture. Schweizer, a German immigrant, had found his way to the Southwest in the 1880s, had jobbed silver and turquoise to Navajo silversmiths, and while working at the Harvey restaurant in Coolidge, New Mexico, had begun buying and selling Navajo arts and crafts—a successful sideline that caught Minnie Huckel's attention. Schweizer spent the rest of his life managing the Fred Harvey Indian Department. He had an eye and a taste for the Indian art business and soon built the Harvey Indian collection into a premiere showcase. This success was further facilitated by the architect Mary Colter, who helped to design the Indian Building at the Alvarado and subsequently went to work full time for the company. Colter was an important force in developing a regional architectural style inspired by local, native design—spaces for the "staged authenticity" that became fundamental to southwestern tourism, and spaces designed for commercial transactions that also offered a seemingly behind-the-scenes view of Indian homelife.[6]

The development of southwestern tourism thus depended on diverse players who illustrate the various and complex forces at work at the turn of the century: Minnie Huckel, a wealthy woman and art patron; Mary Colter, a professional woman finding a career in the Southwest; J. F. Huckel, an elite eastern businessman; Herman Schweizer, a young, ambitious, Jewish immigrant; and a number of Native American artists, including Elle, worked together to invent the modern Southwest and to find a place for themselves within it. Each brought her or his own goals, background, and economic and cultural logic to their meeting. They did not always act out of positions of equality, but each were crucial players in the story. Most analyses of the Harvey Company and southwestern tourism in general tell the story from the Anglo participants' point of view, even when critiquing their use of Indians and Indian imagery. Although the individual, private thoughts and reactions of Indian workers such as Elle may never be known, careful reading of sources left mostly by those Anglo participants can help us examine their roles and experiences within the larger context of turn-of-the-century Navajo and American history.

Much recent scholarship has explored the elevation of Indian imagery in this period, even as Native Americans remained culturally, politically, and economically marginalized. Indian artisans were central figures in the invention of the Southwest. Traveling in the comfort of a berth on the Santa Fe railroad, white Americans could see exotic pockets of the nation where the industrialization, urbanization, and bureaucratization of the era had not yet, it seemed, taken hold. Yet in this period, as industrial capitalism spread and the Southwest was incorporated into the nation and the national market economy, it became, as Leah Dilworth explains, "increasingly clear that the development of the American West would depend on the metropolis for capital and cheap immigrant labor." Ironically, she continues, "The spectacle of Indian artisanal labor resurrected an ideology that declared precisely the opposite: that the rural artisan and the farmer were the backbone of the nation's economy."[7] The presence of hardworking, artistic Indians provided tourists with a heavily mediated—indeed artificially constructed—arena in which to feel they had safely encountered the real West through a glimpse of Indian homelife. Barbara Babcock, Marta Weigle, and others have shown that the prominent place of female Indian artisans and their children in locales like the Fred Harvey Indian Building was crucial to the domestication of the image of the "wild" West. They call such sites "ethnic sets for exotic performances" or "human showcases" where "the companies staged authenticity by controlling the architectural setting, 'live' demonstrations and other expressive performances, museum and sales displays, publications, and virtually all associated exegesis."[8]

Tourists viewed Indians purportedly practicing their naturally artistic, premodern everyday lives, but the artists, too, were travelers who had moved from their rural homes to these tourist spaces in order to incorporate income from such work into their families' economic strategies. The idealized domestic tableaux offered at a Harvey House obscured a gender organization and economic system that differed markedly from that of Euro-Americans. It also ignored the cultural meanings that the Diné, or Navajos, themselves found in their textiles. Weaving was, and is, a highly respected activity that reflects and reinforces Navajo women's economic, cultural, and social centrality.[9] Navajo textiles had long been both market objects and unique cultural expressions embodying *hozho*, the central Navajo philosophical concept that connotes harmony, balance, goodness, and beauty. Weaving also reflects the power of thought and the combination of autonomy and cooperation that is so important to the Diné. Husbands build looms for their wives, and weavers sometimes work side by side at the same loom. At the same time, the design of a rug, as one weaver explains, "just has to be you," and, to quote weaver Mary Lee Begay, "takes a lot of hard thinking."[10] Weavers do not generally sketch out designs but rather conceive and then hold them in their minds as they work. A leading scholar of contemporary Navajo textiles, Ann Lane Hedlund, explains that weaving "represents a proper way to make a living or, putting it more exactly, to live"; weavers practice their art while "caring for their families, homes, and herds . . . and remembering the sacred stories, prayers, and songs that 'go with the weaving.'"[11]

Those "families, homes, and herds" are organized around the principle of motherhood, a term that refers not just to biological mothers, but to the women of one's clan, the family's sheep herd, and the family's land. The Diné are matrilineal, tracing descent from the female side of the family, and matrilocal, with daughters living with their husbands and children near their mother. The primary familial bond is between a mother and child (not between a husband and wife); Navajos belong or are "born to" their mother's clan; and other clan members are their closest relatives. Individual women, men, and children own livestock and other property but share the care of herds and fields. Women generally control range land, and land use is typically inherited from mothers. Weaving, too, has always been dominated by women (though men can, and some do, weave), and weaving knowledge passes from generation to generation through kinship bonds.[12]

At the turn of the twentieth century, livestock products were the primary source of subsistence and of income, supplemented by farming and by trading other items, most importantly textiles, at the local trading post. Living in an often harsh and unpredictable environment, the Diné pooled resources along kinship lines. Economic specialization was not practical, but varied economic strategies and adaptability to changing environmental and historical forces were. Even while becoming more dependent on the national market economy, the Diné did not abandon their diversified subsistence economy or reciprocal economic expectations revolving around matrilineal kinship ties.[13]

Long before trading posts or Harvey houses, weaving had been one of many activities through which women contributed to the household economy. Between the seventeenth and nineteenth centuries, the Diné had increasingly oriented their economy and culture around sheep herds while developing much of what is now considered traditional Navajo culture. Navajo women used their sheep's wool to weave blankets and clothing for family use and for inter- and intratribal trade. By the early nineteenth century, Navajo blankets were prized within a wide regional market for their quality—so tightly woven they were waterproof—and their beauty.[14]

In 1865 U.S. troops that had wrested control of the region from Mexico two decades earlier implemented a scorched-earth policy, massacring herds and burning crops, in order to impoverish and defeat the Diné. Elle probably joined the approximately eight thousand Navajos who were moved to a tiny reservation near Fort Sumner in southeastern New Mexico called Bosque Redondo, or *Hweeldi* in Navajo. There they faced disease, death, and emotional and economic turmoil. Even though they were short on wool and given manufactured blankets and clothing, Navajo women nevertheless "set up looms and created blankets of strength and beauty."[15]

To the army officers at Bosque Redondo, Navajo women's commitment to their looms appeared not as evidence of resilience but proof of conquest. Long accustomed to the association of femininity, domesticity, and textile production, Anglo observers thought weaving augured well for Navajos' ability to adopt "civilized" gender roles. When American officials offered Navajos Anglo-style looms and spinning wheels, however, the Navajo women refused to use them or to work with the white women hired to instruct them, insisting on continuing with "their old plan of spinning and making blankets."[16] Weavers readily adopted some newly available materials, including commercial dyes and yarns, but insisted on controlling the means of production. Nor did they adopt Euro-American gender roles, but continued to ground their social organization and identity in matrilineal kinship relations. Despite cultural misreadings of the Navajo, weaving became a critical point of contact, valued by both groups but for different reasons.

After four years, American officials decided that relocating the Diné to Bosque Redondo had been a costly mistake, making a once self-sufficient tribe an unnecessary economic burden on the federal government. In 1868, eager to return home, a group of Navajo headmen signed a treaty establishing a reservation carved out of their traditional homeland. As soon as they returned, they set about resurrecting a pastoral economy using sheep and goats provided by the federal Office of Indian Affairs and taking advantage of a national boom in the wool market. White traders appeared in Navajo country to broker the sale of wool from Navajo herds to eastern markets. Trading posts sprouted along the new railroad lines and deeper within Navajo country. The Diné traded wool, sheep, textiles and other products for flour, coffee, sugar and other items they could not produce at home. Traders thus helped introduce the national market economy to the Diné while becoming cultural brokers as well. During the 1890s drought and a severe national depression lowered wool prices and ended the Diné's economic recovery, but they continued to center their lives around their sheep herds, grafting elements of the national market economy onto their subsistence economy.[17]

Weavers left traces of these historical changes and continuities in their textiles. They adopted designs from manufactured Pendleton blankets from Oregon that they bought at trading posts, experimented with serrate style designs inspired by Hispanic weaving, and increasingly used commercial yarns and dyes. The Indian Office provided finely spun yarn manufactured in Germantown, Pennsylvania, that allowed weavers to develop ever more intricate and complex designs. Some weavers began to include figurative elements such as trains in their textiles in a new "pictorial" style. When wool prices dropped in the 1890s, women apparently turned increasingly to weaving as a way to increase the value of their wool. New designs reflected changing concerns of the weavers and the changing market. Traders encouraged weaving styles they thought would sell well and regional styles named after neighboring posts emerged. For the most part, Navajos stopped weaving clothing and instead created what would come to be called rugs, meant not to be worn, but to be souvenirs of the West. Military personnel were among the first Anglo collectors, followed by growing numbers of explorers, scientists, government personnel, and finally tourists arriving with the new railroads.[18]

Railroads altered the economic, cultural, and social contours of the region. By the turn of the century, the Santa Fe dominated Albuquerque's economy and had practically built a whole new town around its depot. Railroads also shifted the region's perspective from a local economy oriented along a north-south axis facing Mexico to an east-west trajectory incorporated into the U.S. national economy. One of the byproducts of this process was the introduction of wage work and migrant labor to Native American communities. Many Navajo and other Indian men added income from railroad work to the contributions they made to their household economy. Meanwhile, as the Navajo economy became increasingly incorporated into the modern industrial economy of the United States, the inter-and intratribal blanket trade evaporated as southwestern Indians adopted white-style clothing and factory-made blankets. Navajo weavers adopted their art to a new and changing market that, though it did not generally pay producers well, yet could be crucial to the household economy. Navajo textiles had become a key commodity in southwestern economic development and were central to the income of traders and the growing tourist economy.[19] One of the most famous and successful trading posts, for example, was John Lorenzo Hubbell's in Ganado, Arizona, in the southern part of Navajo country near the New Mexico border. The Hubbell family eventually opened several other posts and became the main suppliers for the Harvey Company. They also became employment brokers, recruiting Navajos and Hopis, including Elle and Tom of Ganado, who were willing to work at Harvey houses as arts and crafts demonstrators.[20] Within the growing trading post economy, Navajo weavers found new and different customers, and they experimented with new materials and designs while maintaining traditional production techniques and continuing to create uniquely Navajo textiles.

While the railroad introduced industrial capitalism to the rural Southwest, it also introduced the Southwest, or a particular image of the Southwest, to the world. Ironically, while some Indian men learned to participate in industrial wage work, the Santa Fe's tourist business perfected the image of Indians as naturally artistic preindustrial craftspeople. Upon disembarking at Albuquerque, train travelers passed through the Harvey Indian Building on the way to the Alvarado lobby. The first thing they saw were weavers, potters, silversmiths, and basket makers, and Fred Harvey sales increased appreciably as a result of this encounter.

The Indian workers' primary job was to be on display for the tourists. In making arrangements for the demonstrators, Harvey Indian Department manager Herman Schweizer explained to the trader John Lorenzo Hubbell that "the principal thing [is] for them to be at work when trains are in. They should be working from 7:30 a. m. to noon. They can work as much or as little as they want to in the afternoon but must come back after supper for about one hour for evening trains." In exchange the Harvey Company provided room and board and on at least one occasion Schweizer promised "double of what they are getting for their stuff on the reservation." This was a good enough deal, apparently, to entice a number of artists and their families away from their homes, farms, sheep, corn, and kin for two or three months at a time, long enough for good weavers to complete a large weaving project "if they bring blankets already started."[21]

Schweizer and Huckel always preferred a mix of women, men, and children to provide scenes of domestic, familial, artistic comradery. The ideal Navajo couple would include a weaver and a silversmith. Navajo women would weave, care for the children, cook, and perform janitorial duties, though accomplishing the latter out of the view of tourists.[22] Navajo silver work was still a somewhat new craft, and silversmiths were harder to find than weavers. Back in Navajo country, economic specialization in weaving or silversmithing would be unusual. Instead, arts and crafts work was integrated into diversified economic strategies. Even the Harvey men did not rely on their demonstrators for quality silver work. More important to them was to have a man who knew enough to act like a silversmith while being "a good man," that is, reliable, honest, and hardworking. His tasks would include cleaning and upkeep on the buildings and usually translating.[23]

Many Indian artists worked at some point for the Fred Harvey Company. The San Ildefonso Pueblo potter Maria Martinez and her husband Julian worked as Harvey demonstrators early in their careers, before developing the black pottery style that brought so much fame. The Hopi-Tewa potter Nampeyo also worked for the Harvey Company on a few occasions, demonstrating her Sikyatki revival style. Nampeyo had already begun to make a name for herself, which the Harvey Company cashed in on when they hired her.[24] Elle, in contrast, was not well-known until her work for the Harvey Company made her one of the only other Indian artists with name recognition in the early twentieth century. Elle's willingness to stay away from home for long periods of time and to be photographed over and over again made her one of the Harvey Company's favorite employees.[25] She and her husband were local celebrities in Albuquerque, their activities documented regularly in the town's newspapers. They met and were photographed with numerous national celebrities, too, from the Chicago Cubs to "America's sweetheart," Mary Pickford. Encouraged by their success in Albuquerque, the Harvey Company began employing demonstrators for other sites as well. Elle and other artists traveled around the country representing the company at expositions in San Francisco, Chicago, and elsewhere. They also worked in other Harvey houses, most notably at the Grand Canyon, where living exhibits of Indian "homelife" were built into the tourist spaces.[26]

Architect Mary Colter based the architecture of the Grand Canyon's Hopi House on that at Oraibi, one of the oldest inhabited villages in the United States. Hopi demonstrators lived upstairs, Navajos camped nearby, and downstairs salesrooms also invoked Indian "homelife." By emphasizing art, and deemphasizing other economic activities carried out in actual Hopi villages, the Hopi House helped to define Native American culture narrowly by its marketable, artistic products. While Harvey publications extolled the Hopi House as a "reproduction of the homes of this tribe as they are found on their reservation," it was not a reproduction but an interpretation of Indian life in which certain characteristics stood in for Indian culture. The inaccuracy of this "staged authenticity" is highlighted by the number of Navajos who enacted their artistic domestic life at the *Hopi* House, where Navajo weaving and silver were especially important commodities.[27]

Authenticity was itself historically constructed, and it changed over time. At the Grand Canyon, Huckel insisted that Navajo women "have and *use* some of their homemade pots to cook." At the same time, Schweizer and Huckel solicited Hubbell's help in securing an "old Navaho forge . . . perhaps a piece of steel rail or whatever there may be that is homemade" for silversmiths working at the Hopi House.[28] Authenticity, then, did not require the complete rejection of technology or industrialization; Navajo silver work, in fact, was not a traditional craft and relied on modern technology, in this case steel. What seemed to be most important in indicating authenticity was the word "homemade," which suggested self-sufficiency: that a Navajo man could build a forge out of a piece of steel rail; that a Navajo woman could feed her family out of homemade pots; that for these Indians art and labor were integrated into everyday life. Such items as Navajo pottery might merely serve as decoration in modern white American homes in which the art of self-sufficiency had been lost, but for Indians they must still be *used*. Harvey images of Indian artisans played off concerns emerging from the arts and crafts movement about the alienation of art from labor in the modern industrial world, the growing dichotomy between the traditional and the modern, and a nostalgia for a mythological past.[29] Still, the art itself did not (yet) have to be so pure: "Modern" designs were especially popular, and weavers could use manufactured yarns and dyes as long as they wove them by hand.

As for the Diné, their identity was less tenuously tied to material objects such as stoves or pots than was the Anglo definition of an "authentic" Indian. On one occasion Tom and Elle asked a Harvey manager to provide buckskin and other materials so that Tom could make moccasins for Elle.[30] This story suggests an impressive level of self-sufficiency that might reinforce Anglo understandings of Indian authenticity: Even if they did not hunt the buck and cure the hide themselves, they also did not buy the manufactured product. But the cost of a pair of shoes may have been less of an issue for the couple than a deeper cultural undercurrent. As a Navajo woman interviewed in the 1990s explained, moccasins "were first worn by the holy people and reflect our culture and our identity as Diné. . . . It is by a Navajo's moccasin the Holy People recognize that a person is a Diné and who that person is." Indeed, establishing this identity may have been especially important to demonstrators like Elle who had journeyed so far from home. Moreover, the construction of the moccasins is critical because the sole "represents mother earth" and the top, which is "dyed red to represent the rainbow . . . is father sky." The sinew that ties together the sole and the top represents lightning and thus the "union of mother earth and father sky [which] brings forth all life." As when a Navajo weaves, the process of making moccasins expresses hozho, harmony between nature and the supernatural, and the power of thought: "We think about how we are going to make the moccasins, we plan out how best to make the moccasins, we use our thinking and planning put into action when we make the moccasins, and when we are done we have moccasins to protect our feet and give us comfort."[31] In other words, the material, the color, and the process of constructing the moccasins would have been more important to Elle and Tom than that the finished product was "homemade."

Diné identity depended on relationships to land, kin, and livestock, relationships that income from weaving could help maintain. In contrast to Elle and Tom, most weavers were unwilling to stay away from home for long periods of time. For that reason, most of the rugs sold in Harvey houses were woven not by demonstrators, who could not in any case have produced the necessary volume, but by women back in Navajo country who combined weaving with their other daily activities. Often these weavers bought packaged dyes at their trading post. Sometimes they spun and carded wool from their own sheep, but often they received wool from a trader as an advance on their rug, or perhaps they paid another woman to process wool for them. Weaving was thus part of both a local and national economy, combining traditional means of production with materials and marketing strategies made available by industrial capitalism.

Presenting "authentic," "traditional," "ancient" Indian culture to the tourist market was crucial to the economic development of the Southwest, yet in both practical and ideological ways it could clash with official federal Indian policy. In day-to-day business practice, for example, the Harvey people took Navajo polygamy—the bane of Christian missionaries—in stride. In fact, polygamy might have made Harvey managers' job easier by providing more adults, especially weavers, per family to take care of various chores. Similarly, the disjuncture between educating Indian children in the Protestant, individualistic, capitalist work ethic that lay at the heart of assimilationist policy ran counter to Huckel and Schweizer's desire for demonstrators to bring along their children who were "one of the chief attractions to the traveling public."[32] The Harvey men had to obtain Indian agents' permission for the children to accompany their families. The agents were employees of the federal Indian Office whose policy was to wean Indian children *away* from traditional culture, the very culture that was being preserved, commodified, and marketed at the Grand Canyon.

Meanwhile, Harvey managers also found some elements of traditional culture trying, and they worried frequently about "spoiled" Indians having a bad influence on other demonstrators.[33] While Indians were asked to demonstrate the appearance of self-sufficiency, attitudes of independence could get them sent home. Demonstrators were to be viewed by, but not interact with, tourists, except within prescribed limits. Most importantly, the Harvey employers wanted demonstrators to act as passive producers rather than active participants in the Indian art market. As anthropologist John Hudson explained to his wife Grace Hudson about the Pomo demonstrators he helped the Harvey Company hire, what "the Harvey's [*sic*] want is the attraction to visitors and monopoly of all work done."[34]

Demonstrators who tried to take business into their own hands, as did a silversmith called Taos, threatened this monopoly. "He is making silver for other Indians and they are selling it," Huckel complained to Hubbell. "He is going over town and selling it and also selling it to our guests on the quiet. Taos has been spoiled by his experience at St. Louis" during the world's fair and, though a "silversmith is quite an attraction," he was becoming uncontrollable. In the end, they sent him home with his wife even before she had completed the blanket she was weaving, which they bought for twenty dollars. Taos received thirty-one dollars, although he asked for $36.50. Harvey manager Snively refused him the additional five-fifty "as I thought he was trying to skin me." He also refused "to pay him $12.50 for putting Pins in 50 buttons for Hat Pins which was about two days' work" but "compromised with him at 12½ cents each."[35]

The dispute with Taos was not the only time that these tourist spaces, primarily dedicated to the commodification of women's work, became arenas for conflicts among men. Shortly before sending Taos home, another Navajo, called Long Man, who in Schweizer's opinion had not been working out well anyway, was "getting troublesome and stubborn. . . . He is pretty much of a mischief maker."[36] "I've had a lot of trouble with the Indians lately in little petty ways," Schweizer wrote Hubbell late in May of 1905 from the Grand Canyon. "The Longman sort of queered the whole bunch, he seems to be a sort of evil spirit reads the stars and all that sort of thing."[37]

This last complaint indicates that although demonstrators willingly traveled into these white tourist sites, they maintained ways of looking at the world that did not always mesh well with their employers' assumptions about market forces and employee responsibilities. Elle and Tom may have been the Harvey Company's favorite employees, but they were not particularly acculturated. Although willing to stay for several months each year, they would go home for reasons that mystified the Harvey people, for example, when Schweizer wrote Hubbell that, "Elle has rheumatism and Tom says Long mans saw the sign and she'd die if she didn't get medicine."[38] In this case, Tom, Long Man, and Elle did not mean western medicine to be found in pills or at hospitals, but the Navajo medicine around which their religious beliefs were organized. Indeed, because the Navajo worldview centers on maintaining well-being through hozho, cultures could clash most irrevocably around the issue of health.

At Harvey houses different worldviews grounded in different economic and gender systems collided. Within this context, it should come as no surprise that even a woman's body could become the site of conflict, as happened to one of the favorite demonstrator families headed by Maria Antonio and Miguelito during the summer of 1905. In May the family began planning to return to the reservation in anticipation of another of Miguelito's wives, Agippa, giving birth. Huckel and Schweizer were not happy with their decision to leave. In a letter to Hubbell, Huckel wrote: "It seems to me he would be much better off if he stays where he is. He is earning a pretty fair salary," and the family was "doing well." Their young daughter, Tonsi-pah, also a weaver, had been ill, but was "quite recovered. Of course, if he is set on going home, I presume it is not advisable for us to object or persuade him not to."[39] The timing was not good for the Harvey Company, as other demonstrators were also "restless," "lonesome," and "homesick," and Elle and Tom were also away.[40] During June, Schweizer and Huckel, with Hubbell's help, tried to make arrangements for replacements while waiting eagerly for Elle and Tom's return.[41]

Then in mid-June Agippa gave birth, probably prematurely. The Harvey people called in a Dr. Pearce who had attended demonstrators before with success. This time he predicted that the baby would not live a month. Huckel told Hubbell, "Agippa was not very ill in Dr. Pearce's opinion, but he would be obliged to attend to her and take her to the hospital."[42] Later Huckel explained,

"We have had so much hospital and other work connected with Migelito's family that I think he believes thoroughly in the 'white man's' doctor."[43] They did not anticipate any problems. Still, Huckel suggested that the family return to the reservation once Agippa was well enough: "I feel if this baby should die at Albuquerque or Agippa should get very ill there the Indians might think it was on account of their living there." He apparently had some understanding of Navajos' need to avoid places associated with death and realized that a death at a Harvey House could be disastrous for the demonstrator program. But Agippa never recovered sufficiently to return home, and, as she got sicker, the limits on this family's acceptance of white ways were severely tested. Schweizer informed Hubbell, "Migelito took his wife out of the hospital and he has her down by the river in a grove of cottonwoods where he built a temporary shelter for her and says he is going to cure her."[44]

Though angry at Miguelito and reprimanded by his boss, Schweizer apparently did not know how to stop this retreat to traditional medicine. In fact, the Harvey men knew that Miguelito was a singer, that is, a Navajo doctor and religious leader. Just the previous fall he had performed a healing ceremony for Tom when doctors at Albuquerque's St. Joseph's Hospital failed to cure his pneumonia. On that occasion Miguelito and Tom's traditional ways brought Fred Harvey good publicity as the Albuquerque paper followed Tom's progress.[45] Born during the Navajos' confinement at Bosque Redondo in the 1860s, Miguelito must have been about forty in 1905.[46] During the 1930s, he and his family would act as important informants for the anthropological work then undertaken with increasing frequency in Navajo country. In her classic studies from that period, anthropologist Gladys Reichard would celebrate Miguelito's knowledge of Navajo religion and Maria Antonio's knowledge of weaving.[47] In the summer of 1905, Miguelito knew what he was doing in that cottonwood grove on the banks of the Rio Grande, although a full-scale sing back home surrounded by a crowd of relatives and friends would surely have been more effective.

When Agippa died, Schweizer, furious, wrote Hubbell, "You can tell Miguelito when he returns that there is no one to blame for her dying but himself." Schweizer insisted that the doctors had told them that she "was bound to die unless she was operated on *immediately.*" In fact, Schweizer finally got her to the hospital, but "It was too late. . . . Dr. Pearce told me that there was no excuse whatever for her dying." He insisted that from then on, they would have a stricter policy in which demonstrators "will have to take [their] physician[']s orders or go back to the reservation on the first train."[48]

Miguelito, Maria Antonio, and Tonsi-pah hurried home after Agippa's death, "too nervous" even "to finish their blankets."[49] But they soon returned. As demonstrators, they moved between their rural homes and Harvey houses and occasionally on longer trips to expositions, integrating demonstration work into their diversified economy. Their movement provides yet another example of the back and forth between "farm and factory" that marked the daily lives of so many Americans in the early twentieth century. But Harvey houses were unusual factories. Rather than wholesale celebrations of technological progress, they were meant to be oases from the modern world. More than mere workplaces, they presumed to display the artistic homelife of what the Harvey Company termed "America's First Families." But for the Indian demonstrators, home was not the Hopi House.[50]

Because the Harvey Company's business *was* tourism, the demonstrator program was, in a sense, far more important to them than to their Native American employees. Schweizer liked "to see my factory in full blast," but he constantly struggled to keep enough demonstrators on hand: "Everybody going to the Hopi House is asking where the Hopi Indians are," he moaned to Hubbell on one occasion, ignoring the fact that many of his favorite Hopi House demonstrators were Navajo. With Miguelito's family gone after Agippa's death, only Tom and Elle remained at the Grand Canyon, making "the Indian proposition . . . really a farce." He pleaded with Hubbell to persuade Miguelito to return or to make some other, really "any arrangement," just, "get some Indians to the Canyon at once."[51]

"It was up to the family when they wanted to quit and go home," remembered one woman who as a child had accompanied her mother to Albuquerque for two months.[52]

And so they did, for dramatic reasons such as Agippa's death or in response to more quotidian or seasonal necessities—to plant their corn, check in with family and friends, attend ceremonies, take care of business, because they just wanted to, or, in the case of one man called the "Old Silversmith," because "people are bothering too much trying to take his picture."[53] Demonstrator work provided some welcome income as well as travel and adventure. It may even have appealed to a few demonstrators as a way to practice and preserve traditional crafts. Most demonstrators, however, were likely less concerned with facilitating cross-cultural exchange than in the satisfaction of earning decent money for work that was of both economic and cultural value to them and their communities. For some, such as Agippa, this decision could lead to tragedy. For others, such as Elle, it may also have entailed sacrifice that was deemed worthwhile. In any case, in the early twentieth century such craftwork was integrated into Navajos' diversified subsistence economy even when practiced in the "staged authenticity" of Albuquerque's Indian Building or the Grand Canyon's Hopi House.

While the Diné brought economic assumptions based on that diversified subsistence economy and reciprocal economic obligations to Harvey houses, their employers maintained faith in market forces and economic specialization. Part of the justification for the marketing of tradition was, according to the Harvey people, that it would benefit all concerned: "The railroad company is very much interested in the success of this project," Huckel wrote Hubbell, "and the tourists are as much so, and I think it will help eventually the . . . Indians by creating a market for their goods."[54]

Through their art, it seemed, Indians could be incorporated into the national market economy and could find a future in modern America, as long as there was a market for their goods. "Staged authenticity" thus suggested an alternative to assimilation: Indian cultures had unique contributions to make, and perhaps they were worth preserving, at least in part. It also served to define Indians as "naturally artistic," a positive but ultimately constraining view.

The conquest of Indian America included not only military force and boarding schools but also the ideological reduction of native cultures to their marketable artistic products—an example, perhaps, of what Barbara A. Babcock calls "modern power," replacing "violence and force with the 'gentler' constraint of uninterrupted visibility, 'the gaze.'"[55] A woman like Elle would not languish in prison like Geronimo, but she was captured many times—on film.

Yet, while in the tourist literature Indians were presented as silent, "beyond expression," a woman like Elle was hardly mute, even if she did not speak English. Remembered decades later as "the boss of the weaving outfit in Albuquerque"[56] she, like her husband Tom and Miguelito and Maria Antonio, found a role in the modern world and a way to support herself by embodying the traditional Indian artisan yearned for by modern Americans. She took on that employment and even met the president without abandoning her ties to her rural home, her kin, her language, her Navajo name, or her religion. In his speech in Albuquerque the day they met, Roosevelt praised those with "adventurous temper and . . . iron resolution . . . who first tempted the shaggy wilderness and turned it into habitations for man." His meeting with Elle is a reminder that the West had been inhabited by "man"—men and women—long before the Anglo conquest, and that diverse groups would continue struggling to make a home there in the twentieth century, a task that might take an even stronger resolution and more adventurous spirit than those manly pioneers Roosevelt had in mind.[57] Historically and historiographically, we have tended to examine more closely the perspective that Roosevelt brought to his meeting with Elle, but just because we do not know what Asdzaa Lichii' said about this encounter does not mean that she said nothing. Despite the lack of written sources from her perspective, we can shift our frame of reference to make the central actor in the story the weaver instead of the president. In doing so, we can deepen our understanding of the ways in which diverse Americans entered the twentieth century and forged our common history.

Much rural women's history has analyzed how women adopted products of domestic labor to the early twentieth century's expanding national industrial economy. The Navajo rug trade fits neatly into this larger historiographical context, but it is worth remembering that Navajo textiles had always been commodities as well as cultural expressions. As Navajo weavers became symbols of the modern Southwest, Navajo women who wove found new markets for their craft. Such marketplaces were sites of compromise and confusion, exploitation and resistance. But, as Diné, weavers continued to expect both financial remuneration and cultural respect for their work. One professional weaver, following in Elle's footsteps, explained in 1986: "Your mind and prayers are connected" to weaving; a rug "just has to be you. . . . I want the Navajo weaver to get lots of money for their weaving. I go several places to teach that." Weaving remains a good way to help face difficult economic circumstances, despite the low return per hour of labor. Younger women, she predicted, will continue to take up weaving because if "there are no jobs for them . . . they think about weaving." Echoing the words of many Navajo weavers over the centuries, she explained, "I raised my children" with weaving, and "with my weaving I get what I want."[58]

Notes

I first told the story of Elle meeting the president at the Fifth Annual Conference on Rural and Farm Women in Historical Perspective held in 1995 in Chevy Chase, Maryland. I would like to thank Lu Ann Jones and Anne Effland for making my participation there possible. Since then the paper has been through many permutations. My thanks go to Jacquelyn Hall, Nancy Hewitt, John Kasson, Marla Miller, and Molly Rozum for their help on the dissertation chapter from which this article is drawn. Participants in the Duke-UNC Feminist History Group and Nancy Shoemaker, as panel commentator, at the 1999 Western History Association meeting provided useful suggestions and lively discussions of earlier versions. Finally, I am grateful to Kathleen Howard, Joan Jensen, Marla Miller, Kathleen Tabaha, and an anonymous outside reader for their thoughtful comments on drafts of the present article and to John Moore and Roberto Mosheim for crucial aid in its completion.

1. Kathleen L. Howard, "Weaving a Legend: Elle of Ganado Promotes the Indian Southwest," *New Mexico Historical Review* 74:2 (1999): 130–31; *McKinley County* (Gallup) *Republican*, April 30, 1903; and Albuquerque *Journal-Democrat*, May 6, 1903, 5.

2. For what little biographical information is available on Elle of Ganado see Howard, "Weaving a Legend," 127–53.

3. Barbara A. Babcock, "'A New Mexican Rebecca': Imaging Pueblo Women," *Journal of the Southwest* 32:4 (1990): 404. A large literature is available on southwestern tourism and on its relationship to the Indian art market. See, for example, Barbara A.

Babcock, ed., "Inventing the Southwest," special issue, *Journal of the Southwest* (1990); J. J. Brody, "The Creative Consumer: Survival, Revival, and Invention in Southwest Indian Arts," in *Ethnic and Tourist Arts: Cultural Expressions From the Fourth World,* ed. Nelson H. H. Graburn (Berkeley: University of California Press, 1976), 70–84; Kathleen L. Howard and Diana F. Pardue, *Inventing the Southwest: The Fred Harvey Company and Native American Art* (Flagstaff, Ariz.: Northland Publishing, The Heard Museum, 1996); Louise Lamphere, ed., "Women, Anthropology, Tourism, and the Southwest," special section, *Frontiers: A Journal of Women Studies* 12:3 (1992): 5–12; Molly H. Mullin, "Consuming the American Southwest: Culture, Art, and Difference" (Ph.D. diss., Duke University, 1993); Scott Norris, ed., *Discovered Country: Tourism and Survival in the American West* (Albuquerque, N.M.: Stone Ladder Press, 1983); Sylvia Rodriguez, "Art, Tourism, and Race Relations in Taos: Toward a Sociology of the Art Colony," *Journal of Anthropological Research* 45:1 (1989): 77–100; Edwin L. Wade, "The Ethnic Art Market in the American Southwest, 1880–1980," in *Objects and Others: Essays on Museums and Material Culture,* ed. George W. Stocking, Jr. (Madison: University of Wisconsin Press, 1985), 167–91; and Marta Weigle and Barbara A. Babcock, eds., *The Great Southwest of the Fred Harvey Company and the Santa Fe Railway* (Phoenix: The Heard Museum, 1996).

4. Scholars have usually viewed the impact of the tourist industry, and the larger market economy of which it was part, on Native American artists and their communities as highly detrimental. See, for example, Edwin L. Wade, "Straddling the Cultural Fence: The Conflict for Ethnic Artists Within Pueblo Societies," in *The Arts of the North American Indian: Native Traditions in Evolution,* ed. Edwin L. Wade (New York: Hudson Hills Press, 1986), 243–54; Tessie Naranjo, "Cultural Changes: The Effect of Foreign Systems at Santa Clara Pueblo," in Weigle and Babcock, *The Great Southwest,* 187–96; and Kathy M'Closkey, "Marketing Multiple Myths: The Hidden History of Navajo Weaving," *Journal of the Southwest* 36:3 (1994): 185–220. Such analyses parallel and sometimes intersect with scholarship on rural women that views Native Americans as losing out as they adopt items of domestic production to an expanding national market economy, and with analyses in Native American women's history that argue that the European and Euro-American economic system disrupted indigenous gender roles to the detriment of women. For an article that combines these themes, see Terry R. Reynolds, "Women, Pottery, and Economics at Acoma Pueblo," in *New Mexico Women: Intercultural Perspectives*, ed. Joan M. Jensen and Darlis A. Miller (Albuquerque: University of New Mexico Press, 1986). In other words, the market economy has long been a villain in Native American studies. Recently, however, historians of Native American women have noted the depth and resilience of cultural systems, evidenced in particular by the fundamental maintenance of gender roles, even as Native Americans adapted to significant historical and material pressures. Other Native American historians have also examined the variety of Native responses to changing economic circumstances and the ways in which Indians brought their own economic rationales to interactions

with Euro-Americans, adapting and adopting aspects of a complex, historically constructed market economy. For an example, see Theda Perdue, *Cherokee Women: Gender and Culture Change, 1700–1835* (Lincoln: University of Nebraska Press, 1998); and Arthur J. Ray, *Indians in the Fur Trade: Their Role as Trappers, Hunters, and Middlemen in the Lands Southwest of Hudson Bay, 1660–1870* (Toronto: University of Toronto Press, 1974).

5. About the Fred Harvey Company I rely particularly on two publications generated by the Heard Museum's recent exhibit on the company: Howard and Pardue, *Inventing the Southwest*; and Weigle and Babcock, eds., *The Great Southwest*. On orientalist southwestern discourse, see Weigle and Babcock, *The Great Southwest*, 6–7. On the Fred Harvey Company and the Santa Fe Railroad, see also Keith L. Bryant, *History of the Atchison, Topeka, and Santa Fe Railway* (New York: Macmillan Publishing Company, 1974); T. C. McLuhan, *Dream Tracks: The Railroad and the American Indian, 1890–1930* (New York: Harry N. Abrams, 1985); and Lesley Poling-Kempes, *The Harvey Girls: Women Who Opened the West* (New York: Paragon House, 1989).

6. Howard and Pardue, *Inventing the Southwest*, 9–15, 103. See also Kathleen L. Howard, "'A Most Remarkable Success': Herman Schweizer and the Fred Harvey Indian Department," in Weigle and Babcock, *The Great Southwest*, 87–101; Matilda McQuaid with Karen Bartlett, "Building an Image of the Southwest: Mary Colter, Fred Harvey Company Architect," in Weigle and Babcock, *The Great Southwest*, 24–35; Virginia L. Gratton, *Mary Colter: Builder Upon the Red Earth* (Flagstaff, Ariz.: Northland Press, 1980); and Marta Weigle, "Exposition and Mediation: Mary Colter, Erna Fergusson, and the Santa Fe/Harvey Popularization of the Native Southwest, 1902–1940," *Frontiers: A Journal of Women Studies* 12:3 (1992): 117–50. On using the concepts of "staged authenticity" and "backstage" views of Indian life in analyzing Mary Colter's architecture, concepts drawn from Erving Goffman's and Dean MacCannell's work, see Weigle, "Exposition and Mediation," 120–30.

7. Leah Dilworth, *Imagining Indians in the Southwest: Persistent Visions of a Primitive Past* (Washington, D. C.: Smithsonian Institution Press, 1996), 147–48, 151.

8. Weigle and Babcock, *The Great Southwest*, 12.

9. Ruth Roessel, "Navajo Arts and Crafts," in *Handbook of North American Indians*, vol. 10, *Southwest* (Washington, D.C.: Smithsonian Institution Press, 1983), 595.

10. Interview no. 27, Hubbell Trading Post National Historic Site Oral History Collection (hereafter HTPOHC), Ganado, Arizona; and Ann Lane Hedlund, *Reflections of the Weavers' World: The Gloria F. Ross Collection of Contemporary Navajo Weaving* (Denver, Colo.: Denver Art Museum, 1992), 30. When the interviews were conducted for HTPOHC in the late 1960s and early 1970s, consent forms were not obtained for the interviews to be used in subsequent research. Kathleen Tabaha, the assistant curator at the Hubbell Trading Post National Historic Site, is in the process of contacting interviewees' family members in order to obtain such permission. In the meantime, she has asked that I not use interviewees' names.

11. Ann Lane Hedlund, "'More of a Survival Than an Art': Comparing Late Nineteenth- and Late Twentieth-Century Lifeways and Weaving," in *Woven by the Grandmothers: Nineteenth-Century Textiles from the National Museum of the American Indian*, ed. Eulalie H. Bonar (Washington: Smithsonian Institution Press, 1996), 47–48. A voluminous literature is available on Navajo weaving. In addition to those works cited above, I am relying particularly on Ellen F. Elsas and Ann Lane Hedlund, *"Well May They Be Made": Navajo Textiles from the Coleman Cooper Collection of the Birmingham Museum of Art* (Birmingham, Alabama: Birmingham Museum of Art, 1987); Ann Lane Hedlund, *Beyond the Loom: Keys to Understanding Early Southwestern Weaving* (Boulder, Colorado: Johnson Books, 1990); Ann Lane Hedlund, "Contemporary Navajo Weaving: An Ethnography of a Native Craft," (Ph.D. diss., University of Colorado at Boulder, 1983); Kate Peck Kent, *Navajo Weaving: Three Centuries of Change* (Santa Fe: School of American Research Press, 1985); Marian E. Rodee, *One Hundred Years of Navajo Rugs* (Albuquerque: University of New Mexico Press, 1995); Joe Ben Wheat, "Documentary Basis for Material Changes and Design Styles in Navajo Blanket Weaving," in *Proceedings of the Irene Emery Roundtable on Museum Textiles* (Washington, D.C.: The Textile Museum, 1976); Joe Ben Wheat, *The Gift of Spiderwoman: Southwestern Textiles, the Navajo Tradition* (Philadelphia: University Museum, University of Pennsylvania, 1984); and Roseann S. Willink and Paul G. Zolbrod, *Weaving a World: Textiles and the Navajo Way of Seeing* (Santa Fe: University of New Mexico Press, 1996).

12. Gary Witherspoon, "Navajo Social Organization," in *Handbook of North American Indians*, vol. 10, *Southwest*, 525–26; and Elsas and Hedlund, *"Well May They Be Made,"* 29–30.

13. Garrick Bailey and Roberta Glenn Bailey, in *A History of the Navajos: The Reservation Years* (Santa Fe, N.M.: School of American Research Press, 1986), argue that even in the twentieth century, as "Navajos diversified into commercial stock raising and wage labor" they did not totally commercialize their herds but "successfully maintained high subsistence value while raising the market value of their livestock. . . . In large part rug weaving enabled them to achieve this balance" because it "gave a dimension to their herding economy that Anglo-American and Spanish-American ranchers lacked" (179–80). David Aberle contends in "Navajo Exogamic Rules and Preferred Marriages" (in *The Versatility of Kinship Essays Presented to Harry W. Basehart*, ed. Linda S. Cordell and Stephen Beckerman [New York: Academic Press, 1980]) that "traditional kinship organization is maintained because of, rather than despite, changes in the Navajo economy—that traditional kinship organization, oriented to the multiple, fluctuating resources of the traditional economy, preserves the same orientation now that the Navajos are marginal participants in the larger United States economy. Relying on multiple, fluctuating resources, which include flocks, farms, crafts, wage work, and welfare, most families have no single source of livelihood sufficient in quantity or reliability to induce them to give up the others. . . . By and large, the nuclear family provides insufficient labor power for all these activities"

(123–24). On the maintenance of matrifocal kinship institutions in the midst of a dramatically changing political economy, see also Klara B. Kelley, "Navajo Political Economy before Fort Sumner," in Cordell and Beckerman, *The Versatility of Kinship*, 315, 317–318, 329. On change and persistence of Navajo women's roles and status, see Laila Shukry Hamamsy, "The Role of Women in a Changing Navaho Society," *American Anthropologist* 59:1 (1957): 101–111; Mary Shepardson, "The Status of Navajo Women"; and Christine Conte, "Ladies, Livestock, Land, and Lucre: Women's Networks and Social Status on the Western Navajo Reservation," *American Indian Quarterly* 6:1/2 (1982): 105–124; and Louise Lamphere, "Historical and Regional Variability in Navajo Women's Roles," *Journal of Anthropological Research* 45: 4 (1989): 431–56.

14. Richard I. Ford, "Inter-Indian Exchange in the Southwest," in *Handbook of North American Indians*, vol. 10 , *Southwest*, 721.

15. Hedlund, "'More of a Survival Than an Art,'" 54.

16. Bailey and Bailey, *A History of the Navajos*, 51.

17. Bailey and Bailey, *A History of the Navajos*, chapter 2. On the Navajo economy and trade networks, see also Klara Bonseck Kelley, "Commercial Networks in the Navajo-Hopi-Zuni Region," (Ph.D. diss., The University of New Mexico, 1977).

18. Bailey and Bailey, *A History of the Navajos*, 59–60; Kent, *Navajo Weaving*, 17–18, 83, 85–86; and Dilys Winegard, ed., *A Burst of Brilliance: Germantown, Pennsylvania and Navajo Weaving* (Philadelphia: University of Pennsylvania Press, 1994). A large and growing literature is available on trading posts in Navajo country. The story of traders and Navajo weavers has often been told as change directed by traders with weavers passively accepting white men's suggestions. Recent scholarship has emphasized weavers' agency and analyzes trading posts as complex sites of transculteration. Three classics are Frank McNitt, *The Indian Traders* (1962, reprint, Norman: University of Oklahoma Press, 1989); William Adams, *Shonto: A Study of the Role of the Trader in a Modern Navaho Community* (Washington, D.C.: Smithsonian Institution, Bureau of American Ethnology, Bulletin 188, 1963); and Willow Roberts, *Stokes Carson: Twentieth-Century Trading on the Navajo Reservation* (Albuquerque: University of New Mexico Press, 1987). Recent studies include Martha Blue, *Indian Trader: The Life and Times of J. C. Hubbell* (Walnut, Calif.: Kiva Publishing, Inc., 2000); Laura Graves, *Thomas Varker Keam, Indian Trader* (Norman: University of Oklahoma Press, 1998); Laura Ruth Marcus, "Moving Towards Nizaad: Exploring the Dynamics of Navajo-Anglo Interaction through Trading and Art," (Ph.D. diss., Indiana University, 1998); Nancy Peake, "Trading Post Tales: Biography of an Indian Trader on the Navajo Reservation, 1930–1980," (Ph.D. diss., University of New Mexico, 1992); and Teresa Jo Wilkins, "Producing Culture Across the Colonial Divide: Navajo Reservation Trading Posts and Weaving," (Ph.D. diss., University of Colorado at Boulder, 1999). A good recent description of the trading post economy is in Robert "Skip" Volk, "'Red Sales in the Sunset': The Rise and Fall of White Trader Dominance in the United States' Navajo Reservation and South Africa's Transkei," *American Indian Culture and Research Journal* 24:1 (2000): 69–97.

19. Marc Simmons, *Albuquerque: A Narrative History* (Albuquerque: University of New Mexico Press, 1982), 234, 275–77, 329; Bradford Luckingham, *The Urban Southwest: A Profile History of Albuquerque, El Paso, Phoenix, and Tucson* (El Paso, Texas: Western Press, 1982), 19, 35–36; and Bailey and Bailey, *A History of the Navajos*, 156, 157–158. On ways in which Navajos combined wage work with a kin-based household economy that often conflicted with their employer's expectations, see Colleen O'Neill, "Navajo Workers and White Man's Ways: Negotiating the World of Wage Labor, 1930–1970," (Ph.D. diss., Graduate School-New Brunswick, Rutgers, The State University of New Jersey, 1997); and Colleen O'Neill, "The 'Making' of the Navajo Worker: Navajo Households, the Bureau of Indian Affairs, and Off-Reservation Wage Work, 1948–1960," *New Mexico Historical Review* 74:4 (1999): 375–405.

20. The Hubbell Trading Post in Ganado is still in operation today, owned by the National Park Service as a National Historic Site. Weavers still visit the trading post's rug room to bargain with the trader in Navajo, while others demonstrate their art for tourists in the visitor's center. These weavers carry on in Elle's tradition, but much has also changed, and tourists are instructed not to photograph demonstrators without their permission.

21. Herman Schweizer to John Lorenzo Hubbell, March 13, 1903, April 29, 1903, and March 6, 1903, Fred Harvey File (hereafter FHF), Incoming Correspondence, box 36, Harvey Trading Post Collection (hereafter HTPC), Special Collections, University of Arizona.

22. Juana Sangre of Isleta Pueblo, interviewed in 1994, remembered constantly cleaning the pots and the floors between trains. She said, "And when they tell us a train is about to be here we used to quit so they wouldn't find us [cleaning]" (quoted in Howard and Pardue, *Inventing the Southwest*, 24).

23. See, for example, Huckel to Hubbell, June 9, June 26, July 1, and July 20, 1905, FHF, HTPC. Unlike weaving, silver work continued to be an important trade item among the Diné. The heavy silver jewelry that Navajos used was inappropriate for the tourist market, so the Harvey Company encouraged some silversmiths to develop a lighter, cheaper style that they could sell in their stores. See John Adair, *The Navajo and Pueblo Silversmiths* (Norman: University of Oklahoma Press, 1944).

24. Howard and Pardue, *Inventing the Southwest*, 74, 76, 105–110.

25. Elle and Tom had no children together, which might have lessened their responsibilities back home. Still, they often brought some of Tom's grandchildren with them to Albuquerque, and Elle was frequently photographed surrounded by children. She was an ideal demonstrator because she could afford to stay away from home while still providing a matronly image (Howard, "Weaving a Legend," 132, 128).

26. Howard and Pardue, *Inventing the Southwest*, 64, 66, 68.

27. *The Great Southwest Along the Santa Fe* (Kansas City, Missouri: Fred Harvey, 1914), n.p., quoted in Marta Weigle with Kathleen L. Howard, "'To Experience the Real Grand Canyon': Santa Fe/Harvey Panopticism, 1901–1935," in Weigle and Babcock, *The Great Southwest*, 21.

28. Huckel to Hubbell, March 4, 1905; and Schweizer to Hubbell, November 17, 1904, FHF, HTPC.

29. I am touching here only lightly on the relationship between "antimodernism," the arts and crafts movement, and Indian art, a relationship that I discuss in more depth in "The Navajo Rug Trade: Gender, Art, Work, and Modernity in the American Southwest, 1870s–1930s," (Ph.D. diss., University of North Carolina at Chapel Hill, 1999). Besides those already cited, related works include T. J. Jackson Lears, *No Place of Grace: Antimodernism and the Transformation of American Culture, 1880–1920* (New York: Pantheon Books, 1981); Eileen Boris, *Art and Labor: Ruskin, Morris, and the Craftsman Ideal in America* (Philadelphia: Temple University Press, 1986); J. J. Brody, *Indian Painters and White Patrons* (Albuquerque: University of New Mexico Press, 1971); W. Jackson Rushing, *Native American Art and the New York Avant-Garde: A History of Cultural Primitivism* (Austin: University of Texas Press, 1995); Wendy Kaplan, ed., *"The Art That is Life:" The Arts and Crafts Movement in America, 1875–1920* (Boston: Little, Brown and Company for Museum of Fine Arts, 1987); Miles Orvell, *The Real Thing: Imitation and Authenticity in American Culture, 1880–1940* (Chapel Hill: The University of North Carolina Press, 1989); Melanie Herzog, "Aesthetics and Meanings: The Arts and Crafts Movement and the Revival of American Indian Basketry," in *The Substance of Style: Perspectives on the American Arts and Crafts Movement*, ed. Bert Denker (Winterthur, Delaware: Henry Francis du Pont Winterthur Museum; Hanover: University Press of New England, 1996), 69–92; Margaret D. Jacobs, "Shaping a New Way: White Women and the Movement to Promote Pueblo Indian Arts and Crafts, 1900–1935," *Journal of the Southwest* 40:2 (1998): 187–216; Molly H. Mullin, "The Patronage of Difference: Making Indian Art 'Art, Not Ethnology,'" *Cultural Anthropology* 7:4 (1992): 395–426; and Teresa J. Wilkins, "The Creation of a Usable Past," in *Diné Baa Hané Bi Naaltsoos: Collected Papers from the Seventh through Tenth Navajo Studies Conferences*, ed. June-el Piper (Window Rock, Arizona: Navajo Nation Historic Preservation Office for the Navajo Studies Conference, 1999), 203–10.

30. Switzer per Snively to Hubbell, July 9, 1903, FHF, HTPC.

31. Interview no. 20: 567 098, in Michael Joseph Francisconi, *Kinship, Capitalism, Change: The Informal Economy of the Navajo, 1868–1995* (New York: Garland Publishing, 1998), Appendix A, 220.

32. Huckel to Hubbell, October 24, 1905, FHF, HTPC.

33. See, for example, Huckel to Hubbell, April 26, 1905, and April 21, 1905, FHF, HTPC.

34. Letter from John Hudson to Grace Hudson, February 6, 1903, quoted in Howard and Pardue, *Inventing the Southwest*, 59.

35. Huckel to Hubbell, April 21 and 26, 1905; and J. Snively to Hubbell, May 6, 1905, FHF, HTPC.

36. Schweizer to Hubbell, April 29, 1905, FHF, HTPC.

37. Schweizer to Hubbell, May 31, 1905, FHF, HTPC.

38. Schweizer to Hubbell, April 6, 1905, FHF, HTPC.

39. Huckel to Hubbell, June 9, 1905, FHF, HTPC.

40. Huckel to Hubbell, June 26, 1905, and May 31, 1905, FHF, HTPC.

41. They got to the Canyon on June 25.

42. Huckel to Hubbell, July 1, 1905, FHF, HTPC.

43. Huckel to Hubbell, July 20, 1905, FHF, HTPC.

44. Schweizer to Hubbell, July 19, 1905, FHF, HTPC.

45. *Albuquerque Morning Journal*, October 3 and October 21, 1904, cited in Howard and Pardue, *Inventing the Southwest*, 61.

46. Interview with Marie Curley, Doris Duke Number 678, the American Indian History Project, Western History Center, University of Utah, September 10, 1970, copy in the HTPOHC, Ganado. Curley says that her father, Miguelito, was four, and her mother, Maria Antonio, was two, when they left Fort Sumner.

47. Gladys Reichard, *Navajo Shepherd and Weaver* (1936; reprint, Enumclaw, Wash.: MacRae Publications, 1977), *Spider Woman: A Story of Navajo Weavers and Chanters* (1934; reprint, Glorieta, N.M.: Rio Grande Press, 1968), and *Navajo Medicine Man: Sandpaintings and Legends of Miguelito* (New York: J. J. Augustin, 1939).

48. Schweizer to Hubbell, July 24, 1905, FHF, HTPC.

49. Schweizer to Hubbell, July 27, 1905, FHF, HTPC.

50. In the 1920s the Fred Harvey Company issued a series of lavishly illustrated publications edited by J. Huckel titled "American Indians: First Families of the Southwest."

51. Schweizer to Hubbell, March 15, 1903; Huckel to Hubbell, May 23, 1905; and Schweizer to Hubbell, September 13, 1905, FHF, HTPC.

52. Interview no. 40, n.d., HTPOHC.

53. Schweizer to Hubbell, May 31, 1905, FHF, HTPC.

54. Huckel to Hubbell, March 23, 1905, FHF, HTPC.

55. Babcock, "A New Mexican Rebecca," 429. Babcock is paraphrasing Michel Foucault's discussion of "the gaze" in *Discipline and Punish: The Birth of the Prison* (New York: Pantheon Books, 1977).

56. Interview no. 7, November 15, 1971, HTPOHC.

57. *Albuquerque Journal-Democrat*, May 6, 1903.

58. Interview no. 1, January 20, 1986, Ganado oral history rug study interviews, HTPC.

CHAPTER 7

Working on the Domestic Frontier

American Indian Domestic Servants in White Women's Households in the San Francisco Bay Area, 1920–1940

MARGARET D. JACOBS

In 1934, "Opal," a young Pomo Indian woman who worked as a domestic servant in the San Francisco Bay Area, wrote in exasperation to the Bureau of Indian Affairs outing matron who had placed her in employment with Mrs. L. N. David of Berkeley: "Mrs. . . . David owes me ten dollars and she won't pay me for it. She accuses me of taking things which I didn't do. Do you remember when I left last July you told me to tell you if I didn't receive my pay to tell you. Well I didn't receive it and besides she accused the girl before me . . . of the same thing. I think it's just a stunt to get out of paying me. . . . I wrote several letters to her, but finally gave it up as hopeless. She only paid me twelve a month." Opal also lamented that when Mrs. David "did let me go to Oakland for the dances she always wanted me to go up to the house to mow the land and kill fleas. The house was just infested with them. That is a terrible job by itself. That meant scrubbing all the ten rooms. She didn't give me a moment's rest, so I think it's terrible that she doesn't want to pay me. Will you please try and make her give me the $10." Opal added in a postscript, "I need the money terribly and I earned it, more than earned it so please make her pay me."[1]

On the face of it, Opal's predicament did not differ significantly from that of other domestic servants in the United States in the early years of the twentieth century. Like Opal, most were female, impoverished, and racially classified as nonwhite, and they had few options for employment other than working as domestic servants.[2] Many other domestic servants also suffered from the same kinds of indignities and toiled for the same low wages as Opal. Moreover, the relationship between employer and servant within the household has always been riven with inequalities that have divided women by class and often by race.[3] This is not a new story.

However, household employment for Opal and other young Indian women did differ from that of other domestic servants in several key ways. First, Opal had not journeyed across the Atlantic or Pacific or trudged across a national border in search of wage labor; nor had she been freed from human bondage only to be enlisted into the lowest rungs of the American economy. Instead it was the colonization of her land and the subsequent federal Indian policy of assimilation that drove her and other young Indian women into domestic service.

Second, employment of young Indian women by white families became more than a private labor transaction between employer and employee; the Bureau of Indian Affairs (BIA) envisioned such employment as a central component of its assimilation policy. From 1880 up to the 1930s, as part of this policy, the BIA had removed thousands of Indian children to boarding schools. Many of the schools developed what came to be called "outing" programs, ostensibly to aid in the children's assimilation, which placed the children for part of each day and usually for entire summers with local families. Boys were usually set to work doing farm labor, while girls were to be employed in domestic service within the home. Even while in school, much of the education Indian children received revolved around training them for such menial positions, a process officials often characterized as making them "useful."[4] Enlisting white women employers in the project of "uplifting" and "civilizing" young Indian women made white women's households more than private homes or workplaces; they became domestic frontiers where colonial relationships continued to play themselves out. As in other colonies around the world, this intimate setting became a significant site for the reproduction and performance of colonial relationships.[5]

Third, the figure of the outing matron—an agent of the BIA—complicated the simple bilateral relationship between white woman employer and Indian servant. By employing outing matrons to oversee the employment of Indian girls and young women within urban households, the BIA attempted to maintain strict control over the young Indian women and to ensure that the white households in which they were employed provided the uplifting environment necessary to the servants' assimilation. Outing matrons in the San Francisco Bay Area compiled copious files from the 1920s through the 1940s on each young Indian woman that they placed in service, a record of documentation that suggests the intense surveillance and scrutiny under which the Indian servants lived and labored.[6]

Interestingly, however, the records also reveal the ways in which these Indian servants partially evaded the BIA's tight control over them. Young

Indian women often refused to be wedged into their assigned roles of obliging servants and rejected attempts to "uplift" them. In hundreds of small acts on a daily basis, young Indian women like Opal asserted their own independence and agendas, chipping away at the façade of colonial hierarchy and order. Most of the young Indian women servants also cast aside or simply ignored the strict Victorian-era sexual codes and gender norms that the BIA promoted in its boarding schools. Instead they appear to have maintained their own Indigenous communities' norms regarding gender and sexuality while embracing the modern gender sensibilities of the city as well.

Ultimately, the state failed in its mission to assimilate young Indian women—that is, less euphemistically, to separate them from their Indigenous communities and make them useful, as domestic servants, in the colonizers' economy. Ironically, many young Indian women used the state's agent—the outing matron—as a mediator in conflicts with their employers. Moreover, most young Indian women apparently engaged in domestic service for just a short period of their lives—as part of a patchwork of economic strategies and perhaps as a youthful adventure—before returning to their reservations and rancherias. Nevertheless, if the state fell short of its goal to assimilate the young women, it still maintained some of its authority over the young women, particularly through asserting control over the children that many young Indian women bore while in service. Thus, as in the more visible conflicts over land and labor between colonizers and Indigenous Californians, the domestic frontier also proved to be a site of ongoing tension, instability, and constant negotiation.

Colonization on the Northern California Frontier

Most of the young Indian women who worked in the Bay Area between 1920 and 1940 came from a variety of Indian groups in northern California, Nevada, and Oregon, including the Pomos, Hoopas, Shastas, Monos, Paiutes, Klamaths, Washoes, and Western Shoshones. It would be impossible to cover the histories of each of these groups in an article, but a brief historical overview of the Pomos provides one example of the ways in which these groups had been colonized in the nineteenth century.

Just a few generations before Opal found herself killing fleas and scrubbing floors in the city for twelve dollars a month, the Pomos had claimed and lived upon a large swath of territory in northern California where the women gathered, leached, and pounded acorns to make their staple acorn mush and collected other edible bulbs, roots, seeds, herbs, nuts, and berries to complement the hunting and fishing that Pomo men usually carried out. Pomo women were (and still are) renowned for weaving the fibers of sedge root, willow rod, and redbud bark (and sometimes colorful feathers) into intricate

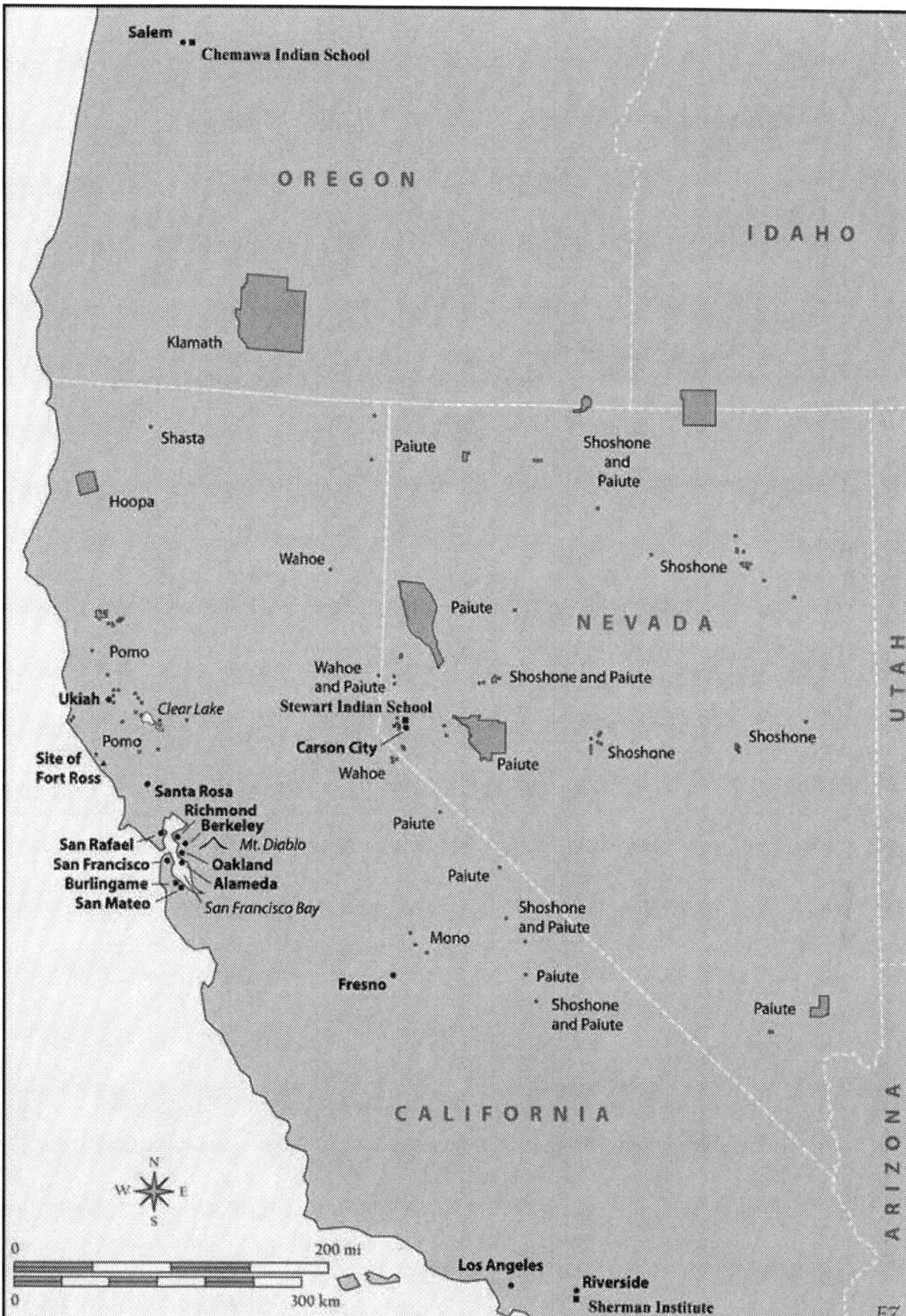

Figure 7.1. Map of California and neighboring states with locations of schools and Indian communities named in the text. Drawn by Ezra Zeitler.

anthill-and quail-patterned baskets ranging in size from the eraser head on a pencil to giant granaries in which to store acorns. In their roundhouse, Pomo women danced and worshipped. Some became highly esteemed healers, and a few Pomo women took leading roles as Dreamers in the revivalistic Bole Maru religious movement that began in the winter of 1871–72.[7]

By the 1870s, four waves of colonization—from the Russians, Spanish, Mexicans, and Americans—had already buffeted the Pomos. In 1812, the Russians had established a trading colony at Fort Ross; five years later, Spanish friars erected a mission at San Rafael.[8] Both the Russians and the Spanish conscripted some bands of the Pomos into forced labor; the Spanish also sought to convert some Pomo groups to Christianity. Europeans had also introduced deadly diseases among the Pomos, who suffered a drastic decline in population, especially as a result of the great pandemic of the 1830s. When Mexico obtained its independence from Spain in 1821 and secularized the missions, it then subjected the Pomos to a new round of slave raiding and trading. By 1842, the Russians had abandoned their fort, but a new crop of colonizers from the United States had begun squatting on land in California. After the Americans conquered the territory from Mexico in 1848, the Pomos suffered from a new and precipitous population decline, brought on by increased disease and starvation. In 1850, the new California state legislature enacted "An Act for the Government and Protection of Indians," which despite its benevolent name, amounted to allowing Indian children to be kidnapped and virtually enslaved.[9] Outright massacres of the Pomos—the most famous at Clear Lake in 1851—also decimated and demoralized the group. The Pomos also lost 99 percent of their homelands to the invaders. Other Indians in the region endured a similar fate.[10]

In the 1850s, U.S. government troops rounded up the remaining Pomos and marched them to two newly established reservations, the Mendocino and Round Valley reservations. With inadequate rations, however, many reservation residents became ill and malnourished. Many Pomos fled the reservations in search of better conditions. By the late 1870s, many groups of Pomos pooled their money to purchase land to create their own small rancherias. When most of these Pomos later lost this land to unpaid taxes or defaulted mortgages, the government in the early 1900s set up other small rancherias to accommodate the dislocated Pomos.[11]

Without their original tracts of land, the Pomos found it more difficult to maintain their earlier subsistence activities. Pomo men gave up their traditional hunting to shear sheep and work in the new logging industry. Beginning in the late 1860s, Pomo women became hop pickers and servants in the new invaders' homes.[12] On the other hand, Pomo women managed to continue some of their gathering and foraging activities in the late nineteenth century; as late as 1900, the Pomos still relied primarily on their traditional diet of clover, bulbs, seeds, nuts, and acorns that Pomo women had harvested for centuries. By the late 1920s, however, the Pomos had become almost wholly dependent on wage labor and new American foodstuffs.[13] Other Indigenous peoples in northern California, Nevada, and Oregon at the turn of the twentieth century also lost their ability to subsist from their land and became increasingly dependent on government assistance, wage labor, or both.

A century of colonization had also undermined Indian social patterns and gender systems in the region. Among the Pomos, according to Elizabeth Colson, who conducted anthropological research among them in the late 1930s, gender relations had been closely regulated before the incursion of American soldiers and settlers, many of whom sexually assaulted Pomo women or took them for their mistresses. "The old marriage system with its permanent binding of families together to ensure the welfare of the children had already suffered somewhat from the disruption of the groups caused by slave raids, massacres, and forced removals," Colson writes. When the Pomos settled on reservations and rancherias, according to Colson, "following the example of the Whites whom they best knew, the Pomo discarded permanent unions."[14] When Juliet Lombard studied the Pomos at the same time as Colson, she found that "a young person almost always has a series of . . . affairs before he or she finally contracts a lasting marriage." Moreover, the Pomos rarely legalized their marriages; as Lombard explains, "[W]hen an Indian man and woman live together for a long period of time, they are considered married."[15]

Assimilation on the Domestic Frontier

By the late nineteenth century, American colonizers in the region had accomplished one of their imperial aims: they had wrested much of the land from its Indigenous inhabitants. Yet, as in the rest of the American West, BIA officials and reformers complained that a so-called Indian problem remained. Although their land base and traditional lifeways had been severely compromised, Indian people still tenaciously held some land, where they could maintain their distinctive identities, innovate new rituals and ceremonies, and evolve new social practices. At the same time, because Indian peoples had lost much of their land and their traditional means of subsistence, they had grown partially dependent on the government for food assistance. In short, the colonization of Indian peoples was not complete.

In the late nineteenth century, to solve this "Indian problem," the U.S. government masterminded a new policy—assimilation—which advocates characterized as a benevolent enterprise to help Indian people adjust to "civilization." In reality, assimilation functioned as an effort to consolidate colonization through attempts, as one white women's reform organization put it, to carry out "the vastly needed work within Indian hearts, minds and souls."[16] On a more pragmatic level, the BIA also hoped to end its trust obligations—including the provision of rations and annuities—to Indian peoples. The BIA set about implementing its new policy by allotting communally held land among several tribes to individual Indians, enacting a Religious Crimes Code in an effort to eliminate many Indian religious ceremonies and practices, and removing thousands of Indian children to boarding schools far from the supposedly harmful influences of their home communities.

Initially, Indian children obtained a varied education at some of these schools, but by the early twentieth century, the curriculum in the Indian schools centered on training boys for menial occupations and girls for domestic service.[17] In 1901, for example, Estelle Reel, the Superintendent of Indian Education from 1898 to 1910, declared that "the importance of holding the work strictly within practical lines can not be too strongly impressed upon the instructor."[18] Another administrator seemed to view the boarding schools as factories that were turning raw material—Indian children—into useful goods. "We must labor with a more definite aim in these schools to fashion this human material into something for which there is a demand," he wrote. "Until we have done this we can not hope for great success in finding locations for our products."[19]

Outing the children to work for and live with white families became yet another part of the assimilation program. White policymakers and authorities characterized the outing of Indian girls for domestic service not just as a job but as a necessary part of their curriculum in "uplifting" Indians from savagery to civilization. As Estelle Reel put it, the outing system "places the student under the influence of the daily life of a good home, where his inherited weaknesses and tendencies are overcome by the civilized habits which he forms—habits of order, of personal cleanliness and neatness, and of industry and thrift, which displace the old habits of aimless living, unambition, and shiftlessness."[20] Thus, authorities ennobled domestic service and invested white women employers with an important role in "civilizing" Indian girls and young women.

At the same time, a growing demand for domestic servants in California and other parts of the American West provided a ready market for the newly trained Indian girls. San Francisco and its environs had grown enormously since the U.S. had seized the territory from Mexico in 1848. At that time, San Francisco had only about one thousand inhabitants, but partly because of the Gold Rush and the completion of the transcontinental railroad, the city's population had increased in size to more than 340,000 by the early 1900s, making it the ninth-largest city in the United States. Until 1920, it was the largest city west of the Mississippi River.[21] New middle- and upper-class women residents of the city would have sought out domestic servants, but found few available in the 1920s and '30s. African American women, who worked extensively as domestic servants in the East, did not make up a sizable pool of laborers in the San Francisco area or in other Western locations until World War II, and at that point they eschewed domestic service for better-paying jobs in ship-building and other defense industries.[22] Mexican women immigrants and Chinese and Japanese immigrant men had served as domestic servants from the late nineteenth century up through the 1920s. Yet during the era in question, immigration from Asia had been curtailed by the 1882 Chinese Exclusion Act and the 1924 Immigration Act. Moreover, at least 500,000 Mexicans were deported or repatriated during the Depression. Therefore, there would have been a scarcity of domestic servants in the San Francisco Bay Area.[23] The superintendent of Carson Indian School noted in 1930, in fact, that in the Bay Area, there were "more applications for girls to assist in families than there are girls."[24]

Although large numbers of Indian women undoubtedly worked as domestic servants in the early twentieth century, especially in the American West, few historians have studied or written about the topic.[25] Scholars have been peculiarly silent about this topic perhaps because of longstanding interest in Indians primarily in their traditional, premodern settings. Works on Indian women have tended to focus on questions of the extent of their status in their traditional societies and how their status changed over time with European contact.[26] As more scholars, however, turn their attention to what Philip Deloria calls "Indians in unexpected places," American Indian women's experience as domestic servants and their encounters with modernity will undoubtedly invite additional research.[27]

The Domestic Frontier as a Contact Zone

As BIA agents placed Indian girls and women in white women's households, the "frontier"—once thought of as the hinterlands on the edge of civilization and more recently conceived by scholars as a contact zone between Indigenous people and their colonizers—moved into new intimate spaces, often within urban areas.[28] Geographer Janet Henshall Momsen explains, for example, "Domestic space can be seen as a contact zone within which negotiations over 'otherness' and identity, based on race, class, religion, age, education, sophistication and citizenship are constantly underway."[29]

This new domestic frontier, in fact, grew out of colonial conflicts on the geopolitical frontier. Evelyn Nakano Glenn has pointed out that domestic service is integrally related to colonialism. She observes that "labor migrants are drawn from 'backward' areas whose economies have been disrupted and subsequent development distorted by western colonial incursions. The distortion of the economy leaves large segments of the population with their usual means of livelihood interrupted. Many are thus free to be torn from their roots and recruited to fill labor needs in the advanced regions, often the source of the original incursion."[30] More recently, the globalization of the economy has created inequities that lead to the migration of impoverished women from a rural to an urban setting or across international boundaries to take up employment in privileged homes within rich countries, a practice that Pierrette Hondagneu-Sotelo calls the "New World Domestic Order."[31] This global colonial phenomenon was already operating in relation to Indian peoples within the boundaries of the United States during the first decades of the twentieth century.

The domestic frontier not only functioned as a side effect of "larger" colonial conflicts but also served to reproduce and re-enact colonial relations on a daily basis. American Indian women's domestic service in white women's homes thus becomes a key arena in which to study what Ann Laura Stoler calls the "intimacies of empire" or "the quotidian shaping of racialized colonial worlds and their disparate sites of production."[32]

American Indian Domestic Servants in the San Francisco Bay Area

In the Bay Area, no Indian boarding schools existed within a convenient distance for Indian girls to be outed on a daily basis, but in 1918, the BIA hired Bonnie Royce, wife of the superintendent of the Stewart Indian School in Carson City, Nevada (often referred to as the Carson Indian School), to place young Indian women from the surrounding area in domestic service. The Commissioner of Indian Affairs stipulated that Royce "give special attention to procuring [employment in] homes for Indian girls after they have left school or for any other Indian women of Nevada and Northern California . . . , in order that they may be protected from the degrading moral conditions which are found in the small mining towns of Nevada and the country adjacent thereto." He also gave Royce strict instructions: "The field [outing] matron should ascertain the character and reputation of the parties wishing Indian help and make regular visits to the homes where such employment is given so that no mistake may be made in placing these girls in homes only where helpful influences are radicated [radiated]."[33]

Royce first established the placement office in Berkeley; it later moved to Oakland, and later still, across the bay to San Francisco. Royce served as outing matron until the early 1930s; she convinced the BIA to hire Jeannette Traxler as her assistant in 1929, and Traxler appears to have taken over from Royce sometime in the early 1930s. In 1934, the BIA hired a new matron, Mildred Van

Figure 7.2. Photograph no. 11, *Girls Sitting on Grass* (photograph of children and grounds of Stewart Indian School southeast of Carson City, ca. 1935). Decimal Subject Files, 1925–1950, Records of the Carson Indian Agency, Records of the Bureau of Indian Affairs, Record Group 75; National Archives and Records Administration—Pacific Region (San Francisco).

Every, who worked in the post until 1946.[34] Although Royce began her work in the 1910s, the outing office did not begin to keep detailed files on the young women until 1925. This article is based on an examination of ninety-seven of the most detailed files.

Given the origins of the program, many of the young Indian women who came to work as domestic servants in the Bay Area had attended the Carson Indian School. During the summer of 1929, for example, of forty-one Indian girls outed for the summer, twenty-seven were from the Carson school. Of the eighty young Indian women permanently outed in the Bay Area in 1929, twenty-eight were from the Carson school. Others had been enrolled at Chemawa Boarding School in Salem, Oregon, or Sherman Institute in southern California or attended unidentified public schools (an increasing trend among Indian children in the 1920s and '30s).[35] Juliette Lombard notes that two-thirds of the Pomo women from the Ukiah valley north of San Francisco who took domestic jobs in the Bay Area had attended Sherman Institute.[36] She also reveals that "by 1941, more than a third of Ukiah Valley Indian women [in northern California] between the ages of fifteen and thirty had worked for some time in the Bay Area."[37]

Young Indian women learned of employment opportunities through the placement service in one of three ways—through referrals from boarding school or reservation officials, through word of mouth among the young Indian women themselves, or through recruitment efforts by the matrons. Matron Van Every visited Sherman Institute every summer and traveled frequently around northern California to recruit young Indian women. The BIA records also indicate that the matrons often corresponded with officials on the reservations or in the boarding schools the girls had attended.[38] Other young Indian women found domestic employment in the Bay Area through a competing private placement service. Royce complained to Superintendent Frederic Snyder of the Carson School in 1930, in fact, that "For the past two years a Mrs. H.C. Roberts, whose husband has charge of a fish cannery at Requa, California, has been responsible for bringing a number of Indian girls to this [East Bay] District to work. When she started this work it was with my knowledge and with the understanding that she would co-operate with this Center. However, as time advanced the girls came without my knowledge and were placed in homes by Mrs. Roberts, who I think, uses poor judgment in the placing of the girls, and ignores our rules and regulations."[39]

In the trilateral relationship that developed along the domestic frontier between the young Indian women, their white women employers, and the BIA outing matron, each group had its own interest and priorities.[40] The records compiled by the outing matrons actually tell us little about the motivations of white women employers and the outing matrons themselves, but understanding the larger context of middle-class women's work and domestic life in the early twentieth century may shed light on why white women became involved in this enterprise. The outing matrons seem to have been motivated in part to take up this line of work through the influence of the Progressive maternalist women's movements. At least one outing matron emerged from a women's reform organization with maternalist orientations. Van Every had close ties to the Young Women's Christian Association (YWCA) and served as Industrial Secretary for the Oakland branch in the 1930s. She also appears on their Indian Girl's Work Committee for 1942.[41] Van Every also relied on maternalist networks in her work with young Indian women and girls. For example, in 1934 Edith Murphey, the chair of the Indian Welfare Committee of the California Federation of Women's Clubs, wrote to Van Every that she wanted to place two Indian sisters in domestic employment in the Oakland area.[42] Working through such women's organizations and clubs for social reform, maternalists often justified women's presence in public reform as a natural extension of their experience or socialization as mothers, upheld a maternal and domestic role as most fitting for other women, and sought to mother other seemingly disadvantaged women.[43]

The outing matrons may also have been motivated to take up these new positions through a desire for professional advancement. In the early twentieth century, many other maternalist reformers maneuvered themselves into unprecedented positions of professional authority through government agencies, including the newly established Children's Bureau and Women's Bureau.[44] The large numbers of white women who worked as teachers and matrons (and less commonly as principals and superintendents) for the BIA represent another way in which white women institutionalized maternalist sensibilities within federal agencies in the late nineteenth and early twentieth centuries. In his study of Indian boarding schools, David Wallace Adams found that "the average teacher appears to have been a single woman in her late twenties." Indeed, Cathleen Cahill discovered that the proportion of women employees in the BIA's School Service "held steady between fifty-five and sixty-two percent" from 1890 well into the twentieth century.[45]

The BIA readily believed that white women's maternalism could be put to the service of its assimilating mission. When he appointed Royce as outing matron, Commissioner of Indian Affairs Sells defined Mrs. Royce's mission as a maternal one. "I feel that there is a great work to be done in Nevada for these Indian women," Sells concluded, "and from the experience that Mrs. Royce has had in Indian work believe that she will be able to give the girls the motherly advice and encouragement which will prove an uplift to those placed in her care."[46] Thus, by building on their associations with domesticity and motherhood, white middle-class women created a new avenue toward professionalism and self-support.

The outing matron's records reveal even less specific information about the white women employers and their motivations, but it might seem obvious why such women sought out domestic servants—simply to help with household work. Yet as many scholars of domestic service have pointed out, acquiring a domestic servant also carried with it a badge of class and racial status that made it possible for women employers—most of whom were white—to meet middle-class standards of cleanliness while escaping the drudgery that such standards required.[47] As Hondagneu-Sotelo explains it,

> Even among wealthy white women born and raised in the United States in the late twentieth century, few escape the fetters of unpaid social reproductive labor. As many observers have noted, their reliance on house cleaners and nannies allows well-to-do women to act, in effect, as contractors. By

> subcontracting to private domestic workers, these women purchase release from their gender subordination in the home, effectively transferring their domestic responsibilities to other women who are distinct and subordinate by race and class, and now also made subordinate through language, nationality, and citizenship status.[48]

Certainly, on a recently colonized frontier with a shortage of domestic servants, white middle-class women in the Bay Area would have been anxious to assert their status through employing a domestic servant. Some white women employers—who were also undoubtedly influenced by the maternalist movements of their time—may also have been drawn to the ennobled mission of participating in the "civilization" of young Indian women.

Young Indian women, of course, had their own distinctive reasons for participating in domestic service. Some Indian girls, who were outed directly from one of the boarding schools for the summer, had little say in the matter. Other young women, who had graduated from or simply left the boarding schools, may have turned to domestic service because they could find little other employment. By the early twentieth century, the notion that Indian women were suited for little else but domestic service predominated. Juliette Lombard, carrying out research in the 1940s among the Pomos in the Ukiah Valley, found that even though many of the young women she encountered had been trained as beauticians, nurses, or in clerical work, none could find work in those occupations.[49]

In contrast to the dearth of documentation regarding white women's involvement in the enterprise, the BIA records reveal a host of other reasons why young Indian women sought domestic service positions. When the Depression hit, Indian women's options narrowed further as their need to earn money became even greater. "Wynona," a Mono Indian, wrote in search of a position because "I am quiet [*sic*] interested, as we certainly feel the depression. I will quit school in a minute to secure a job for fifty dollars per month as a cook."[50] Some supported family members. "Daisy," a Shasta Indian who had three children, wrote to one of the matrons, "[I] have left my husband, he is worthless and cruel. . . . I tried to stay with him for the children's sake but he is just impossible. I am at home with mother now. . . . Must get some work to do soon as my three children and I are without shoes or clothes."[51] During these hard times, many Indian women might have viewed domestic service as one part of an overall economic strategy. Many young Pomo women, for example, often worked picking hops in the summers and serving in white women's households in the Bay Area for the remainder of the year.[52]

While the BIA records do not reveal the larger familial and communal context for these young women's work, other scholars' recent studies on American

Indian labor in the twentieth century suggest that Indian workers conceived of wage work more as a means to contribute to their families' household economies than as a means to gain individual advancement. Moreover, Indian wage earners often modeled their employment on the seasonal round of subsistence economic activities in which their communities had once engaged. As Colleen O'Neill puts it in relation to Navajo wage work, "The Navajos negotiated the encroaching world market selectively, participating in it when it suited their purposes, but refusing to allow capitalist cultural and economic logic to significantly undermine the basic premises upon which they had shaped these new economic strategies."[53]

Some of the young women experienced extreme prejudice and lack of opportunity in their home communities. In the Ukiah Valley, where many of the Pomo women came from, most white families and white-owned businesses refused to hire Indian women. Local Indians there also faced segregation in housing, restaurants, movie theaters, and even beauty parlors. One young Pomo woman from the area declared, "I don't want to live on any rancheria! I want to go away some place and study and study and be left alone."[54]

As this writer's comment makes clear, the young women had other reasons for moving to the city for domestic work beyond a simple lack of money. Some simply wanted adventure and to experience something new. "Irene," from Salt Lake City, "was particularly interested in seeing the Golden Gate International Exposition, and to find out whether she could make Indian articles at the Exhibit."[55] Indian women also seemed to regard domestic employment as a route to some form of independence, sometimes from the paternalism, control, and surveillance they faced within boarding schools or on their reservations, but also on occasion from the abusive situations within their own families. "Elsie," a Washoe, told Van Every that "she did not intend returning to the man with whom she had been living near Fresno but would rather make her own living."[56] Some of the girls envisioned domestic jobs as the means eventually to attain a college education or professional training. "Clara" wanted to work for a while in order to save money to go to Willamette University.[57] "Edith," a Winnebago who had studied nursing for two years at Haskell and then worked for two years as a nurse (and had a "fine contralto voice"), came to the Bay Area to study voice while working as a domestic.[58]

Many young Indian women also sought out domestic jobs in part for the social opportunities they afforded. "Helen," according to her employer, "talked on the telephone a good deal each day, and seemed to have many friends at the University."[59] The YWCA sponsored the Four Winds Club in Oakland for the young Indian women and men in the Bay Area, where they met every Thursday night and held chaperoned dances once a month.[60] "May" wrote one of her friends, "Amelia," "Well, my pal, they had a party Thursday night as usual. I was there, I saw all my pals from Richmond, all of them boys . . . and all the girls."[61] Others relished dancing and drinking in the city out from under the watchful eyes of the matron at the YWCA or their employers. Mrs. Scott let "Caroline," a Western Shoshone girl, go "because she was staying out late—drinking."[62] Notably, these young women largely sought out the company of other Indian women—and a few Indian men—in the Bay Area. Their efforts to connect with other urban Indians, whether from their own tribe or not, laid the foundation for the urban pan-Indianism that would flourish after World War II.[63]

So important was this social life to the young Indian women that many of them refused or resigned from particular jobs if they cramped their social opportunities. For example, "Fern" and Amelia wrote to Royce in 1929 about how unhappy they were working at the Mt. Diablo Country Club (inland from the Bay Area). They pleaded with her, "We can't stand it here any longer. Too hot, lonesome, and everything. We would like to work some place else, where we can see the girls on our day off. It feels terrible not to see them, and that were [*sic*] way off. . . . Can you please get us a better place. We can't stand the heat and we can't cook to suit them. . . . We would rather work there [in] the city than out here. Please get us a place there."[64]

Although some of the Indian women may have taken the jobs for adventure, independence, or social opportunities, they spent most of their time carrying out the duties assigned to them by their white mistresses and expected of them by the matrons. As May put it in a letter to her friend Amelia, "I guess you know that Royce lady make [*sic*] you work. I've been working like hell every [*sic*] since I got here."[65] Indian girls and women who worked as domestics were charged with basic cleaning and additional responsibilities such as caring for children, cooking, ironing, serving the table, and answering the door bell and telephone. Wages varied considerably for young Indian women. In the 1920s, "Jane," a Washoe, made $50 to $65 a month, whereas in the Depression of the 1930s, "Susan," a Klamath, earned just $20 a month while Opal, at one low point, only took in $12 one month.[66]

In their relationships with their employers, the young Indian workers experienced many of the same problems and conflicts that other women did in other domestic service arrangements. The agendas of employers often clashed with the priorities of the young Indian servants, and perennial conflicts that seem inherent to domestic service—over wages, hours, types of work, and leisure—ensued. White women employers wanted obedient and dedicated servants who would work long hours for low wages. After her servant "Hannah" left because "she would rather work in Oakland where she knew someone and where it was a larger place," Dorris Taft of San Mateo wrote to matron Traxler to request a new servant, but one who would work for fifteen dollars a month.

Taft informed Traxler that in San Mateo they did not pay twenty-five dollars and up and "I would like awfully to get a good girl, but one who will stay, this changing and training is a very hard thing both on the girl and on me."[67]

White women employers also wanted to control how their Indian servants—most of whom boarded with their employers—spent their leisure time. Mrs. Parlier of Berkeley was annoyed when her servant "Sylvia" went with her girlfriends to San Francisco in a taxicab. She was "indignant that people who did household employment should spend their [money] in that way."[68] Van Every wrote that Susan "does not accept criticism" and that she "resigned [as] Mrs. Wright's employee because she asked her not to remain out past midnight."[69] Conflicts over leisure had long been a source of friction between white women and African American women servants as well. Many African American women solved this problem by saving up enough money so they could live separately from their employers.[70] Because Indian women were expected to live with white families as part of their "civilization" program, this option was not available to young Indian women servants.

As was common in other domestic service arrangements, white women also sought to command deference and strict obedience from their employees and were upset when many young Indian women seemed unwilling to conform to their demands. On the outing form of "Iris," for example, the matron wrote, "Good girl—slow. Very impudent to Mrs. Lester. Mrs. Maurice says not clean or good worker." "Louisa" "did not make good at first place. Stayed out nights left Mrs. Wilson's. Mrs. Moore let her go because out all night and saucy."[71] Grace Cresap wrote to Royce that her two Indian servants "have been sullen. They do their work, but not in a happy manner; neither Mr. Cresap nor I can stand having ill tempered people about us."[72] As these cases illustrate, white women employers were disappointed in young Indian women who were "impudent," "saucy," and "sullen" and refused to play the role of obedient, humble, and grateful servant in need of guidance, protection, and "civilization."

For their part, like other domestic servants elsewhere, the young Indian women merely sought employment with reasonable hours and decent wages with full control over their leisure time. American Indian girls and women routinely objected to the low salaries white women tried to pay them. Many, like Opal, found it difficult to get their employers to pay them their full wages in a timely manner. "Anne," an experienced young woman from the Colville Reservation in her early 30s and married to a Sac and Fox man who was in the Navy, wrote to Van Every about her employer, Miss Ellis. "I found her very pleasant, and we talked about the work so we are going to try it. One thing I couldn't get her to promise to pay me $40.00[.] And in the future if she still don't see to pay me my price; I am only going to promise you that if she don't I don't want to stay with her for only $35.00 That is after a week's trial."[73]

The type of work the young women were asked to do also grated on them. "Emmeline" lost her "place at Johnstone's because of late hours, swearing and complaining of the wash."[74] In particular, many young women grew weary of having to take care of white women's children. Hannah wrote to Royce, "I am on my way to my sister's. . . . I tried for 2 months to grin and take what came my way—and tell you people I was happy—up till now. I had no privacy what-ever—the kids slept in my bed—used my things—sassed me back." On top of this, according to Hannah, "She [her employer] expected me to take care of the kids and do house work at the same time—which I just could *not* do. They [the kids] wouldn't mind—then she thought I was in the wrong."[75]

Indian servants also chafed at the restrictions their employers placed on their social lives. Hannah complained to Royce, "On my days off I was let off so late, that it really wasn't worth going out. When I went over to Oakland . . . I [had] no time to get ready, and then had to make up for it with a lot of work." Hannah also disliked the sense of being constantly monitored and judged during her leisure time. "Last year I was only at a show and it was told to Mr and Mrs Wright [her employers] that I was 'running wild' down at Oakland," Hannah confided to Royce.[76] "Myra's" intercepted letter to her boyfriend also reveals how much the young Indian women resisted their white women employers' control of their leisure. After staying out late with her "dearie," Myra wrote to him,

> I am writing to tell you what a time I had last night. . . . I was locked out [of her employer's home] so I couldn't come in, I sure wished I stayed with you then. I am here at the YWCA now writing you these few lines. Well, Honey, so I might not get to see you Sunday. . . . Maybe I have to stay Home all-day. It certainly will be tough. If I can't see you. . . .
>
> Well, Mrs. J. call Mrs. Royce up this morning, and told her I was locked out and she told Go right Back to Mrs. Johnson, But I haven't started yet. Hell with Johnsons. They make me sick all over. I might be going Home to Ukiah, on the next Train that pulls out for all I know.[77]

It is clear when looking at cases like those of Hannah and Myra that in a number of significant ways Indian women's experience of domestic service differed significantly from that of other young women who took on the same work. First, another tension complicated the unequal class and race dynamics already inherent in servant-employer relationships in the United States. In this case, in trying to carry out the role envisioned for them by the BIA—as maternalist civilizers of Indian women—white women employers often claimed to be not only employers but uplifters who needed to protect and shape the morals of the young Indian women in their hire and care. Mrs. Harrington of Burlingame, south of San Francisco, for example, asked Royce, "Let me know—how late may she [her servant] stay out at night? She has a friend in the city—an Indian girl and last Sunday they went to a dance. I feel F. is a fine girl and one to be trusted, but I simply wanted to know whether I am responsible for her hour."[78] Like Myra, most of the young servants seem to have resisted their employers as maternalistic and uplifting figures. Wynona, for example, according to Royce was "going with associates whose influence we think is bad; she ignores all our advice and that of her employer."[79]

Second, the presence of the outing matron further muddled the domestic service relationship between white woman employer and Indian employee. BIA records reveal that the matrons scrutinized the work lives and leisure hours of the young Indian women. The matron kept files that rated the girls on many of their household tasks. For Elsie, the matron noted:

Care of Children	Poor
Cooking	Assist, no experience
Ironing	Yes
Answering Door Bell	Yes
Answering Telephone	Yes
Serving the table	No training[80]

The matrons often rated the girls not just on their work skills but also on their behavior in the workplace and their morality. Van Every wrote of Ruth that she was "Moody." Under the Morals category, Van Every wrote simply, if inexplicably, "No Standard."[81] Royce complained of one young woman: "I have had considerable trouble with [Rebecca]. She left her place of employment and claims she went to Santa Rosa but I think she was hiding in Oakland. If so, of course there was a boy in the case. I have tried so hard to keep tabs on [Rebecca] for I really like her and hoped to be able to make something of her."[82] (Royce's comment conveys the strong current of maternalism—a desire to make something of Rebecca—that ran through her work as outing matron.) While other domestic servants certainly had to put up with many of the same conflicts with their employers, only Indian domestic servants were subjected to this level of scrutiny and the presence of a third party, a representative of the federal government, no less.

At times, the young Indian women servants could use the presence of this third party to their advantage; they sometimes called upon the mediating position of the outing matron to gain greater leverage with their white women employers. When Opal "was offered a job with Mrs. Wacs[,] [Van Every] urged her not to take the hob [*sic*] at the low wages offered."[83] And when Opal's former employer, Mrs. Whittaker, refused to pay her the $3.82 she was owed, Van Every "urged her to write Mrs. Whittaker about the money." A few days later,

"Mrs. Whittaker called [Van Every] on the telephone and later came into the office protesting that she would not pay [Opal]. [Van Every] maintained that the amount was due to [Opal]." Just two days later, "Mrs. Whittaker left a check for [Opal]."[84] The Oakland YWCA (with which Van Every was affiliated) also organized its Amicitia and Four Winds Clubs to assist "in the introduction of the Bill limiting the hours of employment in this occupation [domestic service] to fifty-four." These clubs "helped raise a lobby fund and some went to Sacramento at the time of the vote on the Bill, which was defeated."[85] Thus, the matrons, on occasion, could become allies of and mediators for the young Indian women rather than (or in addition to) government agents bent on monitoring and controlling the servants.

As Rebecca's case suggests, however, more often than not, many young Indian women seem to have rebelled against the interference, control, and monitoring of the matrons as much as against the maternalism of their employers. Royce claims she tried to help "Sharon" (Western Shoshone) and another unwed Indian mother find a place for their babies, but Sharon went against her advice and also behaved impudently to her employers. "[Sharon] continued to be disagreeable and gossiped with Mrs. [H.], who was boarding the baby, about her employer and also about her mistreatment from me. [Sharon] evidently got sympathy from Mrs. [H.], as Mrs. [H.] advised her that the Government had no control over them and that they could go on their own if they wished; I understand she consulted a lawyer concerning this. This created an independent spirit in the girls and they became absolutely unmanageable."[86]

The young Indian women particularly resented the control that authorities often still had over their monies, another important difference in the experience of outed Indian girls and women as compared to other domestic servants. "[Sharon] called me on [the] phone last week and demanded the funds I had in my office," Royce wrote to Emmett E. McNeilly, Superintendent of the Western Shoshone Agency. "When I told her I had transferred same to you she was very abusive and talked as no other girl had ever done. All this is very humiliating; considering the patience I have had with her and all the trouble and care she has caused." Royce lamented, "I have done all in my power to advance these girl's [*sic*] welfare and have to acknowledge defeat for the first time, as [Sharon] is the first girl to positively refuse my supervision."[87] "Ruby" had also written to Superintendent Snyder of Carson Indian School to withdraw all of her wages, but Snyder told her that her request had arrived too late and that "we think it is a better way to handle the money than to have the people pay it direct to the girls, we then have a record of what money the girls have earned during vacation."[88]

Other young Indian women butted up against the limited career options open to them and challenged the low expectations of their employers, matrons, and reservation and school officials. "Margaret" shared her frustration with John Collier, the newly appointed commissioner of Indian affairs, in 1933. In her impeccably typed letter, Margaret told him, "I am an Indian girl and a graduate from Sherman Institute. . . . I was sent out to that school to get an education. When I graduated I found I could not get any other job but as a housekeeper. Any girl knows how to do that sort of work I'm sure. My four years wasted. I found I could have accomplished more if I had attended a regular public high school."[89] Margaret also told Collier how her family had lost their land and become destitute. Her grandmother had sold the family's land, and they were living off money from its sale. When her grandmother died, however, Margaret's family could not get the rest of the money, because her grandmother had not left a will. Margaret lamented, "The reason why we Indians in the middle part of California are backward is because we have nothing to get started with. The little we have doesn't amount to anything. We have no money to go to college to be somebody. Why doesn't somebody give us a break?" She explained further to Collier, "I am working here in Hollywood as a housekeeper. My salary is twenty a month. My ambition was to become a nurse; as I am lacking some credits, I can't get in any nursing school. That means I just have to go back and start my four years over again." She concluded, "This is just a glimpse of one Indian family, but there are many more in California."[90]

Collier proved to be of little help to Margaret.[91] She continued to work throughout the 1930s as a housekeeper. Later, she became pregnant and married but separated from her husband. When she could not find a place to board the baby while she worked, she decided to leave the child with her mother and make her mother its legal guardian. Margaret remained resentful that after years of boarding school, she could not find work other than domestic service. In 1941, according to Van Every, a man came into her placement center and told her that "[Margaret] . . . and [her friend] [A.] . . . are violent in their attitude toward our office. . . . They lose no opportunity to make remarks and criticisms and say that we keep Indian girls down."[92] Finally in 1942 Margaret was able to complete a course at the hospital and gain a temporary position there.[93]

Many young women defied the matrons and their employers specifically over the gender roles and sexual standards they sought to instill in the girls. Rather than abiding by the outmoded Victorian mode that was often promoted in the schools, many of the girls embraced the new freer sexual expression for women that had begun to appear in American popular culture during the 1910s.[94] New hairstyles, music, movies, and books lured the young women away from boarding-school fare. Elsie told Matron Van Every that "she wished to stay a while [in a new job] until she got some things she needed including a permanent wave."[95] While hospitalized, Sarah asked Van Every for "two new movie magazines and one Western Romance. . . . If you would please send them to me. Is all I would like to have."[96]

The matrons and some of their employers tried to channel the young Indian women's sexuality into appropriate channels—marriage to respectable, Christian Indian men who were also presumably on the road to assimilation. In 1929, Matron Royce lamented that "the lack of moral standards among the majority of the girls cause [*sic*] great social difficulties; many embarrassing moral questions have been presented during my ten years supervising Indian Welfare, in the San Francisco Bay District; unmarried girls becoming pregnant, girls leaving employment to live with men, married ones leaving wife or husband for others and the contracting of venereal diseases." Royce tried to prevent such outcomes by inviting desirable young men—presumably Indian men—to parties and dances. She reported to her supervisor in 1929, "Special interest has been taken in the young men this year. Many have been called upon and invited and encouraged to call at my home. Their habits have been investigated and if found to be proper associates for the girls they were invited to the social affairs."[97]

Royce also used other means to block young Indian women from socializing with men she deemed unsuitable, as in the case of "Etta," who wrote to her father to protest "against Mrs. Royce having anything to do with her while she is working in Oakland." Etta's father then complained to BIA authorities; Superintendent Snyder countered, however, that it was Royce's job "to look after the interests of young Indian women who work in the coast cities. . . . While [Etta] may be 22 years of age," he noted, "I do not think she should resent any supervision that Mrs. Royce may have over her."[98] Etta and her father disagreed, however. Her father wrote to Royce in 1925,"I wish you would leave [Etta] alone. She's all right when you leave her alone, she old enough to look after her self." Royce seemed to object to the man that Etta had chosen to marry. "If that boy love her and she loves him leave them alone," Etta's father admonished Royce. "We can't pick out her husband and his wife for them so just leave them alone, let them get married if they love each others [*sic*]." Etta's father noted a double standard: "These people here just leave the young pale-face alone, they don't but in when they want to get married, they just let them get married. I thought any people I mean Indians could get married any time as long as they're old enough. If they have their folks consent, But I'm mistaken I see [*sic*]."[99]

Royce's efforts seem to have made little difference. For one thing, as noted by Lombard, there were about five Indian women to every Indian man in the Bay Area.[100] Even had all these men met Royce's criteria as suitable mates for the young Indian women, clearly there were not enough men to go around. Moreover, freed from the constraints of the boarding schools and able to evade their employers and the matrons, many young women seemed to revel in new social opportunities and the chance to flirt and socialize with young men. Some of the young women's relationships culminated in formal or common-law marriage, to Indians and non-Indians, and almost always outside their tribes. Ruth married a Portuguese man in 1934. Wynona "married a white man with the Radio-Post at San Francisco Beach." Bernice, a Winnebago, began living with a "Negro" in 1938.[101] Those young Indian women who did link up with Indian men from outside their communities reinforced the trend that had already begun with the formation of boarding schools—the formation of a pan-Indian identity—and that increased during and after World War II as more Indians moved to urban centers.[102]

Many other young Indian women became single mothers as a result of their sexual relationships in the city. Of the ninety-seven case files I studied, more than one-quarter of the young women became pregnant or already had children while working as domestic servants. Only a couple of these women were married. While the matrons and employers generally viewed this as a sign of the young women's immorality (or their own failed mission to "civilize" and "assimilate" them), within their own Indian communities, it is unlikely that the young Indian women experienced the same degree of disapproval and judgment for becoming single mothers. Among the Pomos, for example, no stigma seems to have been attached to young Pomo women who returned from the city pregnant.[103]

Given the tense climate over their work and leisure in the city, it is no surprise that many of the young women dealt with their conflicts with employers and matrons by simply quitting or running away from their jobs. The files reveal that nine young women abruptly quit their service and that twelve ran away from their positions, a total of almost 22 percent of all the young women I studied. Many young Indian women stayed with an employer only a few months (and in some cases for a period of just days or weeks) before moving on to another employer, returning home for the summer or a brief period, or absconding. On the outing form of "Vera," a Western Shoshone, for example, the outing matron wrote, "In 1928 ran away May 19th, unmanagable [*sic*], detention home May 22." Two years later, the matron added, "In Sept. 1930 Entered Chemawa Indian School. Ran away from same. Placed with Mrs. Bruzzone, Ala[meda]. [A]cted very ugly, impudent and lady would not even keep her over night."[104]

The frequency with which young Indian women ran away from their domestic service jobs demonstrates another important difference between their employment and that of other women who worked as servants. On the one hand, it suggests that at least some of the young women felt a greater sense of compulsion in their jobs and thus a greater need to run away than did other servants. As Vera's experience reveals, young Indian women could even be sent to detention homes for running away. The BIA's outing program thus represented a more paternalistic work situation than other domestic service arrangements.

On the other hand, the fact that large numbers of young Indian women left their jobs after only a few months indicates that they had or felt they had greater options; young Indian women had homes and communities (impoverished though they were) to which they could return or networks of other young Indian women with which they could connect. Other forms of seasonal employment—such as picking hops—also appealed more than continuous employment in the city. As Victoria Patterson puts it, "most [Pomo] girls chose to jeopardize their jobs [in the city] every summer by returning to Mendocino County for the hop season, that time of riverside trysts, easy living, and wages that equaled ten months of dreary housework in someone else's house."[105]

Finally, this phenomenon suggests that the young Indian women had not imbibed the capitalist ethos of the assimilation program. Both Lombard and Colson remarked, with a hint of disappointment, that not one of the young Pomo women they observed and interviewed in the late 1930s had made domestic service a career.[106] Clearly, the outing matrons and the white women employers were also perturbed that they could not get most of the young Indian women to settle down in one position or use their employment as a steppingstone to a "respectable" marriage.

It is tempting to end the story of these young Indian women here as a triumphant tale of a group of women marginalized by their class, race, and gender who managed to pull one over on their would-be oppressors. Within the context of feminist history, we could celebrate these young women's entrance into wage labor and their pursuit of new leisure activities and sexualities as liberatory. Alternatively, we could interpret their experience within the context of recent American Indian history and trumpet the ability of these young Indian women to resist assimilation. Yet for the young Indian women "outed" to domestic service, concepts such as liberation and resistance must be tempered with a view of the larger forces of colonialism that constrained their lives.

The assimilation project may have broken down along this domestic frontier, but the long tentacles of the BIA still reached the young Indian women. When some young Indian women servants—roughly one-quarter of my sample—became pregnant and had children, it is evident that the BIA and its agents still had the upper hand. Having a child while working as a servant often presented an overwhelming challenge to young Indian women, many of whom had delivered their babies, through the arrangement of the outing matrons, at the Salvation Army Rescue Home. One wonders how Jane, unmarried, who bore a baby on December 13, 1928, cared for him after she began work again on January 30, 1929.[107]

Some young Indian women left their children back home with relatives. "Mary," a Pomo, had two children whom she left with her mother while she went to work as a domestic servant for nine months of the year. Apparently, Mary came home in the summers, where she could find work picking hops and see her children.[108] Some young Indian women found this situation intolerable. When "Stella" had a baby, she left it with its grandmother, but eventually Stella left her employer and returned to her home near Ukiah. A field nurse there lamented to Royce, "So another effort to help her has gone wrong. I still believe the girl wants to do right. It was a lot to expect of her to leave her baby and all her relatives to go out alone to earn a living."[109] Interestingly, during an era when most white women reformers pushed for mothers' pensions so that poor women—at least white women—could stay at home with their children, white women in the BIA deemed an Indian woman who came home to take care of her baby as "gone wrong."[110] The field matron's comment suggests a widespread assumption among many white women who worked with Indian peoples that an Indian woman's place was in the (white woman's) home as servant. To such white women maternalists, a young Indian woman who stayed home with her baby and "all her relatives" had not properly imbibed the individualist capitalist ethos promoted by assimilation.

Other young Indian women boarded their children out while they worked. "Ethel," a Paiute, "arrived in Oakland, July 23–1931 With small baby girl." Royce placed Ethel as a domestic and put her baby in a boarding home, but admitted to a field matron among the Paiutes, "I am sure I do not know how we are going to pay for the baby's board, for I fear [Ethel] cannot make enough to support herself and child. The price of the baby's board is $25.00, and [Ethel] has started to work for that amount."[111] Indeed, boarding out one's baby while working was a costly proposition and illustrated that young Indian women were subject to the phenomenon of what Sau-ling Wong calls "diverted mothering," whereby "time and energy available for mothering are diverted from those who, by kinship or communal ties, are their more rightful recipients" to care for the employers' children instead.[112]

The matrons put considerable pressure on some Indian mothers (five of the twenty-five Indian mothers) to give their children up for adoption or to put them in institutions. The case of "Nellie" is a poignant one. When Van Every first began her work, she encountered Nellie, who had a twenty-two-month-old boy, "Sammy," who lived with a Mrs. Upson while Nellie worked. Nellie had since married and had another baby. With former matron Traxler, Van Every called on Nellie and wrote in her file that "she says that she still wishes to have the baby [Sammy] with her, but that her husband has no steady work."

Her husband "does not object to having the child brought home if [Nellie] wishes it. But there is not enough money for their own expenses." Nellie was emphatic that "she does not wish to place the child [Sammy] in an institution."

Despite Nellie's reluctance to part with her son, Traxler and Van Every called upon Mrs. Marie White of the California Children's Home Society. "We gave the account of [Sammy], son of [Nellie], urging steps to be taken immediately in giving [Sammy] a home rather than longer continuing with Mrs. Upson, who is getting too old to care for him longer," Van Every reported. "Mrs. White said that unless [Nellie] can assume the responsibility of the child or some of the girls' family can see the child thru, the child must be adopted out. The mother must give over the case of the child to the Child placing agency and sign a relinquishment or a consent before an agency can do the work need[ed] to take over the case. . . . Mrs. White asked us to advise [Nellie] that we had talked with her and ask for [Nellie]'s full cooperation in the case."

Traxler and Van Every then went to visit Nellie again. By now, economic exigencies seem to have convinced Nellie she had no other choice but to give up her son. "When asked what she intended doing about [Sammy] she said that she would have to let him be adopted out," Van Every reported. "We told her of Mrs. Marie White of the Children's Home Society of California and of the work the Society did. She seemed to understand the steps necessary to placing [Sammy] in a Home. She agreed that she would cooperate fully with Mrs. White." A few weeks later, Van Every learned that "[Nellie] is expecting another baby and is quite willing to give [Sammy] up, not knowing what else to do about him. She signed the relinquishment papers."[113]

Interestingly, the records reveal that the matrons and the adoption agencies with which they worked did not deem all the children of Indian women as suitable for adoption. In some cases, the child welfare agencies discouraged removing children who particularly looked "Indian" from the young women for adoption. Van Every revealed, "The Child Placement Bureau has had Indian placements to make in the past and has found them very difficult, in fact impossible, especially when the child is of such Indian cast of features."[114]

Alternatively, the matrons and other BIA officials sought to have some children removed from their Indian mothers and institutionalized, just as many of them had been parted from their own parents to attend boarding schools or go to work in other families' homes. Losing their children in such a way was often a source of intense pain and anguish for the young women. For example, Etta (the woman whose father had protested against Royce's intervention into her relationship) had been separated from her parents and raised at the Carson Indian School. When authorities removed her four children and sought to place the oldest, a six-year-old boy, at the Carson school, Etta objected strenuously. A probation officer reported that Etta "is most unwilling for this placement, stating that she had been very unhappy there and that she could not possibly consider placing her child there."[115] Despite Etta's wishes, Royce conspired with Superintendent Snyder to place Etta's son at the Carson school. Royce, in fact, declared that Etta's "wishes should not be considered in this case, as she is incapable of judging what is best for her boy."

Authorities not only removed Etta's children but took steps as well to have her placed in a mental institution, claiming that a psychological test had "rated [her] as borderline, mental age 11 years." The matrons' outing records reveal that three other Indian women who had several children out of wedlock and resisted officials' attempts to remove their children were also eventually committed to mental institutions.[116] These cases are a sobering reminder of the high cost that these young Indian women paid for their attempts to live out from under the control of the BIA.

Thus, this is not a simple story of women achieving liberation by pursuing wage labor and embracing modern gender roles. Nor is it merely an uplifting tale of Indian resistance to assimilation. Instead it is an account complicated by not just the legacy of conquest but the ongoing practice of colonialism, now masquerading in the guise of assimilation policy. The households in which young Indian women worked became intimate theaters of colonialism where the roles of gently guiding white mistress and obedient and deferential Indian servant had been scripted and were expected to be played out. This domestic frontier was meant not merely to reflect the new colonial order imposed upon Indian peoples but also to reproduce and perform it in a kind of long-running theatrical production.

However, Indian women domestic servants, as they migrated from their rural homes and communities to the urban Bay Area or from boarding school to workplace, did not passively accept their assigned role in the colonial script—as nameless laborers to be made useful in the "New World Domestic Order." These young Indian women had their own agendas; they wanted to immerse themselves in modern urban life, enjoy the company of other young Indian women, meet men, and use their jobs in the city as steppingstones out of or a temporary respite from the poverty and discrimination they faced in their home communities. Ultimately, for many if not most of the young Indian women who worked in the Bay Area, the period of service constituted a temporary period in their lives. (Lombard found that of all the Pomo women who went to work in the Bay Area, all but one or two eventually returned home.)[117] For some of these young Indian women, working on the domestic frontier in the Bay Area was a carefree adventure, almost a rite of passage, between boarding school (in many cases) and returning to their reservations or rancherias. For other servants, like Etta, working and living on this domestic frontier was a humiliating and harrowing experience that demonstrated the pervasive power of the BIA.

For officials with the BIA, colonization proved to be as incomplete and elusive along this domestic frontier as it did in other contact zones between colonizers and indigenous people. Rather than assimilating what the BIA regarded as appropriate work ethics and gender norms, most of these young Indian women made neither a career of domestic service nor a BIA-approved marriage. The BIA, therefore, did not succeed in solving the "Indian problem," of winning the hearts, minds, and souls of these young Indian women. It settled instead for continuing to exercise a degree of paternalistic control over them. Thus most of the young Indian women servants experienced only fleeting moments of self-determination over their own lives. As May wrote to Amelia, "I'm going to try to be a good girl, if I can make it & try to enjoy myself. It seems though I've lost all my happiness. Ever since I came back here. I hope to be my self some times."[118]

Notes

1. P. Ar. to Van Every, October 30, 1934, chronology, P. Ar. file, Box 1, Relocation, Training, and Employment Assistance Case Records, 1933–1946, Outing Girls, Record Group (RG) 75, Bureau of Indian Affairs (BIA), California Sacramento Agency, National Archives and Records Administration, Pacific Region, San Bruno, California (hereafter Outing Records). These records contain sensitive material that may embarrass or offend the Indian women or their descendants. Therefore, to respect the identity of these women, their families, and their descendants, I have used pseudonyms for each young woman followed by her tribal identity, if identified in the records. The notes give the initials of each young woman.

2. For general coverage of the decline of white, native-born women in domestic service and the predominance of nonwhite women in the field, see Ellen Carol DuBois and Lyn Dumenil, *Through Women's Eyes: An American History with Documents* (Boston: Bedford/St. Martin's, 2005), 285, 543. For more on domestic service specifically in the early twentieth century, see Phyllis Palmer, *Domesticity and Dirt: Housewives and Domestic Servants in the United States, 1920–1945* (Philadelphia: Temple University Press, 1989).

3. Judith Rollins, *Between Women: Domestics and Their Employers* (Philadelphia: Temple University Press, 1985), 6–7. Other works on domestic service include Faye Dudden, *Serving Women: Household Service in Nineteenth-Century America* (Middletown, CT: Wesleyan University Press, 1983); Daniel E. Sutherland, *Americans and Their Servants: Domestic Service in the United States from 1800 to 1920* (Baton Rouge: Louisiana State University Press, 1981); Elizabeth Clark-Lewis, *Living In, Living Out: African American Domestics in Washington, D.C., 1910–1940* (Washington, DC: Smithsonian Institution Press, 1994); and Palmer, *Domesticity and Dirt*.

4. For more on the removal of Indian children to boarding schools, see my articles, "A Battle for the Children: American Indian Child Removal in Arizona in the Era of Assimilation," *Journal of Arizona History* 45, no. 1 (Spring 2004): 31–62; and "The Great White Mother: Maternalism and American Indian Child Removal in the American West, 1880–1940," in *One Step Over the Line: Toward an Inclusive History of Women in the North American Wests*, ed. Elizabeth Jameson and Sheila McManus (Edmonton: University of Alberta Press, 2008), 191–213. Australia followed a similar policy of removing indigenous girls to be trained in institutions and then apprenticed out to white families. See Victoria K. Haskins, *One Bright Spot* (New York: Palgrave, 2005). For more on outing programs and training girls for domestic service, see Alice Littlefield, "Learning to Labor: Native American Education in the United States, 1880–1930," in *The Political Economy of North American Indians*, ed. John H. Moore (Norman: University of Nebraska Press, 1993), 43–59; K. Tsianina Lomawaima, "Domesticity in the Federal Indian Schools: The Power of Authority over Mind and Body," *American Ethnologist* 20, no. 2 (May 1993): 227–240.

5. For some significant works on gender and colonialism within intimate settings, see Ann Laura Stoler, *Carnal Knowledge and Imperial Power: Race and the Intimate in Colonial Rule* (Berkeley: University of California Press, 2002); Margaret Strobel, *Gender, Sex, and Empire* (Washington, DC: American Historical Association, 1994); Julia Clancy-Smith and Frances Gouda, eds., *Domesticating the Empire: Race, Gender, and Family Life in French and Dutch Colonialism* (Charlottesville: University of Virginia Press, 1998); Margaret Jolly and Martha Macintyre, eds., *Family and Gender in the Pacific: Domestic Contradictions and the Colonial Impact* (Cambridge: Cambridge University Press, 1989).

6. Outing Records. These records do not reveal the experiences of all American Indian women who worked as domestic servants in the Bay Area. Many did not use the YWCA's placement service. For example, Mabel McKay, a Pomo healer and basket-maker, worked for a time as a maid for a madam in a brothel. See Greg Sarris, *Mabel McKay: Weaving the Dream* (Berkeley: University of California Press, 1994), 64.

7. For more on life among the Pomos up to 1900, see Victoria Patterson, "Change and Continuity: Transformations of Pomo Life," *Expedition* 40, no. 1 (1998): 3–15. Greg Sarris's *Keeping Slug Woman Alive: A Holistic Approach to Indian Texts* (Berkeley: University of California Press, 1993) and *Mabel McKay* also contain much historical and ethnographic information throughout. The Bole Maru movement was known as the Bole Hesi among the eastern Pomos.

8. According to Greg Sarris and Victoria Patterson, ethnographers designated several indigenous groups of north-central California natives as "Pomos," although they spoke different (but related) languages. See Sarris, *Keeping Slug Woman Alive*, 8; Victoria Patterson, "Indian Life in the City: A Glimpse of the Urban Experience of Pomo Women in the 1930s," *California History* 71 (Fall 1992): 453, n.1.

9. Clifford E. Trafzer and Joel R. Hyer, *"Exterminate Them": Written Accounts of the Murder, Rape, and Slavery of Native Americans during the California Gold Rush, 1848–1868* (East Lansing: Michigan State University Press, 1999), 140.

10. Sarris, *Keeping Slug Woman Alive*, 9–10. Scholars estimate that California Indians once numbered about 300,000 before European contact. Under Spanish and then Mexican rule, their numbers declined to 150,000, but within just ten years of American conquest, their population had dipped 80 percent to 30,000. See Albert Hurtado, *Indian Survival on the California Frontier* (New Haven: Yale University Press, 1988), 1. Sherburne F. Cook carried out the most significant demographic studies of California Indians. As one example of his work, see *The Population of the California Indians, 1769–1970* (Berkeley: University of California Press, 1976). For more on the devastating impact of American conquest on California Indians, see Tomás Almaguer, *Racial Fault Lines: The Historical Origins of White Supremacy in California* (Berkeley: University of California Press, 1994), 107–50; and James Rawls, *Indians of California: The Changing Image* (Norman: University of Oklahoma Press, 1984), 44–217.

11. Elizabeth Colson, "A Study of Acculturation among Pomo Women," (MA thesis, University of Minnesota, 1940), 37; Patterson, "Change and Continuity."

12. Colson, "A Study of Acculturation," 35–36, 44; Patterson, "Change and Continuity."

13. Colson, "A Study of Acculturation," 61; Colson, *Autobiographies of Three Pomo Women* (Berkeley: University of California Department of Anthropology, 1974), 27.

14. Colson, "A Study of Acculturation," 37.

15. Juliette Lombard, "The Migration of Women from the Ukiah Valley in California to the San Francisco Bay Region," (MA thesis, Columbia University, 1942), 18, 17; see also Colson, *Autobiographies*, 28.

16. *Annual Meeting and Report of the Women's National Indian Association* (Philadelphia: Women's National Indian Association, 1883), 10, 11. See also Valerie Mathes, "Nineteenth-Century Women and Reform: The Women's National Indian Association," *American Indian Quarterly* 14 (1990): 1–18; Mathes, *Helen Hunt Jackson and Her Indian Reform Legacy* (Austin: University of Texas Press, 1990); and Helen Wanken, "'Woman's Sphere' and Indian Reform: The Women's National Indian Association, 1879–1901" (PhD diss., Marquette University, 1981).

17. Frederick Hoxie, *A Final Promise: The Campaign to Assimilate the Indians, 1880–1920* (Lincoln: University of Nebraska Press, 1984).

18. *Course of Study of the Indian Schools of the United States, Industrial and Literary* (Washington, DC: U.S. Government Printing Office, 1901), 86–87. Included in Box 1, Folder 13, MS 120 Papers of Estelle Reel, Eastern Washington State Historical Society, Northwest Museum of Arts and Culture, Spokane, Washington.

19. Carl Moore, Supervisor of Indian Education, to Commissioner of Indian Affairs, November 21, 1929, Box 3, Folder: Outing Center–Berkeley, Supervisor of Indian Education, Administrative Subject Records, 1929–1932, RG 75, BIA California, NARA, San Bruno.

20. *Course of Study of the Indian Schools.*

21. Philip J. Ethington, *The Public City: The Political Construction of Urban Life in San Francisco, 1850–1900* (New York: Cambridge University Press, 1994), 2.

22. Shirley Ann Wilson Moore, *To Place Our Deeds: The African American Community in Richmond, California, 1910–1963* (Berkeley: University of California Press, 2000); Gretchen Lemke-Santangelo, *Abiding Courage: African American Migrant Women and the East Bay Community* (Chapel Hill: University of North Carolina Press, 1996).

23. For domestic service in the San Francisco Bay Area, see Evelyn Nakano Glenn, *Issei, Nisei, War Bride: Three Generations of Japanese American Women in Domestic Service* (Philadelphia: Temple University Press, 1986), 105–109. For more on the restrictions on Asian immigration, see Ronald Takaki, *Strangers from a Different Shore: A History of Asian Americans* (Boston: Little, Brown, 1989). For more on the repatriation of Mexican Americans in the 1930s, see Francisco Balderrama and Raymond Rodriguez, *Decade of Betrayal: Mexican Repatriation in the 1930s* (Albuquerque: University of New Mexico Press, 1995).

24. Frederic Snyder to Commissioner of Indian Affairs, January 14, 1930, Box 3, Folder: "Outing Center–Berkeley," Supervisor of Indian Education, Administrative Subject Records, 1929–1932, RG 75, BIA California, NARA, San Bruno.

25. Palmer estimates that between 1920 and 1930, 11–15 percent of employed American Indian women were working as domestics (*Domesticity and Dirt*, 12, 67). Brief examples of work on Indian women domestic servants include Patterson, "Indian Life in the City," 402–11, 453; and Robert A. Trennert, Jr., *The Phoenix Indian School: Forced Assimilation in Arizona, 1891–1935* (Norman: University of Oklahoma Press, 1988), 52–54, 70–73.

26. See, for example, Theda Perdue, *Cherokee Women: Gender and Culture Change, 1700–1835* (Lincoln: University of Nebraska Press, 1998); Lillian Ackerman, *A Necessary Balance: Gender and Power among Indians of the Columbia Plateau* (Norman: University of Oklahoma Press, 2003); Karen Anderson, *Chain Her by One Foot: The Subjugation of Women in Seventeenth-Century New France* (New York: Routledge, 1991); Carol Devens, *Countering Colonization: Native American Women and Great Lakes Missions, 1630–1900* (Berkeley: University of California Press, 1992).

27. Philip J. Deloria, *Indians in Unexpected Places* (Lawrence: University of Kansas Press, 2004). For several books that look at American Indians' encounters with modern wage labor and economic development, see Colleen O'Neill, *Working the Navajo Way: Labor and Culture in the Twentieth Century* (Lawrence: University of Kansas Press, 2005); Brian Hosmer and Colleen O'Neill, *Native Pathways: American Indian Culture and Economic Development in the Twentieth Century* (Boulder: University Press of Colorado, 2004); Alice Littlefield and Martha C. Knack, eds., *Native Americans and Wage Labor: Ethnohistorical Perspectives* (Norman: University of Oklahoma Press, 1996); James B. LaGrand, *Indian Metropolis: Native Americans in Chicago, 1845–75* (Urbana: University of Illinois Press, 2002).

28. For some of the first works to critique earlier conceptions of the frontier and to redefine it, see Patricia Nelson Limerick, *The Legacy of Conquest: The Unbroken Past of the American West* (New York: Norton, 1987); Richard White, *The Middle Ground: Indians, Empires, and Republics in the Great Lakes Region, 1650–1815* (New York: Cambridge University Press, 1991).

29. Janet Henshall Momsen, "Maids on the Move: Victim or Victor," in *Gender, Migration and Domestic Service*, ed. Janet Henshall Momsen (New York: Routledge, 1999), 11.

30. Glenn, *Issei, Nisei, War Bride*, 9.

31. Rhacel Salazar Parreñas, *Servants of Globalization: Women, Migration and Domestic Work* (Stanford: Stanford University Press, 2001); Momsen, ed., *Gender, Migration and Domestic Service*; Pierrette Hondagneu-Sotelo, *Doméstica: Immigrant Workers Cleaning and Caring in the Shadows of Affluence* (Berkeley: University of California Press, 2001).

32. Stoler, *Carnal Knowledge*, 9; Ann Laura Stoler, "Tense and Tender Ties: The Politics of Comparison in North American History and (Post) Colonial Studies," *Journal of American History* 88 (2001): 830.

33. Cato Sells to Superintendent Royce, September 12, 1918, Box 10, Investigative Records of Colonel L. A. Dorrington, Special Agent, 1913–1923, Bureau of Indian Affairs, Nevada, RG 75, NARA, San Bruno.

34. Royce to Supervisor Holst, July 23, 1929, Box 1, Folder: "Los Angeles Berkeley Outing Centers," Supervisor of Indian Education 1928–1929; Royce to Moore, June 10, 1930, Box 3, Folder: "Outing Center–Berkeley," Supervisor Of Indian Education, Administrative Subject Records, 1929–1932; both in RG 75, BIA California, NARA, San Bruno. See also Outing Records. The BIA also established a similar outing program in the Los Angeles area, also presided over by an outing matron. See Box 1, Folder 15–0: "Outing Los Angeles, Supervisor of Indian Education 1928–1929, RG 75, BIA California, NARA, San Bruno.

35. Carl Moore, Supervisor of Indian Education, to Commissioner of Indian Affairs, November 21, 1929, Box 3, Folder: Outing Center–Berkeley, Supervisor of Indian Education, Administrative Subject Records, 1929–1932, RG 75, BIA California, NARA, San Bruno.

36. Lombard, "Migration of Women," 24–25.

37. Lombard, "Migration of Women," 10; Patterson, "Indian Life in the City," 405.

38. Lombard, "Migration of Women," 25; Patterson, "Indian Life in the City," 408.

39. Royce to Snyder, April 9, 1930, Box 3, Folder:"Outing Center–Berkeley," Supervisor Of Indian Education, Administrative Subject Records, 1929–1932; both in RG 75, BIA California, NARA, San Bruno.

40. Victoria Haskins notes a similar geometry between Aboriginal domestic servants, white women employers, and the state's agencies in Australia, where "white mistresses, being positioned between the state and the Aboriginal women, were in fact intermediaries involved in an intimate, day-to-day experience of the practice of

the state's Aboriginal policy." See her dissertation, "My One Bright Spot: A Personal Insight into Relationships between White Women and Aboriginal Women under the NSW Aborigines Protection Board Apprenticeship Policy, 1920–1942," (PhD diss., University of Sydney, 1998), quote p. 59. See also Haskins, *One Bright Spot.*

41. See Van Every to Bertha Eckert, National Board, YWCA, October 5, 1937, J.B. file, Box 1, Outing Records; list of Indian Girl's Work Committee, April 15, 1942, courtesy of YWCA of Oakland. The YWCA was, according to Phyllis Palmer, "the women's organization that was most persistently concerned with the problems of domestic service." Thus it is no surprise that the outing matrons had connections with the YWCA and some sympathy for the young domestic servants. See Palmer, *Domesticity and Dirt*, 113.

42. Murphey to Van Every, November 26, 1934, V.B. file, Box 1, Outing Records.

43. Linda Gordon, *Pitied but Not Entitled: Single Mothers and the History of Welfare* (Cambridge, MA: Harvard University Press, 1994), 55. See also Sonya Michel, *Children's Interests/Mother's Rights: The Shaping of America's Child Care Policy* (New Haven, CT: Yale University Press, 1999); Gwendolyn Mink, *The Wages of Motherhood: Inequality in the Welfare State, 1917–1942* (Ithaca, NY: Cornell University Press, 1995); Molly Ladd-Taylor, *Mother-Work: Women, Child Welfare, and the State, 1890–1930* (Urbana: University of Illinois Press, 1994); Theda Skocpol, *Protecting Soldiers and Mothers: The Political Origins of Social Policy in the United States* (Cambridge, MA: Belknap Press of Harvard University Press, 1992). For more on white women's maternalism toward Indian women, see my article, "The Great White Mother."

44. See especially Gordon, *Pitied but Not Entitled.*

45. David Wallace Adams, *Education for Extinction: American Indians and the Boarding School Experience, 1875–1928* (Lawrence: University of Kansas Press, 1995), 82, 83. Cathleen Cahill, "'Only the Home Can Found a State': Gender, Labor, and the United States Indian Service, 1869–1928" (PhD diss., University of Chicago, 2004), 161, 387. Cahill also believes that the BIA served as an agency in which women were encouraged to enact their maternalist sensibilities. See especially 16–19, 77–82, 227–77.

46. Cato Sells to Superintendent Royce, September 12, 1918, Box 10, Investigative Records of Colonel L. A. Dorrington, Special Agent, 1913–1923, BIA, Nevada, RG 75, NARA, San Bruno.

47. Palmer, *Domesticity and Dirt*, 53.

48. Hondagneu-Sotelo, *Doméstica*, 22–23.

49. Lombard, "Migration of Women," 30.

50. A. Be. to Royce, October 6, 1931, A. Be. file, Box 1, Outing Records.

51. M. Bl. to Royce, August 12, 1930, M. Bl. file, Box 1, Outing Records.

52. Patterson, "Indian Life in the City," 410; Lombard, "Migration of Women," 32–33; Colson, "A Study of Acculturation," 85–86.

53. O'Neill, *Working the Navajo Way*, 13–14; see also 29. In addition, see Hosmer and O'Neill, eds., *Native Pathways*; Martha C. Knack and Alice Littlefield, "Native

American Labor: Retrieving History, Rethinking Theory," in *Native Americans and Wage Labor*, 26; Harold Prins, "Tribal Network and Migrant Labor: Mi'kmaq Indians as Seasonal Workers in Aroostook's Potato Fields, 1870–1980," in *Native Americans and Wage Labor*, 51; LaGrand, *Indian Metropolis*, 25.

54. Quoted in Lombard, "Migration of Women," 21; for lack of employment and prejudice see 14–21; Patterson, "Indian Life in the City," 403.

55. Chronology for I. B., March 5, 1939, I. B. file, Box 1, Outing Records.

56. Van Every to Roy Nash, Superintendent, Sacramento Indian Agency, April 29, 1940, Fr. A. file, Box 1, Outing Records.

57. J. J. to Royce, September 23, 1931, J. J. file, Box 2, Outing Records.

58. E. J. file, Box 2, Outing Records.

59. Chronology for J. B., October 13, 1937, J. B. file, Box 1, Outing Records.

60. Patterson, "Indian Life in the City," 410; A YWCA promotional brochure of 1930 boasts that sixty "individual Indian girls attended winter and summer programs, clubs, parties, Sunday afternoon services and out-door expeditions." See also Oakland YWCA, "A Review of the year 1939," 13–14. Both of these items are courtesy of the Oakland Public Library.

61. M. to A., March 23, 1929, M. J. file, Box 2, Outing Records.

62. A. A. file, Box 1, Outing Records.

63. On urban pan-Indianism, see LaGrand, *Indian Metropolis*.

64. M. and A. D. to Royce, n.d. (ca. 1929), A. D. file, Box 2, Outing Records.

65. M. to A., March 23, 1929, M. J. file, Box 2, Outing Records.

66. Files of Ev. A., El. A, and P. Ar., Box 1, Outing Records.

67. Taft to Traxler, November 13, 1933, H. E. file, Box 2, Outing Records.

68. I. S. file, Box 4, Outing Records.

69. El. A. file, Box 1, Outing Records.

70. See Clark-Lewis, *Living In, Living Out*.

71. V. G. file, Box 2, Outing Records. For more on white women's expectations of deference, see Rollins, *Between Women*, 156–170, 178–203; Mary Romero, *Maid in the U.S.A.* (New York: Routledge, 1992), 97–119.

72. Grace Cresap to Royce, July 3, 1930, Box 1, Folder: "Outing Contracts, Outing Girls, 1930," Records of the Berkeley Outing Matron and Placement Officer, 1916–1933, RG 75 BIA California, NARA, San Bruno.

73. S. M. to Van Every, July 19, 1935, S. A. M. file, Outing Records.

74. G. P. file, Box 3, Outing Records.

75. F. C. to Royce, n.d., Box 1, Folder: "Outing Contracts, Outing Girls, 1932," Records of the Berkeley Outing Matron and Placement Officer, 1916–1933, RG 75 BIA California, NARA, San Bruno.

76. F. C. to Royce, n.d. Box 1, Folder: "Outing Contracts, Outing Girls, 1932," Records of the Berkeley Outing Matron and Placement Officer, 1916–1933, RG 75 BIA California, NARA, San Bruno.

77. V. F. to "Dearie," May 3, 1928, V. F. file, Box 2, Outing Records.

78. Mrs. Harrington to Royce, n.d., Box 1, Folder: "Outing Contracts, Outing Girls, 1932," Records of the Berkeley Outing Matron and Placement Officer, 1916–1933, RG 75 BIA California, NARA, San Bruno.

79. Royce to Mrs. C. B., October 24, 1932, A. Be. file, Box 1, Outing Records.

80. Fl. A. file, Box 1, Outing Records.

81. Fr. A. file, Box 1, Outing Records.

82. Royce to Mrs. Cleland, Ukiah, July 12, 1927, F. E. file, Box 2, Outing Records.

83. Chronology, March 18, 1937, P. Ar. file, Box 1, Outing Records.

84. Chronology, March 22, 24, and 26, 1937, P. Ar. file, Box 1, Outing Records.

85. Oakland YWCA, "A Review of the Year 1939," 13–14.

86. Royce to Emmett McNeilly, superintendent of Western Shoshone Agency, February 16, 1929, A. H. file, Box 2, Outing Records.

87. Royce to McNeilly, February 16, 1929, A. H. file, Box 2, Outing Records.

88. Superintendent Frederic Snyder to P. An., August 17, 1927, P. An. file, Box 1, Outing Records.

89. I. T. to John Collier, August 6, 1933, I.T.(S.) file, Box 4, Outing Records.

90. Ibid.

91. Collier to I. T., August 24, 1933, I.T.(S.) file, Box 4, Outing Records.

92. Chronology, October 13, 1941, I.T.(S.) file, Box 4, Outing Records.

93. Chronology, I.T.(S.) file, Box 4.

94. Many scholars have noted that the boarding schools promoted nineteenth-century Victorian-style gender roles for girls. As just one example, see Tsianina Lomawaima, *They Called it Prairie Light: The Story of Chilocco Indian School* (Lincoln: University of Nebraska Press, 1994).

95. Chronology, March 6, 1938, Fl. A. file, Box 1, Outing Records.

96. S. C. to Van Every, July 18, 1936, S. C. file, Box 1, Outing Records.

97. Quoted in Carl Moore, Supervisor of Indian Education, to Commissioner of Indian Affairs, November 21, 1929, Box 3, Folder: "Outing Center–Berkeley," Supervisor of Indian Education, Administrative Subject Records, 1929–1932, RG 75, BIA California, NARA, San Bruno.

98. Superintendent Snyder to Daniel Robertson, Lovelock, Nevada, May 15, 1925, G. W. file, Box 4, Outing Records.

99. J. W. to Royce, July 6, 1925, G. W. file, Box 4, Outing Records.

100. Lombard, "Migration of Women," 30.

101. S. A. M. file, Box 1; A. Be. file, Box 1; B. L. file, Box 3, Outing Records.

102. See LaGrand, *Indian Metropolis*, especially 161–182.

103. Lombard, "Migration of Women," 35, 38.

104. D. H. file, Box 2, Outing Records.

105. Patterson, "Indian Life in the City," 410.

106. Colson, "A Study of Acculturation," 86; Lombard, "Migration of Women," 29.

107. Ev. A. file; S. A. M. file, Box 1, Outing Records.

108. M. B. file, Box 1, Outing Records.

109. Katherine Martin, field nurse, to Bonnie Royce, August 8, 1932 and September 5, 1932, S. B. file, Box 1, Outing Records.

110. For more on how white middle-class women's maternalism toward Indian women differed from maternalism toward other groups, see my "Great White Mother."

111. Royce to Mrs. Holcomb, field matron, Reno, July 27, 1931, E. M. file, Box 3, Outing Records.

112. Quoted in Parreñas, *Servants of Globalization*, 76. Many Filipina servants have had to leave their children behind in the Philippines while they work in other countries for extended periods; see Parreñas, *Servants of Globalization*, 62, 80, 115.

113. Notes on "outing form," March 1, 1934, March 23, [1934], and March 26, 1934, J. G. file, Box 2, Outing Records.

114. Van Every to Supt. McNeilly, November 13, 1934, A. H. file, Box 2, Outing Records.

115. R. R. Miller, Probation Officer, to Director, Indian Bureau, June 10, 1932, G. W. file, Box 4, Outing Records.

116. Royce to Snyder, July 16, 1932, G. W. file, Box 4, Outing Records.

117. Lombard, "Migration of Women," 32; Patterson, "Indian Life in the City," 410.

118. M. J. to A. D., May 15, 1929, M. J. file, Outing Records.

PART III

Networks and Place

In the previous sections, we describe how networks of social power construct place, but we use the title "Networks and Place" only for this last section. These three articles explicitly focus on the interconnected networks of global capitalism, immigration, and social movements, especially those involving organized labor. All analyze how social movements operate in a city: Bisbee, Arizona; Los Angeles, California; and San Antonio, Texas. All document the social movements' national and international connections, and all consider one particular international place, the U.S.-Mexico border. The authors examine the local, often dramatic, effects of transnational networks that moved people, ideas, symbols, and goods over the border and back. Like the articles in the first section, these essays investigate the relationships between identity and place, but here we emphasize relationships among places, particular kinds of networks, and identities.

In her article "Docile Children and Dangerous Revolutionaries: The Racial Hierarchy of Manliness and the Bisbee Deportation of 1917," Katherine Benton-Cohen details the violent confluence of politics and identity in the copper mining town of Bisbee, Arizona, in the summer of 1917. The town deported local workers—mostly immigrants, one-third of them Mexicans—dumping them in the New Mexican desert. Benton-Cohen uses the lens of masculinity to explain the deportation, a decision that enables her to discuss the intersectionality of gender, race, and class. White mining officials and white workers in Bisbee boasted long before 1917 that the town was a "white man's camp," a boast maintained by discriminatory hiring practices and wage rates. Whites in Bisbee justified these practices by denigrating the manhood of Mexican miners, alleging that they were not man enough to work the hard (and better-paying) jobs underground. In 1917, when a radical American union, the

Industrial Workers of the World (IWW), called for a strike in Bisbee, Mexican miners joined—in disproportionately higher numbers than any other ethnic group of miners—to win equal wages and claim their full manhood. Many of the Mexican miners had additional, transnational reasons for joining the IWW strike. They had participated in or knew about the 1906 copper strike in Cananea, Mexico, where the IWW had assisted Mexican radicals, the Partido Liberal Mexicano (Mexican Liberal Party). When striking Mexican miners in Bisbee demanded to be treated as free men, they spoke a transnational language and called upon transnational memories to end a local injustice.

Transnational networks connecting the United States, Mexico, and Latin America come into play in María A. Gutierrez de Soldatenko's article on labor relations in Los Angeles in the 1990s, "International Ladies' Garment Workers' Union Labor Organizers: Chicana and Latina Leadership in the Los Angeles Garment Industry." These networks linking immigrants, workers, union leaders, and community activists helped women garment workers to forge new identities as urban labor movement activists. Mexicana and Latina women garment workers who became community leaders in the Los Angeles labor movement learned lessons in politics and political skills from their birth families. They used those lessons when they produced garments at home or in factories, and they honed their new skills when they engaged in community activism. The transnational networks in which these women, from three generations, were enmeshed demonstrate the spatiality of lives lived at once locally and globally.

Networks also lie at the heart of Amy Hilsman Kastely's story about San Antonio, Texas, "*Esperanza v. City of San Antonio*: Politics, Power, and Culture." In this court case, the Esperanza Peace & Justice Center, an arts and activist organization, sued the city, charging that it had illegally defunded the arts center. Esperanza went to court not simply against a city government that refused to recognize politicized art as art but also against a city reconstructed since the 1960s as a place where tourists could experience a sanitized Tex-Mex culture. Made and marketed by developers, this San Antonio was a place that papered over conflicts arising from racial and class inequalities. When the Esperanza Peace & Justice Center sought to construct a city that recognized these inequalities and acknowledged its cultural diversity, a powerful network of builders, developers, right-wing political organizations, and conservative art leaders demonized the center, charging that it threatened tourism, social order, and comity in San Antonio. Responding to this smear campaign, the city government stripped Esperanza of its arts funding, but the ensuing struggle was less over money than over the very identity of the city of San Antonio.

The Esperanza Peace & Justice Center drew on several networks, each with its own strategy, to fight city hall. Created by young Chicanas in the late 1980s, the center brought together labor organizers, gay rights activists, those who struggled for the rights of people of color, feminists, artists, and other folk with ties throughout the city and to communities around the world. The center's numerous, inclusive programs and *platicas* (community discussions) made the center a safe place for many kinds of people whose involvement with the center encouraged them further to develop diverse identities for themselves and for the city. The city government labeled Esperanza a troublemaker partially because it could—and did—mobilize hundreds of supporters in political dissent. Through a court decision, the activists succeeded in forcing San Antonio to reverse its decision to defund Esperanza. Supporters of the center—gay and straight; young and old; Mexican American, African American, Native American, and Asian American; men and women—all organized in and for a local place and local identities that stretched in many directions beyond the local. Geographer Doreen Massey writes that places are constructed by networks of social relations that are open, porous, and fluid.[1] Such is certainly the case in the tales of these three cities.

This last section, "Networks and Place," informs us about the crucial role of networks in constituting a modern West and brings together many of the themes we have discussed throughout this book. We declared we wanted to break out of a West contained by Frederick Jackson Turner, to move beyond him in time and space and topic. While each of the three articles deals with a western location, these places—cities constituted by modern transnational networks of intense mobility—are highly contingent. Each of the three articles tells a local western story filled with themes of long interest to Western women's history, such as the regional construction of gender and race and the analytical importance of labor, and each article simultaneously does something new. It makes its local story also a narrative of transnational places in very recent times. Feminist geography conjoined with Western women's history helped us reach these larger understandings of place, and we hope that you find both useful in exploring an ever-changing West.

Notes

1. Doreen Massey, *Space, Place, and Gender* (Minneapolis: University of Minnesota Press, 1994), 121.

CHAPTER 8

Docile Children and Dangerous Revolutionaries

The Racial Hierarchy of Manliness and the Bisbee Deportation of 1917

KATHERINE BENTON-COHEN

On July 12, 1917, three months after the United States entered World War I, a dramatic event in a remote copper-mining town near the U.S.-Mexico border grabbed national headlines. On June 26, in Bisbee, Arizona, the Industrial Workers of the World (the IWW, or "Wobblies") had called a strike on several local copper mines, including the Phelps-Dodge (PD) Corporation's famous Copper Queen Mine. By almost all accounts, the strike had remained relatively uneventful until the wee hours of July 12, when county sheriff Harry Wheeler quietly deputized twelve hundred men, who were normally miners, engineers, doctors, and shopkeepers. Mining company officials silenced all out-going phone calls and telegrams. On the front page of the morning newspaper, Wheeler warned women and children to stay off the streets. By four a.m., the gun-toting deputies "appeared as if by magic," as the front page of the *New York Times* reported the following day. The posse of deputies, led by the charismatic sheriff and armed to the teeth, swarmed the narrow, steep streets of the mountain town.[1]

Throughout the mining district, deputies broke down doors and gathered up men from their homes, rooming houses, or places of business, including not just miners, but also restaurant owners, carpenters, and a lawyer. Amado Villalovas was in a neighborhood store when, as he later explained to the Arizona attorney general, "about ten gunmen all armed came in and told me to get out. I asked them to let me take my groceries home to my family. They dragged me out of the store, hit me and knocked me down."[2] Under the hot July sun,

Figure 8.1. Young girl watches men loaded into boxcars during Bisbee Deportation. Arizona State Library, Archives and Public Records, photo 97-0629.

the deputies forced Villalovas into a line of over a thousand other captives in a forced march through town, past the mines, to a baseball field two miles away. There, local residents gathered to watch as the deputies loaded their charges into twenty-three boxcars and sent them off nearly two hundred miles into the New Mexico desert. Hours later, an army camp in nearby Columbus, New Mexico, rescued the deported men and set up housing for them. Because vigilantes continued to police Bisbee's borders, the deportees were not allowed to go home for more than two months, and many never returned. The event became known across the country as the Bisbee Deportation, although it was not a "true" deportation across international borders.

The deportation captured national headlines, but it was only the most dramatic of a series of encounters during the summer of 1917 between Wobblies and their opponents. The mining West had been the Wobblies' stronghold since disgruntled leaders of the Western Federation of Miners (WFM) had founded the IWW in 1905. Led by colorful characters like "Big Bill" Haywood and Mother Jones, the IWW organized across class, race, and gender lines. Unlike the American Federation of Labor (AFL), which organized along craft lines, the Wobblies' goal was to create an industrial union—"one big union"—that included all workers, from the washerwoman to the foreman.

There were over forty-five hundred work stoppages in the United States that year, but in the patriotic fervor of World War I, the IWW's radical politics and antiwar stance elicited especially deep antipathy. Two weeks after the Bisbee deportation, IWW organizer Frank Little was lynched in Butte, Montana, another copper-mining center. Other towns tarred and feathered Wobblies or deported a few dozen striking workers, as occurred in Jerome, Arizona, just two days before the Bisbee Deportation.[3] But nowhere did anti-Wobbly responses reach the precision and scale of the Bisbee Deportation, a distinction that has generated many attempts at explanation. The event prompted President Woodrow Wilson to appoint a federal commission to investigate the IWW and vigilante activities in war industries in the West.

Today, the event remains a mainstay of the scholarly literatures on the domestic front in World War I, western labor history, and the history of nativism. Interpretations have varied. One view portrays the deportation as a simple example of wartime nativism intended to purge the country of foreign radicals during the Red Scare. The second major interpretation, developed in the only book-length study of the event, portrays the deportation as cynical opportunism by the mining companies that used the war effort as an excuse to rid Arizona mining camps of an increasingly powerful union movement. One scholar has sharpened the anti-nativist thesis by examining nascent interracial collaboration among strikers as a motivation for anti-labor opposition. A women's historian has explored the gendered implications of the deportation and its effects on racial division, specifically the deployment of the concept of "domesticity" by both strikers and deputies.[4] While each of these approaches is valuable, no single theory has the power to explain an event that involved thousands of people. What is missing is an interpretation that captures the variety of perspectives among the deportation's participants.

In this article, I focus on masculinity—or "manhood" and "manliness," as contemporaries would have put it—to show the links between Bisbee's class, race, and gender anxieties and divisions. As Kristin Hoganson has linked diverse interpretations of turn-of-the-century imperialism to "fighting for manhood," I argue that an understanding of the racial hierarchy of manliness can help explain the multiple motives held by Bisbee residents and also help bridge the multiple interpretations the deportation has generated.[5] The deportation was not about labor relations *or* race *or* gender; it was about all of them. Manliness is a useful lens because it colored all of them. Manliness is not a magic interpretive bullet, and I am not arguing that there is only one definition of manliness, even among white men; neither do I argue that manliness is or was inherently violent or militant or pro- or anti-labor. Manliness is a social construct linking male anatomy, cultural identity, and power. What the theme of manliness will do is reveal how several different perspectives on the strike converged in a mass vigilante action.[6] Understanding manliness can help make sense of the links between social categories that we too often isolate for the sake of analytical clarity at the cost of accurate depiction of their deep interconnections. To explore the relationships between manhood and race in Bisbee more closely, I examine their evolution at three stages in Bisbee's history: first in the social world that had developed in Bisbee before 1917; then during the strike, when Mexican workers challenged the terms of Bisbee's social compact; and, finally, in the stunning vigilante response in the form of deportation and its aftermath.

Racial Hierarchies of Manliness

Bisbee's most vivid and public expression of the racial hierarchy of manliness was its reputation as a "white man's camp," which dates to the 1880s. The term's meanings changed over time. At first the term indicated the exclusion of Chinese, who were barred from the town altogether.[7] Mexicans, unlike the Chinese, were allowed to live and work in Bisbee, but the town's status as a white man's camp also referred to its exclusion of Mexican workers from the most lucrative jobs underground. In "Mexican camps" like Clifton-Morenci in Arizona, Mexican workers performed most kinds of work, other than supervisory roles, but in Bisbee they were restricted to only the most menial mining jobs. "Mexican" was a racial label, not a national one, and native-born, lifelong residents of the American Southwest were consigned to the "Mexican" category alongside recent Mexican immigrants.

The place of other ethnic groups in the white man's camp was less clear, however. "Bisbee has always been a 'White Man's Camp,'" insisted one local editorial in 1903, but the new "foreign labor" from Serbia and Italy was threatening that status quo. Eastern and southern Europeans occupied an "in-between" racial category, to use a phrase used by several historians. In Bisbee, workers argued among themselves and with employers over where these "in-betweens" should go in a place self-defined as a white man's camp. Other white man's camps, like Cripple Creek, Colorado, had successfully excluded southern and eastern Europeans in the years before the World War I boom, but not so Bisbee. By 1917, hundreds of Slavs and Italians lived in Bisbee, enough to have their own boardinghouses and distinctive neighborhoods. In part, the Bisbee deportation, occurring in the context of World War I and increasing support for immigration restriction, did reflect fears about foreigners, as many historians have noted. Eighty percent of the men deported from Bisbee in 1917 were immigrants. One third of those counted as foreign-born were of Mexican descent, and another 40 percent were Slavic.[8]

The place of Mexicans and these new "in-between" races in the white man's camp differed, however, and the biggest difference flowed from the dual-wage system of Bisbee's mines. People of Mexican descent doing the same work as other mine employees earned one-half to two-thirds of what their non-Mexican counterparts did. Although northern European workers complained that Slavs and Italians would work for less pay, eastern and southern European workers did not actually occupy a separate racial job category; Mexican workers did. Printed pay scales listed Mexican and white (or "American") wages separately, with Serbs and Italians clustered in mid-level "white" jobs. In a context where race so explicitly equaled class, this distinction was critical because an "American" wage was as racially defined as a Mexican wage. In Arizona, the opposite of a white man's camp was a Mexican camp, *not* a Slavic camp or even a foreigners' camp.[9] This linguistic distinction suggested some room for racial maneuvering for eastern and southern Europeans in contrast to opportunities for Mexicans.

The dual-wage system existed throughout the Southwest's mining industry, but white man's camps buttressed racial divisions of labor by excluding Mexican workers from the better-paid jobs underground—the work of Bisbee's famed "he-men." As the *Bisbee Daily Review* explained in 1903, Bisbee "is strictly a 'white man's camp.' . . . Mexicans are employed only in the common or rough labor" above ground. Sometimes, as at Bisbee's Calumet & Arizona Mining Company (C&A), "Mexican" was a job category as well as a racial label. A detailed "nationality report" compiled by C&A for federal investigators listed categories for "Native Born Citizens," "Naturalized Citizens," and "Foreigners." These were totaled and then, below this total and separated by a line, was a column labeled "Mexicans (not included above)." Wage scales never listed a "foreigner" wage; "Mexican" was the only category that appeared in both nationality reports and wage scales. As a result of this combination of wage and job discrimination, almost all non-Mexican mining employees had better jobs than Mexican workers did. During the 1910s, the average Mexican wage was half the average white wage because of combined wage and job discrimination, and the gap was growing.[10]

The wage system was also highly gendered. Mexican wages were defined as a percentage of white wages, which in turn were defined in terms of "family wage ideology." This principle held that a man working full-time should be not just the primary, but *the* breadwinner, in his family. As Marsha May and Linda Gordon have observed, family wage ideology enjoyed wide consensus among workers, employers, and reformers. Historian Alice Kessler-Harris has shown that women's low wages suffered from the assumption that women were not breadwinners.[11]

As in other industrial communities, in Bisbee the family wage ideology was useful to employers and workers alike: Bisbee had a reputation as one of the best-paid mining camps in the West precisely because the mining companies wanted to entice family men in order to reduce turnover. As one C&A official explained in 1907, "the robust American with a growing family and home ties is a better man for us than a man without these things." To entice these robust specimens, companies supplemented wages with family-friendly philanthropy like home-owning schemes, school-building, park maintenance, and a preference for keeping on married men during lay-offs. These offers benefited mainly those who were earning white wages. Just as David Roediger has summarized W. E. B. DuBois to argue that the "wages of whiteness" include the "psychological wage" of being white, so too did Bisbee's family wage package include forms of compensation not found in a pay envelope. The "wages of whiteness" were family wages.[12]

In theory, white workers and managers agreed on the family wage, but in practice they parted company when it came to defining it in dollars and cents. They had competing visions of the family wage's meaning: employers saw the family wage as an incentive, but those who earned white wages saw the family wage as a right. The mining companies had established a sliding pay scale according to the price of copper; even if these wages were higher than the industry average, this market-determined pay scale conflicted with workers' conviction that wages should be calculated based on a certain standard of living. One of the strikers' demands in 1917 was to replace the sliding scale with fixed wages. In 1917, as wartime inflation deflated salaries, defenders of the strikers invoked the importance of supporting one's family. When the PD company store raised the price of flour, sympathetic newspaper editor John Dunbar argued that the price increase was intended to "starve the miners into subjection," but that all the increases would do was to "starv[e] men out who have families."[13] Dunbar was implicitly admitting that some men *would* work for the current wages, but not the most desirable workers—the family men.

Bisbee's debates about the family wage usually invoked the "American standard of living," a concept that national trade unionists had been developing since the Jacksonian period. Although the term was clearly subjective and rarely explicitly defined, it generally referred to providing the sole support for a wife and several school-age children, and usually to home ownership ("a comfortable house of at least six rooms," wrote one labor leader in 1898). By 1917, these claims were well established. At Bisbee, the strikers were simply "asking the American right to maintain their wives and children," argued editor Dunbar in 1917.[14]

Home ownership was the most potent symbol of the American standard of living in Bisbee. Bisbee had long been known as a "city of homes," where a high percentage of miners were also homeowners, and promotional pamphlets bragged about Bisbee's "domesticated miners." Beginning in 1906, C&A created a subsidiary, the Warren Company, to build an entire suburb to entice "American" miners to purchase homes for their families. PD bought the real estate company in 1917. This corporate commitment to home ownership for workers gave miners some leverage. If it was company policy to offer home ownership, workers argued, it ought to be company policy to pay men wages that covered the mortgage as well as the grocery bill. Defenders of strikers in 1917 repeatedly pointed out that the majority of the men deported were homeowners.[15]

The case of housing shows that the family wage and the American standard of living were racialized as well as gendered. Both white workers and managers used housing to show Mexican workers' unfitness for an American standard of living. Mexican families' "domestic equipment" consisted merely of "an adobe hut with an earth floor." This "lower" standard of living became naturalized in white minds, so that white workers continually opposed the inclusion of Mexican laborers into "white" labor categories by arguing that their lower standard of living allowed them to undercut white wages. Managers did the same. Less than a year after the deportation, PD president Walter Douglas thought it "desirable that American employees should own their own homes," but rejected a home-owning plan for Mexican workers, because "where the Mexican is concerned, it will be difficult to induce him to obligate himself to pay for the house in which he is living." Better to "build tenements or cheaply constructed houses" for rental that "might appeal to the Mexican."[16]

White workers and mining officials believed that the gap between American and Mexican standards of living—indeed, the dual-wage system itself—was a natural product of racial difference. As Linda Gordon has pointed out, most Anglos honestly believed that Mexicans did not need a family wage. A well-circulated government report used Mexicans' "lower standard of living" to justify their low wages: "The wants of the Mexican peon are hardly more complex than those of the Indian from whom he is descended." Mexican wages quite explicitly could not support an "American standard of living," nor were they intended to. In this sense, the dual-wage system, and with it the racial hierarchy of manhood, appeared natural.

Specifically, white critics believed that Mexican workers were not "real" men. If anything, this is an understatement. As Yvette Huginnie has shown, Anglo workers and managers infantilized and feminized Mexican workers to reinforce their exclusion from the family wage and the American standard of living. "The Mexican worker intellectually is a child. He is governed by emotion rather than by reason," explained one technical journal. Another article warned, "The Mexican workman will misunderstand an attitude of social equality toward him. . . . He cannot be your equal; he must either be your superior or your inferior." The superiority of Anglo men over Mexican men meshed quite neatly with the superiority of foreman over laborer in a twinned hierarchy of class and race. Mexican workers needed white bosses they could "look up to," according to such articles.[17] That white workers and managers often expressed these stereotypes in terms of benevolent paternalism only accentuates the ways that their rhetoric aimed to emasculate Mexican workers.

Mexican Workers Strike the Racial Hierarchy of Manliness

These racialized, emasculating characterizations assumed by white bosses and coworkers had little to do with how Mexican workers viewed themselves, however, and the strike was a vivid assertion of their own manly identities. Their strike participation and demands rejected nearly everything about the racial hierarchy of manliness, which, by then, shaped nearly everything about life in Bisbee, from gender to wages, family structure, and housing. No one understood the hierarchy's ideological and material power better than Mexican workers themselves. In the strike of 1917, Anglo Wobbly leaders were calling for an end to the practice of blacklisting, a solidarity strike for copper miners striking in Butte, Montana, and—lastly—a slight wage increase. However, Mexican workers called for dismantling the dual-wage system by demanding the family wage and the right to an American standard of living. Above all, they were rejecting the social compact of the white man's camp, one that denied them full male economic and social citizenship.

Scholars have not adequately explored the challenge Mexican workers raised against the ideology of the white man's camp. Most histories of the Bisbee strike have ignored the prevalence of Mexican workers in the strike or have depicted them as passive, unknowing dupes of Wobbly leaders. One reason, no doubt, is that Wilson's Mediation Commission failed to interview any Mexicans in Bisbee. Few sources exist about Mexicans in Bisbee except quantitative ones (which are difficult to use in the noncensus year of 1917). Others mention groups of Mexicans in only the most vague, stereotypical terms—generally as faceless peons or revolutionaries. The lack of sources on Mexicans in Bisbee is, in fact, prima facie evidence of the power of the white man's camp ideology, because sources on Mexicans elsewhere in Arizona, while not abundant, far outnumber those for Bisbee. I have borrowed from these other sources where necessary. Because of this scarcity of sources, general histories of Arizona's Mexican mine workers have focused on Mexican strikes in Mexican camps—an important story. But that focus has underplayed the ideological significance of their participation in strikes in the white men's camps of Bisbee and Globe-Miami, Arizona. The challenges mounted by Mexican workers in 1917 against the very tenets of the white man's camp were unprecedented. Bisbee had faced union conflict before, in an abortive Western Federation of Miners strike in 1907. But in that incident, strikers had called not for equality for Mexican workers, but for an end to Mexican labor altogether! The 1907 strikers intended to preserve Bisbee's reputation as a white man's camp, not to destroy it. Not so in 1917.[18]

By 1917 Mexicans made up a significant portion of Bisbee's population and workforce. When the strike broke out in late July, the Copper Queen had about three hundred Mexican workers, which added up to nearly 15 percent of the official workforce, second only to "Americans." In addition to the Mexicans employed at the mines, hundreds of new immigrants from Mexico had come to Bisbee looking for work in the month before the strike. The story of Amado Villalovas, the deportee rounded up at the grocery store, is typical in several ways. Countless others suffered injuries and indignities as Villalovas had; two men—a deputy and a deportee—were killed in the confusion of the morning. In addition, at least two hundred twenty-six deportees had wives and families to support, and many of them were Mexican workers like Villalovas, belying the fiction that only white workers needed a family wage.[19] Finally, Mexican workers like Villalovas were disproportionately represented among the deportees. Several witnesses testified that "foreigners," especially Mexicans, were rounded up indiscriminately. It is not even clear that Villalovas was a miner, much less on strike, and in this, too, he was typical, because many of the deportees did not work for the mining companies. A perusal of the deportees' testimonies reveal that they represented many different occupations.

What is clear is that Mexican workers participated in the strike in disproportionate numbers. Several witnesses claimed that at least half of the men on strike were Mexican. Bisbee's mining labor force was about 13 percent Mexican, but at least 27 percent of all deportees were Mexican—and probably more. One mining manager echoed several others when he observed that, alone among the working men, the Mexican workers quit "practically in a body at the first announcement of the strike." At one mine, three hundred of three hundred and fifty Mexican workers appeared on the picket line the first day of the strike.[20] They were the most loyal of the strikers in a workforce of thousands. The question is, why?

Mexican workers had concrete goals and ideological reasons for joining the strike. Above all, Mexican workers were on strike against the dual-wage system. Their chief demand threatened to yank the linchpin from the racial hierarchy of manliness. This demand proposed to raise the wages of *all* surface laborers, regardless of race, from $2.50 to $5.50 per day, while raising wages of underground (white) miners from $5.75 to $6.00—an increase of less than 5 percent. Had both these demands been met, the wages of surface laborers would be within $.50 of what white underground workers earned. If surface workers earned $5.50 per day and underground workers earned $6.00, the dual-wage labor system would have effectively ceased to exist.[21]

Anglo Wobbly organizers had concocted this extraordinary wage demand to entice Mexican workers to their cause, not because of a genuine commitment to it. Strike leaders intended for the Bisbee strike to show support for Wobbly strikes elsewhere, especially in Butte, Montana. As a Wobbly spokesperson explained, "This is a solidarity strike and we must concentrate on that phase of it. The demands made are wholly secondary."[22] Anglo strike leaders were pursuing a national political agenda, while Mexican miners were striking for local demands with broad consequences.

Despite these differences with Anglo leaders, Mexican workers flocked to the Wobblies for sound ideological and practical reasons. The IWW was the first union to take a friendly interest in Bisbee's Mexican workers. The union hired two Mexican organizers, Benito García and Joseph Robles—a first for organized labor in Bisbee. Moreover, while some strikers were surely ignorant of the finer points of Wobbly doctrine, many others would have known about the connections between the IWW and the Partido Liberal Mexicano (PLM), the anarcho-syndicalist organization headed by the Flores Magón brothers. Many Bisbee miners had come from the Mexican copper town of Cananea, where the IWW had participated in the PLM's first important strike in 1906. There, too, PLM members had been striking against the dual-wage system, where "American" workers imported to Cananea earned twice what the Mexican miners earned. In Bisbee, the sheriff's department used the terms "Magonistas" and "Mexican IWW" synonymously, and a year before the strike, the leader of the Mexican IWW was also a representative for the PLM's newspaper.[23] The PLM had close ties with the Wobblies and the Bisbee area. In other words, Mexican workers, far from being the Wobblies' dupes, knew exactly what they were doing.

Mexican workers also challenged the racial hierarchy of manliness by appropriating the language of manhood long denied to them. Federal and state investigators ignored Mexican workers while they were collecting testimony in Bisbee, but statements gleaned from the Mexican camp of Clifton, where Mexican workers represented such an overwhelming majority that investigators had to question them, speak clearly. When New York reporter Robert Bruére asked Mexican miners in Clifton why they were on strike, they said it was "for an American standard of living," and more say in the improvement of working conditions. Federal investigator Felix Frankfurter, then a young Harvard Law School professor and assistant secretary of labor, was even more concise, specifically invoking the role of manhood. After visiting Bisbee as a member of the Mediation Commission three months after the deportation, Frankfurter observed that the strike had been "a fight for the status of free manhood." The Mexicans and Slavs, he concluded, "feel they were not treated as men." One Mexican striker in Clifton touched on this multiracial alliance, casting the racial hierarchy of manhood in the stark terms of slavery. Critics "were sure that the Mexican element and the Spaniards and Italians would not hold together. [But] the times in which the master class were imposing on us are past and gone. . . . The times of slavery are gone forever." Given the racial division of labor, this was a powerful metaphor, even more so because it appropriated a language many white union workers had long used to embrace free labor ideology.[24]

As this Clifton striker recognized, perhaps the most revolutionary aspect of the Bisbee strike was its ability to subvert and reevaluate established "racial" truths. Surviving on a "Mexican standard of living" had been outstanding training for a war between capital and labor. One white carpenter admitted that "the much vaunted superiority of the so-called Anglo-Saxon fades into a myth" in the face of the dedicated resolve of Mexican strikers, who "lived on less than half of what the average [white] striker would consent to remain loyal on."[25] Did it occur to the carpenter that Mexican workers had been enduring similar conditions for decades?

By claiming their manhood and demanding the American standard of living, Mexican strikers pulled up the stakes that secured the white man's camp. Outsiders like Bruére and Frankfurter recognized this, but local Anglos could not. To admit the manhood of Mexican workers would be to topple the teetering racial hierarchy of the white man's camp. This is why the sheriff responded to the strike so forcefully.

Sheriff Harry Wheeler and the Manliness of Patriotic Chivalry

When asked by federal investigators about the strike, Sheriff Wheeler announced, "This is no labor disturbance. We are sure of that."[26] That Wheeler could make the extraordinary statement that a strike was not about labor indicated how deeply racialized the class system was. Race and nation were commingled in a borderlands town populated largely by immigrants, where questions of patriotism and national loyalty were always questions of race. For Wheeler, opposing the strike was a matter of national defense, racialized fears, and—by his own assertion—being a man. Wheeler's commitment to the tenets of American manliness was extraordinary, but it demonstrates the way that divergent views of white manliness could still converge in the decision to participate in the deportation.

For good reason the *New York Times* called Wheeler a "vigorous personage." With his slight stature and modest height, it was not Wheeler's physical stature that made him stand out, but rather his reputation as "a man of splended judgement [*sic*], cool—skillful, daring, and the right man in the right place at all times." Wheeler had authentic and well-known western manly credentials.

The son of a West Point graduate, Wheeler was born and raised on western army forts. After apparently serving in the Spanish-American war, Wheeler worked his way up the ranks until he was captain of the Arizona Rangers, a state militia that patrolled the border, pursued cattle rustlers, and "kept the peace" in labor disputes.[27]

Critics and defenders alike described him as moral and honest. Married with several children, Wheeler was an upright military man and a teetotaler—stern, moralistic, and uncompromising. The Arizona Rangers had sometimes found their captain inflexible and condescending (twenty-six resigned under his watch), but he could also be deeply caring and contemplative. He "grieved" after dismissing an officer whom he had found drunk, praising the fallen man's "exceedingly good character and most lovable traits." Wheeler believed that men were made, not born; he admitted that he had once "fought down some personal habits, but it took me a long time . . . *before I gained the mastery over myself*."[28]

Wheeler's role in the deportation deserves special mention because, unlike company officials who were eastern aristocrats, the sheriff had a good reputation among union members. As captain of the Arizona Rangers, Wheeler had intervened in several strikes in Arizona, most notably the 1903 strike of mostly Mexican workers in Clifton-Morenci. Yet he had gained a reputation as a fair-minded third party who insisted on equal treatment and nonviolence for both sides of labor conflicts. Mother Jones herself had vouched for Wheeler's good character, calling him "a pretty fine fellow," despite her distrust of law enforcement. She admitted that Wheeler "was an exception to that rule." Because of Wheeler's reputation for fairness, he had not been the mining companies' chosen candidate for sheriff. Wheeler once explained to a friend that he had not run for office until 1911 because "The Copper Queen [management] does not want me and that settles it in this County."[29] In spite of his concern, Wheeler was elected twice, and was immensely popular in the mining towns and the large ranching areas that surrounded Bisbee.

Wheeler's moral probity made a strong impression on federal investigators. After meeting with Wheeler for hours, the commission—although they disapproved of Wheeler's actions—dismissed allegations that Wheeler had been paid off by the mining companies. One commission member, an AFL leader from Illinois, echoed the sentiments of several others when he averred, "I believe [Wheeler] is absolutely honest and clean and courageous." The federal secretary of labor called Wheeler "a man of the type" immune "to any corrupt influence of any kind of character whatever."[30]

Wheeler was neither a company man nor crooked. So why the deportation? Why cooperate with the mining officials? Although his plan of action may have converged with theirs, and he may have even worked at their behest, Wheeler fully believed that he did so for his own reasons and on his own terms, and so did the commission. He did not defend the rights of industrialists, but he did believe that maintaining wartime industry was a patriotic responsibility. In Wheeler's mind, he was preserving national interests, not material ones. It was not antilabor attitudes that led Wheeler to organize the deportation, but rather what he called "pure Americanism," and by that he meant patriotism and loyalty. Wheeler believed that anyone striking against a war industry was potentially treasonous. For him, choosing sides became a question of "Are you an American, or are you not?" He defined his Americanism against the actions of "foreigners," and for him, wartime labor activism, foreignness, and disloyalty were inseparable. He insisted, "We intend to make this an American camp where American working men may enjoy life, liberty and the pursuit of happiness unmolested by any alien enemies of whatever breed."[31]

The Mexican Revolution, which had begun in 1910, had a galvanizing influence on Wheeler. For people on the U.S.-Mexico border, the war-related tensions had begun long before America's entry into World War I. The Zimmermann telegraph, in which the Germans promised to return Arizona, New Mexico, and Texas to Mexico, if Mexico would attack the United States, suggested to Wheeler, and to many others, that the strike was the work of pro-Germany provocateurs who had allied with the Mexicans. The telegram—sent just five months before the Bisbee strike—only confirmed Harry Wheeler's worst suspicions. He believed rumors that Mexican workers kept a cache of rifles just over the line, though he had no evidence. After the deportation, he admonished federal investigators that any one of them would have done the same thing, had he "been a sheriff on this border for six or seven years, and a captain of the Rangers years before it[,] and had seen the things which occurred on the border as I have seen them." Living on the border, he explained, "put a new complexion on" the strike.[32] His choice of the term "complexion" unconsciously captured the racial subtext of the fear over labor troubles.

Wheeler and the deputies targeted Mexicans as a group, whether or not they were on strike. As one deputy explained, "It is hard for an American to tell the faces among the Mexicans." As a result, according to one source, "Innocent suffered alike with guilty." Labor Secretary William B. Wilson asked the sheriff how he had ascertained which residents of Mexican descent were revolutionaries or at least "alien." Wheeler responded, "They were practically all aliens, Mr. Wilson." The labor secretary pressed on, "What steps were taken to take charge of those Mexicans" who were explicit supporters of Mexican revolutionary Pancho Villa? To this, Wheeler responded, "How could you separate one Mexican from another?" When Wilson asked whether the deputies had even tried to distinguish among the men, Wheeler concluded the exchange by announcing that, "I honestly believe today that 80 or 85 per cent of these men were foreigners, some of them Austrians and Germans and Mexicans, and none of them loved the country I love." He rounded up many men whose only crime was their foreign appearance—and Mexican men were the most obvious targets. When Secretary Wilson continued to needle Wheeler about his dragnet techniques, Wheeler replied, "I would repeat the operation any time I find *my own people* endangered by a mob composed of 80 per cent aliens and enemies of my Government."[33]

To Wheeler and others, foreigners—especially Mexicans—were a faceless crowd of mindless, dangerous followers. By 1917, the docile children of years past had been transformed into dangerous revolutionaries in the testimonies of deputies and their defenders. No one articulated this metamorphosis of Anglo perceptions better than did Wheeler, with his references to dangerous "mobs," and his repeated mention of rifle-caches. This was a new tune for Wheeler. Just one year before the deportation, Wheeler had received reports from deputies that "there does not seem to be any plotting and organizing going on" among Bisbee's Mexican population. On the contrary, Mexicans in the area were "somewhat timid for fear that they might be molested by the Americans." At the time of the deportation, however, Wheeler claimed that "all Mexicans hate Americans," and his every action flowed from this premise. Wheeler had little patience with federal investigators who questioned his conclusions. "You eastern people haven't had much experience with Mexicans, but . . . we figured they might do anything."[34]

The Mexican Revolution had surprised many people who had assumed Mexicans were simply childish nuisances incapable of insurrection. Close to home, the border towns of Agua Prieta and Naco, both just miles from Bisbee, had been the sites of significant battles to which U.S. residents had flocked to participate as spectators. Sheriff Wheeler repeatedly referenced "border troubles" in general and the Battle of Naco in particular as he defended his role in the deportation. Then, too, the Mexican camp of Clifton-Morenci had been the site in 1903 and 1915 of large-scale strikes led by Mexican workers, as well as wildcat strikes so common that a new Spanglish term arose to describe them—*strikitos*.[35] Both the revolution and this new labor activism forced many Anglos to revise their stereotypes.

The new stereotype of the Mexican as dangerous revolutionary was not as distant from the older one of the docile child as it might appear, however, because neither was manly. Both failed to resemble the ideal resident of the white man's camp: the independent, loyal, family-supporting "American" worker. Even sympathizers reified this ultimately passive vision of Mexican workers. Mining officials warned Bruére, the New York reporter, that the Mexican camps surrounding Clifton-Morenci were "unsafe" because of the "terrible Mexicans," although the muckraking adventurer reported somewhat disappointedly that he found them to be "the most docile people imaginable."[36]

Figure 8.2. A deportee at the camp in Columbus, New Mexico. Arizona State Library, Archives and Public Records, photo 01–3099.

For Wheeler, revolution had not made Mexicans manly and independent, because in his view, they had simply switched their allegiances from American foremen to foreign provocateurs. The Zimmermann telegram indicated to the sheriff that Mexican strikers were dangerous because they had fallen under the sway of "Prussians."

If ideas about manliness shaped Wheeler's understanding of Mexicans' place in the deportation, his own gender identity was inseparable from his decision to take a leadership role in the event. Typical was his statement to investigators that, "I don't shirk anything. If I have done wrong, I am willing to suffer for it. I am not the kind of man who will whimper, and I am not running away from it."[37] Wheeler felt the deportation was necessary to protect Bisbee's most precious social boundaries—those that separated working-class Mexican men from "white women." He worried for weeks, he said, about "foreigners" bothering "women." For Wheeler, the two categories were separate, because "women" were implicitly American, even though thousands of foreign-born women lived in Bisbee.

When Mexican Wobblies approached a group of white female laundry workers to join the union, this was the last straw. In Wheeler's words, "They were so terrorized by visitations of a committee of Mexicans . . . that the women one day left in a body in abject terror. Think of white women in an American town so terrorized by foreigners that they were compelled to quit work in terror of their lives."[38] Like race, gender seemed natural to Wheeler and, thus, the perfect arsenal with which to defend his position. In Wheeler's mind, protecting white womanhood was just as natural as self-defense, and both were at the heart of his understanding of manhood.

Although it was relatively minor, the incident at the laundry came up again and again when vigilantes defended their actions. It was bad enough in their minds when Mexican workers demanded nearly the same wages as Anglo men in Anglo jobs. But when Mexican strikers approached *white women* to join their union—to make common cause with them—the strikers were also challenging *gender* hierarchies that built upon racialized fears. In a world where class differences rested on race and racial boundaries rested on gendered rules, single white women joining a mixed-race miners' union was literally unthinkable. Wheeler could not conceive of it as anything except a potentially violent threat to white womanhood, indeed to "pure Americanism itself."

The deportation was a messy affair, and so were its causes. Unitary theories are tidy, because they insist on parceling race, labor, nation, and gender into separate categories. These interpretations also suppose that one justification trumped another. Yet what is far more striking is the confluence of these ideas. Although the meanings of these categories seemed self-evident, in fact all of them were fluid. The conflation of race and labor was so deeply entrenched in the social system that it was manifested in the most visceral, unself-conscious justifications and behaviors—manliness among them. An emphasis on the role of masculinity—something seemingly natural but never stable—highlights the connections between gender, race, family, labor, and national identity. A threat to one meant a threat to all.

The racial hierarchy of manliness subsumed race, gender, nation, and class into a conception of manliness that did not cause the deportation, but did filter multiple motives into a worldview of white male supremacy that provided a frame for participants to understand their decisions and roles in the strike and the vigilante response to it. For Wheeler, this was the crux of the dual-wage system: to naturalize racial difference to such an extent that any challenge to it was a threat to gender relations and to the integrity of "America" itself.

Ultimately, the strike was a failure by any measure. Many of the deported men never returned. Even worse, Bisbee embraced its status as a white man's camp and "American town" with renewed vigor. As late as 1929, Bisbee advertised as "the last stand of the American miner."[39] Conditions for Mexicans worsened, and with the same circular reasoning they had used before 1917, white workers scapegoated Mexican workers for low wages and labor conflict. Given the odds that were stacked against the workers, it is hardly surprising that the strike was unsuccessful. Still, to attempt it at all meant that the goal of the white man's camp—to make Mexican workers less than men, to deny them agency—had failed.

Notes

I would like to thank Thomas Andrews, Antonia I. Castañeda, Hal Cohen, Flannery Burke, Linda Gordon, Alexander Shashko, and Marienka Sokol Vanlandingham for their readings and assistance.

1. The President's Mediation Commission appointed by President Woodrow Wilson concluded that the strike had been peaceful (U.S. Department of Labor, *Report on the Bisbee Deportation Made by the President's Mediation Commission to the President of the United States, November 6, 1917* [Washington, D.C.: Government Printing Office (GPO), 1918, hereafter cited as PMC], 4; George E. Kellogg testimony, PMC, 13; "Women and Children Keep Off Streets Today," *Bisbee Daily Review*, July 12, 1917, 1; and "Arizona Sheriff Ships 1,100 IWW's Out in Cattle Cars," *New York Times*, July 13, 1917, 17, 1).

2. Testimony cited in reports to Gov. George W. P. Hunt, July, 1917, probably from sworn statements to Arizona Attorney General Wiley Jones, RG 1 Governor's Office, Hunt Papers, box 8, Arizona State Legislative and Public Records, hereafter cited as Hunt Papers and ASLAPR.

3. The classic account of the IWW is Melvyn Dubofsky, *We Shall Be All: A History of the IWW* (Chicago: Quadrangle Books, 1969). Thomas E. Sheridan, *Arizona: A History* (Tucson: University of Arizona Press, 1995), 183. Vernon H. Jensen, *Heritage of Conflict: Labor Relations in the Nonferrous Metals Industry up to 1930* (Ithaca, N.Y.: Cornell University Press, 1950), 400.

4. Major interpretations of the deportation include John H. Lindquist and James Fraser, "A Sociological Interpretation of the Bisbee Deportation," *Pacific Historical Review* 37:4 (1968): 401–22; Philip Taft, "The Bisbee Deportation," *Labor History* 13:1

(1972), 3–40; James Byrkit, *Forging the Copper Collar: Arizona's Labor-Management War of 1901–1921* (Tucson: University of Arizona Press, 1982); Philip J. Mellinger, *Race and Labor in Western Copper: The Fight for Equality, 1896–1918* (Tucson: University of Arizona Press, 1995); Colleen O'Neill, "Domesticity Deployed: Gender, Race, and the Construction of Class Struggle in the Bisbee Deportation," *Labor History* 34:2/3 (1993): 256–73; and Colleen O'Neill, "A Community Divided: A Social History of the Bisbee Deportation" (master's thesis, New Mexico State University, 1989). The most recent study is Christopher Capozzola, "The Only Badge Needed Is Your Patriotic Fervor: Vigilance, Coercion, and the Law in World War I America," *Journal of American History* 88:4 (2002): 1354–82.

5. Kristin L. Hoganson, *Fighting For Manhood: How Gender Politics Provoked the Spanish-American and Philippine-American Wars* (New Haven: Yale University Press, 1998). Other works that have influenced my focus on manliness and masculinity include Susan Lee Johnson, "'A Memory Sweet to Soldiers': The Significance of Gender," in *A New Significance: Re-envisioning the History of the American West*, ed. Clyde A. Milner II (New York: Oxford University Press, 1996), 255–78; Gail Bederman, *Manliness and Civilization: A Cultural History of Gender and Race in the United States, 1880–1917* (Chicago: The University of Chicago Press, 1995); and Matthew Basso, Laura McCall, and Dee Garceau, eds., *Across the Great Divide: Cultures of Manhood in the American West* (New York: Routledge, 2001).

6. I focus here mainly on men. On women in Bisbee, see O'Neill, "Domesticity Deployed," and "A Community Divided"; and Katherine A. Benton, "What about Women in the 'White Man's Camp?': Gender, Nation, and the Redefinition of Race in Cochise County, Arizona, 1853–1941" (Ph.D. diss., University of Wisconsin–Madison, 2002).

7. Bisbee's exclusion of the Chinese was in explicit contrast to Tombstone, its nearby silver-camp neighbor, which included a sizable Chinese population. See Odie B. Faulk, *Tombstone: Myth and Reality* (New York: Oxford University Press, 1972), 199; William B. Shillingberg, *Tombstone, A.T.: A History of Early Mining, Milling, and Mayhem* (Spokane, Wash.: Authur H. Clark, 1999), 130–32; and U.S. Bureau of the Census, *Eleventh Census of the United States, 1890, Population*, Part 1, Statistics of Population (Washington, D.C.: GPO, 1892), 610.

8. "No Foreign Labor Wanted," *Bisbee Daily Review*, May 27, 1903. Robert Orsi, "The Religious Boundaries of an Inbetween People: Street Feste and the Problem of the Dark-skinned Other in Italian Harlem, 1920–1990," *American Quarterly* 44:3 (1992): 313–47. According to Orsi, John Higham coined the term "'in-between' races." James R. Barrett and David Roediger, "In-Between Peoples: Race, Nationality and the 'New Immigrant' Working Class," *Journal of American Ethnic History* 16:3 (1997): 3–44. Elizabeth Jameson, *All That Glitters: Class, Conflict, and Community in Cripple Creek* (Urbana: University of Illinois Press, 1998), 140–60. "Census of the Columbus I.W.W. Refugee Camp," comp. by Ben H. Dorcy, Cavalry Major, Intelligence Officer, Columbus, New Mexico, Hunt Papers, ASLAPR.

9. Mexicans working at the Copper Queen smelter in nearby Douglas earned two-thirds what other men in the same jobs did. I have not found wage scales for Mexicans in Bisbee on the eve of the strike; but the proportional difference between white and Mexican wages would be similar. Copper Queen Smelter Rate Scales, May 16, 1917, Henry McCluskey Collection, MSS 54, box 2, Arizona Collection, Arizona State University. See Phelps-Dodge Corporation Payroll Records, 1885, Arizona Historical Society, hereafter cited as AHS, and "March 13, 1923 Report Re: Wage Scale for Reduction Works Employees in Douglas," Copper Queen Mining Company Wage Scales, Samuel Truett private collection, Albuquerque, New Mexico. The author wishes to thank Truett for access to these materials. See Michael Parrish, *Mexican Workers, Progressives, and Copper: The Failure of Industrial Democracy in Arizona During the Wilson Years* (San Diego: Chicano Research Publications, University of California, San Diego, 1979), 12–13. Linda Gordon describes the ways that Phelps-Dodge manipulated the dual-wage system in her book, *The Great Arizona Orphan Abduction* (Cambridge, Mass.: Harvard University Press, 1999), 181. The racial underpinnings of American identity were best articulated by Theodore Roosevelt, who believed that, as Gail Bederman has summarized, "the manly American race was forged of various immigrant races, [and] all of those contributing races were European" (Bederman, *Manliness and Civilization*, 179).

10. Ralph Rollins, "Labor Situation in Arizona Points to Mexicanization," *Arizona Mining Journal* 4:4 (1920): 13–14. *Bisbee Daily Review*, World's Fair Edition (1904). "Nationality Report of Men Employed on June 26th, and of Men Deported to Columbus on July 12th, Who Were in the Employ of the Calumet & Arizona Mining Company When Strike Was Called on June 26th," PMC reports, 288–89. The Mexican workers were also the only ones whose marital status was not recorded. Roediger and Barrett found that managers drew up elaborate lists of which races should do which work ("In-Between Peoples," 17). On the average Mexican and white wages, see Joseph F. Park, "The History of Mexican Labor in the Territorial Period" (master's thesis, University of Arizona, 1961), 245. Park found the average wage for Anglo workers to be about $4.00, and the average Mexican wage to be about $2.05 during the early 1910s. Phylis Cancilla Martinelli, unpublished manuscript.

11. Linda Gordon defines the family wage usefully as "the sex/gender/family system that prescribes earning as the sole responsibility of husbands and unpaid domestic labor as the only proper long-term occupation for women," in *Pitied but not Entitled: Single Mothers and the History of Welfare, 1890–1935* (New York: Free Press, 1994), 53. For more on the family wage, see Martha May and Ron Rothbart, "'Homes Are What Any Strike Is About': Immigrant Labor and the Family Wage," *Journal of Social History* 23:2 (1989): 267–84. See Martha May, "The Historical Problem of the Family Wage: The Ford Motor Company and the Five Dollar Day," *Feminist Studies* 8:2 (1982): 404, 419. Alice Kessler-Harris, *A Woman's Wage: Historical Meanings and Social Consequences* (Lexington: University of Kentucky Press, 1990), 1.

12. Cleveland Van Dyke report to Kendric C. Babcock, president of the University of Arizona, December 16, 1907, Warren Company Papers, Private Collection of Charles Parrott, Lowell, Massachusetts, 8–9. My thanks to Parrott for sharing these valuable materials with me. On the family wage ideology and its relationship to the homeowning plans in the Bisbee suburb of Warren, see Benton, "'What about Women,'" 192–253. David Roediger, *The Wages of Whiteness: Race and the Making of the American Working Class* (1991; reprint, New York: Verso Books, 1999).

13. Byrkit, *Forging the Copper Collar*, 158. John O. Dunbar, "Editorial Comment," *Dunbar's Weekly*, July 7, 1917, 8.

14. Lawrence Glickman, "Inventing the 'American Standard of Living': Gender, Race and Working-Class Identity, 1880–1925," *Labor History* 23: 2/3 (1993): 221–35. On its relationship to the family wage, see May and Rothbart, "Homes," passim, and, in the Jacksonian period, Jeanne Boydston, *Home and Work: Housework, Wages, and the Ideology of Labor in the Early Republic* (New York: Oxford University Press, 1990). Glickman, "Inventing the 'American Standard,'" 221; quotation from 226. Dunbar, "Editorial Comment: Kill The Strikers," *Dunbar's Weekly*, July 14, 1917, 6.

15. World's Fair Edition, *Bisbee Daily Review*. The census of deportees in Columbus found 773 out of 1003 to be "men owning property," including Mexican and those of Mexican descent (Dorcy, "Census," Hunt Papers). For a published example of such defense, see Edward T. Divine, "The Bisbee Deportations," *Survey*, July 21, 1917, 353.

16. Victor Clark, "Mexican Labor in the United States," *Bureau of Labor Bulletin*, 78 (1908): 477–92, as cited in Dru McGinnis, "The Influence of Organized Labor on the Making of the Arizona Constitution" (master's thesis, University of Arizona, 1930), 18. See Glickman, "Inventing the 'American Standard,'" 228. Walter Douglas, president of Phelps Dodge Corporation, to A.T. Thompson, assistant to the president, Douglas, Arizona, March 7, 1918, Truett collection.

17. Gordon, *Great Arizona Orphan Abduction*, 180. Clark, as cited in McGinnis, "The Influence of Organized Labor," 18. My discussion of Mexican workers is indebted to A. Yvette Huginnie's "A New Hero Comes to Town: The Anglo Mining Engineer and 'Mexican Labor' as Contested Terrain in Southeastern Arizona, 1880–1920," *New Mexico Historical Review* 69:4 (1994): 323–44. Alonzo Crittenden, "Management of Mexican Labor," *Mining and Scientific Press* 123 (1921), 267, as cited in Huginnie, "A New Hero," 330.

18. O'Neill, "Domesticity Deployed," 258. Other scholars have made a similar choice. When Michael Parrish tried to offer evidence of Mexican workers' attitudes in Bisbee, he was forced to cite the testimony of Antonio Rodriguez, an immigrant from Spain who lived on Chihuahua Hill. Rodriguez was the only Spanish-surnamed or Spanish-speaking witness at the Presidential Mediation Commission hearings in Bisbee (Parrish, *Mexican Workers*, 16–7; and PMC, 546–57). On the 1907 strike, see Mellinger, *Race and Labor in Western Copper*, 73–79; and Benton, "'What about Women,'" 216–20.

19. Of the 2,201 surface and underground workers as of June 26, 1917, 314 were Mexican (PMC, 217). These numbers are generally consistent with the testimony of Copper Queen General Manager G. H. Dowell in the PMC reports. Secretary Wilson had eased immigration restrictions from Mexico in June (Parrish, *Mexican Workers*, 18). Mellinger, *Race and Labor in Western Copper*, 188. This figure comes from Dorcy, "Census."

20. Figures cited by witnesses ranged from 50 percent to 85 percent (Strickland testimony, PMC, 502; and Wheeler testimony, PMC, 166, 256). Workforce numbers compiled from statistics at two major companies on June 26, 1917, the last day before the strike. Percentage of strikers (which no doubt included people born in Mexico as well as Mexican Americans) compiled from Army census of deportees conducted in August, the most reliable figures available. Company officials and IWW leaders concurred on this (G. H. Dowell testimony, PMC, 353; and Grover H. Perry, secretary-treasurer of Metal Mine Workers' Industrial Union No. 800 to William [Big Bill] Haywood, July 6, 1917, Exhibits in *State of Arizona v. Henry Waters*, and *Michael Simmons v. El Paso and Southwestern Railroad* [1919], hereafter cited as *Simmons v. EPSW Railroad*, box 1, University of Arizona Special Collections,).

21. O'Neill briefly suggests these same points in "Domesticity Deployed," 258.

22. Jack Norman, Columbus, New Mexico, to Perry, July 25, 1917, *Simmons v. EPSW Railroad*, box 1.

23. O'Neill, "Domesticity Deployed," 82, 83. J. L. P., Report on "Mexican Matters," to Harry Wheeler, June 5, 1916, in *Simmons v. EPSW*, box 8. The best source on the strike is Michael Gonzales, "United States Copper Companies, the State, and Labour Conflict in Mexico, 1900–1910," *Journal of Latin American Studies* 26:3 (1994): 651–81. For a typical example of the claim that the Cananea strike was the opening shot in the revolutionary battle, see Ramón E. Ruiz, *Labor and the Ambivalent Revolutionaries: Mexico, 1911–1923* (Baltimore: Johns Hopkins Press, 1993), 3; and the classic, though now outdated, Rodney D. Anderson, "Mexican Workers and the Politics of Revolution, 1906–1911," *Hispanic American Historical Review* 54:1 (1974): 94–113. Other sources include Jonathan C. Brown, "Foreign and Native-Born Workers in Porfirian Mexico," *American Historical Review* 98:2 (1993): 786–818; and Marvin D. Bernstein, *The Mexican Mining Industry, 1890–1950* (Albany: State University of New York Press, 1965), 65. See also C. L. Sonnichsen, *Colonel Greene and the Copper Skyrocket* (Tucson: University of Arizona Press), 1994.

24. Robert Bruére, *Following the Trail of the IWW: A First-Hand Investigation into Labor Troubles in the West—A Trip into the Copper Camps and the Lumber Camps of the Inland Empire with the Views of the Men on the Job* (New York: New York Evening Post, 1918), 3. Frankfurter, as cited in Parrish, *Mexican Workers*, 30, 29. Critics as cited in Parrish, *Mexican Workers*, 14. See Glickman, 222–23. On immigrant workers and free labor's meanings, see Gunther Peck, *Reinventing Free Labor: Padrones and Immigrant Workers in the North American West, 1880–1930* (New York: Cambridge University Press, 2000).

25. Worker as cited in Parrish, *Mexican Workers*, 11.

26. Wheeler testimony, PMC, 138.

27. "Arizona Sheriff Ships 1,100 IWW's Out in Cattle Cars," 1. Sheriff John White to Gov. Joseph Kibbey, August 15, 1907, Arizona Ranger Papers, ADLAPR, as cited by Bill O'Neill, "Captain Harry Wheeler, Arizona Lawman," *Journal of Arizona History* 27:3 (1986): 303. There is inconsistency regarding documentation of Wheeler's participation in the Spanish-American War. The soundest overview of Harry Wheeler is Bill O'Neill, "Captain Harry Wheeler."

28. Bill O'Neill, "Captain Harry Wheeler," 304. Capt. Harry Wheeler, Naco, Arizona, to Gov. Kibbey, Phoenix, Arizona, October 30, 1908, Arizona Ranger Papers, RG 42, ASLAPR, emphasis added.

29. See John Greenway's correspondence during these years, passim, John C. Greenway Collection, MS 311, AHS, and discussion of Douglas in Byrkit, *Forging the Copper Collar*, 32, 87, 99, 139, 178, 299, 301. Mellinger, *Race and Labor in Western Copper*, 24. Philip Foner, ed., *Mother Jones Speaks: Collected Writings and Speeches* (New York: Monad Press, 1983), 372. Capt. Harry Wheeler to Mr. Sims Ely, secretary to governor, Phoenix, Arizona, February 23, 1908, Arizona Ranger Papers.

30. Walker testimony, PMC, 589, William B. Wilson testimony, 492.

31. "Sheriff Wheeler's Statement on Strike," *Courtland Arizonan*, July 21, 1917, 2.

32. On the impact of the Zimmermann telegram, see Friedrich Katz, *The Life and Times of Pancho Villa* (Stanford: Stanford University Press, 1998), 612, 660, 663—64. Wheeler testimony, PMC, 161.

33. This pro-company miner thought that around 50 percent of the strikers were Mexican (I. H. Strickland testimony, PMC, 502). See testimony cited in reports to Gov. George W.P. Hunt, July, 1917, probably from sworn statements to Arizona Attorney General Wiley Jones, 20–21, box 8, Hunt Papers. Wheeler testimony, PMC, 166, 256, emphasis added.

34. [J.L.P.], police informant, to Sheriff Wheeler, "Re: Mexican Matters," June 5, 1916, in *Simmons v. El Paso*, box 8. Wheeler testimony, PMC, 224.

35. Linda Hall, "The Mexican Revolution and the Crisis in Naco: 1914–15," *Journal of the West* 16 (July 1977): 27–35. Wheeler testimony, PMC, 161–62. See also Bruére, *Following the I. W. W. Trail*, 13–14. A[ndrea] Yvette Huginnie appropriately named her dissertation for these ongoing challenges to management. "'Strikitos': Race, Class, and Work in the Arizona Copper Industry, 1870–1920" (Ph.D. diss., Yale University, 1991).

36. Bruére, "Following the I.W.W. Trail," 1.

37. Wheeler testimony, PMC, 165.

38. Wheeler testimony, PMC, 253.

39. "Bisbee, the Most Southern Mile-High City in North America," *Arizona Labor Journal*, May 31, 1929, 27.

CHAPTER 9

ILGWU Labor Organizers

Chicana and Latina Leadership in the Los Angeles Garment Industry

MARÍA A. GUTIERREZ DE SOLDATENKO

Researchers studying the International Ladies' Garment Workers' Union (ILGWU) and female European immigrant activists at the turn of the century have noted the poor record of this union with respect to women's participation.[1] Latina leaders in the ILGWU tell a similar story about the union in the 1990s. During this period the ILGWU in Los Angeles claimed attempts to organize and represent a predominantly Latina labor force while refusing to acknowledge the contributions, talents, and potential of Latina and Chicana leaders working for them.

While many studies have focused historically on the struggles of European immigrant union leaders in the ILGWU, we do not have a documented history focusing fully on the participation of women of color in the union.[2] Several studies have examined the history and development of the Mexican American and Latina leadership within the ILGWU in Los Angeles.[3] These authors' works celebrate the contributions of Latinas and Chicanas within the historical context of the union, and they are critical of the ILGWU's lack of vision concerning Latinas and Latinos. They also document the labor mobilizations of women in Los Angeles garment industry. Hector Delgado, for example, completely rejects the old stereotypical portrayal of Latino and Latina immigrants working in Los Angeles and shows the ways in which Latinos and Latinas organize.[4]

Many authors have blamed Mexican and Latina women for the lack of unionization, insisting Latina culture is to blame for women's lack of organized or political participation in unions. They argue that Mexican and Latina women are backward and ignorant, difficult to organize, and are not leaders.[5] Yet the evidence demonstrates the active participation of Latina and Chicana garment workers since early times. In both California and Texas, Mexican origin women have organized in independent groups such as *La Mujer Obrera* or *Fuerza Unida*. In Mexico City garment workers organized *La Diecinueve de Septiembre*, an independent union.[6]

My purpose in this essay is not to criticize the union for its policies and actions that continue to perpetuate a system of gender and racial inequality in their ranks.[7] Rather, I want to explore the continual contributions of Latinas within the ILGWU, even in light of difficult union policies affecting Latinas. It is important to document the ways in which Latina and Chicana leaders contribute to the labor struggle in Los Angeles despite the barriers they confront in everyday life and within the union bureaucracy. Latina and Chicana leaders teach us about persistence, intelligence, and courage. I hope union leaders in the newly formed union UNITE will take note and begin to value more highly Latinas in their union.[8]

I met Latinas working for the ILGWU beginning in 1988 while working on my dissertation. In 1992, as a postdoctoral fellow, I had the opportunity to closely observe the Justice Center, created in 1990 by ILGWU to offer free legal advice and provide support for nonunion workers. Eventually I interviewed twenty respondents at the Justice Center, both paid staff and members. From these I made composites of their cases in order to protect their identities. These findings are part of a larger ethnographic study on Latinas in the garment industry in Los Angeles. My method is qualitative and represents a case study in the ILGWU's Justice Center before it was dismantled in 1999. Latina garment workers at the Justice Center not only knew about labor rights; they also knew about the effectiveness or lack of organizing strategies. Some workers had experienced labor struggles before they came into contact with the ILGWU, and they represented the most interesting and inspiring part of the study. These Latinas are crucial in any organizing efforts, and the prospects for workers' mobilization in the industry lay in their hands.

One of the first problems I faced was the need to reconceptualize my vision of "leadership."[9] I will use "leadership" only to point out the active political roles these women took. For lack of a better term and because it embodies both agency and political meaning, I have chosen to call the women I interviewed leaders. All of the women shared certain characteristics that made them stand out from their peers. It is not my intention to discuss or clarify what leadership entails. I also recognize the artificial separation created between leaders and followers and reject such a dichotomy. Successful leadership manifests a constant dynamic between organizers, organizing, and the workers. As demonstrated in this article, the individuals interviewed embody and represent this struggle.

Justice Center for Garment Workers

Latina garment workers came together at the Justice Center and benefited from the experience of running it. One of the goals of the Center was to publicize and transmit knowledge to all garment workers, but the Center was also the site of mobilization planning, where workers discussed strategies and visualized the different possibilities of improving their working conditions and salaries.

The Center had four consecutive directors, all of them Latinas. The first, Beatriz Nava, directed the Center as well as the Immigration project at the ILGWU from 1990 to 1991. Nava was overwhelmed and overworked with the expectation that she work two positions at two different locations, yet she creatively made both projects work without much support or acknowledgment from the ILGWU. When Nava resigned her position for other opportunities, Maria Avila became the new director. Avila, a seasoned community organizer from Chicago, came with a full plan of action, and she energetically involved garment workers with the work of the Center. Avila also networked with community organizations in the garment district. Avila's enthusiasm and commitment reflected her level of involvement at the Center; however, she resigned her position to work at a community organization in South Central Los Angeles two years later. Adriana Meneses then became director, but she also eventually resigned her position by 1994.

During Meneses's directorship many workers became members of the Justice Center. By that time the Center had moved from three different locations and in 1993 was occupying the basement of the ILGWU, close to McArthur Park in Los Angeles. Meneses kept the Center operating with the help of two assistants, Roxana Guevara and Isaura Lucero, and the threesome worked effectively with workers, facilitating weekly meetings and other events. Business was conducted in Spanish, which created an atmosphere of camaraderie the workers came to enjoy. The Center also offered classes in English as a second language. Garment workers met regularly at the Center to exchange stories and job-hunting techniques and to discuss labor laws and rights. Every week a presentation took place whose topic and presenter were decided upon by a group of garment workers. One of the Center's activities was to help workers systematically calculate and document their hours. Every participant completed a form with information on hours of work and pay rates. Workers calculated their wages to check that they were earning the minimum wage. Workers kept a file in the eventuality that they decide one day to take their case to court. The Justice Center collected all such information for future Labor Department hearings on minimum wage.

However, Latina and Chicana directors of the Justice Center held no real power within the union hierarchy but rather worked under the supervision of white males. Many times white supervisors made decisions that undermined efforts by Latina leaders. Although the Center provided a space to prepare a cadre of Latina and Latino garment workers to organize and mobilize the industry, the ultimate result was to contain and restrain such activity. In fact, those invited to join and participate at the Center risked systematic purges by Union leadership, and workers who demonstrated too much independent thinking could come under suspicion at the Center. Workers who showed initiative or questioned the Center's tactics found themselves blacklisted and made unwelcome. To be blacklisted meant not only that a worker was publicly humiliated, but that she could not take part in discussions and would be deprived of her weekly food basket donated to the center by the United Way. I witnessed several incidents in which staff told specific workers they represented a threat to the ILGWU. Latinas and Latinos often felt humiliated and left the Center, accused of not following the union program, which was very limited in scope and rabidly antisocialist and anticommunist. In such ways the Center's mission in support of worker's mobilization actually operated to undercut worker's participation if they disobeyed the ILGWU's mandates.[10]

Many scholars of organized labor agree that the ILGWU does not have a good record when it comes to women or people of color. Women of color are present in the struggle, yet they have remained invisible. Despite union's blacklisting, Chicana and Latina organizers persevere in their work on behalf of garment workers. At the Justice Center, for instance, the work of Latinas and Chicanas lend credibility to the ILGWU when it comes to the organization of Latinas in Los Angeles. We must come to terms with these women's backgrounds in order to understand what motivated them to participate in the labor struggles in the garment industry.

Profile of Latina Leaders in the Garment Industry

Even though the union has not treated Latinas and Chicanas as equals, they have been pivotal to ILGWU's efforts to organize workers in Los Angeles. Young Chicanas and Latinas have brought with them a legacy of organizing; they have not arrived at ILGWU as blank slates waiting to be led by white male leadership. It is important that we understand the background of Latina leaders to dispel distorted representations about them. I have assembled below information about Latina leaders—including family background, educational level, Chicana or Latina role models, and their roots as garment workers—that discounts persistent notions that Latinas and Latinos lack political culture.[11] Lisa Schlein, for example, in her work on the garment industry in Los Angeles, argues that Latinas lack a sophisticated political culture and therefore need Anglo Americans to organize for them.[12]

The family backgrounds of Latina and Chicana leaders interviewed had several similar characteristics. The majority of the women came from large families that lived under harsh economic conditions. Children in these families had to work and struggle from an early age. These women developed a strong sense of identity within their families. Most of these individuals learned to be assertive and thrived when given responsibility. In all cases, the women realized the leadership role they played within their own families. Family members instilled in them a strong sense of justice and egalitarian ideals, as well as a work ethic and collective consciousness. Some interviewees said:

> *Yo fui criada por mi abuelita y un tio socialista. . . .* I was raised by my grandmother and a socialist uncle. Thus I grew up in a more or less socialist environment, helping others and knowing that there should be equality among all of us.[13]

> *Yo creci en un sindicato con mi tia. . . .* I grew up in a union hall with my aunt. She cooked for the workers in a small town. They worked for a British oil company in Ancon, Ecuador. I remember the meetings in the union hall; they left a lasting impression in me.[14]

Chicana and Latina families provided the environment in which these women learned about social issues. Some interviewees noted that they learned about political participation and radical ideas from their spouses. Many of their mates had a history of unionism or community organizing behind them. One woman explained:

> *Yo pienso que en parte mi esposo me indujo a participar. . . .* In part, I think my spouse induced me to participate. He belongs to a union. My husband always gets involved with the work of his union.[15]

However, we must not forget the dynamics of gender inequality in these households. While families could provide environments for growth, families could also be contested sites for women organizers. In households and within the family, divisions between women's and men's work appeared at two levels. The households enacted a strict division of labor, placing women at a disadvantage. In terms of labor organizing, these women also faced resistance from some family members. For many Latina leaders, their home was the site of discontent and resistance as a result of their active political participation. In many instances the expectation for women was that they fulfill their organizing duties at the union without modifications to family arrangements that included strict gender division of labor. They were expected to be superwomen. These labor organizers understood the unfairness of this arrangement and struggled with this every day of their lives, but, because they were vocal and defended their rights at home, tensions were always present. For instance, I often conducted interviews with Latina leaders with their children present:

> *Yo nadamas tengo dos hijos pero es mucho trabajo. . . .* I only have two kids, but it is a lot of work. Look at my little one, how he moves around. I am always busy. . . . I could not attend my ESL classes. My husband could not help me. I had to do it all![16]

In some cases the mothers of Latina organizers disapproved of their daughters' line of work. Other family members could also obstruct the development of a Latina organizer's participation. Susana Rendon remembers the difficulties she faced when she began to work for the union:

> *Yo llegaba a mi casa a las once de la noche y mi mama furiosa. . . .* I would get home at eleven at night, and my mom was furious. Sometimes my mother would slap me for getting home so late. She never understood what type of work I was doing.[17]

Rendon's mother often reminded her that working at the union was not an appropriate job for a *señorita*.

If employed at the union, Chicana and Latina organizers had to have at least a high school diploma, and some college or its equivalent was desirable. By comparison, those garment workers not employed by the ILGWU or the Justice Center generally had lower levels of education. Many Latina organizers believed that their economic and social position resulted from their inability to further their education:

> *Mi padre era bracero el venia de Mexico a trabajar por temporadas. . . .* My father was a bracero. He came from Mexico to work seasonally. My mother came to work as well, and they worked very hard to support us. I left school in sixth grade to help my parents out. I worked in anything I could find.[18]

> *Yo fui asta el segundo año y ya fue todo. . . .* I went to school until the second grade and that was all. When I was older there were teachers from the city coming to my small town. I went to the teacher. I asked her to come and

> live with my family so that she could teach us something (laughter). . . . She invited me to enroll in adult classes. That is how I finished the sixth grade.[19]

> *Cuando yo vine de Sudamerica ya vine graduada de secundaria. . . .* When I came from South America I had graduated from high school. Later on I had to learn English. I graduated from high school, and I attended Los Angeles City College and California State University at Los Angeles. By this time I was already working for the union.[20]

Latina and Chicana leaders were very proud of their mothers, grandmothers, aunts or older sisters, who had taught them to be strong and to build their character. Older women set good examples, and they instilled a sense of pride in their younger relatives. Chicana and Latina leaders learned about who they were and what things they could do independently through these other women. They learned from these role models how to be survivors and to persevere in all their activities in life. One interviewee said:

> *Mi abuelita siempre me enseño (sobre) la justicia. . . .* My grandmother always taught me about justice. . . . The land belongs to those who toil in it, she used to say. It is better to die on your feet than to die on your knees. My grandma used to tell me defend yourself, speak up, and she was always a fighter. She could not speak much English, but she would always argue for her rights.[21]

The majority of Latina organizers had experiences working for the garment industry, and their mothers or grandmothers had worked in the garment industry in Latin America and the United States. Some Latina organizers remembered working at home as children. The majority helped their mothers and grandmothers with their sewing "homework." They recalled doing straight sewing, turning up collars and waistbands, or cutting threads as children. They also remembered the harshness of the industry's working conditions and the low wages their families had to endure. Their perspective on labor organizing and level of commitment remained closely related to their experiences as garment workers, which were initiated in childhood:

> *Mi mamá todavía es costurera. . . .* My mother is still a garment worker. There were six girls and three boys at home, and there were too many of us. We used to do industrial "homework." When we would come from school we had to clean up. We did our schoolwork, then we would sit and work all afternoon turning waistbands. During the summer we worked at the shop as well.[22]

> *Mi mamá era costurera ella hacia "homework."* . . . My mother was a garment worker who did "homework." She used to go to a store that made shirts, and she would take work home. When we children were there we would help with trimming, we folded the shirts, and we placed a piece of material inside of collars to make them stiff.[23]

To summarize, all Chicanas and Latinas I identified as leaders had similar family backgrounds and a highly developed sense of social justice. These women shared a sense of equality and an awareness of social issues that began in their own households or with their extended families. Latinas and Chicanas simultaneously struggled against the gender division of labor within their own households. Most Latinas and Chicanas had strong roots as garment workers through their own work experience or through family members.

Garment Workers Make the More Effective Organizers

One particular debate among the women interviewed was over the best way to organize. Should all organization of workers occur within the factory? Could one successfully organize from without? For some Latina organizers, having family members in the industry or having had their own previous garment work experience seemed adequate for effective organizing. Others believed that such connections were not sufficient because it was possible to forget one's "garment roots." According to studies in unionization, one of the most effective strategies is worker-to-worker recruitment and mobilization.[24]

The Latinas I interviewed considered working in the garment industry as the prerequisite for effective organizing. They admired and respected the paid staff at the union, yet they visualized an even better organizing staff who would also be garment workers. This remains an unresolved issue, and one not easily settled. Garment workers wanted to see people like themselves occupying important positions in the union, and so they viewed those Latinas working behind a desk in the union and at the Justice Center with ambivalence. Constant tension existed between those who worked at the shops and those who did not.

Some organizers had worked for the garment industry and had recently stopped because that work was extremely difficult. Nevertheless, they understood the need to continue the struggle from the inside and not to lose touch with workers. One organizer said:

> *Hay veces que digo, bueno si queremos organizar a la costura debo trabajar en la costura.* . . . There are times that I say, "Well, if we want to organize the garment industry, then I should be working in a shop." The truth is that

> working for thirteen years at the sewing machine weighs a lot on my back. I get so tired. I do not get tired of struggling with the owners—that is a daily battle. [But] physically, I cannot sit at the sewing machine anymore.[25]

Some garment workers believe that only working in the shops could give organizers an edge for doing their union work:

> *No es la misma urgencia. . . .* They do not have the same urgency that we have. We are being exploited the whole day. We see what owners pay us. Then it is that *coraje* (rage) that you feel. This rage pushes you to do something to change things. I feel some people in the union do not have a lot of contact with the workers.[26]

The closer the organizer stays to garment workers, the more successful her organizing practices become. The most effective women leaders maintained close ties with the membership and with nonmember garment workers. Latinas and Chicanas could always relate to women like themselves or those sensitive enough to understand their language and cultural nuances. In contrast, the top leadership of Los Angeles ILGWU remained distanced from the base, which led to increasingly counterproductive acts. A group of garment workers meeting outside the Justice Center in 1995 complained that they were not heard or taken seriously in planning activities at the Center. They perceived some of the leadership and volunteers at the Center as arrogant when they tried to teach workers about working conditions and about how to organize. Thus the tension between the Latina and Chicana leadership and the ILGWU became an ever-present threat to successful organizing.

Organizing Among Latina and Chicana Garment Workers

Women who are successful in organizing, whatever their political or organizational background, bring a gendered and ethnic politics to their activism.[27] They know how to relate to other women in order to achieve their goals for the organization. Furthermore, they recognize the importance of ethnicity and race in their politics. This recognition helps Latina organizers assist workers with various resistance strategies. Even though differences over strategies may arise, their success rests in part on the leader's ability to work with the gender and racial/ethnic politics of the workers.

Many of the Latina and Chicana leaders in the ILGWU had some experience in organizing before coming to the union. They had learned about labor organizing through their involvement in struggles in their communities, grass-roots organizations, and at factories and shops. Other Latina organizers learned their skills while participating or working as volunteers with community organizations. Some had worked with the various Cesar Chavez campaigns. There were even those who had actively participated with Marxist organizations in Los Angeles. Some of these women had also been active in their home countries in Latin America. All of these women were articulate and knew the issues, and most had interacted with political activists in different settings. The end result was developed awareness of social and political issues in their communities or at their place of employment. They applied this knowledge in their everyday lives and, of course, to the garment workers' struggle.

Some Latina organizers learned about political and organizational involvement before their arrival at the ILGWU. A few examples help dispel the notion that these individuals were somehow apolitical or organizationally naive. Cristina Ramirez Vasquez began visiting the Center for Autonomous Social Action (CASA), an organization that helped develop some Chicana and Latina leaders in the Los Angeles area, after she immigrated from Ecuador.[28] She explained:

> *Cuando me mandaron al ILGWU a entrenar a New York yo llegue verde. . . .* When the ILGWU sent me to train in New York, I was so "green." I knew nothing. I used to go to CASA, the organization on Pico, to listen to Bert Corona, and he used to speak about the undocumented immigrant workers. I used to cry with my sister listening to the injustices. So at the gut level, I knew about immigration, but I wanted to learn [more], and I wanted to help.[29]

In the case of Maria Elena Durazo, her initial participation in community activities was as a college student and while working with CASA. Durazo went to work for the ILGWU with a group of Chicanos from CASA. CASA's strategy was to work with unions to train more *raza* for the struggle of the Mexican community in Los Angeles.[30] Durazo eventually returned to finish her law degree and now is the president of the Hotel and Restaurant Employees Union in Los Angeles. Durazo is one of the most highly visible Chicana leaders occupying an important position in organized labor in Los Angeles.

Alicia Lepe's training and preparation occurred at the Head Start Program. She began as a volunteer and later became a paid staff member with the program:

> *Yo aprendi a desenvolverme en el Head Start. . . .* I learned to speak in public and to interact with the public at the Head Start program. They taught me a lot. I learned to address a group of people, to conduct meetings and take notes. Later I went to work with the Latino Community Justice Center

in East Los Angeles. I worked as well for the Rodriguez brothers and for Cesar Chavez. I worked in their campaigns and translating at meetings.[31]

Some Latina organizers joined communist groups, where they participated in study groups and learned about strategies about organizing:

> *Yo aprendi mientras trabajaba con un grupo comunista en una huelga en Los Angeles. . . .* I learned while working with a communist group in a strike in Los Angeles. We were winning the struggle, but the owners started a campaign accusing us of being communists, and that was the end of it. It happened so fast, and it was badly organized. The boss fired everyone involved in the strike. We lost at the end. The owner claimed that since it was a communist group, he would not negotiate with us.[32]

In the process of participating in struggles from different political perspectives and at different levels, women learn to act politically and to provide leadership, but what stood out from all the experiences of the women interviewed was their ability to relate to other women. This characteristic has been extensively discussed in the cases of Jewish, Italian, and Irish organizers in the ILGWU, but it was also important to Chicanas and Latinas in labor struggles.[33] Latina organizers relied on their abilities to relate to women workers to facilitate their recruitment, organization, and activism.

Latinas and Chicanas mobilized in unions along gender and racial /ethnic lines.[34] Feminists have also noted that women organize differently than men.[35] Women transform the culture of unionism.[36] I found that Chicana and Latina leaders created alternative ways to reach out and intervene for Latina garment workers. Networks developed among women at the Justice Center centered on gender and race. For instance, women came together to participate in their own endeavors. Women organized birthday parties, held potlucks at their homes, or got together to sell household products to each other. In these settings, Latinas also discussed issues of work and organizing. To paraphrase Karen Sacks, "The potluck was political."[37]

The political action and mobilizations of working-class women of color continue to unfold. There is much to learn about the multiple oppressions of gender, race, ethnicity, and social class in grassroots mobilizations and unions. Chicana researchers emphasize the ways in which women develop a critical consciousness through interactions with other women.[38] While studying cannery workers in organizing drives, Patricia Zavella observed that "Chicanas began developing a critical consciousness about their experiences through the discussions they had with one another."[39] Chicanas and Latinas politicized each other at the union and at the Justice Center, and Latina leaders recognized the impact they had on women workers. At the same time, women workers sought out women leaders to work with. This was not as much about leaders and followers as it was an example of the way in which Latinas shared a commonality of lived experiences. Latina organizers called upon their commonality to mobilize other women and to develop their own organizing skills. They did not think their work was only to labor on behalf of other Latinas, but to teach Latinas to help themselves. Leaders knew they had to communicate self-reliance and assertiveness among their Latina sisters because they wanted all Latinas to be able to survive on their own.

Another important aspect related to Latina leadership development was the affirmation leaders derived from their interaction with the Latinas and Chicanas they served. Admiration and support were always present, and it went both ways. This dynamic realization of support coming from Latina workers motivated Latina leaders to continue their work. One Latina leader said:

> *Yo siempre soy mas efectiva con las mujeres. . . .* I am always more effective with women. Women seek my help because they know that I am very strong. The other day I went with one of my Latina clients to the Immigration and Naturalization Service office. . . . They had to let me in to see a supervisor after I argued with them. . . . My client said, "If you had not come, they would not let me in." I told her, "Yes, they would let you in. You just have to be more forceful with them. You can do it, too."[40]

Cristina Ramirez Vasquez, a political educator of the ILGWU in Los Angeles, explained how her vocation as an organizer called for an effective way to empower Latina garment workers:

> *Simplemente como organizadora uno tiene que sentir la vocacion. . . .* Simply stated, as an organizer, one has to feel the vocation to try to help people so that they can help themselves. In this job, that is how I get satisfaction.[41]

In other instances, Latinas demonstrated a concern for the Latina union organizer who invested all her energy in the union. Vasquez recalls how devastated she felt after a strike defeat, feeling that she had let the workers down. However, Latina garment workers understood her position and tried to console her for all her work and commitment toward their struggle. Vasquez recalled:

> *El dia que perdimos la campaña, yo fui a hablar con las compañeras. . . .* The day we lost that campaign I had to go and talk to the compañeras, and I

> could not do it. I was crying. Everybody noticed my despair. I went home and began to cry, and then someone was at the door. All the women in the strike committee were there. They came to see that I was doing all right; we all had a shot of tequila and cried together. . . . *Cuando las trabajadoras se dan cuenta que tu eres sincera.* . . . When the workers notice that you are sincere, when you really try to do something. We work because we love what we do, we are dedicated to garment workers and they know it.[42]

Women who have participated in different union campaigns constantly approach Vasquez. They come to her and hug her, remembering her fondly. For Latina organizers, their participation in the union is a labor of love.

Unfortunately, the top leadership at the union level manipulates this commitment to their own advantage and to the detriment of Latina leaders within the organization. Latina leaders are so busy with immediate, everyday concerns of the union organization that they have little time to establish themselves effectively within the bureaucracy. When Latinas look after themselves, they are accused of not supporting the goals and ends of the union. Martha Samano, a political educator who preceded Vasquez, left the ILGWU after an open struggle with the union over harassment by a white male staff member. Picket lines of workers in support of Samano marched in front of the union hall.

In another example, Connie Moreno, an ex-ILGWU organizer who earned the respect and affection of many Latina workers, left the union in 1989. I had a chance to see Moreno's excellent work with Latina workers, as she was my main informant at the beginning of my research. One of the reasons union officials gave her for her dismissal was that as a single mother, she had a duty to raise her daughter and to clean up her house first:

> They said at the union that I did not have enough time to take care of my family, and to clean my house [laughter] . . . I said to them, that is my decision. . . . I was very naive, very idealistic. I felt, if I worked and busted my butt, then there will be recognition.[43]

Latina leaders developed various tools and forms of resistance in the shop. At the same time, they struggle with the ILGWU hierarchy. Latina leaders work actively against a system of exploitation of garment workers. Simultaneously, they resist the male union supervisors who block their attempts to organize independently and effectively with Latina workers. In terms of resistance at work, strategies arise out of particular problems workers encounter, such as bargaining for a better price on a particular operation, asking for breaks, or demanding better work conditions. These acts of resistance help workers figure out the system as they practice protesting and contestation. A garment worker explains:

> *Hay que exigir un poco no hay que bajar la vista. . . .* We must demand a little—we do not need to keep our eyes downcast. One sees instances of both conformism and resistance every day at the shop. Sometimes people in a section get together to fight a particular price. That is really encouraging. I feel great when that happens. I tell my coworkers *hechenle ganas* (keep up the good work).[44]

In another example, Bracamonte, an outspoken garment worker, said:

> *No! Con los patrones siempre he tenido la tendencia de pelear. . . .* No! With the bosses I always have the tendency to fight in the factories. They have fired me from many shops because I speak up. Even if we do not fight for a union, they fire us, but one continues struggling. I used to get people together to fight for better piece rates.[45]

Workers occasionally back up other workers when they are fired, or when they feel a worker has been mistreated. These are small triumphs that feed into the feeling of solidarity among these workers. In a particular instance, a worker complained about the price of piece rate, the boss called him into his office, and he left with his severance pay. Everyone became upset, and the boss had to reinstate him. Olga Fuentes, a sample maker, vividly recalls this incident when all her coworkers stood together. They told their boss:

> *No vamos a dejar que corras a Rene. . . .* We won't allow you to fire Rene. If you fire him, we won't show for work tomorrow. So you make the decision—either Rene stays or we do not come to work tomorrow! Nobody comes to work tomorrow—listen everyone! The next day Rene came late. We stopped working until he arrived, [and] everyone felt relieved Rene came to work, even the *canijos* bosses [laughter].[46]

Most workers feel that instances of resistance at work are important lessons in their political learning process. It is at work that working conditions, wages, and abuses first become contested. Contestation takes different forms but boils down to workers' actions. As Bracamonte explains:

> *Yo pienso que se aprende peleando en la fabrica. . . .* I believe that one learns in the factory struggling. That was the way in which I learned.[47]

Susana Rendon, a garment worker, was always confronting her bosses:

> *Y me dieron trabajo. . . .* And they gave me a job. I was a "trimmer." I was always making trouble for the owner, always fighting prices. There was this sexist guy always harassing me, and I would go and report him as well.[48]

Latinas maintained their outspokenness even if it meant risking their jobs. Vasquez said:

> *Una vez abri mi bocota para defender a unos trabajadores y alli me corrieron.* . . . Once I opened my big mouth to defend some workers and there they fired me! I had just worked there for a short time.[49]

Instances of resistance occur in the everyday experiences of garment workers, but more organized large-scale resistance occurs as well. The owners have the advantage because they can move their factories overnight or file for bankruptcy, as occurred in a shop in Hollywood, California, in 1992. Workers camped outside the factory doors, though, so that the owner could not move the machinery without paying them for their last month of work.[50]

According to Latina leaders, the most effective methods of resistance tend to occur at shops where workers were able to pull together, either with the help of the union or on their own. The Latinas interviewed all recounted several strikes or mobilizations they each took part in. They did not always win, but in terms of experience such actions affected their lives. Mobilizations imprinted a memory of struggle and hope that affirmed these Latinas as politically active.

They learned how to mobilize in real-life situations, and they felt prepared for any struggle in the future. They understood the difference between spontaneous, unorganized struggle and long-term struggles in factories. One organizer said:

> *Yo creo que la gente tiene que ver algo bien concreto para aventarse. . . .* I think people have to see something very concrete to participate; it has to be very well organized. Spontaneous struggles have always existed in the garment industry. People get together, they struggle. They stop working, and they never return. Where I used to work [on organizing labor resistance], we worked quickly, and then we felt nobody wanted to do anything anymore. That is not the way to struggle![51]

Together with organized or sporadic resistance, workers also sought some official response from the Labor Department; however, when workers took cases to the Labor Commission they were not taken seriously. Workers who experienced firsthand the inaction from the Labor Commission toward employers did not trust government agencies to resolve work disputes. Workers distrusted the Labor Commission when it failed to protect workers' rights:

> *El trabajo en la fabrica llego a un punto que ya no aguantabamos. . . .* Work at the factory reached a point that we could not take it anymore. We worked for forty hours [but] they paid us for twenty. We got mad. I offered to go to the Labor Commission. I went there, and I visited different offices. I filed a complaint. They said they would send somebody, but nobody showed up![52]

In some instances workers mobilized in reaction to a particular action taken by the owner or supervisor. Rendon recounted an incident in retrospect:

> *En esta fabrica resulto que el patron nos hizo enojar. . . .* At this shop the boss made us mad. He passed down a list for us to sign. It had all kinds of restrictions at work—we could not make noise, speak to each other, listen to the radio, to whistle, go to the rest room. All of us refused to sign it, and we came up with our own demands. We asked him to sign a letter we all signed and notarized. In this letter we asked for fair wages, vacation, and all the rights that were legal.[53]

The union has faced several defeats that the union leadership has not evaluated seriously. For example, in 1991 La Mujer Obrera (LMO), an independent garment workers' group, launched a strike against four garment manufacturers and invited the ILGWU to lend technical support. ILGWU's team of white male organizers made the tactical mistake of ignoring women workers in LMO as if they were incapable of fighting for their own rights. The ILGWU tried to negotiate with employers without consulting with LMO and instead lost all support from workers due to their sexist and racist practices.[54]

In the case of Latina and Chicana garment workers in Los Angeles we can clearly see the practices of a union that has failed to learn to work with women and specifically with women of color. Chicanas and Mexicanas in Texas have not had good relationships with either the ILGWU or ACTWU. Judging from their record, these two unions have tried to work with employers rather than with workers.[55]

By examining the lives of Chicana and Latina leaders, we can learn about their participation, commitment, and strategies. It is important to note the way in which Latina organizers develop leadership skills in response to both Anglo and male union bureaucracy and the needs of Latina garment workers. Chicanas and Latinas come from a variety of ideological backgrounds, but they all face similar barriers of gender and race in their work. Although Chicana and Latina leaders faced barriers at almost every step of their efforts to organize Latina garment workers, they made considerable progress on behalf of the workers. For example, Cristina Ramirez negotiated contracts and organized strikes using her effective social skills; Alicia Lepe helped undocumented Latina workers with their immigration, empowering them to do things for themselves; Roxana Guevara and Adriana Meneses addressed Latinas at Justice Center meetings, effectively explaining labor rights while joking with them in Spanish. These leaders knew enough about both labor relations and cultural nuances to be accepted and respected while they were able to draw on their own working experiences to mobilize Latina workers.

Latina and Chicana leaders know the complexity of unionization efforts and keenly resent exclusion, being used as tokens, or not being taken seriously. They clearly know who the perpetrators are—the mostly male hierarchy of the ILGWU in Los Angeles and the International headquarters in New York. The union leadership must act and willingly recognize the innovative potential of Latina and Chicana leaders to improve the work of the ILGWU that has now merged with the Amalgamated Clothing and Textile Workers Union (ACTWU) to form UNITE.

As I was writing this paper, I received faxed messages from two Latina organizers at the ILGWU informing me that they had been fired. Accusations against them included the charge that they manipulated the membership of the Justice Center because they could communicate in Spanish (an absurdity because they were hired because they were bilingual and could communicate with monolingual Latinas). Latina and Chicana leaders have an authentic desire to fight for workers' rights, end exploitation, and improve working conditions. They understand the plight of garment workers better than anybody else because they are closer to workers. It is time for UNITE to reconsider old policies and traditions that retard unionization possibilities for Latinas in Los Angeles. The future calls for more effective inclusion of members in racial/ethnic groups so greatly affected by the efforts of the union.

Notes

This piece is dedicated to all the Latina and Asian garment workers and women union organizers and leaders at the ILGWU, some of whom must remain anonymous. Special thanks to Connie Moreno, Rocio Saenz, Maria Davila, Martha Samano, Beatriz Nava, Rina Tamayo, Maria Elena Durazo, Cristina Ramirez Vasquez, Alicia Lepe, Roxana Guevara, Adriana Meneses and Isaura Luceno. Michael Soldatenko provided critical comments and unconditional support. This research was funded by the Institute of American Cultures at the Chicano Studies Research Center at UCLA.

1. For example, see the work of Carolyn Daniel McCreesh, *Women in the Campaign to Organize Garment Workers, 1880–1917* (New York: Garland, 1985); Rose Pesotta, *Bread Upon the Waters* (Ithaca NY: ILR Press, 1987); Elaine Lereder, *The Gentle General: Rose Pesotta, Anarchist, and a Labor Organizer* (Albany NY: SUNY Press, 1993); and Annalise Orleck, *Common Sense and a Little Fire: Women and Working-Class Politics in the Unites States, 1900–1965* (Chapel Hill: University of North Carolina Press, 1995). The discussions in these works center on the contributions of Irish, Jewish, and Italian activists to the ILGWU in its early period and also explain the constant alienation and dismissal of women by the mainly male leadership.

2. There are a few works on individual participants, including, for example, the oral history account of Esperanza Mendoza Schechtor, an ILGWU organizer in the 1940s. See the interview with Schechtor conducted by Malca Chal in *Activist in the Labor Movement, the Democratic Party, and the Mexican American Community* (Berkeley: The Bancroft Library, University of California Berkeley, Regional Oral History Office 1977–1978); the narratives of Clementina Duron, "Mexican Women and Labor Conflict in Los Angeles: The ILGWU Dressmakers' Strike of 1933," *Aztlan* 15:1 (1984): 145–61; and Douglas Monroy, "La Costura en Los Angeles, 1933–1939: The ILGWU and the Politics of Domination," in *Mexican Women in the United States: Struggles Past and Present*, ed. Magdalena Mora and Adelaida R. del Castillo (Los Angeles: UCLA Chicano Studies Research Center, 1980), 171–78.

3. See Duron, "Mexican Women and Labor Conflict in Los Angeles"; Pesotta, *Bread Upon the Waters*; Monroy, "La Costura en Los Angeles"; John Laslett and Mary Tyler, *The ILGWU in Los Angeles, 1907–1988* (Inglewood CA: Ten Star Press, 1989); and Benjamin Márquez, "Organizing Mexican American Women in the Garment Industry: La Mujer Obrera," *Women and Politics* 15:1 (1995): 65–87; Miriam Ching Yoon Louie, *Sweatshop Warriors: Immigrant Women Workers Take On the Global Factory* (Cambridge MA: South End Press, 2001), 202–4.

4. We need to problematize this identity to show its complexity. For a further discussion of this issue, see Maria Angelina Soldatenko, "Made in the USA: Latinas/os?, Government Work and Ethnic Conflict in Los Angeles Sweat Shops," *Cultural Studies* 13:2 (1999): 319–34. As I stated there, "Latino ethnicity is increasingly constructed as a 'universal,' 'classic,' and genderless pan-ethnicity" (319).

5. Here, I distinguish among Chicana, Mexican, and Latina women because demographically the majority of workers in the garment industry in Los Angeles is and has been Chicanas and Mexicanas. In the 1970s more women from other Latin American countries entered the industry. Most authors erroneously refer to all of them only as Latinas. For a profile of the garment industry in Los Angeles, see James Loucky, María Soldatenko, Gregory Scott, and Edna Bonacich, "Immigrant Enterprise and Labor in Los Angeles Garment Industry," in *Global Production: The Apparel Industry in the Pacific Rim*, ed. Edna Bonacich, Lucie Cheng, Norma Chinchilla, Nora Hamilton, and Paul Ong (Philadelphia: Temple University Press, 194), 345–61. For a statistical breakdown on the ethnicity of workers in officially registered shops

only, see Edna Bonacich and Richard P. Applebaum, *Behind the Label: Inequality in the Los Angeles Garment Industry* (Berkeley: University of California Press, 2000), 169. Scholars and journalists alike have insisted that the lack of organizing among Latina garment workers is due to their ignorance. According to this view, Latinas do not know about their labor rights and are unwilling or too scared to organize effectively. See Lisa Schlein, "Los Angeles Garment Industry Sews a Cloak of Shame," in Mora and del Castillo, *Mexican Women in the United States*, 113–16; and Walter Foguel, *Mexican Illegal Aliens in the United States* (Los Angeles: Institute of Industrial Relations, University of California, 1978).

6. For an account of the Fuerza Unida battle over relocation of Levi Strauss from San Antonio, Texas, to Mexico and the massive layoffs of Chicana and Mexican workers, see Louie, *Sweatshop Warriors*, 206–9. The work of La Mujer Obrera in El Paso, Texas, opposing Farah since the 1970s, is documented in Márquez, "Organizing Mexican-American Women in the Garment Industry"; and Swasti Mitter, "On Organizing Women in Casualized Work: A Global Overview," in *Dignity and Daily Bread*, ed. Sheila Rowbotham and Swasti Mitter (London: Routledge, 1994). To learn more about garment workers in Mexico City and the ways they have organized the first independent union recognized by the state, see Marisol Arbaláez, "Impacto Social del Sismo, Mexico 1985: Las Costureras," in *Between Borders: Essays on Mexicana/Chicana History*, ed. Adelaida del Castillo (Encino CA: Floricanto Press, 1990), 313–35; Teresa Carrillo, *Working Women in the '19th of September' Mexican Garment Worker's Union: The Significance of Gender*, Working Paper 179 (Michigan State University: Women in International Development, 1989); and Silvia Tirado, "Weaving Dreams, Constructing Realities: The Nineteenth of September National Union of Garment Workers in Mexico," in Rowbotham and Mitter, *Dignity and Daily Bread*, 100–113.

7. For my previous work analyzing racism and sexism in unions, particularly the role of the ILGWU in the lives of Latina garment workers in Los Angeles, see María A. Gutierrez Soldatenko, "Organizing Latina Garment Workers in Los Angeles," in *Las Obreras: Chicana Politics of Work and Family*, ed. Vicky Ruiz (Los Angeles: UCLA Chicano Studies Research Center [CSRC], 2000), 137–57.

8. The International Ladies' Garments Workers' Union (ILGW) joined the Amalgamated Clothing and Textile Workers' Union (ACTWU) in 1995 to form the Union of Needle Trades, Industrial, and Textile Employees (UNITE).

9. We need to find a better language with which to discuss and understand women's leadership. Our traditional language is laden with gendered and ideological perspectives about what defines a leader and leadership. Furthermore, how do we escape from turning this discussion into another example of the "women worthies," that is, of deeming some women worthy of attention for accomplishing great deeds while ignoring the acts of everyday women? While I recognize the problems in my language and its political implications, I have not developed an adequate response. Karen Sacks resolves this conundrum by coining the term "center-woman" for those

women who lead in the struggle to organize other women (Karen Brodkin Sacks, *Caring by the Hour: Women, Work, and Organizing at Duke Medical Center* [Urbana: University of Illinois Press, 1988], 137–42).

10. The ILGWU developed with ongoing ideological struggles over purging communists from the organization that date back to the 1920s. For background on this, see Paul Berman, *A Tale of Two Utopias: The Political Journey of the Generation of 1968* (New York: W. W. Norton and Company, 1996). See also Xiolan Bao, *Holding More than Half the Sky: Chinese Women Garment Workers in New York City, 1948–1992* (Urbana: University of Illinois Press, 2001), 32–40.

11. Earl Shorris, in his *Latinos: A Biography of the People* (New York: Avon Books, 1992), states:

> Politics has no purchase on Latinos, except for Cubans, who lived once in their island in a public way, as if it were Athens. All the rest have a latent sense of freedom, a Christian sense, freedom in the soul instead of the Agora. They are metaphysicians, the children of God; the public realm interests them less than home or heaven. . . . They did not practice politics, for metaphysicians do not believe people can be free except in dreams (406).

12. Lisa Schlein, "Los Angeles Garment Industry Sews a Cloak of Shame," 116.
13. Interview by author with Alicia Lepe, February 20, 1993.
14. Interview by author with Cristina Ramirez Vasquez, March 4, 1993.
15. Interview by author with Mariana Bracamonte, February 12, 1993.
16. Interview by author with Muriel Mora, March 8, 1993.
17. Interview by author with Susana Rendon, April 7, 1993.
18. Interview with Mariana Bracamonte, 1993.
19. Interview with Muriel Mora, 1993.
20. Interview with Cristina Ramirez Vasquez, 1993.
21. Interview with Alicia Lepe, 1993.
22. Interview with Alicia Lepe, 1993.
23. Interview with Cristina Ramirez Vasquez, 1993.
24. For an account of how the ACTWU mobilizes members to work for the union, see Jose La Luz, "Creating a Culture of Organizing: ACTWU's Education for Empowerment," *Labor Research Review* 17 (1991).
25. Interview with Muriel Mora, 1993.
26. Interview with Mariana Bracamonte, 1993.
27. For discussions regarding gender issues, see Sheila Cunnison and Jane Stageman, *Feminizing the Unions: Challenging the Culture of Masculinity* (Aldershot, England: Avebury, 1993); and Brigid O'Farrel and Joyce L. Kornbluh, *Rocking the Union Boat: Union Women's Voices, 1915–1975* (New Brunswick NJ: Rutgers University Press, 1996). For discussions regarding ethnicity/race issues, see Patricia Zavella, "The Politics of Race and Gender: Organizing Chicana Cannery Workers in Northern California," in *Women and the Politics of Empowerment*, ed. Ann Bookman

and Sandra Morgen (Philadelphia: Temple University Press, 1988); and Mary Pardo, "Creating Community: Mexican American Women in Eastside Los Angeles," in Ruiz, *Las Obreras*, 107–35.

28. For information about CASA, a community organization founded by Bert Corona, see Marisela R. Chavez, "'We Lived and Breathed and Worked the Movement': The Contradictions and Rewards of Chicana/Mexicana Activism in El Centro de Acción Social Autonomo-Hermandad General de Trabajadores (CASA-HGT), Los Angeles, 1975–1978," in Ruiz, *Las Obreras*, 83–105; and Carlos Muñoz, *Youth, Identity, Power: The Chicano Movement* (New York: Verso, 1989).

29. Interview with Cristina Ramirez Vasquez, 1993.

30. Among other "Casistas" who worked for the ILGWU were Mario Vasquez and Miguel Machuca, who worked in various campaigns in the 1970s and 1980s.

31. Interview with Alicia Lepe, 1993.

32. Interview with Mariana Bracamonte, 1993.

33. See Lederer, *The Gentle General*; Orleck, *Common Sense and a Little Fire*; and Pesotta, *Bread Upon the Waters*.

34. See Pardo, "Creating Community"; Zavella, "The Politics of Race and Gender"; and Vicky Ruiz, "A Promise Fulfilled: Mexican Cannery Workers in Southern California," in del Castillo, *Between Borders*, 281–98.

35. See Orleck, *Common Sense and a Little Fire*; Pesotta, *Bread Upon the Waters*; and O'Farrel and Kornbluh, *Rocking the Union Boat*.

36. See Ruth Needleman, "Women Workers: A Force for Rebuilding Unionism," *Labor Research Review* 1 (1988).

37. Karen Brodkins Sacks, *Caring by the Hour: Women Work and Organizing the Duke Medical Center* (Urbana: University of Illinois Press, 1988), 125.

38. See the work on Chicana activists and mobilizations in Zavella, "The Politics of Race and Gender"; Pardo, "Creating Community"; and Ruiz, "A Promise Fulfilled."

39. Zavella, "The Politics of Race and Gender," 206.

40. Interview with Alicia Lepe, 1993.

41. Interview with Cristina Ramirez Vasquez, 1993.

42. Interview with Cristina Ramirez Vasquez, 1993.

43. Interview by author with Connie Moreno, June 10, 1989.

44. Interview with Muriel Mora, 1993.

45. Interview with Mariana Bracamonte, 1993.

46. Interview by author with Olga Fuentes, May 18, 1993.

47. Interview with Mariana Bracamonte, 1993.

48. Interview with Susana Rendon, 1993.

49. Interview with Cristina Ramirez Vasquez, 1993.

50. See Jessie Katz, "Workers Camped at Closed Factory," *Los Angeles Times*, March 5, 1992, B3.

51. Interview with Mariana Bracamonte, 1993.

52. Interview with Muriel Mora, 1993.

53. Interview with Susana Rendon, 1993.

54. See Márquez, "Organizing Mexican American Women in the Garment Industry"; and Mitter, "On Organizing Women in Casualized Work."

55. See Louie, *Sweatshop Warriors*, 225. The ILGWU has demonstrated historically its insensitivity to issues of race and gender. Such practices are rooted and have been cemented since early times in its dealings with black, Puerto Rican, and Chinese garment workers in New York. For an excellent discussion of sexist and racist policies and practices at the ILGWU in New York, see Bao, *Holding More than Half the Sky*, 38–42.

CHAPTER 10

Esperanza v. City of San Antonio

Politics, Power, and Culture

AMY KASTELY

I first visited San Antonio, Texas, in 1958, when I was seven. I remember a downtown with many houses and lots of people sitting outside on porches and stoops. My older cousin explained that the people we passed on the street were speaking Spanish. Crisp, spicy smells and lively music came from the homes and restaurants. I wanted to dance. My white relatives lived in a house that was air-conditioned and cold, even when it was hot outside. Everybody at my aunt's house was white except a man who mowed the lawn. My aunt took my cousin and me to the Alamo, and we learned that the Mexicans killed everyone. I was afraid.

I moved to San Antonio in 1993. The downtown neighborhoods have been replaced by huge buildings surrounded by manicured grass and cement, hotels, and restaurants for tourists. You rarely hear Spanish spoken in these downtown streets.[1] Songs such as "La Bamba" and other "crossover songs" boom from shops selling Alamo T-shirts and ceramic Mexican hat dancers. Burger King offers breakfast tacos. The people in my aunt's neighborhood, on the near-Northside of town, are still mainly white, but most will tell you that San Antonio is fully integrated and culturally diverse. Many white San Antonians will explain how racial equality has come to the city without the conflicts experienced in other cities. Indeed, many white San Antonians experience diversity as living near several Latino families in suburban neighborhoods, working with Latinos as professionals or trained staff, and having a favorite Mexican restaurant, staffed by working-class Chicanos and Mexicanos. Some may also interact in similar ways with black Americans and Asian Americans.

Remarkably, in San Antonio, the largest city in the United States with a majority Latino population—the "capital" of Mexican-America—few white people experience genuine cultural difference. Although different cultures exist in San Antonio, the city and its business leaders have successfully corralled genuine diversity and replaced it with a commodified, "feel good" version of cultural difference.

I do not mean to say that authentic cultural diversity must be painful. However, unmediated exposure to another culture will force one to realize that other intelligent, healthy, well-meaning, and clear-thinking adults perceive the world very differently and value aspects of the world very differently. And in the United States, unmediated exposure to minority cultures will require one to see the destructive effects of cultural imperialism and forced assimilation. These experiences can be painful. In *The Color of Fear*, filmmaker Lee Mun Wah asks David, a white man, what it would mean for him if he were to believe what the men of color were telling him about racism. With a trembling voice, David responds, "Oh, that's very saddening. You don't want to believe man can be so cruel to himself or to his own kind. I do not want to accept that it has to be that way or maybe it is."[2] For many white people in the United States, it would be very upsetting and disturbing to experience genuine cultural difference. This disturbing feeling will not sell hotel rooms and investment packages.

As Arturo Madrid observes, the dominant view in the United States embraces diversity as "desirable in principle, not in practice. Long live diversity . . . as long as it conforms to my standards, my mind set, my view of life, my sense of order."[3] This is the kind of "cultural diversity" that sells airplane tickets, hotel rooms, and restaurant seats. This is the "cultural diversity" embraced by San Antonio's wealthiest business leaders and promoted by city policies.

But it is not easy to hide genuine cultural difference, particularly when members of a "minority" culture constitute a majority of the population, as in San Antonio.[4] Historically, public and parochial schools have subjected Chicanos and Mexicanos to mandatory assimilation. In the Westside barrio of San Antonio, for example, high schools have followed an "Americanization" curriculum since the 1930s.[5] This curriculum focuses on the skills of culture-crossing. Even today, the city's children are taught a highly-filtered version of San Antonio's history in which Chicanos, Mexicanos, and black Americans are portrayed as moving with easy acceptance into the highest places of San Antonio's professional, religious, and social life. In the 1960s, while downtown Chicano, Mexicano, and black neighborhoods were replaced with tourist facilities, poor and working-class neighborhoods of color were isolated in the Westside, Southside, and Eastside. Placement of highways and bus lines ensure that most middle-class people never see the neighborhoods where most working-class Chicanos, Mexicanos, and black Americans live. Police violence is routine in San Antonio and is particularly prevalent when police intervention is used to keep poor people out of the downtown area and off the streets. As a result, downtown streets cannot be used for traditional community activities and street commerce, except for the few strolling *helado* and *raspas* (ice cream and snow cone) vendors that are allowed to continue selling—quaint or exotic remnants of a once-active street life.[6]

City leaders work hard to promote a comfortable concept of cultural diversity in which all San Antonians share a love of "Tacos, Tequila, and Tenderloin," and celebrate Juneteenth and Cinco de Mayo along with the Fourth of July, Columbus Day, and, for a full week, the victory of Anglos over Mexicans at the Battle of San Jacinto. According to the 2002 San Antonio Visitors Bureau promotion, "San Antonio has always been a crossroads and a meeting place. Sounds and flavors of Native Americans, Old Mexico, Germans, the Wild West, African-Americans and the Deep South mingle and merge."[7] There is no mention of the genocide of Native Americans in this region, of lands taken, nor of forced segregation of Mexican and black Americans. There is no mention of the use of military force to subdue Mexican and black workers in the 1930s, or of the city's refusal to install sanitation equipment, flood protection, and health care facilities to brown and black neighborhoods during the 1950s and 60s.

In 1989 the city of San Antonio created a Department of Arts and Cultural Affairs (DACA) to administer grants to arts and cultural organizations and projects from money generated by the Hotel Occupancy Tax and other funds granted to the city by the National Endowment for the Arts and the Texas Commission on the Arts. DACA was short-lived. The decision to create a separate department had been made as a reform effort, to remove cultural arts funding from political influence and to extend public funding to community-based organizations that had never been included before. Working in the spirit of reform, the first DACA director, Eduardo Díaz, and his staff sought to fund numerous Latino and black arts and cultural organizations, to require the large European-oriented arts organizations to diversify their staffs and programming, and even to encourage the revival of cultural arts and practices that had been weakened by years of exploitation.

DACA's open recognition of the dominance of Anglo and other European-based cultural arts in San Antonio's major arts organizations was angrily criticized by many city leaders. Tourist industry leaders, conservative arts leaders, and others in city government denounced DACA's explicit focus on race and ethnicity as "divisive" and "exclusionary." Others spoke in favor of DACA's commitment and called for an even more profound commitment to cultural justice.

One critical moment came in 1994, when DACA recommended a 5 percent reduction in funding to five organizations, including, most notably, the San Antonio Museum of Art, because these organizations had failed to take reasonable steps toward developing an ethnically-diverse programming staff. At the Museum of Art, despite repeated promises to diversify, every department head and every programming curator was white. City and tourist industry leaders responded that the museum was incorporating cultural diversity in its programming, citing the "Chicano Art: Resistance and Affirmation" and "The Harmon and Harriet Kelley Collection of African American Art" exhibits.[8] The Esperanza Peace and Justice Center, a community-based center for cultural arts and activism, led a coalition of individuals and organizations, the Coalition for Cultural Diversity, formed to support and extend DACA's diversity initiatives.[9] A coaliton statement identified the heart of the dispute over DACA: "The issue, so often distorted, is not about some ill-defined notion of 'cultural diversity,' but about who gets to decide what 'cultural diversity' is."[10]

The 1994 cultural diversity debate ended with the DACA director refusing to implement the 5 percent reduction.[11] In the wake of this victory for "non-divisive" cultural diversity, business and city leaders sought greater control over the city's arts and cultural funding and sought to focus funding on the promotion of cultural expression that would be attractive and comfortable for "the whole city" (which many people understood as a code word meaning class-privileged Anglos) and "tourists" (which many understood as indicating Anglo and Hispanic middle-class travelers). In addition, the city eventually fired the DACA director, dissolved DACA's status as a city department, and replaced it with a much smaller, less autonomous Office of Cultural Affairs (OCA). Recognizing its vulnerability, OCA abandoned the earlier commitment to cultural diversity in favor of a funding program based on the model of "cultural tourism" that included evaluation of an organization requesting funding based in part on its attractiveness to tourists.

During this debate, city officials identified Esperanza as a group that would challenge the ways in which city funding favored Anglo interests and discriminated against Chicano and African American communities. Esperanza could mobilize hundreds of people for public protest, letter writing campaigns, and petition signing. Esperanza was, and is, committed to cultural rights—the right to maintain and participate in one's cultural tradition and the corresponding obligation of government to protect and nurture the cultural traditions of all people. For city officials—particularly those concerned with public election—Esperanza was a troublemaker. For the next three years, city officials worked to silence the debate over cultural diversity, and defunding Esperanza was one piece of this effort. In 1995 some members of the city council argued for complete defunding, but could not muster a majority vote for more than incremental defunding.[12]

The 1997 Defunding: Esperanza Was (and Is) a Target

Esperanza was created in 1987 by a group of young Chicana women, some queer and some straight, who dreamed of a place for community-based organizers, activists, and cultural artists to meet, discuss, and act against all forms of social, political, and economic oppression. Most of the women grew up in working-class San Antonio and wanted to do progressive political work in their hometown.

For fifteen years, women of color have led, worked, and shaped Esperanza as a vital cultural arts and activist organization. Today, Esperanza is alive with women and men, old and young; Latinos/as, black Americans, Asians, Native Americans, and whites; queer and straight; working class, poor, and middle class. The organization is feminist, politically progressive, outspoken, and deeply rooted in San Antonio. Esperanza is run by a very hardworking volunteer board, a full-time paid staff of only four people, scores of volunteers, and hundreds of participants and supporters. As a community of people working for and within larger communities, we are committed to multi-issue work for social justice, and to long struggle for change in the world and in ourselves.

Esperanza has organized hundreds of programs, *platicas* (community discussions), classes, and activities that have explored complex issues and enlarged understanding of diverse cultures and histories. The organization has been active in women's reproductive choice, human rights, and the rights of Spanish-speaking workers. Esperanza has organized antiwar protests, low-cost housing actions, and demonstrations against the Klu Klux Klan. Esperanza has presented the work of hundreds of artists and cultural workers, particularly those who have been ignored or silenced in mainstream arenas. Individually, the women and men of Esperanza have done the work at home. They have talked, challenged, and learned with their own families and with neighborhood friends. With great courage, they have strived to live the changes they advocate and to empower the people they love.

Throughout its history, Esperanza has worked hard to maintain a cooperative relationship with city government, recognizing that city officials are not the source of oppression against the people of San Antonio, although they have often been the agents of oppression. Yet, in 1994 and thereafter, as Esperanza articulated and organized in favor of genuine cultural diversity, this work threatened the deep entanglement of the city with the tourist and development industries.

Emboldened by the success of the anti-affirmative action movement, some—both in and out of city government—decried Esperanza for raising issues of race, ethnicity, class, and sexuality in connection with public funding. Esperanza and its leadership, particularly Graciela Sánchez (Esperanza's longtime executive director), Gloria Ramirez (current chair of the board of directors and longtime editor of the newsjournal *La Voz de Esperanza*), and Michael Marínez, (activist artist and longtime Esperanza volunteer), were demonized by the news media and hounded by anonymous threats.[13]

Howard Peak, who had been a new city council member during the 1994 DACA controversy, was elected mayor in 1997. Peak, trained as an urban planner and closely tied to San Antonio builders and developers, believed that city officials must promote the city's tourist and development industries. He also felt that cultural diversity could advance these goals, but only in its "feel good" form. Toward this end, Peak sought to silence and isolate Esperanza as the principal voice for cultural rights. As we discovered later in litigation, it was Peak who guided the defunding of Esperanza. Peak encouraged the involvement of right-wing organizers by personally appearing on conservative radio talk shows, garnered support for the defunding from a network of conservative white gay men, and secured the unanimous agreement of the city council in a closed meeting at City Hall late in the evening before the defunding vote.[14] Throughout, Peak's position was that Esperanza's social justice programming and its vision of cultural diversity were political, that art is not political, and therefore Esperanza did not qualify for "arts" funding.

Community Response: Todos Somos Esperanza

The Esperanza community deliberated for almost a year about how to respond to the 1997 defunding. It was difficult to survive. In addition to the city funding, the city withheld state funding, some local private foundations rejected funding applications because of the adverse publicity, and some individual donors were frightened off. The Esperanza board, staff, and community worked hard to keep the organization strong.

The politics of the defunding were difficult to address. In 1997 Esperanza was attacked by an unusual alliance among city officials, conservative white gay men, and the Christian Right. We had been defunded by an eleven-member city council that had six Mexican American members and one black American member. We knew that many people, both Anglos and Latinos, would assume that Latino and black council members would not discriminate against a group that promoted the rights of people of color. And further, the media and city officials had emphasized Esperanza's cosponsorship of a lesbian and gay film festival, Out at the Movies, as the reason for the defunding, thereby driving a wedge between Esperanza and other progressive arts and social justice organizations who were frightened by the political strength of the right wing and by the fury of the homophobic attacks.

We knew both the power of the homophobic wedge and irony of its role in city politics. Not only were the mayor and city council willing to fund the Alamo Gay Men's Chorale, but Dennis Poplin, coordinator for the Lesbian & Gay Media Project—producers of Out at the Movies and the only organization to receive public funds for the film festival—was advised by the city's arts department officials that the Media Project would be funded if it broke its association with Esperanza.[15] The more we learned of the actual events leading to the defunding, the more clear it became that Esperanza's cosponsorship of the Lesbian & Gay Film Festival was being used by city officials to fuel right-wing protests against Esperanza and to drive a wedge between the center and other Latino and African American organizations.

Esperanza responded by joining with other arts organizations to create the Arte es Vida campaign. The campaign focused on the importance of art to the lives of individuals and communities, and asked people to send postcards to the city council to express their support for public funding for the arts. As a direct result of this campaign, arts funding rose in the city council's list of priorities from forty-second in 1997 to tenth in 1998.

Meanwhile, during 1997 and 1998 Esperanza participants met in a series of weekly and then monthly meetings. People worked hard in these meetings to analyze the defunding in the context of ongoing political struggles in San Antonio. María Berriozábal shared insights from her ten-year experience on the city council and took members on an "economic tour" to emphasize the lasting social, economic, and cultural effects of city government decisions. Petra Mata and Viola Casares talked about their experiences in organizing Fuerza Unida and the frustrations they endured in their lawsuit against Levi Strauss.[16] Dulce Benavidez shared the lessons she learned as organizer of the San Antonio Lesbian and Gay Assembly. Linda Morales and Terry Ramos spoke of their experiences as AFL-CIO organizers working with Boeing employees. Mike Sánchez reported on his discussions with members of the carpenters' union, and numerous others shared their experiences and insights.

The Esperanza community was cautious about the possibility of filing suit against the City of San Antonio, in part because the Civil Rights Movement in the 1960s lost some community momentum when legal action was taken. Through discussions, the Esperanza community decided to file a lawsuit only if the legal claim would not distort the truth of the defunding and would support a focused organizing and community education campaign.

It was important to pursue the issue of cultural rights and to engage others in discussions of the power of culture and art in the historical survival of our communities and in our daily lives. Regardless of the outcome of the legal case, it would provide a focus for these discussions and illuminate the connections between cultural dominance and other forms of oppression.

We filed a federal lawsuit alleging an unconstitutional targeting of Esperanza.[17] We also undertook the Todos Somos Esperanza campaign utilizing door-to-door organizing, small house parties throughout the city, street theater, and a variety of formal and informal discussions and programs focusing on the importance of culture to the survival of oppressed communities and the obligation of government to respect the cultural expression of all of the city's communities.

Central to the defunding of Esperanza was the city's lack of support for authentic cultural expression in Chicano and black communities, its insistence on production for the tourist industry, and its pervasive commitment to European-derived cultural norms and practices. The lawsuit alleged that the mayor and city council responded to Esperanza's advocacy for cultural rights by targeting it for defunding. This targeting was successful because of the power of homophobic attacks against Esperanza. In both public and private justifications for the defunding, the mayor insisted on the idea that art and politics were distinct. This idea of "art for art's sake" is itself a product of fairly recent European American, middle- and upper-class cultural thought, and is quite different from the understanding of art in Mexican American communities and throughout Latin America. The city's insistence on a separation between art and politics is an insistence on European American culture and Anglo-centered cultural diversity.

Distinguished art historian Tomás Ybarra Frausto, who appeared as an expert witness, explained:

> Latin American art was born out of political struggle. As countless academics and artists have written, Latin American art for the last hundred and fifty years has been predominantly characterized by intense social concern. While much of European art has focused on the individual experience or on experience between the genders, the most important works of Latin American literature and much of its painting are concerned with social phenomena and political ideals. Art has been a critical vehicle for exploring social and national identity, political violence, racial and national integration both in Latin America and by Latinos in the United States.[18]

The lawyers working with Esperanza were challenged to shape claims and arguments that would accurately reflect the complexity of the defunding, including the racial and ethnic dimensions. This was difficult because the law of racial discrimination was severely limited by Reagan-era decisions. Further, the right to free speech, the center of First Amendment law, has been defined and elaborated as an individualistic, even class-based privilege. The words to describe genuine cultural diversity and a group's right of cultural integrity barely exists in First Amendment law.

When we researched the legal precedents, we were tempted to tell the defunding story as a simple case of antigay governmental action because that claim had been successfully raised before. That was, indeed, the advice offered by national groups such as the American Civil Liberties Union (ACLU). As lawyers, we are shaped by the law's structures, and so it was difficult to find ways to speak about Esperanza's experience. In addition, we knew that the formalities and practicalities of a courtroom trial would not allow us to tell the entire history of the Esperanza defunding. Every legal case requires that reality be simplified. We worried that if we simplified the story enough to prove our case, we would risk losing the complex truth.

Moreover, the core group of three lawyers who worked to shape the claims—Carol Bertsch, Mary Kenney, and I—are all white. Although Carmen Rumbaut, a Cubana, and Chicanas Elvia Arriola and Ilene Garcia provided helpful guidance at the beginning, and the trial team included Chicanas Isabel de la Riva, Denise Mejia, and Judy Saenz, (together with Lynn Coyle, a white attorney), most of the analysis, research, and drafting was done by white lawyers. We did not see the issues of race and ethnicity as clearly as other members of the Esperanza community. Because of this, we had difficulty knowing how to analyze the information we were collecting and how to present the evidence we had discovered. Esperanza and its lawyers solved this problem by making sure that Esperanza staff and community members were involved with every step in the legal decision-making.

As the lawyers worked with the Esperanza community to shape the lawsuit to reflect the actual story of the defunding and to define the racial and ethnic significance of the city's arts funding decisions, we came to understand the power of grassroots discussions of law and justice. Through the sometimes-painful process of listening, agreeing, and disagreeing, we came to a much deeper understanding of race and ethnicity, and the many differences among us. The community focused the lawsuit on issues of respect and cultural integrity, and held to this focus throughout the litigation.

The participation of Esperanza community members in decisions regarding legal strategy is very different from traditional lawyering practice, but Esperanza lawyers embraced it as an important part of our work. Yet, as we tried to bring in other attorneys to help us on the case, most resisted our decision-making process as unprofessional. As a result, Esperanza lawyers experienced a level of distancing and disrespect that was unfamiliar. This was particularly clear when we attempted to work with young white lawyers from the national ACLU. Although we were older and more experienced lawyers than they, and although we had been working on the case without them for two years, the young lawyers treated us as if we simply did not understand the law or the legal process. They were not comfortable in the cramped, mosquito-infested law office we had set up at Esperanza and repeatedly suggested that we should bring in a big firm attorney, who they thought could better "handle" the case. They resisted the Esperanza community's participation in legal decisions and disagreed with legal claims we shaped to reflect Esperanza's experiences and politics. Repeatedly, they spoke as if we simply had not thought enough about the case and did not understand the world. After a few months, the Esperanza board of directors and the ACLU agreed that the national organization should withdraw from the case.

After reflecting on this failed collaboration, I see that Esperanza staff and lawyers were treated as brown and black people are often treated by white Americans. Somehow, white Americans assume, without conscious thought, that they are the moral judges of people of color.[19] We assume, without thought, that we can assess and measure the thoughts and perceptions of others. "Yes, that is reasonable," we say, or, "No, your fear is unfounded." And we assume, without thought, that people of color who graciously or gently express disagreement with our evaluations are simply misinformed or misunderstanding some aspect of our conclusions. This unseen assumption often presents people of color with the unhappy choice between being "confrontational" and being patronized. If people of color are not confrontational, white people tend not to hear them, and if they are confrontational, we tend to dismiss them as "too angry."

The ACLU lawyers treated Esperanza lawyers as if we were brown or black, primarily because we did not distance ourselves from our clients. Positioned as merely part of the Esperanza community, we became legal outsiders, in need of education and guidance. I am glad for this experience, for it helps me to understand the tremendous pressure on lawyers of all races to separate themselves from poor, working-class, lesbian or gay, and brown or black clients. Sadly, lawyers too often give in to these pressures.

The Alchemy of Cultural Rights

The Todos Somos Esperanza campaign brought the issues of cultural diversity and public funding for cultural arts to discussions throughout the city. The campaign was most intense during the four years between the defunding and Judge Orlando Garcia's decision in favor of Esperanza. During this time thousands of people engaged in or with *cafecitos*, *platicas*, street theater, yard signs, community meetings, bumper stickers, a community mock trial, and a evening vigil at the federal courthouse. The issues raised by the defunding were actively discussed by people in their homes, on the streets, in community meetings, and at neighborhood gatherings.

At these gatherings, people talked about the power of culture. The Chicano community has survived because of its careful maintenance of its language and cultural practices. The black community has survived because of its conscious commitment to nurture cultural identity and traditions. Dance, song, and verse have held the pain and joys of life. They have taught the lessons of survival despite political domination, theft, rape, and betrayal.[20]

The vitality and visibility of the Todos Somos Esperanza campaign was crucial to the success of the lawsuit. The discussions engendered by this campaign informed the legal strategy at every stage of the litigation. During the trial, the courtroom was packed with Esperanza supporters: old people and youth, gay and straight, women and men, brown, black, and white people.

We were lucky to have been assigned to Judge Orlando Garcia (assignment of judges is done randomly). Garcia was raised in San Antonio and served as a state legislator prior to his appointment as a federal judge. Although reputed to be tough on lawyers, he is also known as intelligent, skillful, and hardworking. It was helpful that Garcia has a deep understanding of San Antonio and the importance of culture to the Mexican American community. At the beginning of the trial, the first witness, Eduardo Diaz, used the word " *quinceañera*" and quickly translated for himself, "that means a fifteenth birthday celebration." Judge Garcia smiled and instructed the witness, "This is San Antonio," he said, "I don't think you have to translate."[21]

The next witness, Esperanza Executive Director Graciela Sánchez, identified herself as a lesbian and a woman who had grown up working class in San Antonio's Westside barrio. Graciela used numerous Spanish words as she testified about the work of Esperanza, speaking in a bilingual weave that is familiar among Chicanos in San Antonio. Judge Garcia listened closely, and the courtroom filled with the power of Spanish spoken openly, without translation, in the formal atmosphere of federal court. The audience was completely silent in recognition of the moment. Sánchez testified to the judge and to her family, friends, and allies. The determined, engaged presence of community members was essential as a testament to that moment.

Later in the trial, the crowded courtroom witnessed as Mayor Peak testified to his belief that art and politics are necessarily distinct. When asked whether a program like MujerArtes, in which low-income women learn to tell their

Figure 10.1. Vigil held at the federal courthouse, the evening before the trial of *Esperanza v. City of San Antonio.* Courtesy of the Esperanza Peace & Justice Center.

Figure 10.2. Preparing for a women's day march with the banner of "Todos Somos Esperanza," one of the slogans used to raise awareness of cultural rights. Courtesy of the Esperanza Peace & Justice Center.

stories through the art of ceramics, is a "political" program, Peak responded that it could be, "depending on the program and what the purpose is, and what the people are that go through that program."[22] At that moment, a collective gasp arose from the back of the courtroom as members of the community reacted to the unexamined racism in the mayor's statement.

With members of the Esperanza community present for the trial, the focus on issues of cultural integrity and genuine cultural diversity remained at the center of the legal strategy. And the visible interest of community members in the lawsuit brought home to the judge the importance of the case. Following the trial and months of careful thought and research, Judge Garcia issued an eighty-five-page decision in favor of Esperanza, finding that the city had violated the First and Fourteenth Amendments of the United States Constitution, as well as the Texas Open Meetings Act. The Judge ordered the city to refrain from favoring or disfavoring grant recipients on the basis of their views on culture and cultural diversity, and required the city to compensate Esperanza for lost funding.

There is an alchemy to rights, as Patricia Williams teaches.[23] The concept and content of rights is nothing more than a manifestation of political power—a slogan invented by one European group in struggle with another.[24] Yet when communities use the concept and commit to the belief that they, too, are entitled, the obtuse logic of law can sometimes benefit the less powerful. If people believe that their cultural practices should be respected and protected by city government, if people yearn for a vital, liberating cultural diversity despite the multifaceted pressures of assimilation and accommodation, then legal decision-makers may begin to recognize and protect these values and activities.

Alchemy happened in the Todos Somos Esperanza campaign. Liberating cultural diversity existed for moments at Esperanza and other community-based venues. It is glimpsed in honest public discussions. In the Esperanza case, a place was found within First Amendment law that could protect and engender cultural rights. As we come to see the importance of culture in our lives, we grow closer to Indigenous peoples throughout the world who are fighting for cultural and political autonomy. Within international law, a human right of cultural integrity is increasingly recognized. This right requires that the cultural identities of minority groups be preserved and developed and that nations support the economic, social, political, and cultural institutions necessary to ensure the survival of minority groups.[25]

The United States has actively opposed efforts for international recognition of cultural rights over the past several decades.[26] Our government has tended to see cultural rights as inconsistent with global capitalist development and international trade.[27] The present regime in Washington shows no willingness to alter this policy. Sadly, U.S. rejection of international cultural rights is just one of many ways that the U.S. government now stands against the deep yearnings of people around the world to maintain something of their own values and cultural practices in the face of U.S. economic and cultural domination.

Esperanza v. City of San Anotonio and the Todos Somos Esperanza campaign engaged many in the struggle to understand and enact dynamic and liberating cultural diversity. Together we forged a vision of cultural rights and a place for such rights in U.S. domestic law. Similar work is being done by others in the United States and throughout the world. This work is important, and it suggests the possibility of more fully understanding ourselves and others. If we can imagine cultural diversity, if we can see the deep and precious significance within different cultures throughout the world, perhaps we can understand our own fears in the face of such difference. If we can do that, perhaps we can then understand the anger and fear directed against us.

Notes

1. This is true even though 41.9 percent of the people in San Antonio speak Spanish in their homes (U.S. Census Bureau, *2000 Census* [Demographic Surveys Division, Washington, D.C., 2002,]), available at http://www.census.gov.

2. Lee Mun Wah, *The Color of Fear*, video, 90 min., StirFry Productions, 1995.

3. Arturo Madrid, "Diversity and Its Discontents," in *Racial and Ethnic Diversity in Higher Education*, ed. Caroline Sotello Viernes Turner, et al. (Needham Heights, Mass.: Simon & Schuster Custom Pub., 1996), 526.

4. The 2000 Census reported 59.4 percent of the population of San Antonio as Hispanic, 30.8 percent as white, and 6.8 percent African American (U.S. Census Bureau, *2001 Supplemental Survey* [Demographic Surveys Division, Washington, D.C., 2002]), available at http://www.census.gov/acs/www/Products/Profiles/Single/2001/SS01/Tabular/160/16000US4865000l.htm.

5. This curriculum is discussed in Eugene E. Garcia, *Hispanic Education in the United States: Raíces y Alas* (Lanham, Mass.: Rowman & Littlefield, 2001), 49–55.

6. A U.S. Department of Justice study found that the leading jurisdictions in number of complaints filed in federal court alleging police use of excessive force were New Orleans, Louisiana; Los Angeles, California; Jefferson Parish, Louisiana; San Antonio, Texas; Houston, Texas; and El Paso, Texas (United States Department of Justice Report, Crime Control Digest 26:1 [June 1, 1992]). See also Macarena Hernandez, "Video's Violence Angers Viewers in S.A.: Blacks Say Scene Familiar to Them," *San Antonio Express-News*, July 11, 2002, 10A; and John Gutierrez-Mier, "Protest Targets Police Abuse: Groups Say Incidents Rising," *San Antonio Express-News*, Dec. 2, 1999, 3B. The loss of street vendors is examined in Regina Austin, "'An Honest Living': Street Vendors, Municipal Regulation, and the Black Public Sphere," *Yale Law Journal* 103 (1994): 2119.

7. San Antonio Visitors Bureau, *Welcome to San Antonio*, http://sanantoniovisit.com/visitors/com_history.asp, accessed on October 10, 2002.

8. Dan R. Goddard, "Definition of Diversity at Center of Arts Battle," *San Antonio Express-News*, August 6, 1994; and "Editorial," *San Antonio Express-News*, August 11, 1994, 16A.

9. I joined the Board of Directors of the Esperanza Peace and Justice Center in 1996 and was lead attorney in the case of *Esperanza et al. v. City of San Antonio* et al.

10. Mike Greenberg, "Coalition Seeks Arts Funding Cut for Groups Failing Diversity Test," *San Antonio Express-News*, August 30, 1994, 16A.

11. Mike Greenberg, "Arts Board, Director Still Split on Diversity," *San Antonio Express-News*, September 1, 1994, 16A.

12. That year, funding was cut from Esperanza's MujerArtes collective and the Center's Visiones de Esperanza: Inner-City Youth Media Project.

13. The Esperanza building suffered repeated break-ins. Threats were written on the walls, and in one episode, human feces were smeared on the building and hung in a bra from a tree. Esperanza members were followed and received threatening phone calls at their homes, and their cars were scratched and damaged.

14. These events were cited in the testimony of City Director Terry Brechtel, Mayor Howard Peak, City Council Member Jeff Webster, City Council Member Tim Bannwolf, and City Council Member Ed Garza in *Esperanza v. City of San Antonio*, trial transcript, United States District Court for the Western District of Texas CA No. SA98-CA-0696-OG, 102; and in the Declaration of Graciela Sánchez, 65.

15. Testimony of Dennis Poplin, trial transcript, *Esperanza v. City of San Antonio*.

16. The history of Fuerza Unida and its struggle against Levi Strauss is reported at http://www.accd.edu /pac/lrc/chicanaleaders/fuerzaunida.htm.

17. Two smaller, unincorporated organizations for which Esperanza served as fiscal agent were defunded along with the Esperanza and were coplaintiffs in the lawsuit. These were the San Antonio Lesbian & Gay Media Project and V~N, an artists' networking organization.

18. Affidavit of Tomás Ybarra-Frausto, para. 8, in Plaintiff's Motion for Summary Judgement, Exhibits, July 14, 1999, *Esperanza v. City of San Antonio*.

19. Marilyn Frye explores this idea in her book, *Willful Virgin: Essays in Feminism, 1976–1992*, (Freedom, Calif.: Crossing Press, 1992), 153.

20. Valarie Boyd's wonderful biography *Wrapped in Rainbows: The Life of Zora Neale Hurston* (New York: Scribner, 2003) records the complexity of black cultural survival in Hurston's vision and practices.

21. Testimony of Eduardo Díaz, *Esperanza v. City of San Antonio*, 59.

22. Testimony of Howard Peak, *Esperanza v. City of San Antonio*, 429.

23. Patricia Williams, *The Alchemy of Race and Rights* (Cambridge, Mass.: Harvard University Press, 1991).

24. This was a basic insight of the Critical Legal Studies movement of the 1970s and 80s (Costas Douzinas, Peter Goodrich, and Yifat Hachamovitch, eds., *Politics,*

Post-modernity and Critical Legal Studies: The Legality of the Contingent [New York: Routledge, 1994]).

25. See, for example, Halina Niec, "Cultural Rights: At the End of the World Decade for Cultural Development" (background paper for UNESCO, 1996), available at http://www.unesco-sweden.org/Conference/Papers/paper2.htm; and Terri Janke, "Report on Australian Indigenous Cultural and Intellectual Property Rights" (Australian Institute of Aboriginal and Torres Strait Islander Studies and the Aboriginal and Torres Strait Islander Commission, 1999), available at http://www.icip.lawnet.com.au/index.html.

26. The United States is the lone industrialized nation that has refused to ratify the United Nations's International Covenant on Economic, Social, and Cultural Rights (see http://www.hri.ca/fortherecord2002/vo16/usarr.htm). Also see Philip Alston, "U.S. Ratification of the Covenant on Economic, Social, and Cultural Rights: The Need for an Entirely New Strategy," *American Journal of International Law* 84 (1990): 365.

27. This view is reflected in a recent United Nations report that states: "The most fundamental flaw reflected in the approach of the independent expert is the idea that economic, social, and cultural rights are entitlements that require correlated legal duties and obligations" ("Report of the Open-Ended Working Group on the Right to Development," United Nations Doc. E/CN.4/2001/26, 45–46); and by Padideh Ala'I, who writes: "The United States has been, for the most part, opposed to the recognition of economic, social, and cultural rights as 'rights,'" ("A Human Rights Critique of the WTO: Some Preliminary Observations," *George Washington International Law Review*, 33 [2001]: 545–46).

EDITORS AND CONTRIBUTORS

Editors

Susan E. Gray is an associate professor of history in the School of Historical, Philosophical, and Religious Studies at Arizona State University. She was co-editor of *Frontiers: A Journal of Women Studies* from 2003 to 2012. She is the author of *The Yankee West: Community Life on the Michigan Frontier* (University of North Carolina Press, 1996) and co-editor of *The Identity of the American Midwest: Essays on Regional History* (Indiana University Press, 2001). At present, Gray is completing *Lines of Descent: Family Stories from the North Country*, a multigenerational history of a mixed-race (Odawa and white) family based on their personal narratives.

Gayle Gullett is an associate professor of history in the School of Historical, Philosophical, and Religious Studies at Arizona State University. Her publications include *Becoming Citizens: The Emergence and Development of the California Women's Movement, 1880–1911* (University of Illinois Press, 2000) and articles on women's politics in the American West. Her current project, "New Women in a New City: Gender, Modernity, and Los Angeles, 1910–1920," asks how relationships between Los Angeles and the city's activist women shaped Southern California modernity. Gullett was co-editor of *Frontiers: A Journal of Women Studies* from 2003 to 2012.

Contributors

Brett L. Abrams is a cultural and urban historian who has written about media and sports. He received his PhD from the American University in 2000. After publication of his first book, *Hollywood Bohemians: Transgressive Sexuality and the Selling of the Movieland Dream* (McFarland, 1998), his focus has been on how sports in Washington, DC, illustrate political issues and changes in the business of sports. Along with *The Bullets, The Wizards, and Washington DC Basketball* (Scarecrow Press, 2012), Abrams has also written *Capital Sporting Grounds: A History of Stadium and Ballpark Construction in Washington, D.C.* (McFarland, 2008). He is an active member of the North American Society for Sports History and works as an electronic records archivist.

Katherine Benton-Cohen is an associate professor of history at Georgetown University. She graduated summa cum laude from Princeton University and received her PhD in the Women's History Program at the University of Wisconsin–Madison. She previously taught at Louisiana State University. Benton-Cohen is the recipient of many grants and awards, including ones from the Woodrow Wilson Center, the National Endowment for the Humanities, the Coordinating Council for Women in History, and the National History Center. She is the author of *Borderline Americans: Racial Division and Labor War in the Arizona Borderlands* (Harvard University Press, 2011) and is currently writing a book about the Dillingham Commission of 1907–1911 and the invention of the "problem" of immigration in public policy.

María A. Gutierrez Soldatenko is the chair of the Intercollegiate Department of Chicana/o–Latina/o Studies at the Claremont Colleges and teaches in the Chicano/Latino/a Transnational Studies Department at Pitzer College. Her research interest and publications discuss the lives of garment workers in Los Angeles in terms of labor, union organizing, their ways of resistance, and their ways of knowing.

Margaret D. Jacobs is the Chancellor's Professor of History at the University of Nebraska–Lincoln. She is the author of *White Mother to a Dark Race: Settler Colonialism, Maternalism, and the Removal of Indigenous Children in the American West and Australia, 1880–1940* (University of Nebraska Press, 2011), which won the 2010 Bancroft Prize from Columbia University. Her current project, "Taking Care: The Indigenous Child Welfare Crisis and the Conscience of Settler Colonial Nations, 1950–2000," examines why Indigenous children came to be overrepresented in the child welfare systems of the United States, Australia, and Canada, and how Indigenous women activists mobilized to confront this crisis.

Amy Kastely is a lifelong activist, working in New York City, Chicago, Honolulu, and, for the past twenty years, San Antonio. Kastely is a community lawyer, believing that justice comes not from the courts but from the yearnings of working people, the solidarity of communities, and the human values of love and respect. She shuns the regnant model of legal practice, in which the lawyer is centered and the client marginalized. Working with the Esperanza Peace & Justice Center and other community organizations, Kastely has participated in organizational, educational, and activist work on civil rights; anti-war; race and gender discrimination; environmental racism; lesbian, gay, and trans rights; low-income housing; and other issues affecting our communities. She is also a professor of law at St. Mary's University School of Law, and she previously taught at the University of Chicago Law School and the University of Hawaii–Manoa William S. Richardson School of Law.

Laura Jane Moore received her PhD from the University of North Carolina in 1999. She researches and writes about Navajo women and the Navajo rug trade at the turn of the twentieth century. Her essay "Elle Meets the President" was awarded the Joan Jensen–Darlis Miller Prize by the Coalition for Western Women's History. Moore is currently an independent scholar in Washington, DC.

Catherine S. Ramírez is an associate professor of Latin American and Latino Studies and director of the Chicano Latino Research Center at the University of California–Santa Cruz. She is the author of *The Woman in the Zoot Suit: Gender, Nationalism, and the Cultural Politics of Memory* (Duke University Press, 2009). Ramírez has also published several essays on popular culture, feminist theory, and science fiction. Her current book project, *Assimilation: A Brief History*, examines the history of assimilation as a concept, practice, policy, and ideology in the United States. She holds a PhD in ethnic studies from the University of California–Berkeley.

Amy Sueyoshi is the associate dean of the College of Ethnic Studies at San Francisco State University. She holds a PhD in history from the University of California–Los Angeles and a BA in history from Barnard College. She has written on a range of topics, including cross-dressing, same-sex marriage, romantic friendship, and Asian American pornography in journals such as *Frontiers, Amerasia*, and the *Journal of American Ethnic History*. She is the author of *Queer Compulsions: Race, Nation, and Sexuality in the Intimate Life of Yone Noguchi* (University of Hawaii Press, 2012) . Her second book project, tentatively titled *Sex Acts: Race, Leisure, and Power in Turn-of-the-Century San Francisco*, traces how white middle-class expansion of gender and sexual norms constricted Asian Americans; the manuscript is currently under review at the University of Colorado Press. She is a co-curator and founding member of the GLBT History Museum and the recipient of the Willie Walker Award for Community Service from the GLBT Historical Society.

Yolanda Venegas received her PhD in ethnic studies from the University of California–Berkeley in 2004. She teaches at Santa Clara University.

Mary C. Wright is a senior lecturer in the Department of American Indian Studies at the University of Washington. She received her PhD in history from Rutgers, The State University of New Jersey, in 1996. She is the author of many articles related to Indigenous history and co-editor of *More Voices, New Stories: King County, Washington's First 150 Years* (Pacific Northwest Historians Guild, 2003).

INDEX

African Americans: as domestic servants, 169n69, 201, 209; Esperanza and, 231, 279, 282; perceptions of, 69, 78n99, 114; in San Antonio, 278; as zoot suiters, 111, 115
Alvarado Hotel's Indian Building, 171, 172–73
American Civil Liberties Union (ACLU), 284–85
American exceptionalism, 4, 10
American Federation of Labor (AFL), 163, 233, 282
American Indians: and adoption, 217–19; art by, 173–74; as domestic servants, 223n25; and forced institutionalization of children, 218–19; holocaust of, 155, 158, 278; inclusion in histories, 7, 9; Indian princesses, 158–59; limited career options of, 212–13; modernity and, 144; prejudices against, 207; in *Ramona* (book), 157; segregation of, 207, 278; and single motherhood, 215; tourism and, 145, 152, 187n4
American Indian tribes: Cherokee, 31; Colville, 34–36, 209; Klamath, 37; Klickitat, 37; Lillooet, 28, 31, 39; Nez Perce, 28, 30, 32–33, 35–36, 38–39; Okanagan, 28, 33; Pomos, 181, 196, 198–99, 203–4, 215–16, 219, 221n8; Salish, 37; Shuswap, 31; Tenino, 33; Thompson people, 28–29, 32–36, 39; Western Apache, 37; Yakama, 28, 30, 35–38; Yurok, 33. *See also* California Indians; Navajo (Diné); Plateau peoples; Plateau women
"American standard of living," 237, 238–39, 242
"America's Orient," 143, 172
Angel Island Immigration Station, 55, 70, 72–73n33
Asdzaa Lichii. *See* Elle of Ganado
assimilation: of American Indians, 15, 159, 185; of Chicanos, 26, 117, 276; of Chinese immigrants, 25, 48, 64, 66–67; of Japanese immigrants, 46, 48, 55, 64, 66–67, 69; of Mexican Americans, 276; schools as methods of, 199–200, 276

Battle of Naco, 245
Battle of San Jacinto, 278
Bean, Babe, 52, 54, 67–68, 77n93
Bisbee, AZ: demographics of, 239, 252n19, 253n33; dual-wage system, 235–36; homeownership in, 237–38; immigrants in, 235, 239, 249n7; reason for strikes in, 239; as white man's camp, 235
Bisbee Deportation: aftermath of, 233, 248; "border troubles" and, 245; demographics of deported, 238, 240, 252n20; description of, 232–33; injuries during, 240; investigations of, 234; Mexican Revolution and, 244, 245; motivations for, 232, 234, 242, 244–45, 247; non-miner inclusions in, 240; World War I and, 244; Zimmerman telegraph and, 244, 246
boarding schools, 40, 185, 199–200; Carson Indian School, 203, 212, 218; Chemawa Boarding School, 203, 215; Sherman Institute, 203–4, 213; Stewart Indian School, 202, 203
body, as used by geographers, 25–26
Bosque Redondo, 175–76, 183
Brown Derby, 84, 88–89
Bureau of Indian Affairs (BIA): assimilation efforts of, 200; maternalistic reformers and, 205, 210–11; resistance against, 195–96. *See also* Office of Indian Affairs; outing

Café International, 80, 82–84
California Indians: devastation of Native communities, 155, 222n10; as laborers, 150; Luiseño, 37, 153–54, 157; missions and,

155–57; report on, 159; San Pasquale people, 154, 159; Toypurina, 157
Californio: American Indians and, 157; conquest of, 150, 164; construction of, 150; cultural celebrations and, 164, 165–66; culturalistic racism and, 150–51, 160–61; depiction in art, 163–64; historic preservation and, 164–65; identity of, 150–51; Manifest Destiny and, 152, 166; masculinity of, 162; missions and, 145; myths of, 149–50, 152–53, 155, 160, 162, 165; perceptions of, 151–52, 162–63
caló. *See* pachuco slang
Center for Autonomous Social Action (CASA), 263, 274n28
Chicana and Latina union leaders: backgrounds of, 269; CASA and, 263; collaborative unionization and, 264–65; development of, 264–65; egalitarianism and, 258; ethnicity and, 262; family structure of, 258–59; gender and, 262; industry experiences of, 261–62; qualities of, 255; union history of, 257, 263; white union officials and, 269–70; work experiences of, 260, 262–63
Chicanas/os: 258–60, 269; assimilation of, 26, 117, 276; gender norms of, 26, 118, 120–22, 123, 128–30; inclusion in histories, 7, 9; in literature, 120, 128, 130; of movement era, 117–18, 120; perceptions of "real" Americans held by, 117; position of in American society, 113. *See also* garment workers
childbirth, 38–39; and afterbirth, 36
Chinese immigrants: American perspective of, 64, 66; assimilation of, 25, 48, 64, 66–67; and clothing, 64–66; as domestic servants, 201; gender blurring of, 64; ideas of femininity of, 65–66; Japanese immigrants and, 48, 57, 65; literature of, 65; masculinity of, 64; mining and, 235, 249n7; pejorative parodies of, 68; photos of, 64, 66; prejudices against, 234; work experiences of, 260–63
civilized-savage dyad, 157, 159, 161–62, 200
colonialism, 143, 150; and the American West, 10, 11, 15; Amerindian women and, 145; conquest of Indigenous inhabitants and, 199; domestic service as, 195, 201–2, 219; global, 20n28; rebellion and, 157; settler, 17n5; sexualized imagery of, 147–48, 157–58; spatial dimension of, 143–44
communism, 257, 264, 273n10; and Red Scare, 234
conquest, 149, 185
"cool," 111, 114–18, 128–29, 136n59
Copper Queen Mine, 232, 240, 243, 250n9
cross-dressing: acceptance of, 25, 71n10, 80–81; as compared to race, 67; in film, 85–86; in Hollywood, 80–81, 89–90; homosexuality and, 86, 89, 91; Mercedes de Acosta and, 92–93; movie industry and, 88–91; prohibition of, 53–54, 89–90, 100, 106n32; social status of, 78n97; "Stuart," 50; by women, 52, 53, 67, 68, 77n88, 86–88, 98
cultural celebrations, 164–66, 278
cultural diversity, 276, 281, 283, 288

"dark white," 69, 79n102
Department of Arts and Cultural Affairs (DACA), 278–79, 281
dime novels, 5–6
domestic servants, 194, 200–201, 205–6, 223n25, 224n40
dual-wage system, 236, 238–40, 248, 250n9

1882 Chinese Exclusion Act, 201
1893 Columbian Exposition, 165
"El Bracero y la Pachuca," 120–22
"El Louie," 115–17
Elle of Ganado: Fred Harvey Company and, 172, 178–79, 185; importance of, 185; personal history of, 172, 191n25; Theodore Roosevelt and, 171–72, 185; tourism and, 145–46; as traditional demonstrator, 172, 178–79, 185; weavings of, 171–72
Eltinge, Julian, 54, 100
English as second language classes, 256, 259
Esperanza Peace and Justice Center: African Americans and, 279, 281–82; capabilities of, 279, 283, 285–86; and conflicts with City of San Antonio, 279–80, 282–83, 290n12, 290n17, description of, 280; funding of, 279–83, 288, 290n12, 290n17; GLBT community and, 281–82; harassment of members of, 290n13; history of, 280; *La Voz de Esperanza*, 281; Mexican Americans and, 281; mission of, 279–80; mobilizations of, 279, 283, 285–86; perceptions of, 279; unions and, 282; vandalism of, 290n13. See also *Esperanza v. City of San Antonio*

Esperanza v. City of San Antonio, 282–86, 288–89
ethnic studies, 6–7, 48

family wage ideology, 236–38, 250n11
femininity, 74n59, 121–26, 129–30, 176. *See also* Japanese femininity
feminist geography, 4, 23–24, 201–2
flappers, 82–83
Franciscan Order, 155–56
Fred Harvey Company: American Indian art and, 172–73; "America's Orient" and, 172; Elle of Ganado and, 145–46, 172; monopoly of, 181; Tom of Ganado and, 177, 180, 182–84; tourism and, 172–74, 184; traditional demonstrators and, 172, 177–79, 181–85
Fuerza Unida, 225, 272n6, 282

gaimenteki doka, 69–70
Garcia, Orlando, 286, 288. See also *Esperanza v. City of Antonio*
garment workers: Chicana and Latina union leaders and, 265; demographics of, 271n5; exploitation of, 266; mobilizations of, 268; resistance by, 266–68; sexual harassment of, 268; strikes by, 268; wages for, 260, 262, 266–67, 269; worker solidarity of, 267–68; working children of, 259–61; working conditions of, 260, 262, 266–67, 269
gender construction: and gender blurring, 52–53, 64; cross-dressing and, 54–55, 65–67, 80–82; of gender norms, 82–83, 91, 93; ideology of motherhood and, 107n38, 107–8n48, 124; of Mexican Americans, 120–22; missions and, 72n29; outing and, 196; of Plateau peoples, 29, 32; by society, 48; through dress, 24, 60. *See also* femininity
gender illusionists: acceptance of, 46, 50–51, 68, 77n94; as entertainment, 50–51, 54–55, 67, 71n10, 77n94, 84; gender construction and, 50, 76n87; history of, 70n4; in Japanese attire, 51
Great Depression, 113, 201, 206, 208

"hip," 26, 111, 114, 117–18, 129, 136n59
Hollywood, 83–84; advertising focus of, 82–83, 86–88; criticisms of, 94; in film, 85–86; gender construction and, 80–82; gossip in, 86–87, 96–98; in literature, 95–96; movie industry and, 84, 88–91; nightlife of, 23, 83–85, 85–86, 88–90; vulgarities of, 96; and women screenwriters, 91–93; World War II and, 99–100
Hollywood players: acceptance of, 91, 93, 96–98; caricature of, 86; and gender norms, 81–82, 90–91, 94–95, 101–2; in films, 85–86, 98–99, 102; description of, 25, 94, 104n11; environs of, 83; freedom of, 96–98, 101–2; homes of, 90–94; in literature, 95–96, 100; nightlife and, 85–86, 89; private parties and, 94–98; prohibition of, 89–90; and publicity, 25, 83, 87, 89, 96–98, 101–2; success of, 87
homoeroticism, 61
homosexuality: African Americans and, 78n99; definition of, 100; in films, 83, 104n10; fear of, 103n5; and Gay and Lesbian Alliance against Defamation, 71n13, 77n88; in Hollywood, 80–81; homophobia and, 282–84; Japanese femininity and, 61, 69; lesbians and, 75n66, 83, 89, 91, 100–101; in literature, 103n8; marriage and, 92; *pachuquismo* and, 118; prevalence of, 75n66; and queer theory, 48; romantic friendships and, 75n66; and San Francisco Lesbian and Gay History Project, 77n88; in urban areas, 82
Hopi House, 179, 184
"How to Sin in Hollywood," 80, 81
hozho, 180, 182
Hubbell Trading Post (Ganado, AZ), 172, 177, 188n10, 191n20
Hweeldi. *See* Bosque Redondo

identity: construction of, 67, 69; effect of modernity on, 24; of Hollywood stars, 82; of Navajo (Diné), 180; pan-Indian, 215; regional, 13; sexual, 23, 75n67, 82
industrial capitalism, 178, 180
Industrial Workers of the World (IWW): AFL and, 233; in Bisbee, 232; history of, 233; investigations of, 234; membership of, 233; Mexican Americans and, 241; Partido Liberal Mexicano (PLM) and, 241; purpose of, 241; resistance to, 234; violence against leaders of, 234; WFM and, 233; Woodrow Wilson and, 234; World War I and, 234
International Ladies' Garment Workers Union (ILGWU): blacklisting and, 257; Chicana

and Latina union leaders and, 254, 262, 269–70; communism and, 257, 273n10; focus of, 269; merger with Amalgamated Clothing and Textile Workers' Union (ACTWU), 272n7; racism of, 257, 269, 272n7, 275n55; relationship with garments workers, 262; sexism of, 269, 272n7, 275n55; successes of, 264
Issei, 55, 57, 73–74n50

Jackson, Helen Hunt, 144–45, 152–55, 159
Japanese femininity: American womanhood and, 61–63, 74n59, 75n67; appeal of, 24–25, 60, 63; romanticism of, 61
Japanese immigrants: American perspective of, 57, 73n50; Andrew Carnegie and, 24; arrival of, 24, 49, 55, 70; assimilation of, 46, 48, 55, 63–64, 66–67, 69, 70, 72n31; Chinese immigrants and, 57, 65; and clothing, 56, 59–60, 72n31; defense of, 68; desire for American acceptance, 57, 59, 64; as domestic servants, 201; *gaimenteki doka*, 69–70; pejorative parodies of, 68; photos of, 55, 56–57, 59–60; social status of, 57; women, 60–61; *youfuku* and, 55
Japanese Noh Theater, 51, 71n12
Japanese-themed teas, 60–62
Justice Center, 255, 256; blacklisting and, 257; directors of, 256, 257; successes of, 264; white union officials and, 257

"Kid Zopilote," 116
kimono, 55, 56, 70; American perspective of, 63–64, 69, 74n59, 75n67; femininity of, 48, 60; identity and, 24–25; in literature, 61
Ku Klux Klan, 280

Landmarks Club, 163, 165
leadership, 255–56, 272n9
Levi Strauss lawsuit, 272n6, 282, 290n16
Los Angeles Sheriff's Office, 84, 90
Lummis, Charles Fletcher, 152, 164–65

Malcolm X, 116–18
Manifest Destiny: admitted destructiveness of, 145, 157, 165; Californio and, 152–53, 166; culturalistic racism and, 159, 166; descriptions of California and, 151–52; justification of, 149; in literature, 161; nostalgia and, 149; sexualized imagery of, 148, 157–58, 163; Spanish-heritage myth of, 152–53
Marble, Mary, 46, 47, 50–51, 70 n1
masculinity: Bisbee Deportation and, 242–47; of Californio men, 162; as defined by Turner thesis, 4–6, 8, 13; definition of, 234–35, 239; of jive, 116–17; language of, 241; of Mexican Americans, 241–42, 245–46; of pachuco slang, 116–17, 124; in *pachuquismo*, 116–17, 118–19, 128; perceived Mexican lack of, 238; raw food and, 36; strike as proof of, 241–42; white male supremacy and, 247
maternalist reformers, 204–6, 217
matrilineage, 175
McCarthyism, 6
menstrual lodge: archaeological studies of, 30; attire in, 36–37; challenges to, 39–41; construction of, 32–33; description of, 30; effect of modernity on, 24; and gender construction, 23, 36, 37–39; influence of, 30; placement of, 31–33; purpose of, 28–29; spiritual power of, 36; use of, 36; utensils used in, 35, 36. *See also* women's lodge
menstrual seclusion: diet and, 34–36; disposal of waste during, 36; guardian spirits during, 35; metaphysical characteristics of, 32; Plateau language for, 31; purpose of, 31; of Thompson people, 34–35; use of time during, 38
menstruation: cultural significance of, 31–33; synchrony of, 33; water and, 35, 36; wood and, 36
Mexican Americans, 235, 239; assimilation of, 276; cultural hybridity and, 113, 116; deportation of, 201, 229, 232–33, 240; discrimination of, 236, 278; as domestic servants, 201; in literature, 161; masculinity of, 238; Mexicanas, 162, 255; prejudices against, 235, 238; unionization and, 255; white perceptions of, 238–39, 244–45
Mexican Revolution, 113, 244–45
"Mexican standard of living," 238, 242
missions, 145, 155–56

modernity, 14–15, 21n41, 24, 26, 144–46
Mourning Dove. *See* Quintasket, Christine
movie industry: depictions in films, 98–99; gossip about, 99; in literature, 100; publicity of, 25, 88–91, 94, 96–98, 101–2

multiculturalism, 8–9
Murrieta, Joaquín, 163

Nahl, Charles Christian, 152, 163–64
Navajo (Diné): assimilation of, 181, 185; at Bosque Redondo, 175–76, 183; conflicts with Fred Harvey Company, 181–83; economy, 174–77, 178, 180, 189n13; family structure, 175, 181; gender roles, 174–76; ideas of death, 181; identity, 180; impact of railroad on, 177; importance of weaving to, 174–77, 186; medicine and, 182–83; migrant work and, 177; perceived marginalization of, 171–72; polygamy and, 181; pottery, 178; self-sufficiency of, 176, 179–80; silversmithing, 173, 178–79, 191n23; trade by, 176–77; as traditional demonstrators, 172, 177–79, 181–85, 191n22; wage work and, 177, 189n13, 207. *See also* Navajo textiles
Navajo textiles: Anglo collectors of, 173, 177; designs in, 174, 176–77, 179–80; economy of, 174, 186; of Elle of Ganado, 171; materials for, 175–76, 179–80
Nazimova, Alla, 90–93, 98
New Western history, 3, 7–8
"New Woman," 60, 63, 82–83, 91, 103n6
"New World Domestic Order," 202
1913 Alien Land Act, 69
1924 Immigration Act, 201

Office of Indian Affairs, 145, 176. *See also* Bureau of Indian Affairs (BIA)
Orientalism, 71n11, 143–44, 147, 166n2
outing, 195, 202–3, 207, 209–11, 213–14, 215–16; American Indian compliance with, 206–9; as assimilation method, 199–200; boarding schools and, 200, 202, 207; childcare during, 216–17; employment and, 207–9, 215–16, 219; gender norms of, 196, 213; marriage and, 214–16; maternalist reformers and, 204–6, 217; matrons of, 195, 202–3, 211–12; and mental health, 218–19; motherhood and, 214, 217–19; purpose of, 195–96, 200, 204–6; records of, 195, 203–5, 211, 220n1, 221n6; resistance to, 196, 212, 214, 218–19; sexual standards of, 213–14; social opportunities during, 207–8, 215; subservience in, 209; working conditions of, 194, 208, 210
Overland Monthly, 50–51, 60

pachuco slang, 112, 113; dictionary of, 84, 120, 137n84; failed mimicry of, 113; failure to assimilate and, 114; profanity in, 115; rebellion and, 115, 118–19; songs with, 120–21, 137n86; use of with family, 118–19; women and, 118–23, 126, 128–30
pachuquismo: defining features of, 110, 131n3, 132n4; depictions in the media of, 112–13; disdain for, 116; ducktails, 116, 131; in literature, 115–16, 127–29; masculinity and, 116–19; rebellion and, 26, 117, 126–27; resistance by, 111; as symbol of ethnic pride, 115, 116. *See also* pachuco slang
pandemic of the 1830s, 198
People v. Zammora, 119–20, 122–27, 138n93
petting party, 96, 108n55
Photoplay, 82, 90–91
place, 8–9, 11–12, 23
Plateau peoples: challenges of, 39–41; culture of, 29; divorce in, 29; gender construction of, 32–33, 40–41, 45n43; shelter types of, 29, 45n43; lodges of, 29, 33. *See also* Colville; Plateau women; puberty rites
Plateau women: childbirth and, 38–39; divorce and, 29; duties of, 29, 38, 41, 45n44; menstruation and, 32–33; power of, 29, 37–41
pochismos, 111–13, 116
"Pocohantas perplex," 158–59
puberty rites: challenges to, 39–41; counting ball, 37; descriptions of, 34–35; diet and, 34–36; in menstrual lodge, 28–30; in Plateau culture, 30, 32, 34; of Thompson people, 32–33, 34–36

Quintasket, Christine, 34, 38

race: as compared to cross-dressing, 67; construction of, 24, 48, 68–69, 77–78n94, 78–79n101, 235–36; division of labor by, 242; evolutionary hierarchy of, 78n101; fluidity of, 69; and racial project, 167n11; wages and, 236–38
racism: culturalistic, 153, 159–61, 166, 235–36; of DACA, 278–79; in San Antonio, 278, 283, 286, 288; and segregation, 113, 277–78; of Turner thesis, 5–6; of unions, 257, 269, 272n7, 275n55
Ramona (book): Catholicism and, 153–58; culturalistic racism and, 161; main character

of, 161–62; Manifest Destiny and, 144–45, 148, 155, 163; message behind, 144–45, 154–55, 159–60; missions and, 155–56; setting of, 161; *Uncle Tom's Cabin* and, 155
Roosevelt, Theodore, 5, 57, 171, 185
Royce, Bonnie, 202–5, 207–8, 210–11, 214, 217–19

San Antonio: assimilation in, 276; conflicts with Esperanza, 280, 282–83, 290n12, 290n17; cultural diversity of, 276–77; demographics of, 289n1, 289n4; institutionalized racism in, 278, 283, 286, 288; police brutality in, 278, 289n6; sanitized history of, 276. See also *Esperanza v. City of San Antonio*
Sánchez, Graciela, 281, 286
sexually transmitted diseases, 65
Sleepy Lagoon incident, 122–27
Snyder, Frederic, 204, 212, 214, 219
Social Darwinism, 148
social networks, 11–12
Southwest, 173–74, 178, 180, 185–86, 187n4
Spanish-American War, 243
Spanish-heritage movement, 151–53
Spanish-heritage myth, 150, 152–53, 155, 164–65
"squaw," 153, 158–60

Texas Open Meeting Act, 288
Tirilis, 112, 119
tlo'gamug, 31
Todos Somos Esperanza, 283, 285–86
Tom of Ganado, 177, 180, 182–84
tourism: American Indian art and, 172–74, 187n4; American Indians and, 145, 152, 177–78; authenticity of, 179–80, 184, 230; as conquest, 185; cultural diversity and, 283; "cultural tourism," 279; Fred Harvey Company and, 172–74, 184; Navajo textiles and, 174; nostalgia and, 143–44
transcontinental railroad, 14, 24, 143, 152, 200
Traxler, Jeannette, 202, 208–9, 217–18
Turner, Frederick Jackson, 13–15; and Turner thesis, 3–9, 13, 148–49

Union of Needle Trades, Industrial, and Textile Employees (UNITE), 255, 270
unions, and unionization, 257, 259–61, 264, 282. *See also* union strikes; *and specific unions*
union strikes: in Bisbee, 235, 237–42, 244, 247–48; in Clifton-Morenci, 241–42, 245; colonialism and, 156; by garment workers, 264–65, 268, 269; Harry Wheeler and, 242–44, 246; by IWW, 229–30, 232; masculinity and, 239; by Partido Liberal Mexicano (PLM), 241; race and, 234, 247–48; by WFM, 239–40

Van Every, Mildred, 202–4, 207, 209, 212–13, 217–18
Vasquez, Cristina Ramirez, 263, 265–66
Ventura School for Girls, 122, 126, 128–29, 140n126
virgin-whore dyad, 118, 128–29, 161–62
von Sternberg, Josef, 87, 89, 105n22

wafuku, 55, 72n31
wage work, 177, 189n13, 207, 216
Wasp Magazine, 50, 53, 61, 64, 71n8
Western Federation of Miners (WFM), 233, 239
Western women's history, 3–4, 6–11, 13, 18n13
Wheeler, Harry, 242–46
"white man's camp," 235, 239, 242, 245
Wilson, William B., 244–45
Wilson's Mediation Commission, 239, 243–44, 248n1
women's lodge, 38–41. *See also* menstrual lodge
World War I, 232, 234, 235, 244
World War II, 99–100, 110, 201

youfuku, 55, 67, 72n31
Young Women's Christian Association, 70, 208, 210, 212, 225n41

zo'met, 31
Zoot Suit (play), 120, 127–30
Zoot Suit Riots, 110, 114, 130, 131n1